England's National Nature Reserves

Dedicated to the wardens of the Nature Conservancy Council
and the site managers of English Nature

England's National Nature Reserves

by Peter Marren

for English Nature

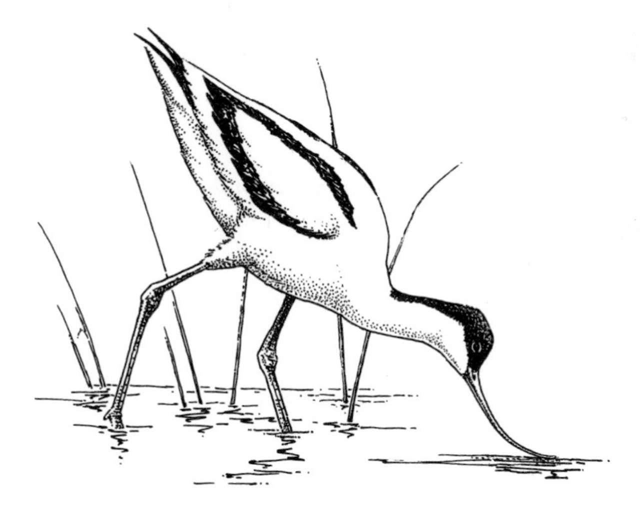

Photographs by Peter Wakely
Illustrations by Ruth Lindsay

First published in 1994 by T & A D Poyser Ltd
24–28 Oval Road, London, NW1 7DX

This book is printed on acid-free paper

Typeset by Phoenix Photosetting, Chatham, Kent
Printed and bound in Great Britain by
Bath Press, Bath, Avon

A CIP record for this book is available from the British Library

ISBN 0–85661–083–6

Contents

The colour plates can be found between pages 10 and 11, 42 and 43, 74 and 75, 106 and 107, 138 and 139, 170 and 171, 202 and 203.

List of Colour Plates

Foreword

I WELCOME the first book on the National Nature Reserves (NNR) of England! It tells of the origins, development and current status of English Nature's present holding of NNRs, and emphasises the contribution made by these areas to future sustainable management of the natural environment as a whole, and to the enhancement of biodiversity in the United Kingdom.

The story is progressive.

Policies for these reserves, and the uses of the expanding resource that they represent, have modified over the years. Opportunities and challenges have arisen and knowledge has increased of the practical measures needed for nature conservation. In these pages, written with the support of English Nature but not at our dictation, the author expresses his own views, presents his own analyses and some of his own doubts. He tells the stories of the people most closely involved, with details of the ways in which management of land for nature conservation has been carried forward. Also important are the additional uses, equally valued: research, public enjoyment, education and demonstration. The challenges faced by reserve staff, told in the book, illustrate all too well the problems of meeting such varied demands, whilst never disregarding the needs of nature.

Today, the protection, management and sustainable use of NNRs lie at the heart of English Nature's strategy, absorbing about one-fifth of our resources. A few NNRs are private places, where the wishes of the owners (with whom English Nature may have a Nature Reserve Agreement or a lease) or the needs of nature conservation are incompatible with open access. Most are already public open spaces or are traversed by rights of way, and can be managed positively for visitors.

In particular, from 1991, English Nature has made increasing use of statutory provisions that allow us to declare as NNR, land that is held and managed by others, whose commitment and capabilities we recognise as 'approved bodies'. We see that many organisations now have the necessary expertise. We believe that nature conservation in England will be best served through the development of partnerships with other owners and managers of reserves of national importance, and it is gratifying that many of these are managed with visitors in mind.

A carefully selected assemblage of NNRs is essential for the sustainable management of the nature conservation resource and for the security of England's biodiversity and variety of geology and natural features. English Nature's programme of declaration is planned to continue. Ultimately, we aspire to build a suite of reserves which will contribute to wider policy objectives and will fulfill a mixture of functions, including:

- conserving England's most valuable nature conservation resource, the best places within each recognised natural area, especially fragile or threatened habitats and nationally important assemblages of species;
- safeguarding less tangible qualities, such as wilderness and untamed wildlife;
- gaining, for our own understanding, and disseminating to others the management skills required for practical nature conservation;
- contributing to allied functions, especially field experience, research, environmental education, and the promotion of understanding of nature conservation;
- in all these matters, supporting and supplementing the activities of the voluntary movement.

This book tells the story so far. Its gazetteer records the wildlife store of existing reserves. It ends with the author's review of options and likely future directions, in which the building of partnerships is emphasised as the key to secure the integration of nature conservation in sustainable development and to carry forward the UK Biodiversity Action Plan.

I welcome his open approach, and I commend his book to all who want to know and understand the rich sample of our natural heritage in England that is designated as National Nature Reserve.

Lord Cranbrook
5 May 1994

Introduction

THERE must be close to 2 000 nature reserves in England today, run by a wide variety of bodies and ranging in size from the famous field pond at Badgeworth, Glos (celebrated in the *Guinness Book of Records* as the world's smallest nature reserve) to the vast expanses of intertidal sand and mud at the Wash. On some the emphasis is on public amenity and education; others serve as sanctuaries for wildlife where access has to be limited or even prevented. Not all of these sites are of the highest nature conservation importance in national terms, though virtually all of them are in some sense special.

Nature reserves managed directly by Britain's official nature conservation bodies, or with their formal approval, are 'declared' to be National Nature Reserves. These sites represent some of the best examples left of our semi-natural downs and heaths, woodlands and wetlands, estuaries and uplands. Because of the fragmented character of our wild landscape, not all National Nature Reserves are large. A few, like the Cairngorms and the Wash, are among Europe's larger nature reserves, but at the other end of the scale are others of less than 10 ha—no bigger than a typical late-twentieth century field. But large or small, the National Nature Reserves are the nation's most significant holding of first-rate wild habitats; the jewels, as it were, of our wildlife heritage crown. In Britain as a whole, over 200,000 ha of land is so protected. This might sound a lot, but much of the area consists of mountainous terrain in Scotland and Wales or estuarine marshes and mudflats in England. Away from the coast and the uplands, most National Nature Reserves extend over a few score, or at most, a few hundred hectares, and are often surrounded by intensively managed farmland.

In 1991 the government organisation for nature conservation in Great Britain, the Nature Conservancy Council, was reorganised into separate agencies for England, Scotland and Wales. Although the three new bodies retain formal links, they are already developing individual policies and styles to suit their different local circumstances. For better or worse, England, Scotland and Wales are now separate countries so far as nature conservation is concerned. In this book I am concerned only with National Nature Reserves in England. This regrettably means that many of the more scenically dramatic National Nature Reserves, like Snowdon, Rhum and the Cairngorms have to be omitted.

The body which looks after most of England's National Nature Reserves, English

Nature, came into being in April 1991. It inherited the same conservation policies and legislative background as its predecessor, the NCC, but is rapidly evolving a philosophy of its own. One of its main aims is to 'enhance the public awareness of nature'. It was in that spirit that English Nature invited me to write this book. I have done so with the full cooperation of English Nature and with free access to internal documents. I have been generously allowed to write a personal interpretation of National Nature Reserves and their evolution over the past 40 years, not all of which English Nature would necessarily agree with. I can only hope that in return I have succeeded in conveying a sense of the dedication, expertise and good humour I met everywhere as I travelled around England's network of NNRs during 1992. These places are in good hands.

I hope it will not be considered unduly chauvinistic to suggest that there *is* something indefinably English about the way in which the National Nature Reserves south of Hadrian's Wall and east of Offa's Dyke are looked after. Because, until 1981, Reserves were selected in a British context, England has few mountain Reserves or dramatic 'seabird cities' along the coast. Most of England's NNRs consist of softer landscapes, many of which have been the workplace of generations of countrymen as commons, rough grazings, hay-fields, managed reedbeds or coppices. To maintain them requires continued management to prevent scrub invasion or the replacement of herb-rich swards with coarse grass and bracken. For some Reserves, moreover, management goes further than mere maintenance to the enhancement of their interest for wildlife, and this has produced mosaics of different habitats producing a finely tuned landscape that probably never existed in the past. It is one of the anomalies of the English landscape that much of our wildlife requires human activity to survive. In terms of manpower, our National Nature Reserves are among the more intensively managed parts of the countryside. The decline of traditional land husbandry, the smallness and isolation of many of our natural habitats, our preference for being in the driver's seat, all have influenced the way in which we look after our wild places. If it were possible to sum up these ancient, interesting and often beautiful landscapes in a phrase, I would suggest 'unostentatious neatness'. On National Nature Reserves the fences, gates and footbridge rails will be well maintained, and often new; the grassland is flower-rich and scrub free; the ditches run with clear water, with sluices and elbow-pipes at the angles; and everywhere there will be signs that people have been hard at work: recently cut stumps and pollarded trees; nest boxes and piles of brushwood; paddocks of flexi-netting and electric fences; tractors and landrovers; cattle and sheep. There is an air not of Shakespeare's 'desert inaccessible' but of a wild garden, of the kind that the Englishman has for centuries felt at home in: controlled wilderness; contrived drama; a sense of the best of both worlds. Nature reserves are, after all, part of the English scene, and foreign visitors frequently liken the whole of our rural landscape to a large, well-tended garden.

This book attempts to tell the story of England's 140 or so National Nature Reserves, to explain their various functions and guises and to give at least an idea of what happens on the Reserve from day to day. Rather than repeat the 'traditional' format of a gazetteer of individual nature reserves, I have approached the subject through a series of themes, linked to the Reserves' aims of habitat protection, scientific research, amenity, species safeguard and management. This is a story concerned at least as much with the aspirations, foibles and fashions of the human race as it is about wild animals, trees and insects. But it will also, I hope, be read as a celebration of what has been achieved on England's National Reserves since 19 May 1952, when the first batch of seven was 'declared' by the then Nature Conservancy. We were fortunate in Britain to have made an early beginning—well in advance of public opinion (and of most other European countries)—in the days when 'ecology', 'conservation' and even 'environment' were words used only by specialists. Today, when nearly everyone professes concern for the 'environment', National Nature Reserves remain something of a conservation backwater. They deserve to be appreciated more than they appear to be. In today's topsy-turvy England, when so much land is no longer serving a useful function, nature reserves might be a useful reminder of what has been and what some land could yet become.

Acknowledgements

THE subject of this book was first suggested to me by Derek Langslow, the chief executive of English Nature, and developed by discussions with Keith Duff, Mark Felton and Eddie Idle. I am grateful to them for helping to turn the notion into a reality. Mark Felton was my anchorman in English Nature throughout and I owe thanks to him for his problem-solving, wisdom and restraint. I thank Mark and Eddie for reading and commenting on the full manuscript.

It was a rare privilege and pleasure to be able to spend so much time on the Reserves in the company of those who look after them. English Nature's site managers helped me in many ways, sharing their knowledge and experience, ferrying me about the Reserves, reading chunks of the text and putting up with my questions over cups of tea and glasses of beer. Their hospitality made my research all the more enjoyable. This book is dedicated to the site managers and to their forerunners. I thank in particular the following: John Bacon, Graham Bellamy, Alan Bowley, Robbie Bridson, Colin Campbell, Steve Clarke, Roger Cook, Rees Cox, Martin Davey, Bill Elliott, Malcolm Emery, Chris Gardiner, Michael Gee, Douglas Gilbert, Ian Findlay, Ron Harold, David Henshilwood, Phil Holms, Martyn Howat, Dick Lambert, Ray Lawman, Bob Lord, David Massen, Maurice Massey, Frank Mawby, David Maylam, Martin Musgrave, David O'Connor, Phil Page, Robin Prowse, John Robinson, Tony Robinson, David Rogers, Peter Roworth, Bob Russell, Peter Singleton, Rick Southwood, Paul Toynton, Mike Tuck, James Venner, Tom Wall, Chris Waller, Richard Williamson and Malcolm Wright.

The photographs in this book are all the work of Peter Wakely, and many of them were taken specially for it. The quality of Peter's work speaks for itself. For me they capture something of the essence and individuality of each Reserve. Seeing some of these lovely images projected onto a screen, I felt rather like Alice looking through the too-small door into the wonderland garden beyond. Many have an intimate quality—in a phrase that Peter used once during our long and enjoyable slide selection sessions, like 'looking through the keyhole'. This is his book as well as mine, and I can only hope he thinks that the text lives up to the pictures.

I am also grateful to the following for their help: Dick Seamons for library services; Stefa Kasnowska for reading and editing several chapters, Rick Keymer, Ian McLean and Mike Henchman for reading and commenting on parts of the book; John Lincoln and Jonathan Wray for their help in finding illustrations and leaflets; and to Adam Cade, Simon Elliott, Tony Gent, Basil Lindsay and Alan Pritchard for information. Maureen Symons turned my illegible scripts into faultless type with her usual speed and efficiency; to Mo, my continued, undying thanks.

Finally, my thanks to Andrew Richford of T. & A.D. Poyser for organising things, smoothing pathways and for being the ideal publisher. I hope that this book will not be the last of a fruitful collaboration.

Peter Marren
Ramsbury, 1993

CHAPTER 1

Origins

Because of the close interdependence of animals and plants as they live in nature, any effective action to conserve wild life necessarily implies comprehensive measures directed not only to the preservation, but to the control, so far as practicable, of native plants and animal populations . . . In short, wild life conservation cannot be separated from nature conservation at large. We have been compelled therefore to place a wide interpretation upon our terms of reference.

From the Wild Life Conservation Special Committee White Paper, *Conservation of Nature in England and Wales* (Cmd. 7122), July 1947.

NATURE reserves are barely a century old. But the idea behind the word, the notion of *sanctuary*, is as old as history itself. The first wildlife sanctuaries in Britain for which there is historical evidence were the Norman Royal Forests. Yet it is unlikely that they had no predecessors. Hunters of wild animals and hewers of wild timber know that they have to exercise restraint in order to sustain their game bags and harvests of wood. It is difficult to imagine how the builders of the vast wooden temples at Flag Fen, near Peterborough, for example, could have laid their hands on such quantities of wood and timber in what was probably already a predominantly agricultural area, without some sort of woodland protection. The Norman Forests were, however, the first *national* system of sanctuaries of which we have knowledge. They were tightly regulated, with their own laws and courts, and their officials were responsible to the king personally. The Normans recognised that in order to preserve stocks of wild deer and boars, it was not sufficient merely to ban indiscriminate hunting and impose a close season: it was necessary also to protect their leafy habitat.

Forest law seems élitist and arbitrary to us, but the Forests were very close in conception to the idea of National Parks, if for the nation one substitutes the king. Forest magistrates were given considerable, some said tyrannical, powers, and the chief forester was a senior figure in the royal household (the equivalent today would be a place in the Cabinet for the head of English Nature). Yet Forest law only added another layer of legality to the existing Common Law. It did not displace the rights of commoners to graze their animals, fish, dig turf or gather dead wood. Nor were the Forests unpopulated wildernesses, although many of them did contain a core of uninhabited woodland or heath. In practice they were closer to the present day Norfolk Broads, where an authority with regulatory powers acts on behalf of government, but most of the land is privately owned and many competing users have a claim on its resources. Life goes on, subject to special restrictions.

Even so, the extent of the Forests at their brief height, when they covered about a third of all England, was regarded by most as an abuse of royal authority, and the king was soon forced to reduce their area to more modest proportions. The Forests were possible because the countryside was underpopulated—the population of The Conqueror's England was less than that of present-day Hampshire; there were probably more rooks than human beings. In the later Middle Ages, the role of Forests as sanctuaries for the beasts of the chase began to take second place to their income-earning possibilities. And later still the Forests were sold off, bit by bit, one by one, to wealthy subjects who enclosed them, evicted the peasantry, grubbed up those woods they didn't want and kept the rest for the deer, the pheasant and the fox. The direct conservation legacy of the Forest system is probably small. The only large Forest to have survived in a recognisable form is the New Forest, although we have its commoners to thank for that, not the foresters of the Crown. The smaller, more compact, Hatfield Forest in Essex preserves the physical appearance of a medieval Forest, although the law which sustained it was long ago abolished. Without the Forests, there might be fewer ancient woods and heaths surviving today, but that possibility is hedged around with so many ifs, ands or buts that the contribution of the Forests to the present-day landscape is hard to estimate. The idea behind them might have persisted, at least at a subconscious level, in the continuing rural preoccupation with game and hunting.

Of more enduring benefit for nature were the private parks of medieval England, which were true sanctuaries and somewhat reminiscent of twentieth century nature reserves in the carefully managed variety of habitats they contained—copses, fish-ponds, grassland ('launds') and heath. Because England has suffered few revolutions and no conquests since 1066, a single family or institution has often owned the same piece of land for hundreds of years, nurturing a sense of stewardship, a useful safeguard against the temptations of the moment. Hence England still contains private parks full of venerable trees that are the envy of Europe—as at Moccas, Boconnoc, Melbury, Duncombe, Staverton, and, above all, the royal Great Park of Windsor. Moccas Park and Duncombe Park are now National Nature Reserves. They are the proof that what conservation needs most is not so much the law as conservatism.

In a sense, then, nature reserves already existed before the term came into fashion. Today 'nature reserve' is used as an umbrella term in so many contexts and for such a wide variety of places, from tiny ponds and railway cuttings to vast moors and estuaries, that we may be losing sight of its original meaning. For whereas the concept of sanctuary implies a safe haven, a *refuge* for wild animals, reservation implies something rather different: the deliberate *setting aside* of land for nature. Nature reserves surfaced in the late nineteenth century as a means of preserving wild or, in the contemporary phrase, 'primitive' land from development. They were the product of a growing sentimentality towards wild animals and (especially) birds, engendered by the growth of towns and cities. There was suddenly a widely felt longing for the sights and sounds of nature now that they were no longer on most people's doorsteps. It was not at first scientific necessity so much as the strange workings of the human spirit that nurtured the ideal of nature reserves. In a sense, they represented a fantasy world, a peaceful scene of wild nature unsullied by man. Freud was intrigued by the dichotomy between the universal will to harness the landscape for mankind's requirements on the one hand, and the individual's desire for islands of calm and solace on the other. Nature reserves were a means of having it both ways:

> The creation of the mental realm of fantasy finds a perfect parallel in the establishment of 'reservations' or 'nature-reserves' in places where the requirements of agriculture, communications and industry threaten to bring about changes in the original face of the earth which will quickly make it unrecognizable. A nature reserve preserves its original state which everything else has to our regret been sacrificed to necessity. Everything, including what is useless and even what is noxious, can grow and proliferate there as it pleases.
>
> Sigmund Freud, *Introductory Lectures on Psycho-analysis*, quoted in Thomas (1983).

It was only with the conviction that he has achieved an absolute mastery over his environment that the Englishman can condescend to offer nature its own patch. This would have made no sense to his ancestors: to them nature was everywhere and it was clearly there to be *used*.

There was, arguably, no great need for nature reserves (in the strict sense) before industrial times. It might have been useful to preserve areas of virgin woodland or pristine bog, but for that we would have had to have made a start in the Bronze Age. Most of the English landscape has been under more or less intensive use for perhaps 3000 years, and our wildlife has adapted well to traditional land management—hay making, coppicing, reed harvesting, open-range grazing and the like—since this is based on regular cycles and mimics natural events. The only animals to be exterminated between the Normans and the Victorians were large species which found no hiding place, like the Wolf and the Wild Boar, or large, edible birds like the Great Auk or the Great Bustard. We lost very few insects and possibly no wild flowers at all. It is easy to overlook the fact that, even now, relatively few wild animals, insects and plants have become extinct in England (and several of those few have since returned). But what *has* to a great extent been lost in the present century is the ancient *fabric* of the countryside, the patchwork of wood and wet, roughs and commons that is felt instinctively to represent the heart of rural England. The transformation of the English landscape from a fabric to a food factory began in the eighteenth century under the

Parliamentary enclosures, themselves fuelled by improvements in farming and drainage technology. These enclosures were at first patchy, and were never the wholesale transformation that has sometimes been claimed; some counties, like Kent or Devon, were hardly affected at all. But in the more agricultural counties, naturalists were finding fewer and fewer wild places between the cornfields— and the corn itself was gradually losing its colourful weeds. In Cambridgeshire, for example, the ploughing of the ancient turf had, by 1860, already confined 'the peculiar plants' of the chalk to roadside verges, quarries and the few banks that were too steep for the plough.

The Great Exhibition of 1851 celebrated the wonders of the new technology, and that year, appropriately enough, saw the drainage of the last of the great fenland fastnesses, Whittlesey Mere. The shallow mere proved surprisingly easy to drain; steam engines pumped out the water through a network of channels and, a few years later, almost the entire area was not only dry but was under crops. This was universally celebrated as a technological triumph. Only a handful of entomologists felt a pang of regret for the old fen with its acres of myrtle and reedbed, and the Large Copper butterflies seeking the water docks in the weedy dykes. And even the entomologists managed to put such feelings into perspective. The Rev. F O Morris, for example, an early conservationist who was later to campaign against the trade in wild bird plumage, regarded such drainage as necessary, and right:

> The industry of man has stopped the 'Meeting of the waters' . . . and, condensed in the steam-engine, [has] driven all before them, as if with the force of the rising tide of the ocean. Science, with one of her many triumphs, has here achieved a mighty and a valuable victory, and the land that was once productive only of fever and of ague, now scarce yields to any in broad England in the weight of its golden harvest. . . . The entomologist is the only person who has cause to lament the change, and he, loyal and patriotic subject as he is, must not repine at even the disappearance of the Large Copper Butterfly, in the face of such vast and magnificent advantages.
>
> The Rev. F O Morris,
> *A History of British Butterflies*

Fenland was the first wild habitat to be faced with wholesale destruction. Unlike most other wild places, fens could be converted into first class agricultural land at relatively low cost. Fortunately not all of the fens could be drained for some land had to be set aside to store the winter flood water. In a few cases the local commoners, long accustomed to cutting turf and reed-thatch from the fen, insisted that the land could not be drained without their consent. Wicken Fen in Cambridgeshire was one such place. But by the late nineteenth century there were only a few remaining wild corners left in Fenland, islands of wilderness and wet in an otherwise treeless landscape of crop fields, and forming the starkest possible contrast between nature and farmland. They were, in effect, nature reserves even before the Rothschilds began to take active steps to preserve them.

But that is to anticipate. The Victorians saw no great need for nature reserves. There was some popular revulsion against the more gratuitous forms of cruelty and the grosser forms of commercial exploitation, and this eventually resulted in the first wild bird protection act and the formation of a Society for the Protection of Birds (later the

RSPB). But the most significant move towards the protection of wild places was made by a body that had nothing to do with nature conservation: the Commons, Open Spaces and Footpaths Preservation Society, formed in 1865 to protect the rights of commoners. In the year in which Whittlesey Mere had been drained, the ancient forest of Hainault, close to the northern edge of London, had been enclosed and grubbed up by the Crown. Noting the improved land rents which resulted, the manorial lords of Epping Forest also began to make enclosures, some of them making proper arrangements with the commoners, others not. Matters came to a head in 1865 when the newly formed Society championed the cause of one of the dispossessed families which had been fined for exercising what it regarded as its ancient right to lop branches. As luck would have it, the Society uncovered documentary evidence proving that the Corporation of London itself owned common rights in the Forest, and could therefore challenge any recent enclosure. It chose to do so and, after a famous legal battle, won its case. The enclosures were declared unlawful and returned to the Forest. In order to settle the matter once and for all, the Corporation bought out the interests of the manorial lords and in 1878 became the sole lord and, by Act of Parliament, the effective owner. The Forest was acquired primarily as a public amenity for Londoners. But the terms of the Epping Forest Act made it a nature reserve in all but name, by ordering the Corporation to protect the 'timber and other trees, pollards, shrubs, underwood, heather, gorse, turf and herbage'. All the more pity, therefore, that the Act was filed away and ignored. None the less it was a conservation milestone, the first implicit acceptance in law that 'man does not live by bread alone' and that city dwellers have a claim on the countryside. Furthermore, it was effective: Epping Forest is still there.

THE FIRST NATURE RESERVES

It was but a small step from taking the responsibility for wild lands on behalf of the City, to accepting the custodianship of land and property on behalf of the nation. This was the aim of the National Trust, which was founded in 1895. The National Trust began with a major advantage: it had been blessed with corporate status, enabling the Trust to acquire and manage land as a charitable body. These powers were underlined in 1907 by a Private Bill declaring its properties inalienable (except by decision of Parliament) under the principle that the only certain way to protect a site was to own it, freehold and for ever: wise words. The Trust's original terms of reference stipulated that the acquisition of lands 'for the preservation of their natural aspect features and plant and animal life' should be on an equal footing with those 'of beauty and historic interest'. And in its early years, the National Trust did indeed acquire places for wildlife preservation. Wicken Fen, in 1899, was the first and has been described as Britain's first nature reserve. It was followed in the first quarter-century by Derwent Water (1902), Hindhead Common (1906), Cheddar Gorge (1910), Blakeney Point (1912), Box Hill (1914), Scolt Head Island (1923) and the Farne Islands (1925), all places of the first importance for nature. Yet the Trust's record of involvement in nature conservation was ultimately disappointing. Some of the early properties, like Scolt and the Farnes, required little maintenance. Others, like Wicken and Hindhead, needed, but did not receive, urgent management. The Trust ultimately refused to acquire sites deemed to be of interest only to naturalists, and was only with the greatest difficulty persuaded to take on places like Blakeney Point and Scolt Head Island. In the case of Wicken Fen, the Trust had failed to require the donor, N Charles Rothschild, to endow his gift, expecting to off-set the costs of maintaining the Fen against the expected revenue from sales of sedge. When these proved less than adequate, the Trust had reluctantly to dip into its own limited resources. Perhaps it was experiences of this sort that led the National Trust subsequently to concentrate its resources on castles, ruined abbeys and stately homes.

That the National Trust had taken on so many important wildlife sites in its early days was due partly to the influence and thick wallet of N Charles Rothschild (1877–1923), who began in 1899 to purchase parcels of land with the original intention of handing them over to the Trust. Realising at length that nature conservation was the least of the Trust's many interests, however, Rothschild established his own Society for the Promotion of Nature Reserves (SPNR) in 1912. This was, during Rothschild's lifetime at least, very much a one-man show. Membership was by personal invitation and was regarded as a honour: there was no subscription. The Society's object, to 'preserve for posterity as a national possession some part at least of the native fauna, flora and geological features of the British Isles', was a recognition of the failure of the National Trust to take on this responsibility. Rothschild hoped that the Board of Agriculture, rather than the Society itself, would assume responsibility for looking after nature reserves. He saw the Society's chief task as one of enabling the Board to make the right choices. Rothschild gamely set to work compiling a comprehensive list of the British wildlife sites 'most worthy of protection', intending eventually to extend it to the whole of the British Empire (he was working on New Zealand and the South Seas shortly before his death). The list of 273 sites in Britain was presented to the President of the Agricultural Board in 1915. But the timing was unfortunate. There was a war on, and the Board decided that its priority lay in the reclamation of land for agriculture, not its abandonment for nature.

The SPNR did, in a roundabout way, become the owner of one important nature reserve: Woodwalton Fen in Cambridgeshire. Having purchased the Fen in 1910 as a private hunting ground for moths, Rothschild had intended to donate the site to the National Trust, as he had done in the case of Wicken Fen. The Trust refused to accept the property, however, claiming that the Fen had no scenic beauty and was of interest only to naturalists. So instead, Rothschild gave it to the SPNR. Relics of Rothschild's period of tenure survive to this day in the form of a balconied wooden house, rather like a colonial ranch, with its garden of sunflowers (*Buckthalmum*), Broad-leaved Ragwort and other flowers, originally planted to attract butterflies. Concepts of nature conservation were different then! Unfortunately looking after this single site overstretched the Society's resources. It was obliged to sell its only other nature reserve, Ray Island, in order to pay for the Fen's maintenance.

A similar experience led to founding of the first County Naturalists Trust in England. In 1912 Dr Sidney Long and Professor F W Oliver had launched a successful public appeal to raise funds to purchase Blakeney Point on the North Norfolk coast, which was then taken on by the National Trust. A similar appeal, 9 years later, succeeded in securing the greater part of Scolt Head Island for the nation. But when the Trust refused to add the nearby Cley Marshes to its portfolio, and stood out against *any* further coastal properties in Norfolk, Sidney Long reacted by helping to found the Norfolk Naturalists Trust in 1926 as 'a special non-profit paying company to hold and manage [important sites] as nature reserves'. F W Oliver prophesied that one day every English county would have its own County Trust. He was right, but that day was still 45 years away.

Despite the efforts of naturalists like Rothschild and Sidney Long, only a handful of nature reserves (in the strict sense) had been established by 1939. It was not until 1930 that the RSPB, originally conceived of as a campaigning body, acquired its first reserve, although as early as 1911 it had promoted a remarkable scheme to establish a chain of 'national sanctuaries' across the European continent. The RSPB's first experiences in site-based conservation were unhappy. Its small reserve at Romney Marsh was ruined by land drainage; its Dungeness reserve failed to save its main object, the Kentish Plover, and no more than a handful of other reserves were created before 1939. But despite the Romney Marsh débâcle, or perhaps because of it, the RSPB became committed to a policy of land purchase as *faute de mieux* the only realistic way of establishing sanctuaries for wild birds. Elsewhere local campaigns had saved a few well-known places from the developer. Hadley Great Wood near Southend was the focus of a well-publicised battle between local people, supported by the press, and the local planning authority. The wood was eventually purchased and turned into a nature reserve, but a sense of bewilderment lingered at County Hall: "why do these people want to preserve a wood—do they not have the sea?". To most people in 1939, nature reserves were the hobby of a few eccentrics—bird fanciers and bug hunters—a slightly frivolous luxury. Without the sea change in culture brought about by world war, they might have so remained. But if the preservation of nature was at a low ebb (the word 'conservation' was not in popular parlance until the 1960s), the scientific study of living plants and animals was approaching its flood tide. The new science of ecology was taking the study of wildlife outdoors, away from skins, bones and pressed flowers and back to its natural setting, the English countryside.

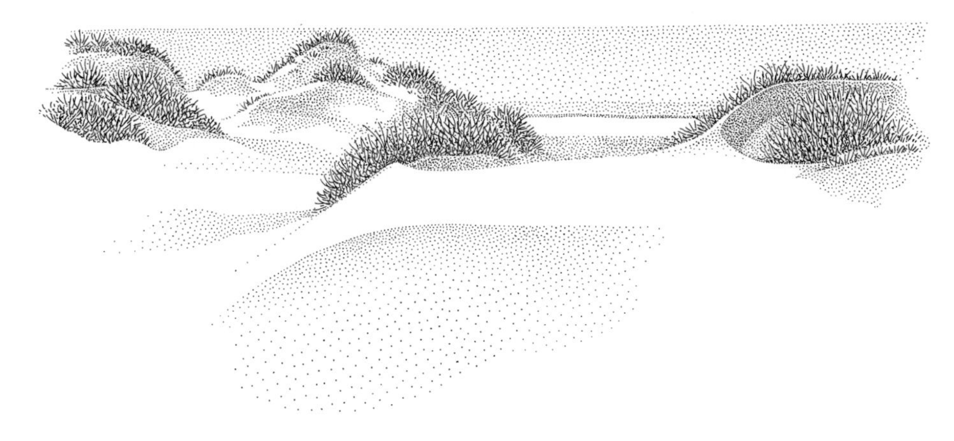

THE ENGLISH TRADITION OF NATURAL HISTORY

The word 'ecology', so familiar now that it has all but lost its proper meaning, was coined in 1866 by a German disciple of Darwin, Ernst Haeckel. It derives from the

Greek *oikos*, meaning 'home' or dwelling place, and Haeckel used the word for a new form of field study that related the animal or plant to its natural surroundings or environment. Haeckel was really dignifying with a modish 'ology' what had for more than a century passed as field study. Darwin was certainly an ecologist, and before him we can trace an English tradition of field study based on observation that takes us back to Gilbert White, the eighteenth century vicar of Selborne.

There must have been scores of curate–naturalists in those relatively leisured times, when there was plenty of time to potter about one's estate, contemplating nature and cultivating one's vegetables. Gilbert White was special because he happened to possess a first-rate inquiring mind allied to literary gifts, and was persuaded to publish his observations. *The Natural History of Selborne* is the most successful nature book in the history of publishing, more talked about than read perhaps, but capable of inspiring new generations of naturalists still. The book defines, indeed virtually invents, the English tradition of natural history and, since it is written as a series of letters, one can follow the processes of Gilbert White's mind. He sees something in an animal's behaviour that he doesn't understand. Rather than accept the received wisdom, or lack of it, he reasons with the facts, sometimes constructs a theory to explain them, and occasionally tests his theory with a simple experiment. Unlike most of his predecessors he is not interested in the man-centred view of nature, but in the fascinating details of the lives of living creatures for their own sake. White's intense interest in nature communicates to us directly across the centuries, so that we too are caught up in the excitement, even though we can reach for the answers from our bookshelves. White was lucky to inherit a parish that lay on a crossroads of chalk, sand and clay, and hence was particularly rich in wildlife, but his approach to natural history was potentially open to anyone with a patch of green in their back garden.

Nature study became fashionable in Victorian England, but for many it became a matter of taking nature indoors. The best minds concentrated on the dissection of bodies and the naming and classification of (necessarily dead) organisms, especially obscure ones: slime-moulds, sea anemones and desmids. Darwin, with his White-like observations of backyard earthworms and insect pollinators, was something of an eccentric in this world; besides, he was just passing the time, having completed his greatest work early on in his career.

By the early years of the present century, the study of wild nature had become stale and rather trivialised, as a collecting hobby or as something to amuse the children. The essential sorting and classification of organisms had been completed. Virtually every bird, beetle, moth or liverwort inhabiting the British Isles had been named and described, and its distribution recorded. But, despite Darwin, relatively little effort had gone into the natural behaviour of living plants or animals, nor of their relationship with one another and with their environment. If ever it became necessary to protect wild places or particular wild species, the knowledge of how to do so was woefully incomplete. Some form of dynamic impulse was needed, to lead naturalists, professional and amateur, back to the practice of field observation that was the legacy of Darwin and White.

The new science of ecology was slow to take root in England, at least under that name, and its appeal was at first confined to the Plant Kingdom. At the turn of the century a number of botanists interested in the living environment began to call themselves 'ecologists', among them F W Oliver, who was interested in the vegetation of the ever-changing Norfolk coastline, and the Yorkshireman C E Moss, the first person to classify and map the vegetation of the Pennine moors. The most influential of them was a pupil of Oliver's, A G Tansley (1871–1955). Tansley was in touch with fellow ecologists on the European mainland (he read and spoke German fluently), and was intent on creating a forum for promoting the study of natural vegetation in Britain. In 1904, with 11 others, he set up the British Vegetation Committee, which led to the founding of the British Ecological Society in 1913. Although Tansley had a rather diffident personality, and his written work rarely sparkles, he excelled as an editor of journals and as a correspondent. He made things happen. Some of his contemporaries, like W H Pearsall and E J Salisbury, published more papers than he ever did, but without Tansley it is uncertain whether there would have been a society or a journal in which these early ecological luminaries could shine so brightly. He, more than anyone else, is the mainspring and forerunner of the National Nature Reserves. His talent for organisation gave British naturalists a forum, a direction and ultimately a crusade.

Ecology was a new way of looking at the lives of wild animals and plants. Because it was concerned with the natural home or 'environment' of species, it was bound to be primarily an outdoor science. It encouraged new ways of surveying and monitoring wildlife. It was also a great unifying influence. This was potentially a science to which the gifted amateur could contribute as well as the professional. The British Ecological Society would eventually include evolutionists, plant geographers, animal behaviourists, geneticists, entomologists and bird watchers. It produced a broadening of individual outlook and a mixing of hitherto rigid disciplines at seminars and field excursions. This rubbing together of different intellects produced some glorious sparks. In retrospect, the 1920s and 1930s can be seen as the start of a golden age of British natural history. Few 'laymen' were aware of this at the time, since, with the exception of ornithology, the results were largely confined to scientific journals. After 1945, much of this work was popularised in the remarkable New Naturalist library published by Collins. 'New Naturalist' was a fortunate phrase. Much of the detail was indeed new, unfamiliar and sometimes difficult, but it was based on solid traditional foundations: the distinctive English approach to natural history.

The physical nature of England inevitably shaped the approach of English ecologists. The English landscape has little in common with, say, the Alps, whose zones and relatively uniform slabs of vegetation was the basis of the plant biogeography schools at Zurich and Montpellier, or the prairies of the American Midwest, where the more abstract and mathematical form of American plant ecology took shape under Frederic Clements. England's wild areas are small in scale, unusually diverse and profoundly influenced by man. Our open downs and heaths will eventually turn into woodland unless maintained by grazing, cutting or burning, and even our native woodlands were kept in an unnaturally youthful state by coppicing. It followed that even the wildest places in England needed continued management to stay as they were. Simply putting up a fence was unlikely to prove an adequate means of preserving wildlife. The English landscape had been shaped by the needs of its human inhabitants over centuries and millennia, and many of our wild plants and animals had grown to depend on the maintenance of early seral stages, like short, close-cropped grass and even ploughland. The management of nature reserves in a country like England needed a sound knowledge of the dynamics of wild vegetation, part natural, part man-induced. The science of plant ecology, as developed by Tansley in his *magnum opus The British Isles and their Vegetation* (1939), was the key. And the acquisition of National Nature Reserves would soon convert plant ecology from a fundamental science to an applied one.

The other half of ecology—the Animal Kingdom—lagged well behind. It was far from clear whether animals formed communities at all, except in the simple sense of being commensal. At the turn of the century, most professional zoologists worked in zoos and museums or in the agriculture and fishery laboratories. Science was highly compartmentalised: few fish biologists had much to say to entomologists; soil scientists kept their own council; oceanographers cruised the equatorial seas, mammal experts to the Arctic or to tropical Africa; and there were no professional ornithologists at all. Ecology, like animal behaviour, was potentially a unifying theme, but the work was difficult and time-consuming, and funds were hard to come by. The subject demanded someone who combined all-round competence as a field naturalist with an original mind and an ability to communicate. These qualities were happily personified by C S Elton (1900–91), who was in some ways Tansley's zoological counterpart. He was the founder, and for many years the editor, of the *Journal of Animal Ecology*, he wrote the first text book on animal ecology and set up the famous and influential Bureau of Animal Population at Oxford. Elton was one of the first professional zoologists since Darwin to be chiefly concerned with animal behaviour in the wild. He won his spurs in the Arctic, studying the peculiar fluctuations in the numbers of voles and lemmings, which seemed to boom and crash like bad investments on the Stock Exchange. What caused the 'good' and 'bad' years? What

1. Right: *The old brick pit at Wicken Fen in Cambridgeshire.*
2. Below: *The famous hydrosere at North Fen, Esthwaite Water.*

3. Above: *The thatched bungalow in the midst of Woodwalton Fen.*
4. Below left: *Gibraltar Point on the Lincolnshire coast.* 5. Below right: *The Swanscombe Skull site.*

regulated the numbers of animals? Was it predation or some other factor? The secret, which, as it turned out, was the unifying principle of animal ecology, lay not in the behaviour of individuals but in that of populations. Except at the most primitive level, animals, unlike plants, do not form communities capable of classification. Instead they form food relationships—food webs—within a habitat, be it a pond in the corner of a field or the plains of the Serengeti. In *Animal Ecology* (1927), Elton introduced the useful idea of an animal's "niche". By this word, he meant not so much the animal's home as its 'profession': its relationship with its food and with predators under the implacable laws of Eat and be Eaten. Elton represented the relationship as a pyramid, his now famous 'pyramid of numbers', with bushels of grass and gallons of plankton at the base and just a few big fierce animals at the top.

Like Tansley, Elton spent much of his later life promoting the study of British natural history. Unlike him, Elton attracted a strong student following and brought an accessible touch to his broadcasts and writings. Formal recognition of his achievements came late in his career—a belated FRS in 1953; but no knighthood or Nobel Prize, probably because Elton could not abide bureaucracy and was useless at committee work. But, again like Tansley, he soon became interested in the practical application of the new forms of knowledge, especially to wildlife management. For example, the natural regulation of Grey Seal populations, and the seal's relationship with its fishy prey, were a matter of considerable interest to fishery managers. Such knowledge could help man and seals to live together, not to mention fishermen and conservationists. Elton was interested in conservation, long before the term became attached to nature protection. To him it was a far more fundamental principle: the 'co-existence between man and nature, even if it has to be a modified kind of man and a modified kind of nature'.

The achievements of outstanding ecologists like Tansley and Elton were to transform traditional English natural history. Ecology encouraged field study by providing a framework in which naturalists could discover the relationships of wild animals and plants with each other, and with their environment. It also provided a new understanding of how to manage land for nature by introducing the concepts of succession and competition. And above all it established a respectable *scientific* case for nature reserves as outdoor laboratories. No longer was the idea of sanctuary based only on sentimentality. At a time when respect for science was great, nature conservation had at last become a worthy scientific objective, and nature reserves the open air analogy of research centres. All that was needed now was a catalyst.

PLANNING FOR NATIONAL NATURE RESERVES 1941–1949

For a generation that has never known world war, it is hard to appreciate the tremendous impact of the national war effort between 1939 and 1945. One obvious effect was physical—new roads, quarries and aerodromes, coupled with the felling of woods and the sealing off of many wild places for military training. Another was the weakening of the landowning class by heavy taxation and death duties, and the consequent break up of large estates. A change of hands, with the consequent loss of continuity and tradition and the relative stability they bring, is a dangerous time for wildlife. Indeed, Tansley regarded it as the greatest threat facing our wildlife and

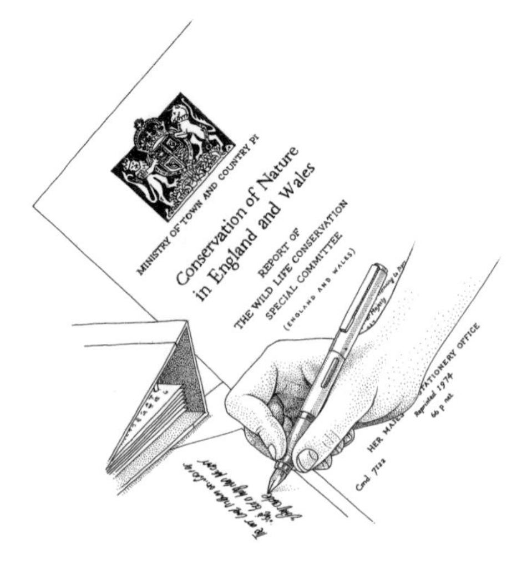

believed that 'some kind of public action will be the only means by which rural beauty can be preserved'. Fortunately such action was much more likely in 1945 than it had been in 1939. The nation had grown used to planning and regulation, and believed that these held the key to prosperity in peacetime also. Hence a third effect was cultural. After decades of *laissez-faire*, Britain was forced to find a more competent and rational approach to land management. Planning for peace began well before 1945. Most people seem to have been confident that Hitler would be defeated sooner or later; and in the meantime 'Britain can take it'. Post-war thoughts were being penned even as the bombs rained down and London burned.

National planning was a concept that some academic geographers and ecologists had long advocated. During the 1930s, a Land Utilisation Survey, under the direction of Dudley Stamp, had mapped the use of land over the whole of Britain, field by field. An *ad hoc* committee convened by another planning enthusiast, Lord Abercrombie, called for the establishment of a National Survey Commission to produce a kind of land-use atlas of Britain. Both Elton and Tansley were members of the committee. Once war broke out, the ecologists began to peddle their wares: they proposed a survey of British grasslands (with large-scale agricultural improvement in mind) and the application of ecological principles to pest control and crop breeding. The botanist W B Turrill pointed out how useful a national survey of coastal vegetation might have been to the defence of Britain (to find out, for example, which beaches held the best cover for defending troops). But for all their enthusiasm, the ecologists got nowhere with the agriculture and forestry departments. The foresters said they knew it all already, and had been applying sound ecological principles for years. The agriculturalists, like their forebears in 1914–18, just weren't interested.

And so it was by a roundabout route that a few influential naturalists and scientists were brought to think about nature conservation and nature reserves. Much of the ecological work of the previous three decades seemed, in retrospect at least, tailor-made for the selection and management of land for nature. At the same time nature reserves offered an unprecedented opportunity for promoting ecology, as ready-made open-air laboratories and demonstration sites. A great deal was now known about natural vegetation and man's influence upon it. A priority list of nature reserves existed and could be refined. A certain amount was known about animal behaviour and the way animal populations worked; less, but a little, on how wild animals, birds and invertebrates could be 'managed'. The blueprint for a system of nature reserves was ready and in place; it awaited only the necessary resources and organisation to bring it about.

As it happened, such machinery was already being developed, quite independently. A committee headed by Lord Justice Scott had been established in 1941 to look into the question of land utilisation in rural areas. The Scott Report, published in 1942 and drafted largely by Dudley Stamp, recommended the 'long overdue' establishment of National Parks. But it recognised that nature reserves were something separate from the Parks; indeed, in access terms, they were the very opposite. In a crowded country, public amenity and nature conservation could not, as in America, go hand-in-hand. The relevant clause in the Scott Report is worth quoting:

> *Nature Reservations*—While some of the larger National Parks will naturally form or contain 'nature reserves' and it may be possible to set aside portions of them specifically for the purpose, it is essential in other cases that prohibition of access shall be a first consideration, and for this reason nature reserves should also be established separately from National Parks. We recommend that the Central Planning Authority [of the Parks], in conjunction with the appropriate Scientific Societies, should prepare details of areas desired as nature reserves and take the necessary steps for their reservation and control—which must be strict if rare species are to be safeguarded.

Ten years earlier, Stirling Maxwell had made the same point with greater elegance: 'to the ordinary man a National Park and a National Nature Reserve imply the same things, while in fact they are essentially and vitally different. The one is for man and welcomes man. The other is for Nature and the protection of Nature from the dominance of the human race'.

The Scott Report, then, held the germ of the eventual separation of 'scientific' nature conservation and public amenity in Britain. Other European countries proved less obsessed with access and prohibition than Britain, and have often found ingenious ways of combining nature and people. But Britain's concentration on the scientific aims of nature conservation to the virtual exclusion of any educational or recreational aim reinforced the Scott Report's tendency to see the public as the problem. Whether or not this has helped the development of nature conservation in the long run is debatable.

The post-war construction minister asked for expert guidance on 'reserves, sanctuaries and sites'. By coincidence, a conference held in 1941 under the auspices of the RSPB and the SPNR had already considered the role of 'nature preservation' in Britain. To their great surprise, delegates from the conference were invited to join the Standing Committee on National Parks and develop their proposals. The result was the Nature Reserves Investigation Committee (NRIC). Its intellectual fire-power was considerable. As well as Tansley and Elton, both by now committed advocates of nature conservation, it included the veteran plant ecologists E J Salisbury and O W Richards, the ornithologist A W Boyd, the Scottish naturalist John Ritchie and, as a useful link with Whitehall, a leading amateur naturalist who also happened to be a professional Parliamentary clerk, Cyril Diver—new naturalists all. The Committee was, in effect, the British Ecological Society in a new role as government advisor. It produced a stream of reports between 1943 and 1945, all bursting with ideas and emphatic in tone. Most of the proposals on nature reserves that surfaced two years later in the now famous White Paper 'Cmd. 7122' were based on the work of the NRIC. It considered a range of possible roles for nature reserves: as outdoor laboratories, sanctuaries for rare species ('species reserves'), educational reserves, 'geological monuments', even 'economic reserves' to 'encourage the breeding of species beneficial to agriculture'. The Committee specifically proposed 47 outstanding sites as future 'National Nature Reserves' (the first time this term had been used), in addition to a number of more vaguely defined 'conservation areas' and 'scientific areas'. Administering these should become the responsibility of a National Wild Life Service staffed by 'persons with expert knowledge of plants and animals' and supported by 'such administrative officers as may prove necessary'. It thought that there was no need to separate 'species reserves' from 'habitat reserves'. Ecologists had shown that the first depended on the second, and that such a distinction was not only meaningless but unscientific. In its conclusion, NRIC seized the high moral ground: we had a duty as a nation to make certain that no more species or habitats were lost. Wildlife conservation should become the formal responsibility of government. More than one writer has found 'something heroic' about the Nature Reserves Investigation Committee, thinking about a future for nature in the darkest days of the war.

Tansley and his fellows must have hoped that their recommendations could be packed into the forthcoming Town and Country Planning Act, and this might well have been a much tidier solution than what actually happened. Unfortunately the government decided instead to convene another committee to report on the report. That piece of procrastination meant that National Parks, nature reserves and conservation areas would miss the planning boat; they would require separate legislation and have to work within the existing planning framework. Tansley decided it was time to 'go public'.

Our Heritage of Wild Nature: a Plea for Organised Nature Conservation was drafted by Tansley at the behest of the British Ecological Society and published in 1945. It presents a comprehensive if somewhat bloodless overview of Britain's natural habitats, followed by a discussion of the ideas of the Nature Reserves Investigation Committee, including an argued case for more and better managed nature reserves. Tansley was well aware that the Committee's proposals were in advance of public opinion, riding the post-war planning wave; hence the cultivation of public support was vital. But the astonishing aspect of *Our Heritage* lies less in its largely sensible arguments than in its conclusion that, in 1945, 'the limits of profitable agricultural land must have been reached'. Tansley even felt able to claim that wartime ploughing had been an improvement, having replaced the 'monotonous and often practically deserted and derelict grass-fields by the varied and stimulating activity associated with ploughing', and concluding that 'the total loss [of wild habitat] has not been very severe'.

Tansley cannot be blamed for failing to predict what actually did happen: that the continuance in peacetime of the war economy of subsidies and guaranteed prices, coupled with advances in agrotechnology and crop breeding, would vastly expand 'the limits of profitable agriculture'. At the time, most people seem to have shared his rather complacent assumptions. That not everyone did so is evidenced by the minority

Report to the Scott Report, published in 1942, to the effect that it was by no means certain that agriculture and 'rural amenity' would remain compatible for the forseeable future. Unfortunately that view was ignored. Perhaps the preservation of the consensus within Whitehall departments was regarded as too precious to risk by raising alarm calls over the future direction of agriculture. The founding fathers of nature conservation seem to have found it convenient to believe that habitat destruction was a thing of the past. It followed, therefore, that the main purpose of nature reserves would be for scientific study.

Meanwhile the last and most famous of this confusing archipelago of committees had been set up. The membership of the Wildlife Conservation Special Committee, like that of its predecessor, reads like a Who's Who of the great names in ecology and nature conservation. It was nominally chaired by Sir Julian Huxley, although he in fact attended only a couple of meetings before being whisked away to become the first director of UNESCO. Tansley, as usual, bore the main burden of correspondence in his role as vice-chairman. Particularly influential among the members were Cyril Diver and Max Nicholson, both of whom had the ear of Ministers and an insider's knowledge of the Whitehall machinery. A young London naturalist, Richard Fitter, acted as secretary. The Committee's final report, published as a White Paper in July 1947, is generally known by its 'Whitehall-ese' name, Cmd. 7122. Its title in English is *Conservation of Nature in England and Wales*. Its language was confident, practical, to-the-point and written with a rare and refreshing absence of gobbledegook. Nicholson was on hand to ensure that its proposals met a more sympathetic understanding than was usual in Whitehall. So far as nature reserves were concerned, Cmd. 7122 adopted most of the NRIC recommendations, though dropping one or two of its wilder flights of fancy. It recommended six types of 'reserved areas' to meet all the needs of the community. These were:

(1) National Nature Reserves (biological, geological and physiographical, or purely experimental)
(2) Conservation Areas (biological, physiographical, geological or landscape)
(3) National Parks
(4) Geological Monuments
(5) Local Nature Reserves
(6) Local Educational Reserves

The 'Conservation Areas', watered down both in size and empowerment, were eventually enshrined in the legislation as 'Sites of Special Scientific Interest'. 'Geological Monuments' were subsumed within the National Nature Reserves category, as were the Educational Reserves. For the authors of Cmd. 7122, National Nature Reserves were much the most important recommendation: the flagships of nature conservation in England and Wales. The Reserves should be acquired and administered by a biological service akin to the US Fish and Wildlife Service (Huxley's transatlantic experience was coming in useful here), with an independent budget and its own management and research functions. The main purpose of the 'National Reserves', stated the Committee, would be 'to preserve and maintain as part of the nation's natural heritage places which can be regarded as reservoirs for the main types of community and kinds of wild plants and animals represented in this country, both common and rare, typical and unusual, as well as places which contain physical features of special or outstanding interest'. National Nature Reserves could be designed to cater specifically for research and experiment, or for educational purposes or as 'places where the nature lover can go to enjoy nature'—in that order.

The Committee was broadly in favour of open public access to the National Reserves, and thought that any restrictions should be 'strictly limited to those essential for the conservation of wild life . . . and for the protection of any research in progress'. It was essential, it thought, fatally echoing the Scott report, that the National Nature Reserves must be kept separate from the National Parks. This was the last coffin nail in the late John Dower's idea of the National Parks playing a major role in nature conservation. It also meant that, while the National Parks received a great deal of publicity, the National Nature Reserves received almost none. An opportunity to gain popular support was lost. It did at least ensure that potential conflict with other land use departments and land users was minimised. National Nature Reserves were envisaged as being small, cheap and private. There were to be no Serengetis or Yellowstones in England.

Cmd. 7122 proposed the 'setting aside' of 73 Reserves in England and Wales—an advance on the 47 original sites suggested by NRIC—covering some 28,350 ha. This area, which 'could be enclosed within a rectangle of less than 10 by 11 miles', represented less than 0.002% of the land surface. The whole network, thought the Committee, might cost about half a million pounds, with annual running costs estimated at £10,000 per year. The Committee was optimistic that most of the proposed Reserves lay on land almost useless for any other purpose; they were effectively 'waste land . . . beyond the margins of economic development, or woodland which is not being exploited commercially to any extent' (that fateful complacency again!). It followed, therefore, that National Nature Reserves were unlikely to conflict with the interests of the agriculture departments or the Forestry Commission. On the contrary, the Committee added hopefully, the ecological know-how of the biological service might be helpful to their work. Each Reserve should have a warden, whose responsibilities would include the keeping of daily weather records and a logbook. The role would be part park keeper, part naturalist. Furthermore, added Tansley and company firmly, the warden should be protected against excessive paper work (I fancy they would be aghast at the volume of paper that passes through a modern Site Manager's in-tray!).

The recommendations of Cmd. 7122 applied only to England and Wales. Before they could be acted on, there was yet another delay while the equivalent Scottish report was produced. The Scottish committee under John Ritchie had the harder task, since the NRIC had confined its work to England and Wales. In its final report, 'Cmd. 7814', the Scottish Committee, like its predecessor, considered it tactful to stress the potential economic benefits of a science-based service. It recommended 50 National Nature Reserves in Scotland and called (in vain) for a separate Scottish Wildlife Service. Under the inhibiting gaze of Scottish politicians and landowners, the Committee found no need for National Parks in Scotland (thus ensuring that Scotland became the only country in Europe without a single National Park). With the completion of the Scottish report, the stage was clear at last for legislation. In a last twist to an already serpentine tale, the Wildlife Service was set up not by Act of Parliament but by Royal Charter. Max Nicholson, then secretary to the Lord President of Council, thought that by making the new body a research council directly responsible to the Privy Council it would help to safeguard its independence. He had in mind John Dower's warning of what had happened to the Old Lady of Riga who went for a ride on a tiger: 'they finished the ride/with the lady inside/and a smile on the face of the tiger'. Nicholson's chief, Lord President Morrison, agreed that the Big Brother ministries must be kept at bay. He had, he added, thought of a 'more convenient' title for the Wildlife Service: the Nature Conservancy.

TABLE 1 *Proposed NNRs 'already in safe-keeping' in 1947 (as listed in Appendix 6, section 10 of Cmd.7122)*

Site	*Owner*
Farne Islands, Northumberland	National Trust
Askham Bog, Yorks	Yorkshire Naturalists Trust
Alderley Edge, Cheshire	National Trust
Dovedale Ashwood, Staffs	National Trust
Box Hill, Surrey	National Trust
Burnham Beeches, Bucks	The Corporation of the City of London
Epping Forest, Essex	The Corporation of the City of London
Barton Broad, Norfolk	Norfolk Naturalists Trust
Hickling and Horsey, Norfolk	National Trust and Norfolk Naturalists Trust
Blakeney Point, Norfolk	National Trust
Scolt Head, Norfolk	National Trust
Wicken Fen, Cambs	National Trust
Woodwalton Fen, Hunts	Society for the Promotion of Nature Reserves
North Fen, Esthwaite, North Lancashire	National Trust (part)
Aston Rowant Woods, Oxfordshire	National Trust (part)

TABLE 2 *National Nature Reserves in England proposed by the Huxley Committee (1947) and their present status*

Northern group	
Farne Islands, Northumberland (73 ha)	Owned by National Trust (1925); NNR (1992)
Naddle Low Forest, Westmorland (101 ha)	RSPB nature reserve (part)
North Fen, Esthwaite Water (8 ha)	NT (part); NNR (1955)
Roudsea Wood, N Lancs (263 ha)	NNR (1955 and 1981)
Hawes Water, N Lancs (8 ha)	Part of Gait Barrows NNR (1977)
Colt Park, Yorks (60 ha)	NNR (1956 and 1993)
Askham Bog, Yorks (24 ha)	Yorkshire Naturalists Trust nature reserve
Skipwith Common, Yorks (405 ha)	
Ainsdale Sand-dunes, Lancs (223 ha)	NNR (1965)
Rostherne Mere, Cheshire (134 ha)	NNR (1961)
Alderley Edge, Cheshire (65 ha)	Owned by NT
Wybunbury Moss, Cheshire (12 ha)	NNR (1955)
Dovedale Ashwood, Staffs (28 ha)	Owned by NT

TABLE 2 *Continued*

Western group (mainly sites in Wales)	
Clarepool Moss, Shropshire (20 ha)	
Sweat Mere, Shropshire (12 ha)	
Avon Gorge, Bristol (162 ha)	Part owned by NT; NNR (1970)
Cheddar Wood, Somerset (40 ha)	Somerset Wildlife Trust nature reserve (part)
Shapwick, Ashcott and Meare Heaths, Somerset (1012 ha)	Part NNR (1961), much damaged by peat digging
Braunton Burrows, Devon (810 ha)	Part NNR (1964)
Isles of Scilly (c. 121 ha)	Informal agreement with Crown Commissioners over intertidal and marine habitats
Southern group	
Morden Bog and Old Decoy Pond, Dorset (263 ha)	NNR (1956)
Heaths from Studland to Arne, Dorset (1215 ha)	Part NNRs (1954–1981), RSPB nature reserve
Hurst Castle and Keyhaven, Hants (365 ha)	
Matley and Denny Area, New Forest, Hants (810 ha)	
Old Winchester Hill, Hants (182 ha)	NNR (1954)
Kingley Vale, Sussex (263 ha)	NNR (1952)
Basingstoke Canal, Surrey (243 ha)	Multi-ownership, threatened by navigation
Box Hill, Surrey (356 ha)	Owned by NT
High Halstow Marshes, Kent (770 ha)	Part NNR (1958) and RSPB nature reserve
Blean Woods, Kent (770 ha)	Owned by consortium of charitable bodies. Small part NNR (1953)
Deal Sand-hills, Kent (101 ha)	
Wye and Crundale Downs, Kent (608 ha)	NNR (1961), rest ploughed
Ham Street Woods, Kent (405 ha)	NNR (1952), rest replanted
Birdlip and Painswick area, Glos (567 ha)	Part NNR (1976), part owned by NT
Wychwood Forest, Oxfordshire (486 ha)	Part NNR (1955)
Aston Rowant Woods, Oxfordshire (227 ha)	Part NNR (1958), part owned by NT
Pulpit Hill and Lodge Wood, Bucks (279 ha)	
Tring Reservoirs, Herts and Bucks (122 ha)	Former NNR, since disestablished
Burnham Beeches, Bucks (405 ha)	Owned by London Corporation
Windsor Forest, Berks (365 ha)	Managed under informal agreement with Crown Commissioners
Bricket Wood Scrubs, Herts (122 ha)	
Water End Swallow Holes, Herts (20 ha)	
Wormley Wood, Herts (202 ha)	Owned by Woodland Trust
Eastern and central group	
Epping Forest, Essex (1417 ha)	Owned by London Corporation

TABLE 2 *Continued*

Hales Wood, Essex (32 ha)	Part NNR (1955), part Essex Naturalists Trust nature reserve
Horsey Island, Essex	Part NNR (1983), Essex Naturalists Trust reserve
Shingle Street (Orfordness), Suffolk	NNR (1954)
Minsmere Level, Suffolk (891 ha)	RSPB nature reserve
Cavenham Heath, Suffolk (518 ha)	Part NNR (1952), part ploughed
Lakenheath Warren, Suffolk (1077 ha)	Military airbase, small part Norfolk Naturalists Trust nature reserve
Barton Broad, Norfolk (202 ha)	Norfolk Naturalists Trust nature reserve
Hickling Broad and Horsey Mere, Norfolk (1036 ha)	Most owned by NT or Norfolk Naturalists Trust. Hickling declared NNR (1958)
Winterton Dunes, Norfolk (174 ha)	NNR (1956)
Blakeney Point, Norfolk (445 ha)	Owned by NT
Scolt Head Island, Norfolk (324 ha)	Owned by NT, NNR (1954)
Chippenham Fen and Poor's Fen, Cambs (81 ha)	NNR (1963)
Wicken Fen, Cambs (275 ha)	Owned by NT, NNR (1993)
Fenland Wildfowl Reserve, Cambs (486 ha) [Includes part of Ouse Washes and Whittlesey Wash]	Part RSPB nature reserve
Monk's Wood and Bevill's Wood, Hunts (243 ha)	NNR (1953)
Woodwalton Fen, Hunts (3888 ha)	NNR (1954)
Holme Fen, Hunts (243 ha)	NNR (1952)
Castor Hanglands, Northants (486 ha)	NNR (1954)
Holywell and Pickforth Woods, Lincs and Rutland (344 ha)	
Nottingham Sewage Farm (405 ha)	
Creswell Crags, Derbys and Notts (24 ha)	
Leighfield Forest, Leics (251 ha)	Part private, part Leics Naturalists Trust reserves
Wren's Nest, Dudley (49 ha)	NNR (1956)

Present NNRs listed by Cmd. 7122 as proposed SSSIs (then envisaged as larger sites than NNRs) include Northumberland coast (including Lindisfarne), Upper Teesdale, Ingleborough and Malham, Lizard Peninsula, Thursley District (including Thursley Common) and North Norfolk Coast (including Holkham).

CHAPTER 2

The Nature of the Reserve

Moor House NNR, high up in the northern Pennines

> I know few pleasures greater than standing in a newly established nature reserve which one has helped to set up. You feel that you have made a special link with the plants and animals around you and with the people who will come to look at their descendants in the future. It is difficult to analyse why this is so satisfying. It is not just because a conservation battle has been won. I suspect that the underlying pleasure—relief is almost a better word—is connected with a desire to produce something permanent in today's world, in which so much else is subject to unpredictable change. Of course, nothing can be predicted with absolute certainty—political madness or war may undo one's work or mismanagement may mar it—but what can be done has been done.
>
> Norman Moore on Choosing National Nature Reserves
> (from *The Bird of Time*, 1987)

THE Nature Conservancy was the love-child of a small number of naturalists and ecologists. Its birth in 1949 brought an end to the prolonged period of gestation. By riding on the band wagon of post-war planning and popular respect for science, nature conservation had at last become a national priority. The tasks of the infant Conservancy were daunting—more so, perhaps, than it knew—but there were solid foundations to build on: a measure of independence under a friendly minister, direct access to the Treasury and a detailed legacy of ecological knowledge, including a carefully worked-out 'shopping list' of nature reserves. The Conservancy had remarkably few formal duties. Under the National Parks and Access to the Countryside Act 1949, it could notify sites which, in its opinion, were of special scientific interest for their biological or physiographic features. It could, if it wished, conduct scientific research to promote the study of British wildlife and wild habitats. And lastly, of course, the Nature Conservancy was empowered 'to establish, maintain and manage' nature reserves.

It was hoped and expected that the leading lights of the old Nature Reserves Investigation Committee and the Wild Life Special Committees would help the

Conservancy to put their ideas into practice. The Royal Charter required that the latter should be headed by a Board, consisting of between 12 and 18 members, all of them chosen 'on account of their scientific qualifications or interest in matters connected with nature conservation'. The septuagenarian Tansley became its first chairman; he was deservedly knighted for his services to science and conservation in 1950. Among others appointed in the early years were Charles Elton, E B Ford, Harry Godwin, Max Nicholson, W H Pearsall and J A Steers, all of whom had been members of one or other of the committees. Captain Cyril Diver, the main draftsman of Cmd. 7122 and a member both of the NRIC and the Wild Life Committee, was appointed the Conservancy's first director-general.

The Nature Conservancy could acquire land by purchase, lease or gift. The National Parks Act further enabled it to enter into agreements with land owners and occupiers so that 'suitable land not so acquired may yet be managed as a Nature Reserve'. These Nature Reserve Agreements were expected to operate in a similar way to the forestry dedication schemes on privately owned land, set up by the 1947 Forestry Act. In effect, the land would be 'dedicated' to nature conservation, with an appropriate sharing of costs and the payment of compensation for any restrictions on the owner. The Conservancy could also make bye-laws on any land declared as a National Nature Reserve, whether it owned the land or not.

What exactly did the word *National* mean? The Reserves were clearly meant to be of national importance for wildlife, though no objective means of identifying such sites had yet been devised. They were also 'national' as opposed to 'local'. The Wildlife Conservation Special Committee was at pains to distinguish National from Local Nature Reserves, whose selection was a matter for the local authority. They were also 'national' in that they were run by a government body funded from the public purse and under a unified scientific policy. What they were *not* was nationalised property in the sense of the recently nationalised railways or coal industry. Most National Nature Reserves would remain private property. Neither would people necessarily have rights of access. The Reserves were places preserved in their wild state for the business of scientific study. As such they were not politically important. They were not even formally recognised in the legislation: the 1949 National Parks and Access to the Countryside Act mentions them only briefly and only as 'nature reserves', lower case. The National Nature Reserve label was not in fact enshrined in the legislation until the Wildlife and Countryside Act of 1981.

It was not until two years after it was set up that the Nature Conservancy established its first nature reserve. Before that it had to recruit staff and find premises, and both proved unexpectedly difficult. In the first year, only £36,185 out of a sanctioned grant of £100,000 was actually spent. Part of the sum went on acquiring a handsome Victorian house at 12 Hope Terrace in Edinburgh, at a knock-down price, to serve as a headquarters that was 'reasonably far from St Andrews House [the Scottish Office] and reasonably near the University'. It proved more difficult to find suitable premises in London. Many locations were inspected, but the Conservancy had to fall back on temporary accommodation before eventually leasing a grand but bomb-damaged Regency house among the embassies at Belgrave Square which housed its Great Britain headquarters until the move to Peterborough in 1984. The new ambassadors for nature shared the Square with those of Norway and Portugal.

Suitably qualified scientific staff were even harder to find. This may seem surprising today, but in 1949 there was a singular dearth of people with the right qualifications, despite the achievements of the British Ecological Society. Many of the Nature Conservancy's original scientific team had gained their spurs in the Colonial Service, as foresters and agriculturalists in East Africa and elsewhere. Twelve scientists were appointed in the first 18 months of the Conservancy's existence, all of them botanists or geologists. But easily the most significant appointment was that of E M ('Max') Nicholson, who became director-general in 1952, after the resignation through ill-health of Cyril Diver. Described by the naturalist, D E Allen, as 'that always rare being, the practical visionary', Nicholson supplied the direction and forceful drive that the organisation so desperately needed during its first decade. To do so, he had abandoned his Whitehall career to take on what seemed a forlorn little Cinderella, under the thumb of a great many ugly sisters. But his attitude as director-general was anything but humble. Nicholson shared with Julian Huxley the conviction that science in general, and ecology in particular, held the key to the future, to the bridging of the widening gulf between human needs and the health of the environment. More than any of his associates, he saw his role as a promoter of new ideas: sooner or later, he thought, the truths of ecology would gain acceptance, for 'one thing in the world is invincible—an idea whose time has come'. Nicholson's book *The Environmental Revolution*, written immediately after his spell at the head of the Nature Conservancy, positively bubbles with that innate sureness and confidence. For the 'ill-trained' bureaucrats and the cloistered academics who had failed to heed the call of the trumpet he had, by that stage, nothing but contempt. But even Nicholson admitted that the odds were not favourable. 'We desired a paradise to care for, but what we found called rather for the improvisation of a field hospital'. The Conservancy had arrived very late in the day. To have succeeded in 1949, it needed to have made a start in 1914.

Nicholson's book *Britain's Nature Reserves* (1957) provides an interesting insight into the philosophy of National Nature Reserve acquisition in the early days. The idea was 'not to choose places on impulse or indiscriminately, but to build up a carefully balanced selection' of the best examples of the different types of habitat found in the British Isles. But the aim in so doing was at least as much to provide 'open-air laboratories' for scientific study as it was to protect Britain's wildlife. From our perspective, 40 years on, the implied assumption that wild nature is the preserve of the professional scientist and his students seems unduly narrow. But, with public support then so obviously lacking (there were only five County Naturalists Trusts in 1957 and even the RSPB then had only a few thousand members), the choice was between that sort of nature reserve and no nature reserves at all. The use of publicly owned land was then seen in rather exclusive terms. The forester had his quota of land for growing trees, the ecologist had his outdoor laboratories, and the public was allowed the National Parks. What was already beginning to be overlooked was Cmd. 7122's idea of setting land aside for nature study and the simple quiet enjoyment of the country-side. That seemed to be the responsibility of no one.

Thanks to the work of British ecologists, the Nature Conservancy was fully aware that nature reserves would have to be managed if they were not to dry out, or become overgrown by scrub or rank grass, or harbour the 'wrong' sort of wildlife. But to begin with its priority lay in a thorough survey of what the Reserve contained and what made it tick. Much of the work described in *Britain's Nature Reserves* was of this sort: a kind of stocktaking of the plants and animals, of the soils, of the man's impact on the land, and a hundred other things which might have 'a bearing on the maintenance of the best conditions for wildlife'. By implication, all this might take a long time. Some of the Reserves would be subjected to trial and experiment to see how best to adapt current agricultural and forestry practices to nature reserve management. As Nicholson noted, it seemed paradoxical that 'we can ensure the survival of wild places in Britain only by finding out what happens when we interfere with them'. With hindsight, they ought perhaps to have known rather more. There was a great deal to be learned from traditional land husbandry and the craft industry, from coppicing and shelterwood systems in woodland to the commoning practices of rough grazing, turf digging and reed harvesting. Many species depended on the continuation of these, by then, failing practices. But such an approach was presumably judged unscientific. There is little evidence that the scientists talked to the woodmen, the commoners or the thatchers. Theirs was a hermetic world of seminar rooms and laboratories, and they thought in terms of the future rather than the past. As a result, they were in danger of having to reinvent the billhook.

THE FIRST NATIONAL NATURE RESERVES

The first English National Nature Reserves were a batch of seven, 'declared' on 19 May 1952. 'Declared' is one of those formal words that the Civil Service is so fond of. It conveys the impression that the news is cried from the steps of the Town Hall to the gathered multitude. The truth is more prosaic: the only step the Conservancy is obliged to take is to advertise the declaration in the columns of the *London Gazette*, a journal read by almost nobody. In more recent times there have been celebratory openings in a fête-like atmosphere, complete with symbolic plantings, unveilings or, in one case, the 'releasing of a herd of bullocks'. It has also become customary to issue a press release containing details about the new Reserve. But there were to be no ceremonial openings for any of the earliest National Nature Reserves and their public launch was distinctly muted. Possibly people were worried that publicity might attract too many visitors.

The first National Nature Reserve in Britain was Beinn Eighe in Ross & Cromarty, a mountain vastness of wild crags, boggy moorland and native pine forest. Curiously enough, Beinn Eighe was not on anyone's 'shopping list', and its purchase came about largely by chance. The vast, almost uninhabited, estate had come on the market in 1950, and the brief of the Conservancy's then Scottish Director, John Berry, was to bid for the 284-ha native pinewood at the foot of the mountain. But Berry knew the area and thought highly of it, and his successful bid was for the entire estate of 4374 ha. Representing a sale of about 74p per hectare, this was probably the best bargain the Conservancy ever made. Cyril Diver gave in with fairly good grace and accepted the *fait accompli*.

It is worth looking in a little detail at the first batch of National Nature Reserves in England, as between them they reveal much about contemporary attitudes towards Reserve selection and management. They were a mixed bag, an *ad hoc* jumble of conservation reserves, geological monuments and outdoor laboratories. They came first because most of them were acquired by the relatively speedy means of freehold purchase at auction or from the Crown Commissioners, involving the straightforward transfer of land from one Crown body to another. Of the seven, only three—Kingley Vale, Ham Street Woods and Cavenham Heath—were then considered to be among the best examples of particular wild habitats. The others came about by opportunity.

The Piltdown Skull site seems to have been the first property to have exchanged hands—a cruel trick of fate, for England's first National Nature Reserve turned out to be a scientific hoax. The site, a disused gravel pit near Uckfield in East Sussex, was presented in good faith by its then owner, Mr W T Lutyens. Part of the pit was thereupon drained to allow access to the fossil-bearing gravels. Piltdown Man was at that time believed to be the most important, certainly the most baffling, Hominid remains ever found. Early in the century, a few fragments of skull, a detached lower jaw and various 'crude implements' had been unearthed. They proved a puzzle, since the remains defied all that was known about human evolution. Finds elsewhere had indicated that early man had a modern jaw bone but an ape-like braincase, yet here was evidence of a being with a modern braincase but the jaw of an ape! That such a being had never existed and that the remains had been carefully buried there became apparent 2 years later. A practical joker, probably a curator of fossils at the British Museum, had planted the remains, using bits of a human skull and the jaw bone of an orang-utan, skilfully 'damaged' and stained and with neatly filed teeth to give the impression of antiquity. Once the fraud was uncovered, the Nature Conservancy quietly revoked the declaration and returned the site to the estate. But the memorial stone remains in place, and the initial drainage work there did at least permit the investigations that were to expose the fraud.

A second 'geological monument', the Swanscombe Skull Site in Kent, was offered in 1952 and became a National Nature Reserve a year later. Fortunately in this case the fragments of 'the English Adam' proved to be genuine, and the site has also yielded thousands of flint hand-axes as well as bones of elephants, rhinos, bison, horses and other large beasts that roamed over southern England 100,000 years ago. Possibly the Piltdown fiasco discouraged the acquisition of more such sites. In future only one more 'geological monument' listed in Cmd. 7122—Fyfield Down—was declared, and there were to be only three more geological nature reserves in the whole of Britain. In future the Conservancy would concentrate its resources on securing the best habitats for living animals and plants. It was felt that perhaps time was on the side of rocks and bones, compared with the uncertain future of a wood or a heath.

Cavenham Heath was exceptional among the early Reserves in that it represented a first-class example of a threatened habitat. After the East Anglian fens, the Breckland heaths of Norfolk and Suffolk were regarded as the most endangered landscape in England. The Second World War had had a devastating effect on the once extensive Breckland commons. The finest of them was Lakenheath Warren, which contained an incomparable wealth of Breckland wild flowers, insects and birds and had probably changed very little in eight centuries. But the pressures of wartime left little sympathy for such considerations. In 1942 half of the Warren was turned into an air base while the rest became a training area for tanks and artillery (the experimental plots of the ecologist A S Watt were bombed in succession by the Luftwaffe, the RAF and the US Airforce!). Elsewhere in the Breck, much of the former open heathland had been bought by the Forestry Commission to plant with conifers, or else had been expensively reclaimed as third-rate farmland. E B Ford regretted that 'the Nature Conservancy has come too late . . . for the areas which it may be possible to save will almost certainly be too small to maintain the general characteristics of the region'. It wasn't quite that bad. Cavenham Heath was on the Cmd. 7122 list, and, although it too had been knocked about by wartime activities, was regarded as the next best site after Lakenheath. The Conservancy entered into negotiations with the Crown Estate Commissioners and was able to declare 53 ha of the heath, hardly one tenth of the proposed area, as the first step in a policy 'to preserve for further study a few good examples from the little that remains'. While negotiations proceeded, the Ministry of Agriculture approved a land improvement grant over another part of Cavenham Heath, neglecting to mention the fact to the Conservancy. The land was ploughed.

The Ham Street Woods in the Weald of Kent was also under threat, this time from felling and replanting. This place of standard oaks and a regularly cut underwood of hornbeam and hazel was famous for its rare moths, and included the only known breeding place of the large and handsome Blue Underwing or 'Clifden Nonpareil'. When the property came on the market following the first Tree Preservation Order made by a local authority, the Conservancy dug into its pockets and purchased about a third of the wood. The rest was acquired by the Forestry Commission who immediately clear felled the natural woodland and replanted it with conifers. Unfortunately the best area for the Blue Underwing lay in the latter part of the wood. The entomological fraternity was not amused.

Sir Arthur Tansley himself seems to have been responsible for the purchase of Kingley Vale in West Sussex. He had known the place for 40 years, and, with A S Watt in the 1920s, had published a scientific paper about its famous forest of yews, reputed to be the finest in Europe. Tansley was particularly fond of the view from the head of the Vale across the coastal plain towards Chichester. The Vale's two owners were happy to sell, so long as the Conservancy allowed them to continue to use the land for rough shooting. Like so many wild places at that time, Kingley Vale had been mutilated by war and neglected in the peace; it was in fact in a mess. Fortunately large yews are almost immortal. The purchase was one of the last acts of Tansley's long career. He died in 1955, having retired as the Conservancy's chairman two years before. In 1957, a large sarsen stone was transported by lorry from the Fyfield Down National Nature Reserve in Wiltshire and laid at his favourite viewpoint at Kingley Vale. The metal plaque reads:

> In the midst of this Nature Reserve which he brought into being this stone calls to memory Sir Arthur George Tansley, FRS, who during a long lifetime strove with success to widen the knowledge, to deepen the love and to safeguard the heritage of nature in the British Islands.

Kingley Vale, Ham Street Woods and Cavenham Heath were the 'conservation reserves', though none of them in fact received much management for at least a decade. The last three of the 1952 batch—Yarner Wood, Moor House and Holme Fen—were regarded as 'scientific reserves', that is, habitats in no way outstanding that were considered suitable for ecological research. The record leaves the reader in no doubt that it was this class of nature reserve which most interested the Conservancy's scientists. Fortunately the early purchase of these places has safeguarded them from the growing pressures on semi-natural land, and they have turned out to be special after all. Yarner Wood is now the largest ancient broadleaved wood on Dartmoor. And Moor House has become the only substantial tract of unmanaged heather moorland in northern England.

The Yarner Estate came on the market in 1950. It was snapped up by London property speculators and resold in lots at auction 3 months later. The Conservancy bid successfully for Yarner Wood. It was obliged to pay roughly double the original price, but at £77 per hectare this was still a fairly nominal sum compared with today's land prices. The Wood was virtually unknown and had not been listed in Cmd. 7122, but a quick inspection by the Conservancy's chief scientist, Verona Conway, suggested that it was 'representative of the general ecological conditions obtained in the sessile oak woods that characterise the valley slopes fringing the east side of Dartmoor'. One of its advantages lay in the absence of public rights of way. The Conservancy was looking for just such a private, robust, fairly uniform wood to conduct woodland management experiments. The main problem lay in its remoteness, scores of miles from any of its regional offices or field stations. The services of the Yarner Estate gamekeeper, Mr Fred Toby, who lived nearby and had worked in the wood for over 30 years, were retained. He became the first full-time Reserve warden (see Chapter 3).

At 4050 ha, the purchase of Moor House, in the high Pennines between Cross Fell and the Tees, represented a commitment on an altogether grander scale. It too had come up for auction on the break up of a large estate—that of Appleby Castle in 1950—and cost the Conservancy £5000 (£1.24 a hectare). A barren sweep of moorland and bog, enlivened only by streams and broken crags, it boasted Britain's highest occupied house—Moor House itself—and the earliest upland weather station. It was from the latter that Gordon Manley had undertaken the first scientific investigation of the climate of Britain's uplands in the 1930s, which revealed that Moor House is more like Iceland than Kent—almost perpetually cold and windswept, with deep-frozen winters and dull, wet summers. It is probably the harshest climate in England. This unprepossessing place held a number of advantages as a scientific reserve. It was reasonably close to the planned field station at Grange-over-Sands on the Lancashire coast and included a building in good order that could be converted to laboratories and accommodation for staff and visiting scientists. There were a few snags. The Conservancy would be liable for the maintenance of the private road across the open fell to the 'Wuthering Heights' of Moor House. And, since this area was mostly common land, it had no means of controlling grazing levels or erecting enclosures without the consent of the numerous commoners from villages west of the Reserve, who grazed their flocks there during summer. Nor did the purchase include the mineral rights. Like Yarner Wood, Moor House was not listed by Cmd. 7122, but Verona Conway, a peatland specialist herself, saw in it great scientific potential. She was right. Today, with more than 400 published scientific papers about the moor, representing the cream of an entire room-full of documents, Moor House is probably the most thoroughly studied wasteland in the world (see Chapter 5).

Finally there was Holme Fen in what was then Huntingdonshire: the classic example of a lake that turned into a birch wood. When Whittlesey Mere was drained in 1851, 'a man called Wells' saw, with greater perception than most of his contemporaries, that as the peat dried out it was going to shrink. In the interests of science, he sunk an iron post, said to have been taken from the Great Exhibition at Crystal Palace, through the thick mantle of fen peat until it rested on the Oxford Clay beneath and the top lay flush with the ground. The peat did indeed shrink—initially at the rate of 0.3 m every 2 years (though a lot of it probably blew away in the wind)—and the post now stands proud, secured by hawsers. Today the ground lies 4 m beneath the original

surface and has in fact sunk below sea level. Such fame as Holme Fen enjoys is centred on this early ecological experiment. It had attracted the interest of Sir John Fryer, a member of the Wild Life Conservation Special Committee, who suggested that, since it was now clearly impossible to raise the water level, the best way to reinstate the fen was to dig through the present surface until water was reached. 'Much fundamental ecological knowledge should be gained by this work', he thought (though the idea was never put into practice). Holme Fen was Crown property, but the Commissioners agreed to transfer all 259 ha to the Conservancy (reserving, as usual, the shooting rights, though these were surrendered voluntarily two years later). Holme Fen represents perhaps the least complex ecosystem in wild Britain, much of it consisting of little more than bare peaty ground and birch trees. Its very simplicity makes it useful for teaching some of the basic principles of ecology, such as primary production. But it was hardly the most exciting place in England for wildlife.

The first seven National Nature Reserves in England typified the kind of Reserves which the Nature Conservancy would acquire over the next decade: small areas of wild land which would be managed as outdoor laboratories for a new generation of ecologists and to preserve the special features of the site. Most of the seven were smaller than the nature reserves envisaged by Cmd. 7122, and some were not listed in that White Paper at all. The Conservancy was forced at the very outset of its Reserve acquisition programme to temper the ideal aims of the founding fathers with a necessary pragmatism.

'IT'S NOW OR NEVER'

A nature reserve is perhaps the most tangible goal of nature conservation. In the public mind it embodies everything that conservation sets out to achieve. The formal

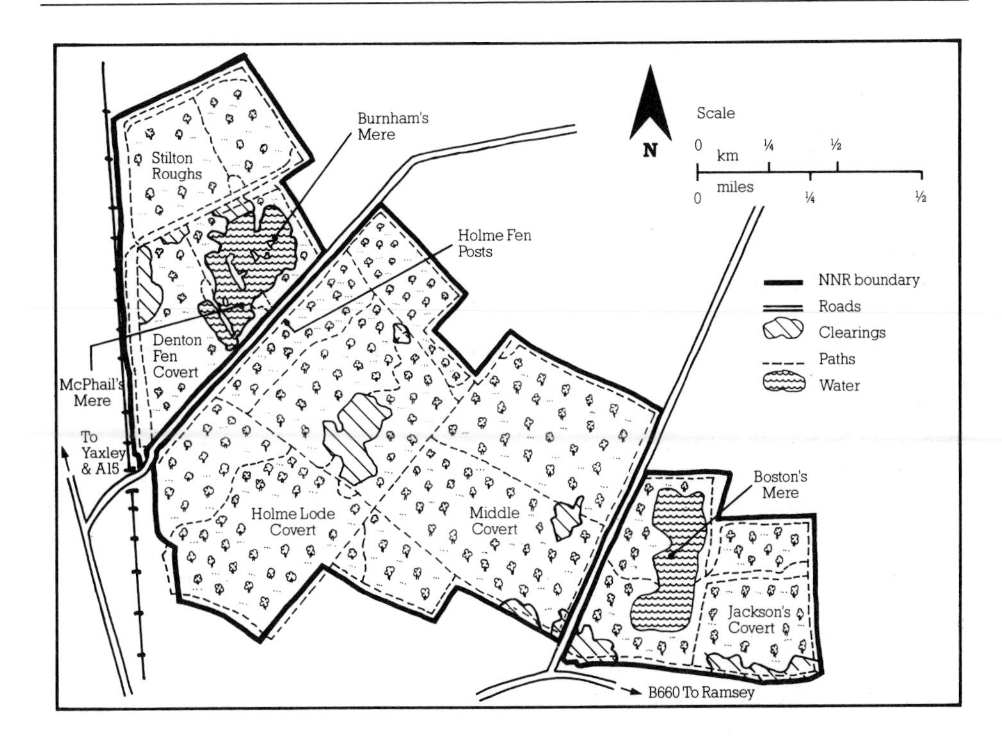

MAP 1 *Holme Fen NNR, Cambridgeshire*

declaration of a National Nature Reserve after many months hard bargaining is always a happy occasion, and with a new Reserve often comes the desire to make this one the best so far. There is often a great deal of estate work to be done: new gates and stockproof fences to be installed, ditches to be dammed or slubbed, access ways to be improved. There is also an understandable desire to try to find out all about the new holding; indeed I suspect that the surveys and stock-takings envisaged by the founders of the National Nature Reserves had as much to do with a child-like curiosity, the flipping open of a watch to discover the mechanism within, as in any particular principle of scientific management.

As we have seen, four types of tenure are possible on a National Nature Reserve. The first, and most desirable, are Reserves which are owned by the Conservancy and wholly under its control, such as Yarner Wood or Old Winchester Hill. Then there are Reserves like Moor House which, although owned, have some form of inbuilt constraint such as a sitting tenant or common grazing rights. Together these owned Reserves account for slightly less than a third (30%) of the present NNR estate in England (see Appendix 2). Some Reserves have been leased, often from a Department of State, the Crown or a heritage body, and usually on a long-term basis. An example is Scolt Head Island, which is leased from the National Trust and the Norfolk Naturalists Trust. In practice, the terms of leases generally allow the Conservancy a fairly free hand.

About a third of England's National Nature Reserves are neither publicly owned nor leased but remain private land, subject to a Nature Reserve Agreement between the landowner and the Conservancy. A common form of agreement runs for 21 years and allows the Conservancy a limited range of rights in exchange for an annual payment. The payment has varied from the purely nominal sums of the early days to the substantial sums offered more recently in compensation for loss of profits. This type of Reserve is usually managed to some compromise formula which, although often very much less satisfactory than outright purchase, and sometimes almost as expensive, allows the Conservancy to manage the site to an acceptable standard.

In practice, then, the label of National Nature Reserve covers widely varying levels of protection from the near absolute to the decidedly partial. The unifying factor is that the conservation of nature takes precedence over all other forms of land use: this is essentially what distinguishes National Nature Reserves from Sites of Special Scientific Interest. On some owned Reserves, like Yarner Wood or Scolt Head Island, there may be *no* other use of the land other than that of nature conservation. More often there is a shared use: wildfowling at Lindisfarne, for example, or the reworking of old lead mines at Moor House.

Why does the Conservancy not opt for outright purchase in every case? One answer is that it lacks the resources to do so. Another is that the landowner may not wish to sell. The Nature Conservancy and its successors were granted compulsory purchase powers because, since the Crichel Down case in the 1950s, such powers are normally granted to Departments of State or agents of the Crown that own land. Such orders are made, not by the Conservancy, however, but by the Minister of State, once he is convinced that all alternatives have been exhausted. This might take years. Moreover, the Conservancy was always reluctant to upset the landowning establishment, on whose co-operation it relied. It was therefore often a choice between imperfect agreements and no protection at all. And it gradually dawned on people that protection, and not scientific study, was to be the name of the game. Tansley's prediction that post-war agriculture and forestry would settle down to an unaggressive *status quo* was proving wildly wrong. Natural habitats of all kinds were disappearing under the plough or the spruce at a rate unprecedented in history. And there was no mechanism in place to protect fully the best sites, save for their declaration as National Nature Reserves. The safeguards allowed for Sites of Special Scientific Interest were directed towards housing and industrial development and changes in land-use, not agricultural intensification. And since the private sector of conservation was almost non-existent at this date, the National Nature Reserves became, for lack of an alternative, the most important instrument for site protection. They were being made to fulfil a conservation function that their founders had not envisaged, but which was now recognised as vital. As Dudley Stamp remarked at the time, 'it was a case of now or never'. He was mindful of his recent search for a single patch of undeveloped habitat among the prairies of Nebraska—ironically the very place where Clements had pioneered quantitative methods in plant ecology, 50 years earlier. In the end he had had to give up. The prairies had become an ocean of swaying wheat—an ocean without islands. Parts of eastern England seemed to be going the same way. The then Chairman of the Nature Conservancy, Sir Arthur Duncan, suggested to the Commons Committee on Estimates in 1958 that 'the completion of the programme of Reserves that is done in 1950 would not be as good as the one that was done in 1900, and the one done in AD 2000, I should think, is probably not worth doing at all'.

The agricultural advances of the 1950s had therefore made the original proposal of

73 National Nature Reserves obsolete. That area of 258 km^2, scattered in penny packets over the whole of England and Wales, was unlikely to save much of the detail of the wonderfully intricate nature of our traditional countryside. From picking out (like favourite chocolates) particular examples of wild habitats in Britain, it became an urgent matter of finding *all* the best examples. This would eventually multiply the original candidate list of 73 sites by a factor of 12.

Conservationists are habitual list makers, and this faculty makes the sorting and classification of candidate nature reserves a fit and congenial task. As we have seen, N Charles Rothschild produced such a list as long ago as 1915. The Nature Reserve Investigation Committee's list, drawn up in 1943, sought a reasonably objective basis, what people now like to call a *rationale*, for selecting nature reserves. They tried to find 'a fair balance . . . between the conservation of representative types of flora and fauna and the protection of populations, aggregates of species, individual species and communities that are peculiar, rare or unique'. They recognised that ancient or 'primitive' habitats such as long-established woodland or virgin peat bogs had a special value, and they knew that large areas were better than small ones. In general, their work was informed and thorough, and has stood the test of time.

In 1965, the Treasury professed itself concerned about the apparently open-ended commitment of National Nature Reserve acquisition. How many Reserves, it asked, did the Conservancy require? When would the series be complete? It was partly to answer awkward questions of this sort that the Nature Conservancy began what was to become a 10-year programme to identify the areas of 'national biological importance to nature conservation' in Britain. To do so, methods of classifying vegetation and habitats had to be defined, and dozens of surveys were made by in-house and contract scientists, combing the overlooked and forgotten corners of England, Scotland and Wales. It was the last and most significant phase of ecological exploring in Britain, and it produced in 1977 the famous two-volume tome, *A Nature Conservation Review*. The review made Britain the most thoroughly ecologically-documented country in the world, and the English lowlands the most thoroughly documented of all. Such a review presupposes of course that the best sites *can* be pulled out of their matrix and evaluated reasonably objectively. An elaborate system was devised that took into account a variety of factors, notably the relative size, diversity and 'naturalness' of the site. Only a handful of places stand out as unique, as head and shoulders above any others of their type: Dungeness, the New Forest *en bloc*, St Kilda, Upper Teesdale, the Flow Country of the far north of Scotland. More often sites have to be weighed up against a range of criteria. The Review is a continuous state of flux along the margins as new sites are found and old ones re-evaluated, or, in a few cases, when the site ceases to exist. The published Review listed and described 735 areas as 'key sites'. Most of the existing National Nature Reserves proved to be key sites, which was rather convenient. The few that failed to make the grade, such as the Tring Reservoirs or the little island of Haaf Gruney in Shetland, were eventually disestablished or, as the phrase has it, 'de-declared'. The Review prescribed no means of safeguarding the key sites, but made clear that each deserved a degree of protection *equivalent* to that of a National Nature Reserve. This in itself was a radical shift of policy. In 1977 there were about 150 National Nature Reserves in Britain. But there were 735 'key sites', and most of these had only the then inadequate SSSI mechanism to protect them.

EXPANDING THE NETWORK

In considering the *Nature Conservation Review* we have jumped ahead in time. Back in the 1950s, the Nature Conservancy was acquiring Reserves at a steady and, considering its resources, rapid pace. Some of the best known Reserves were declared during this decade: in 1953, Monks Wood, the site of the future experimental station, part of the Blean Woods in Kent and Scolt Head Island; in 1954, Old Winchester Hill, Hartland Moor and Castor Hanglands; in 1955, Lullington Heath and Wybunbury Moss. We will not follow the story of the acquisition of the network of National Nature Reserves in detail here, except to note a few general points from these formative years. First, many of the Reserves at this time were outright purchases, something that became less usual later on except as a last resort. Probably the main reason for opting for purchase was to secure land for long-term scientific experiments from which the public could be excluded. Monks Wood, Hartland Moor and Lullington Heath were examples. At Roudsea Wood in Lancashire (now in Cumbria) the Conservancy even managed to persuade the local authority to remove the existing rights of way from its maps in order to safeguard the scientific equipment which strewed the woodland floor.

A few properties were acquired by deed of gift, such as Calthorpe Broad, presented by the widow of the naturalist Robert Gurney. Rostherne Mere in Cheshire was another gift. Its owner, Lord Egerton, was persuaded to bequeath the secluded lake to the Nature Conservancy so that it could continue 'to enjoy the strict protection which it enjoyed in his lifetime'. For several other sites the Nature Conservancy took on the responsibility for management on behalf of the owners, namely at Woodwalton Fen, Weeting and Thetford Heaths, Ranworth and Cockshoot Broads and Scolt Head Island. Hickling Broad was exceptional in that, although it was declared a National Nature Reserve, it continued to be looked after by a conservation charity, the Norfolk Naturalists Trust. In 1956, two more geological Reserves were added to the list: Fyfield Down, a dense scatter of sarsen stones amid Wiltshire downland, and the Wren's Nest in the Borough of Dudley, a noted locality for limestone fossils.

Understandably, the choice of some Reserves seems to have reflected the individual interests of members of the Conservancy's scientific committee. Tansley's advocacy had secured the early purchase of Kingley Vale and W H Pearsall's of Moor House. In 1954, North Fen on the shores of Esthwaite Water in the Lake District and the nearby Blelham Bog were leased from the National Trust. Both were well known through Tansley's writings, which were based in turn on the research papers of Pearsall. Tiny Cothill Fen in Oxfordshire, already an informal nature reserve named after John Ruskin, became a National Nature Reserve at about the same time. This 2-ha rectangle of reedbed might have been considered rather small, even by English standards, but E B Ford had studied tiger moths there, and it too was conveniently owned by the National Trust. These 'flyspeck' sites form a special category among National Nature Reserves as 'classic' research sites which, because of their thoroughness of documentation over a long period, have become scientific assets.

Most of the above-mentioned sites were already well known to ecologists. Bridgwater Bay on the Somerset coast, on the other hand, was *terra incognita*. Nevertheless, when the Somerset River Board offered 2430 ha of intertidal saltmarsh and mudflats in the bay to the Nature Conservancy, the latter agreed to take it on as another experimental reserve. Like most of these *ad hoc* acquisitions, it eventually justified its selection. The Bay has its fair share of migrant wildfowl, including the Shelduck, which chooses to stay and moult here when most English Shelduck fly off to Heligoland. The Reserve was to play a useful part in establishing the successful *rapprochement* between wildfowlers and conservationists in Britain (see Chapter 9).

The Reserves at Hartland Moor in Dorset (1954) and Roudsea Wood (1955) were established mainly for their nearness to the recently established field stations at Furzebrook and Merlewood, which made them useful for research in heathland and woodland ecology. Both Reserves were large, relatively undisturbed and private. And, as with Yarner Wood and Bridgwater Bay, their conservation value eventually overtook their original function as outdoor laboratories. The full significance of Roudsea Wood, as a wonderful place whose present composition is mirrored by the ancient tree pollen in the bogs at its feet, was not appreciated until 30 years later; the choice of Roudsea above all the other alluring woods of the district was a lucky fluke. Hartland Moor was another: it is now the largest continuous area of wet heath in Dorset and, despite being burned to a cinder in 1976, is still one of a handful of places that contain virtually all of the rare and special birds, reptiles, flowers and insects of the glorious Purbeck heaths.

Rodney Stoke NNR in the Mendips of Somerset was the first Reserve to be selected as the result of a comprehensive habitat survey, in this case a review of the Mendip ashwoods. England is the premier country in Europe for ashwoods, our oceanic climate and limestone soils being well-suited to this most elegant of trees. The authors of Cmd. 7122 had recognised that the Mendip-type of ashwood should be represented in the national series of Reserves, and had singled out Cheddar Wood as the best example. It was certainly the best known. However the Regional Officer responsible, Norman Moore, thought it would be as well to compare the site with other large ashwoods in the area, and undertook a thorough survey of them with the help of a local naturalist, Noel Sandwith. The results suggested that the outstanding site was not Cheddar but Asham Wood, but unfortunately that wood was owned by a quarry company with planning permission to extend its workings further. Rodney Stoke was the next best choice, containing most of the characteristic species of the area like Blue Gromwell, Meadow Saffron and the Bulin Snail. Moreover the owner was willing to sell. Rodney Stoke was duly declared a National Nature Reserve. As it happened, some parcels of scrubby grassland and old strawberry fields were included in the purchase. These were little regarded at the time, but as perceptions of the value of old grassland changed they assumed a much greater importance and their management is an important function of today's Reserve.

There was, inevitably, a political reaction to the rapid acquisition of National Nature Reserves. The Nature Conservancy began life in a friendly *milieu*, with close and useful ties between it and government. This did not long survive the fall of the Attlee government and the Conservancy's protector, Herbert Morrison. The climate soon grew chilly, especially when the Nature Conservancy sought to acquire a large chunk of the Cairngorms in 1953 and, a few years later, to purchase the Hebridean island of Rhum. The new Lord President of the Council, Lord Salisbury, expressed himself concerned at the extent of these plans, especially when 'much of the land was being sought for its ecological character and value to scientific research, rather than merely because it contained rare species'. The Forestry Commission chimed in with a complaint that the Conservancy had been declaring land that was suitable for growing timber. Behind the scenes the politicians briefly considered imposing restrictions on the type of land the Nature Conservancy could acquire. Fortunately, Max Nicholson was robust in his defence of the Conservancy's independence, and an investigations committee established under Treasury chairmanship pronounced itself 'reassured'. Nevertheless the latter insisted that all actual and potential differences should in future be resolved with neighbours and other land users before a Reserve was declared. Taken literally this would have amounted to a brake on Reserve acquisitions, as it was no doubt meant to be. There was a difference in opinion in the Conservancy's own ruling body. Against those, like Nicholson or Dudley Stamp, who wished to press on and preserve as many sites as possible, stood others like W H Pearsall, chairman of the scientific policy committee responsible for drawing up criteria for Reserve selection, who liked to do only one thing at a time, and that thoroughly.

In 1959, the Nature Conservancy was subjected to further persecution in the form of a Commons Committee of Estimates, where it was made to account for every brass farthing spent on Reserves to a sceptical and astonishingly ignorant panel of MPs. Nicholson was pressed particularly hard on the matter of raising revenue from National Nature Reserves. Could he not, for example, let the grazing or sporting rights? But even this Committee could not deny that England's first 40 or so National Nature Reserves, covering some 4860 ha, had been acquired at negligible cost to the taxpayer. The establishment of a useful core of Reserves in less than a decade was a great achievement and one that showed true foresight. It was aided by the relatively stable financial climate and the low land prices of the 1950s, and pushed through by a certain native grittiness in the Conservancy's leadership. When one considers that, of the other Cmd. 7122 nature reserve proposals, the geological monuments and educational reserves flopped at the first hurdle, the Local Nature Reserves were for many years a lame duck and the conservation provisions of Forest Nature Reserves proved so weak as to be barely worth having, the success of the National Nature Reserves is all the more admirable. The idea worked because a few people knew that a great deal depended on it. Today most people might agree that they were right.

CHANGING PERSPECTIVES

By 1961, the Nature Conservancy looked after some 70 National Nature Reserves in England, Scotland and Wales, covering 52,000 ha. Just under half the area was owned or held on long leases at an average cost of £4.44 per hectare. The most expensive Reserve, the island of Rhum, had cost £23,000—about the contemporary price of a medium-sized house in inner London. The other half was held under various shorter-term agreements at purely nominal payments that averaged an incredible 7.4p per hectare per year. The network continued to expand steadily in succeeding years and not a year passed between 1962 and 1983 without at least one new Reserve being declared. The rate did slow between 1965 and 1973, however, when the Nature Conservancy lost some of its former independence after being made an arm of the newly constituted Natural Environment Research Council (NERC). Scientists take a pride in their impartiality, and the Conservancy's advocacy of nature protection was viewed with suspicion in some quarters of the Council. Some of the governing scientists began to question the protectionist role of National Nature Reserves. If their purpose was to provide scientists with living laboratories, why then were there so many? Could the Reserve network not be trimmed, and the surplus released back to the private sector and the charitable bodies? It was not the last time such loaded questions were to be asked.

By 1973, the government had decided that science and nature conservation were no longer comfortable bed fellows, and that it would be better for the Conservancy to buy in research under a customer–contractor arrangement than to have it provided in-house. Accordingly, the old Nature Conservancy was demolished. Most of its administrative functions, including the setting up of National Nature Reserves, were taken over by the newly appointed Nature Conservancy Council. The former research arm remained in NERC as the Institute of Terrestrial Ecology (ITE). The Minister claimed that the NCC, as the Nature Conservancy Council inevitably became known, would be able to take a stronger and more independent line on important issues. The Chairman and members of its governing Council were appointed by Ministers with a view to ensuring that the NCC would not over-estimate its new-found strength and independence. There is no doubt that the loss of its scientific function left the Conservancy (as I shall continue to call it for the sake of convenience) with a changed outlook, more concerned with protecting habitats than with conducting original ecological research. Most of its contracted research in future lay in the empirical fields of survey and monitoring. On the Reserve there was more estate work and less experimental management than before. In some ways this was well and good, as most Reserves were badly in need of basic management, such as coppicing or stock grazing. The new circumstances (or the Split as the reorganisation was universally but inelegantly known) left the Reserves in something of a policy vacuum. If they were no longer functioning as 'outdoor laboratories', as envisaged in the original White Paper, did they have any new role to play? Evidently not, for the Nature Conservancy Council Act did nothing but repeat the 1949 dispensation for National Nature Reserves. This seems not to have bothered anyone unduly. The NNRs bumped along under their site protection role. It is only in recent years that a new role for them has emerged as erstwhile farmland has begun to go out of production (see Chapter 10).

Despite its important changes in other areas, the Wildlife and Countryside Act 1981 had relatively little to say about National Nature Reserves, apart from introducing the term to the legislation for the first time. Section 35 of the Act did, however, extend the concept of a National Nature Reserve to cover land held and managed by others. Such land had to be 'of national importance' and owned by 'an approved body' (approved by the NCC, that is) and to be managed in a suitable way. Unfortunately the approved bodies were slow to queue for the honour, since the law made no promise or allowance of additional funding. It is only in the past few years that 'Section 35 Reserves' have begun to multiply, under an agreement that the NCC's successor, English Nature, will provide modest funds for any refinements of management it believes to be necessary. There is no question of Big Brother-style intervention. The Section 35 NNRs remain firmly under the control of their owners. Section 35 has far-reaching implications for the future of National Nature Reserves, however, since they could eventually result in a situation where more Reserves are run by approved bodies than by English Nature.

If so, the role of the latter would become increasingly one of enabling rather than managing directly. In the long run, this would probably be harmful to nature conservation, though no doubt politically cute.

By placing the spotlight on management agreements and SSSIs, with all the brouhaha that has sometimes resulted, the Wildlife and Countryside Act diverted public attention away from nature reserves. In the early Annual Reports of the Nature Conservancy, the National Nature Reserves appear as 'jewels in the crown', and page after page is devoted to their story. By the 1980s, their allotment had shrunk to a notional page or two: from mainstream to backwater in less than 30 years. It was not that the Reserves themselves were being neglected—far from it, the 1980s were the years of great advances in Reserve management through mechanisation, the use of Manpower Services teams and increased staffing. But public attention was focused on the sterile conservation battles north of the Border and on what the Conservancy has always called 'the wider countryside'. There was a brief surge of interest in 1988 when the late Nicholas Ridley announced that he wanted to privatise some of the National Nature Reserves (how many he had in mind was never made clear. The NCC had 11 sacrificial sites ready as 'a sop to Cerberus'). This had at least the useful effect of obliging the NCC to think about its strategic aims and about the future of the Reserves. Ridley's intervention seems to have amounted to little more than his instinctive aversion to anything with National in its name, and his successor as Environment Secretary announced that the plan, which had been roundly derided by the press, 'was not on his agenda'. But the privatisation proposal may yet prove to have been unexpectedly benign, for it put the spotlight back on National Nature Reserves once more. The ways in which our Reserves may develop in the immediate future is explored in Chapter 10.

THE WIDER SCENE

International agreements on nature conservation now offer a welcome reinforcement to legislation, although the amount of extra protection they provide on National Nature Reserves is not great. Rather, the existence of National Nature Reserves makes it possible for governments to designate sites under the various conventions without having to commit themselves to increasing resources. The earliest was the Ramsar Convention on the Conservation of Wetlands and Wildfowl (named after the town in Iran where the Convention was formulated), which was ratified by the United Kingdom in 1976. The Convention commits governments to the 'wise use' of sites listed under the Convention. Among the first Ramsar sites designated by the Department of Environment on 5 January 1976 were a batch of existing National Nature Reserves, namely Lindisfarne, the Norfolk Broads (including the Bure Marshes NNR), Bridgwater Bay, and Walberswick. A great many coastal and wetland NNRs are now Ramsar sites (see Appendix 3), for, since much of the English coast is of international importance for passage waders and wildfowl, a great many estuaries and soft shores qualify for Ramsar status. The Convention provides an internationally accepted yardstick for evaluating sites of importance for birds, so that any area holding over 20,000 waterfowl or at least 1% of the estimated world population of a particular species or race is considered to be of international importance.

Another accord, this time under the EC Bird Directive, commits governments to designate Special Protection Areas (SPA) on the habitats of certain rare species (especially lowland heaths or places where large numbers of migratory birds congregate regularly). Governments are expected to take steps to prevent 'SPAs' from pollution or undue disturbance, and take action where necessary to prevent them from 'deteriorating'. Once again, National Nature Reserves are places where governments can honour their agreements without undue difficulty. In practice SPA and Ramsar designations often overlap. The NNRs at the Lower Derwent Valley, Walberswick, Thorne Moors and the North Norfolk Coast, for example, are both Ramsar sites and SPAs. On both designations, the government has a let-out option if it considers it to be 'in the national interest' to destroy the site. Of more tangible value is the system of 'Environmentally Sensitive Areas', introduced by the Ministry of Agriculture under an EC farming directive in the 1980s to provide a means of farming in ways more sympathetic to the qualities of the landscape and its wild places. In certain areas like Upper Teesdale or the Breckland, ESAs have helped to provide a useful buffer zone around National Nature Reserves. Set-aside land has the potential to achieve much the same aim on a more local scale, and has created some much-needed buffer land on several Reserves in the agricultural south and east, notably Barton Hills in Bedfordshire and the Lewes Downs in East Sussex (see Chapter 10).

Protective legislation is a rolling conveyor belt, sometimes slow, sometimes fast as at present. The number of schemes and designations offering enhanced rates of grant-aid or 'presumptions' against development is becoming bewildering to those unversed in the language of acronyms and civil service small-print. Since government ministers often claim that the cumulative effect of these measures is to 'improve the delivery of nature conservation', it is as well to bear in mind that virtually all of these schemes offer only partial protection and are generally underfunded. A site may have a six-fold layer of protective mechanisms yet may still be damaged—as at Twyford Down, where the national interest in the form of a four-lane motorway demands its sacrifice. The protection offered by nature reserves, and National Nature Reserves in particular, is of a different order because it recognises that here, at least, wildlife comes first. It is unlikely that their role will be superseded by 'wider countryside' legislation in the foreseeable future, because on no other sites do conservation bodies have direct control over how the land is managed. What actually happens on nature reserves, and what makes them different from the rest of the land, is the subject of the chapters that follow.

A QUARTET OF NATURE RESERVES

I want to conclude this chapter by looking at four National Nature Reserves declared during the past 20 years, which I believe to have a significance beyond that of a single site. These are the North Meadow at Cricklade (1973), Gait Barrows (1977), the Ribble Marshes (1981) and the Wash (1992). Each in its different way has extended the concept of the National Nature Reserve so that this has become more of an umbrella term than ever. At least two of the sites would probably have been destroyed without a National Reserves network in place to offer an alternative. And not one of them was listed by the founding fathers as a possible National Nature Reserve.

Most of the early Reserves were recognisably *wild*, that is to say uncultivated and in many cases unfarmed, apart from some rough grazing. This was the Cmd. 7122 view of nature reserves as 'land which has suffered the least disturbance by man'. To the plant ecologists of Tansley's generation, permanent pasture on neutral, alluvial soils was part of the 'disturbed' farm landscape. It is arguable, however, that the hay meads of Oxford, say, or the water meadows of Wiltshire, are just as natural as the chalk downs. They are ancient and are composed mainly or wholly of wild grasses and flowers growing in recognisable communities. They often lie on land that has never been cultivated and may even, as the landscape historian Oliver Rackham has suggested, represent strong echoes of the subalpine flora of the remote past. Perhaps because ecologists were slow to take much notice of enclosed meadows, they failed to realise that such places, with their ponds, Black Poplars and Green-winged Orchids, were fast becoming things of the past. Hay meadows and riverine fields often lie on excellent soil, and, once drained, can be converted into arable land. And that is more or less what happened, except in areas subject to ancient customs, or owned by reactionary people who happened to like wild flowers, cows and big hedges. Such places have become perhaps the least expected form of National Nature Reserve, the very opposite of popular notions of wild heaths and estuaries. In another sense, though, the old meadows may be nearest to our hearts: the familiar sights and sounds of half a century ago, now so rare that not one parish in ten has a hayfield or a really good field pond. They may be 'tame', but they are the quintessential old England of

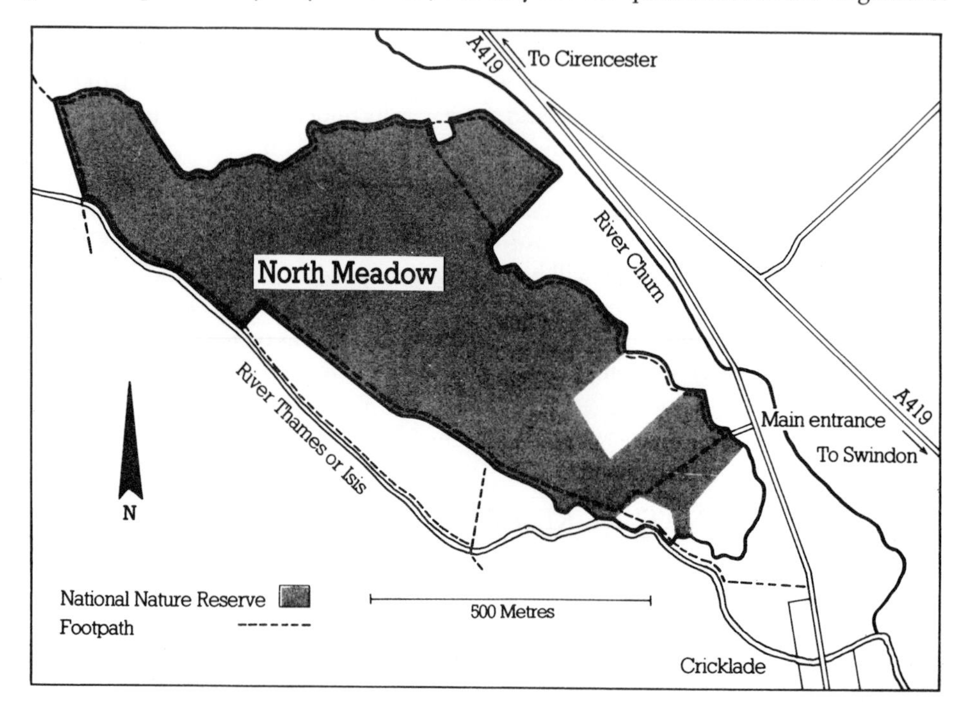

MAP 2 *North Meadow NNR, Wiltshire*

Rupert Brooke and Elgar, and most of us respond more to a field full of flowers and butterflies than to a bleak moor or a mudflat.

The first of the dozen or so meadowland Reserves in England was the celebrated North Meadow at Cricklade in Wiltshire, a place that the poet and botanist Geoffrey Grigson urged everyone to visit at least once before they died. This is the big broad field along the infant Thames which at the end of April becomes filled with the nodding purple bells of the Snake's-head Fritillary lily, thousands upon thousands of them. It is one of those places that has been managed in the same way for centuries in an annual cycle of grazing and haymaking, broken by seasonal floods, that harmonised with the communal needs of the farming people of Cricklade. By the 1960s, the old ways were threatened here as everywhere else, but the Conservancy was able to guarantee the meadow's survival by buying up plots of the land as they became available. Now the main freehold owner of the meadow, the Conservancy sells the hay as a standing crop to local farmers, and also rents part of the land to wild flower seed merchants who harvest this novel form of crop with a sort of giant hoover. The meadow's future has been safeguarded, and, equally importantly, it continues to be farmed in ways that resemble the traditional uses of this famous field (see Chapter 9).

Until the 1970s, few Reserves were declared to avert an immediate threat to their survival. As we have seen, the Conservancy was reluctant to play the compulsory purchase card and, until the advent of the Wildlife and Countryside Act, was obliged to rely on the planning system and local council enforcement action to prevent development on SSSIs. In any case, it could not afford to purchase sites that had planning permission for development. Fortunately the occasions when the Conservancy was faced with an all-or-nothing case of purchase or destruction were few, but when they did arise the casework could become extraordinarily arduous. Gait Barrows, in Silverdale on the coast of Morecambe Bay, was a case in point. This is one of our finest and most beautiful limestone pavements, and a peculiarly massive form of pavement it is, bare waterworn stone penetrated by deep fissures and scooped into by circular 'solution cups'. Gait Barrows is tucked away on private land behind a screen of scrub and woodland and was hardly known to the outside world except by local naturalists. Its beautiful stone was unfortunately a valuable commercial commodity for there was a big demand for waterworn limestone by rockery nurseries, especially in London. As it is only the eroded surface of the pavement that fetches the top prices, a large expanse of pavement can soon be ruined by the use of explosives and hydraulic machinery to strip away the best stone. Gait Barrows lay outside the National Parks, and the 'winning' of stone there lay in one of the grey areas in planning law about which lawyers enjoy bickering for years on end. Meanwhile the blasting and shovelling went on, and between 1965 and 1975 more than half of the pavement was badly damaged or destroyed. Eventually Lancashire County Council was persuaded to bring enforcement action against the owners, who thereupon agreed to sell the site for a six-figure sum. Gait Barrows NNR was duly declared in 1977. This single case had tied down regional staff and land agents for years, and at one point the NCC had even considered the compulsory purchase route (never before used, except in a couple of technical cases where no owner was known). Time has healed some of the scars at Gait Barrows, and it is now one of the most attractive Reserves, the much-abused pavement lying at the core of a wild expanse of woodland, reedbed and a marl lake. None the less, the Conservancy could not afford to fight many such battles.

A few years later, there was a similar all-or-nothing case, but on a much larger scale. The Ribble Estuary is among the wildest places in England, and is used by thousands of geese, ducks and wading birds during the winter months as a staging post to and from the Arctic, along the great East Atlantic flyway. The south bank of the Ribble is the largest continuous area of grazing marsh in England, and a remarkable spectacle at low tide in summer when hundreds of cattle graze the vast open range of sweet grass (and more remarkable still, I'm told, at the dead of a freezing winter when snow flurries over the flats and icebergs move up the Ribble on the tide). The estuary was not, however, a Cmd. 7122 site, nor one for which the Conservancy, in normal circumstances, would have considered bidding. The choice of nature reserves is constrained by financial reality and, to some extent, by limitations of scale. The Conservancy was used to thinking in terms of tens of hectares, not horizon-to-horizon expanses measured in square kilometres.

The south shore of the Ribble estuary, formerly part of the Scarisbrick Estate, was put on the market in 1978. A bid from the RSPB to purchase the crucial 2200 ha of saltmarsh and tidal flats, backed by promises of financial support from the NCC and the World Wildlife Fund, failed and the land was sold instead to a Dutch farmer and an engineering contractor who planned to embank most of the marsh and drain it for intensive agricultural production. They were legally entitled to do so (indeed, they would probably have received grant-aid), and it was only the cross-party support of 226 MPs, and the threat of compulsory purchase, that prevented the reclamation of the entire estuary. Even so, the NCC could not have found the asked-for price of £1,725,000 (plus costs) from its own resources—for it amounted to a quarter of its entire annual budget. Fortunately press interest and back-bench murmuring had encouraged the then Environment Minister, Denis Howell, to take an interest in the case, and he pledged government support for the purchase of the estuary as a nature reserve. Sensing the mood, the developers decided to sell. Contracts were exchanged in March 1979, and later that year the Ribble Estuary became England's second largest National Nature Reserve. But despite the apparently happy outcome, there were disquieting aspects to the case. It exposed the possibility of blackmail over important sites. There seemed to be no alternative to the most expensive option of freehold purchase to save such sites. And, of course, the developers were in a no-lose situation for, whether the site was sold or whether it was reclaimed, they stood to profit at the expense of the British taxpayer. In the event, one of them went on to purchase and reclaim an adjoining area of saltmarsh. This land is now Set-aside, and the owner is paid for not growing crops on it. The price of safeguarding places like Gait Barrows and the Ribble was several orders of magnitude away from the 84 p a hectare freehold purchase of Beinn Eighe.

The Conservancy's Annual Report voiced frank concern about the implications of the Ribble case. With the high tide of agricultural reclamation and the consequent soaring of land prices, the Conservancy feared that in future it might be helpless to prevent the loss of irreplaceable sites (despite the extra demands of the Ribble purchase, its annual grant had not been increased, but cut). Fortunately public opinion was forcing a change in the law, partly as a result of the publicity given to cases like this. The Wildlife and Countryside Act greatly improved the protection for SSSIs by introducing a mandatory period of negotiation before a 'potentially damaging operation' could take place. This reduced the immediate threat of all-out destruction and improved the conservationists' hand at the bargaining table. In effect it produced an alternative to purchase and the declaration of the site as a nature reserve. Land prices remained high, but at least the Conservancy's annual budget was increased to meet the massive administrative burden imposed by the Act. Furthermore it could now grant-aid voluntary bodies to purchase their own land, a factor which was to increase vastly the nature reserve portfolio of the English County Trusts.

The ebb-tide of agricultural improvement has opened up many new opportunities for nature conservation and for more positive co-operation between conservationists and farmers and landowners. Until the late 1980s, it would probably have been a waste of time to negotiate for a National Nature Reserve agreement on an area the size of the Wash, despite its evident national importance for migrant birds and seals. The Dutch and Germans have felt more confident, and the Wash's continental counterpart, the Waddensee, is among the most impressive nature reserves in Europe. In the end, negotiating for nature reserves boils down to a matter of confidence, and of the imagination to 'think big'. The Conservancy's first steps to safeguard parts of the Wash were in the familiar territory of penny packets, a couple of scraps of foreshore at Kirton and Lutton Outmarsh, purchased in the mid-1980s to save them from reclamation. What made the difference was a test-case public inquiry over the proposed reclamation of part of the Wash at Gedney Drove End. If the applications had been approved, a flood of similar applications would have followed. But since it was turned down, a 100 years of gradual attrition of grazing marsh and intertidal mud was suddenly brought to a halt. The way was open for a new initiative to provide for the future of the Wash as an estuary.

The Conservancy decided to go for the big solution—a nature reserve agreement covering almost the whole of the tidal flats and saltings of the Wash. The task called for considerable organisational and diplomatic skill, for the Wash is not what it sometimes seems—an empty tidal waste—but a valuable resource used by grazers, shell fisheries, shipping companies, wildfowlers and the military, among others, to say nothing of its potential as a source of tidal energy. The significance of these eventually successful negotiations was that, for the first time, conservation was being widely accepted as a *unifying* force, as the one interest capable of bringing together and seeking to reconcile the different livings and uses that are made of an area. It has brought a significant change to the work of the Reserve's site manager, Bob Lord, for the Wash requires almost none of the traditional husbandry and estate work associated with nature reserves. Instead, Bob is responsible for putting into practice a strategy worked out with the more traditional users of the area to establish sanctuary areas and to improve the quality of the intertidal marshes. This is a different kind of National Nature Reserve: not so much land set aside for nature as a *forum*, a framework in which people with a common interest in preserving the Wash can work together instead of pursuing their separate and conflicting interests in isolation. Significantly, too, this was the first National Nature Reserve to be the subject of a formal international accord, in which scientists and reserve managers from several European countries are pooling their experience and knowledge. There is an indisputable logic to developing common international standards: the birds and seals that visit the Wash also use the Waddensee and the Rhine estuary.

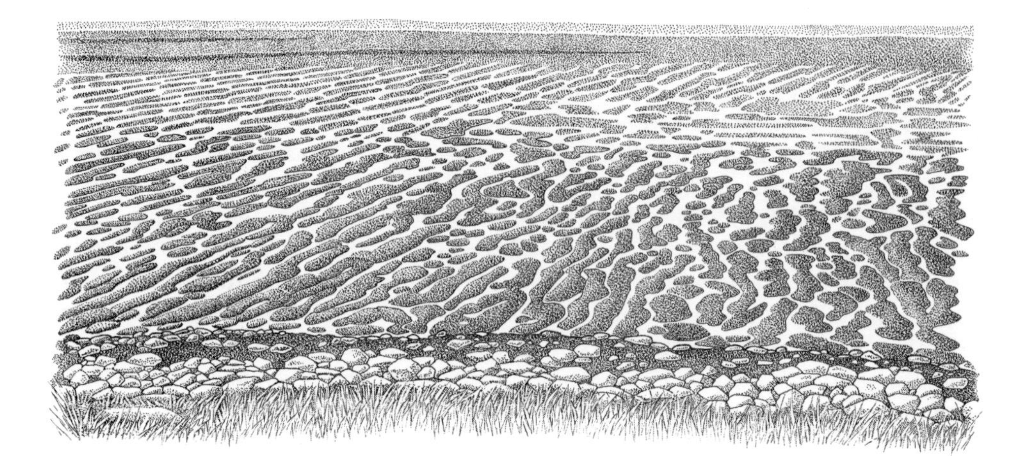

6. *The great yew at Kingley Vale.*

7. Above left: *A study in landscape perspective at Holme Fen.* 8. Above right: *Cavenham Heath in the Suffolk Breck.*
9. Below: *Managed coppice-with-standards woodland at Ham Street Woods.*

10. Left: *Massive fissured limestone pavement forms the heart of Gait Barrows.*

11. Below: *The Wash, the Breast Sands area in Norfolk.*

12. Below: *The North Meadow at Cricklade.*

13. Left: *The Derwent Gorge in County Durham.*
14. Below: *The edge of Parsonage Down.*

15. Below: *Naturalists searching for orchids along the nature trail at Old Winchester Hill.*

CHAPTER 3

Managing the Reserve

THE responsibility for the day-to-day running of National Nature Reserves belongs to the Reserve wardens, or 'site managers' as they are now known. Most site managers are assisted in their work by one or two estate workers and, often, a summer warden. They are helped further by small teams of voluntary wardens, who are members of the public who act as guides and generally keep an eye on things. The responsibilities of Reserve wardens vary a good deal. A few spend much or all of their time looking after a single large Reserve, like Douglas Gilbert at the Derbyshire Dales or Ian Findlay at Upper Teesdale. More often, nowadays, he or she is responsible for a suite of Reserves. Mike Cox, for example, is in charge of all six of the Oxfordshire Reserves and Peter Singleton has no fewer than seven Reserves in the southern Lake District under his care. Increasingly their duties are being broadened to include advice on management on SSSIs and other sites where nature conservation is a primary aim (see below). It was mainly for that reason that the title of Reserve warden was changed in 1991 to 'site manager'. Be that as it may, the bulk of most site managers' time continues to be spent on National Nature Reserves.

'A PECULIAR CLASS'

The grade of Reserve warden was recognised by the Treasury in 1956 as 'a departmental class peculiar to the Nature Conservancy'. It has counterparts in the voluntary sector and local recreation authorities, but in the Civil Service the warden has always been in a class apart. Reserve wardens at that time were expected to have experience in estate management or some other practical accomplishment, but not necessarily to have academic qualifications. In 1958 a new grade, that of warden–naturalist, was created to cover those nature reserves where a scientific qualification was deemed necessary. The first such post in England was made to cover the Reserves in the Breckland of Norfolk and Suffolk. The distinction between estate management experience and scientific expertise has become increasingly blurred over the years, and the difference between site managers and other 'operations' staff today is more a matter of philosophy than intellectual attainment. Many of the former are now graduates.

At the outset, it was considered desirable for a warden to live on or close to the Reserve. This often meant living in remote areas with relatively primitive facilities. Many of the early Reserves had a 'tied house' which the warden rented from the Conservancy. Some, such as Yarrow Lodge at Yarner Wood, continue to be so occupied, though, with increased responsibilities elsewhere, it is no longer quite so important for the warden to live 'over the shop'. In the early days it was often difficult to find suitable people who were willing to live nineteenth century lives for the benefit of working with nature. At Yarner Wood, the warden, Fred Toby, 'came with the land'. Fred Toby had been the gamekeeper of the Yarner Estate since the 1930s, and had an unrivalled knowledge of the area and its wildlife. He was used to the living conditions, which were certainly tough, with no telephone, and no vehicle either until the Conservancy allocated a Land Rover to the post in 1960. His wife, Lily, ran a bed-and-breakfast service for visiting scientists at Yarrow Lodge.

Conditions at Moor House NNR in the middle of one of the bleakest moors in the North Pennines, were, if anything, even more austere. Until it was metalled in the 1960s, the 6.4-km track to the lonely house on the moors was so rough that only Land Rovers could tackle it (and even then only at 16 km per hour and at the risk of a hefty repair bill). It was shared by Ken Park, the officer-in-charge of the field station, and the Reserve warden, Tom Hodgson and his family. Phil Holms, who was the estate worker there much later in the 1970s, recalls the long hours spent clearing the track of snow in the winter (which at Moor House can last for 5 months), and the endless battle to bolster up the old house against the prevailing cold and damp. Taking readings from the weather station and digging sheep out of the snow were regular winter occupations. The drinking water was piped from a nearby stream. Most of the work on the Reserve was undertaken with hand tools: hay was cut by scythe on the few rainless days and stored as winter feed. Drainage channels, walls, fences and the road needed constant repair, and in frosty weather grit had to be scattered from buckets to pave a passage for the much-needed oil tanker. Frosts were possible at any time of the year except July. The logistics of supplying and maintaining Moor House were almost akin to those of a polar base; temperatures of −20°C were not unusual. In the end, with its declining use for scientific research, the house became too great a financial burden to maintain, and it was finally boarded up in 1980 (see Chapter 5). In Labrador and the North Sea, workers are paid high wages for putting up with such conditions. Not so the Conservancy staff. Max Hooper recalls that for casual and contract staff at Moor House in the 1950s, the pay was £6 a week. 'But the Conservancy deducted £5 for board and lodging, so for a week of point quadrats you took a pound home! That was before the road was metalled so you couldn't slip down and blow it all in Alston or Garrigill.'

The main compensation for primitive living conditions and low pay was a healthy outdoor life, studying nature in beautiful surroundings. In those days there seems to have been plenty of time to stand and stare. The warden's reports from the 1950s and 1960s are full of what might now be regarded as unnecessary detail and atmosphere, lovingly compiled and preserved in green buckram ledgers embossed with the Reserve's name (what a contrast with the dossiers of today with their cheap laminated covers and horrible plastic spines!). Here, for example, is Norman English on a few days spent at Rusland Moss in 1960:

> *29th March*
> Along the main ride cotton grass was in flower. A roe buck with two does browsed among the heather on the fringe of the pinewood. I watched a red deer stag for some time until swirling currents of a stiff breeze took the scent, and he was quick to make for thicker cover, taking with him a hind which until then had been out of sight. Long-tailed and great tits scurried about in the birch; a pair of mallard rose from the marsh. A hen pheasant flushed from deep heather glided into the marsh scrub.
>
> *12th May*
> Growth buds are lengthening on the pines, the cones 'cracking' in the warm sunshine. Birch in young leaf, buckthorn flowering. Willow and wood warbler and cuckoo are in song. A pair of curlew rose from the old pasture, a heron was flushed from the boundary ditch. A sparrowhawk sweeping over open ground.
>
> *31st August*
> Birch leaves tinting, alder buckthorn berries ripe. Heavy fruiting of rowans. Peacock butterflies feeding on scabious, Ichneumons flying together with hoverflies and bees in great numbers. Marsh and great tits working the willow fringe.

In his fine account of Kingley Vale, *The Great Yew Forest* (1978), Richard Williamson gave a vivid impression of life on a National Nature Reserve. At the time of writing, Richard is probably English Nature's longest serving Reserve warden, having devoted the past 30 years to looking after the Vale and its famous yew groves. He arrived there in 1963, aged 28, having obtained the relevant experience from 'summer jobs helping [Reserve] wardens along the Norfolk coast, forestry jobs gaining knowledge of management, farming jobs learning about machinery, and above all minute and prolonged observation of wildlife in all its intimate aspects'. The Reserve at that time had hardly been touched since the 1940s, when it had been a military training area. The scars were still livid: tree stumps, tank tracks and dug-outs, fungi growing on the yews where they had been scored with bullets and a great crater where a rusting Centurion tank had been blown to bits with dynamite. The downs were scrubbing over, and had become infested with ragwort since myxomatosis. But it was still a beautiful place with its ancient groves and the circular sweep of the downs with their matchless view over the Sussex plain. With the limited resources at his disposal, Richard's custodianship was restricted to what he could manage with hand tools, until 1968 when he managed to purchase for £25 a 'beaten-up faded red Massey-Ferguson tractor' named Betsy, together with a low-loader trailer and a silage cutter. 'At last some real management was about to begin.'

Making-do and local ingenuity characterised the management of most National Nature Reserves in the 1960s, when conservation was still the poor hand maiden to the scientific field stations. Plate 10 of Sir Dudley Stamp's *Nature Conservation in Britain* (1969) depicts what he describes as an 'abandoned farm implement' a wooden-shafted meccano-like device, which he thought had been left there by some previous owner. The 'abandoned implement' was in fact none other than warden–naturalist Derek Ungley's precious mowing machine, bought at some agricultural junk sale and used to cut coarse grass and scrub at Aston Rowant NNR!

It was not until the late 1960s that increased staffing levels on Reserves allowed the latter to be taken properly 'in hand'. The Bure Marshes, for example, received its first full-time estate worker in 1966. That post was 'promoted' to Reserve warden 3 years later, and in 1978 the warden was allocated a new estate worker post to cope with the increasing level of dredging, mowing and scrub clearance. Today, the Reserve manager Rick Southwood is helped by two estate workers, but between them they have to cover three Reserves—Ludham Marshes and Winterton Dunes as well as the Bure Marshes. In 1958 there were only 15 Reserve wardens to cover the whole of Britain's NNRs—roughly 2430 ha to every man employed. Estate workers were even thinner on the ground with only seven posts, of which no fewer than three were based at Woodwalton Fen to cover 'the Peterborough group' of Reserves: Woodwalton Fen, Monks Wood, Holme Fen and Castor Hanglands.

Today estate workers are still regarded like gold dust even though there are more of them. Apart from the Peterborough team, two estate worker posts are attached to

each of the six most labour-intensive regions: the Breck Reserves, the Norfolk Broads, Ainsdale, the Oxfordshire Reserves, Parsonage Down, Castle Eden Dene and the Lizard. Most of the other site managers are assisted by a single estate worker. Like the warden/ site managers, estate workers often work unsocial hours and on their own. Many are young men (two are young women), gaining experience of Reserve management until they reach the magic age of 26 when they become eligible to apply for a site manager post.

Woodwalton Fen stands out among the earlier National Nature Reserves in that from the very start considerable resources were devoted to its management. The reasons for this were part moral obligation and partly urgent necessity, for immediate action was necessary to prevent the Fen from drying out and losing most of its special interest. The Fen had been leased to the Nature Conservancy by the SPNR precisely because the latter could not afford to run it properly. The Conservancy's commitment to maintaining the Fen was underlined by the establishment of an 'all star' management committee, including Miriam Rothschild, Max Walters, Cyril Diver, Eric Duffey and J A Steers. It was underlined further when the Monks Wood Experimental Station was established nearby in 1962 and for several years took over formal responsibility for running Woodwalton Fen. It became a kind of scientist's playground with all kinds of 'hobbies' going on from Eric Duffey's Large Copper cages to Norman Moore's experimental ponds. The actual wardening of the Peterborough group of Reserves was the responsibility of a unique team of estate workers under the late Gordon Mason, son of the George Mason who had looked after the nature reserve for Charles Rothschild. The Mason team were officially classed as 'Fen men'; as the 1958 Annual Report puts it, 'these men retain those peculiar skills which enabled the Fen men of one hundred years ago to wrest a living from the fen country before its almost complete reclamation to arable cultivation'. In winter the team moves to Monks Wood to coppice the hazel, but it was (and is) otherwise based mainly at Woodwalton, clearing and 'brinking' the dykes, cutting reeds and scrub and maintaining records. Gordon Mason used to spend months in summer cutting the miles of rides with a hand scythe. He deserved his BEM, awarded in the Queen's Birthday Honours of 1968. Today a third generation of Masons is represented at the Fen by Gordon's son, Andrew.

WARDENSHIP

Over the years, the warden's job has grown in complexity—more Reserves, more machinery, more paperwork and above all far more management. As some compensation, the material comforts of the job have also grown. English Nature's site managers (and their equivalents in Scotland and Wales) are probably the best paid nature workers in the country, thanks to a pay award made in 1979 that took into account the sometimes long and unsocial hours worked and the need to be on stand-by most of the time (Mike Tuck tells of a time he was interrupted half-way through his Christmas dinner by someone demanding to be taken to see 'Keith Corbett's sand lizard patches'). Much of the former manual labour has been replaced by machines or put out to contract, but some jobs, like sheep-dipping and putting in fence posts, remain much the same.

Reserve wardens come from a wide variety of professional backgrounds. In the early days, they were likely to have had experience in forestry work, estate management or gamekeeping, but in a few cases the appointees were retired servicemen. The first warden of Old Winchester Hill, for example, was a former military policeman and security guard! Jim Kennard, later Chief Warden in south-west England, spent 12 years planting trees for the Forestry Commission and three teaching climbing at an outward bounds school in Sussex before joining the NCC as the second warden of Old Winchester Hill, taking over from the security guard in 1969. Most wardens recruited in recent years have already had experience working for other conservation bodies, or looking after country parks or National Trust properties. Many were estate workers on National Nature Reserves before being promoted to warden/site manager at the mandatory minimum age of 26. Several Reserves have served as *de facto* 'nurseries' for young estate workers who later became Reserve Wardens, notably Yarner Wood, where more than a dozen Reserve wardens once served as estate workers or volunteers. Some wardens have a background particularly appropriate to their own patch, such as Ian Black, a former trawlerman who works the Essex coast Reserves. For a few Reserves, a son has taken over the work of a father. Charles and Bob Chestney were successive wardens at Scolt Head Island for sixty years, and David Maylam, now site manager of Blean Woods, is son of John Maylam, the former warden of Ham Street Woods. Dick Lambert and Peter Roworth are among several who have teaching experience. Joan Daniels, the first woman Reserve manager to be appointed, has a doctorate in peatland hydrology.

John Bacon, the Chief Warden in English Nature's former West Midlands region, told me that all Reserve wardens should have four main qualities. First and still (thank heaven) foremost is a love of nature and the countryside, a sense of *vocation*. This is, or should be, true of all posts in conservation agencies, but it is the Reserve warden/manager above all who needs the all-round knowledge and experience to census breeding birds, count waders and wildfowl, record butterflies along a transect and monitor environmental change. The nature of this work varies from place to place, but most wardens still spend some time on what might be called 'pure natural history'—though far less than their forebears did. Every warden is an all-round field naturalist, and a few are among the most impressive observers I have ever met, with what I can only describe as extrasensory perception. Although the job calls for all-round field craft, many wardens, especially the older generation, were primarily interested in birds. Bob Chestney, for example, knew his tern colony so intimately that he was able almost to think like a tern. The character of the Reserve has always tended to shape a warden's personal interests and outlook. Rees Cox, at the popular Studland Reserve, is an all-round field educationalist. With the Stiperstones and Downton Gorge on his patch, Tom Wall is not unnaturally interested in the historic and cultural context of nature reserves. John Bacon, formerly of Old Winchester Hill, was a pioneer in management for butterflies; John Robinson at the very photogenic Wyre Forest is a first-rate wildlife photographer.

The second essential quality of good wardenship is practical-mindedness. This qualification might well exclude many otherwise excellent naturalists. Depending on the Reserve, wardens may need to handle livestock, maintain dykes and ditches, build hides, repair machinery and supervise contractors and voluntary helpers. Maintaining the fabric of a nature reserve has become a more involved and demanding task in recent years, as increased resources and power machinery enable the warden to manage on a much more ambitious level than in the early years. The nature of the job requires him not only to implement management plans but to see further into the *potential* of the Reserve. An increasing amount of a warden's time is spent not only on habitat maintenance but on habitat restoration, especially on wetland Reserves.

With this necessary pragmatism comes an increased need for technical skills. Most wardens now use a variety of vehicles and power tools. For example, the equipment for the Ribble NNR includes a four-wheel drive tractor, the trusty Honda 'Big X' All Terrain Cycle, which is becoming almost standard issue on nature reserves, and a VeePee All Terrain Vehicle, useful on soft ground for, among other things, pulling cows out of gutters. Some technical skills can be taught at training courses: virtually all wardens have been trained in the proper use of a chainsaw for example, and in first-aid. But increasingly new staff are expected to possess such experience already. The recent advertisement for the post at Fenns, Whixall and Bettisfield Mosses demanded, among other things, 'familiarity with bog ecology and hydrology, practical expertise in bog management, and forestry skills'. The next generation will doubtless need postdoctoral experience in remote sensing and a pilot's licence.

Last, but not least, on John Bacon's list, a warden must be a good communicator and negotiator. Talking to parties on the Reserve and in draughty village halls is a traditional part of the job, but a warden also has to win the confidence of a host of other people and organisations who in one way or another have interests that impinge on the Reserve—neighbours, tenants, river engineers, shooting syndicates, local authorities, coastguards and grazing licensees to name but a few. Increasingly, some Reserves are part of a co-operative management scheme, such as Ainsdale NNR on the Sefton Coast, or are managed in alliance with other authorities, like Wren's Nest. The managers of large estuarine sites, like Bob Lord at the Wash and Ian Black along the Essex coast, spend much of their time in a co-ordinating role, working with a range of agricultural, fishing, military and sporting interests to achieve a balanced and sustainable use of the area. The work is becoming increasingly managerial, and portable telephones, filofaxes and accountancy skills are becoming as much part of the furniture of the job as binoculars and a Land Rover. The days when a Reserve warden's job consisted mainly of bird watching and keeping people off the grass are long over, if they ever existed.

I find it surprising, given the nature of their work and abilities, that more warden/managers do not reach out to the public, by writing for their local newspaper, for example, or appearing more often on radio and television. The former occupation has its hazards, of course. Bob Lord contributes regular articles to the *Boston Target* under the byline, 'Eyes on the Wash'. Wildfowling around the Wash is one of those subjects which it is wise to treat with circumspection, and so it was unfortunate that Bob's account of circular walks in areas used by the shooting fraternity was misprinted as circular 'walls'. This evidently caused a stir, and the next thing he knew the local authority had received an angry letter from the local wildfowler's association demanding to know more about a matter 'of grave concern to our members'.

Bill Elliott is unique among wardens in that he grew up on what is now Parsonage Down NNR and has been the farm manager there ever since 1954. The story of Parsonage Down is an extraordinary one which deserves a book to itself. This wonderful oasis of wild grass survived because from 1927 until 1979 it was owned and farmed by one man, Robert Wales, who was a rare practitioner of the art of farming in harmony with nature. While, for example, most farmers would regard ant-hills as a nuisance and flatten them with harrows and rollers, Robert Wales retained them for the extra 'bite' of grass they supplied, especially in early spring when the sweetest grass often grows in the lee of an ant-hill. He farmed for quality rather than quantity, maintaining a low-level all-year-round grazing of both cattle and sheep that over time has produced a tight downland turf that is wonderfully rich in wild flowers. The NCC was lucky when, on taking over responsibility for the down after the death of Robert Wales in 1979 as provided in the latter's will, it was able to retain the services and lifetime skills of his right-hand man, Bill Elliott. There is, in a sense, no mystery to why Parsonage Down is so special, even to jaundiced scientists who thought they had seen every form of chalk vegetation. It is all down to good old-fashioned animal husbandry and treating the land for what it is—a living tapestry rather than a factory floor kitted out for maximum production here and now, and the devil take the consequences. Bill Elliott has not turned his back on agricultural advances, but he uses them as a rapier rather than a bludgeon. 'I keep up with the changes in agriculture that take place but I know what's right for this place. There is no substitute for experience—I know each field and what the stocking ratios are, how they're affected by drought, by frost—I alter things before it becomes apparent to anyone else that damage might occur.' By contrast, for the 138 ha of the farm that the Conservancy was forced to sell to repay the Treasury's loan, the ploughs were waiting at the gates on the day the land changed hands. 'That one field down there used to be five lovely fields, hedged and ditched. They bulldozed the lot to make a 130-acre field. Gone so quickly after all those years. Another man bulldozed the lynchets (medieval hillside terraces)—just levelled them off.'

When it comes to pointing the way to alternative ways of farming that preserve the natural and historic features of the land instead of brutally obliterating them, Parsonage Down has much to offer. Probably no other nature reserve has such potential as a demonstration of how husbandry and nature conservation can be wheels of the same cart.

SITE MANAGERS AND TEAM LEADERS

The post of Reserve warden/manager continues to generate an unusually high level of job satisfaction. During my tour of England's National Nature Reserves during the summer of 1992, I found not a single person who was anxious to move away from his 'patch'. Some site managers, like Dick Williamson, Ian Findlay and Cliff Waller, have looked after the same Reserve, or group of Reserves, for more than 20 years. Their absolute commitment to work which can sound very pleasant and relaxing to the armchair conservationist, but which in practice can at times be stressful and demanding, impresses anyone who has had dealings with nature reserves. Wardens tend to be self-motivated people, used to working on their own and making their own decisions. Their contributions have sometimes seemed to me to be underrated by the Conservancy, particularly during the 1980s when all the attention was on 'wider issues'. In the early years, nature reserves lay at the very heart of the Conservancy's strategy, both in their role as outdoor laboratories and as places where conservation techniques could be tried and tested. As their contribution to science seemed to wane, and the emphasis of nature conservation switched to national and global environmental problems, many wardens felt somewhat side-lined by events. One of them told me that on his visits to the Conservancy's Peterborough headquarters he felt like 'the man who comes to mend the radiators'. The perspective of the man in the office and the man on the ground had diverged sharply.

The damage that such rifts can cause to the conservation effort is recognised by English Nature's management board. At the time of writing, it is undertaking a major internal reorganisation aimed at increasing the sense of pulling together as a team and at breaking down some of the social and organisational barriers that have developed in recent years. In practice this will mean the replacement of the old regional structure with a series of smaller units, each with their own 'team leader' and their own budget, under the overall direction of a 'general manager' trained in the techniques and language of a businessman. Some site managers I have spoken to have welcomed the changes as a means of combining the disparate threads of science, land agency and field staff. Others fear that the new system may generate even more paperwork and gobbledegook than the old, while perpetuating existing divisions. They point out that few administrators have had much experience of running National Nature Reserves, and that the post of chief warden, traditionally the champion and troubleshooter of the region's field staff, has now been abolished along with the regions themselves.

One means of overcoming this perceived marginalisation of the field grades might be better promotion prospects. Hitherto, these have been poor. A warden could, after qualifying through the submission of a 'project' analogous to a university thesis, be promoted to 'senior warden' level, with a commensurate rise in pay, but beyond that there was only the now abolished chief warden grade. Under English Nature's recent reorganisation, three erstwhile chief wardens, Martin Howat, David Henshilwood and Robbie Bridson have been made team leaders, a senior post now available to 'all the talents'. There is no reason why one or more ex-wardens should not one day rise to the most senior posts in the organisation, and bring with them the measures of practical experience and resourcefulness learned on nature reserves. But the majority of warden/managers will probably remain content to continue looking after nature reserves. The job is well paid and brings its own rewards. They may not make the headlines very often, but I suspect that most would agree with Dick Williamson that the fascination of their work continues to lie in the 'combination of its creativity, its variety and the utter conviction that it is worthwhile'.

VOLUNTARY WARDENS

Ever since the 1950s, local naturalists and other members of the public have helped the Conservancy to look after its Reserves as voluntary or honorary wardens. Such people come from all walks of life, but in many cases are near neighbours of a Reserve who know it well and have become very fond of it. The 20 or so persons who help Mike Tuck to look after his heathland Reserves in Dorset include a businessman who sells computers, a local councillor, a handyman at a Sainsbury store, a wealthy lady who hunts and several retired people. One of them is interested in deer, and keeps meticulous records of deer numbers and movements in the area. Another is a keen 'twitcher' and helps to census breeding and migrant birds.

In 1992 there were some 800 voluntary wardens in all from all corners of England. Exceptionally a Reserve like Shabbington Wood Forestry Nature Reserve may have

40 volunteers, in this case mainly butterfly watchers and recorders, but most busy Reserves average about 10, and the less-visited ones only one or two. That wonderful jumble of clay, rock and woodland of almost tropical luxuriance, the Axmouth–Lyme Regis landslip NNR is exceptional in that it is wardened almost entirely by volunteers, who have acted as guides and helped to maintain the notoriously unstable footpath. The teams have been directed by two dedicated honorary wardens, Laurie Pritchard (1955–1979) and Norman Barns (1979 onwards), who reported directly to the South-western region's chief warden. Without their help, the Conservancy would have found it difficult or impossible to look after this Reserve adequately, since the peculiarities of internal organisation mean that it is a long way from any wardening base.

The duties of voluntary wardens vary considerably according to their aptitudes and interests, and to the nature and relative popularity of the Reserve. Each is sent an official letter of appointment, and supplied with an armband, a badge and a warrant card. The volunteer is expected to visit the Reserve fairly frequently, and be acquainted with any local bye-laws or fire plans. He or she is empowered to examine permits and warn trespassers, guide parties around the Reserve and contribute to the Reserve record and some of the wildlife monitoring schemes. In some cases volunteers also help with management tasks such as scrub removal and fencing. Roughly 10% of the work on Reserves is done by volunteer support. Their work is largely unpaid, but volunteers do receive basic travel expenses and the more responsible posts carry an honorarium. Each region of the Conservancy holds a volunteers' 'get-together' at least annually, and usually based at a particular Reserve. In the south region, for example, some 100 wildlife volunteers met at the North Solent NNR in 1992 and at Old Winchester Hill in 1993. The meeting is invariably a relaxed, informal occasion giving volunteers the chance to meet one another and to see what happens on other nature reserves in the area. The Conservancy also holds an annual award scheme when people with long or exceptional records of service are thanked and presented with a certificate. It is a token way of rewarding the helpers, some of whom knew the site well long before it became a National Nature Reserve. Twelve people given awards in 1992 were reckoned to have contributed 220 years of service between them! Tom and Cath Weston, for example, were voluntary wardens at Old Winchester Hill ever since it opened in 1954. Cyril Lane was the principal voluntary warden at the rather isolated Reserve of Wychwood in Oxfordshire for almost as long until his 'retirement' at the age of 93! It is always a pleasure to see such service recognised in a national award, such as the BEM which Mr Lane received in the Queen's Birthday Honours of 1990.

OBLIGATIONS

In a country as crowded as England, there are very few areas of genuine wilderness on which human society makes no demands at all. Even our remotest places, like the sand banks of the Wash and Morecambe Bay or the north Pennine moors, are respectively overfished and overgrazed and full of conservation problems. As everyone who owns a large garden or helps to run a country estate will know, freehold ownership of a nature reserve rarely carries the freedom to do as you like. The greatest constraint on Reserve management is the conditions of tenure, but even owned Reserves may be covered by wayleaves, shooting rights, dedication schemes, access rights, common rights and a variety of other interests, not to mention moral obligations, that have a bearing on how English Nature looks after them. To take a rather extreme case, Dendles Wood at the edge of Dartmoor is a small (29 ha) woodland Reserve, which was purchased by the Conservancy in 1965 to preserve it from the advance of the spruce. It is a fairly representative Dartmoor oakwood, except for some very large spreading beeches which are believed to represent an earlier, more open phase of development. Like most English 'wild woods', Dendles Wood represents not so much a wilderness as a record of silvicultural fashion and past management. Even so, one might assume that such a small patch of inaccessible woodland in a remote upland valley might not matter very much to anyone except a naturalist or country sportsman. One would of course be wrong. To begin with, the bed of the River Yealm, which flows through the wood, was expressly excluded from the title deeds. The sporting rights are owned by a neighbour, and several nearby farms have rights of access along the narrow tracks of the wood (which are nevertheless the responsibility of the Conservancy when it comes to repairing them). The South-western Water Authority has an intake within the wood. And before the Conservancy could purchase the freehold, the wood had been dedicated so that the land could be used only for growing timber 'in accordance with the rules and practice of good forestry'. In other words, as the management plan admits, the use of Dendles Wood is conditioned by the views of its neighbours. The Conservancy even inherited obligations *outside* the Reserve. It was supposed to maintain a 10-m firebreak along one boundary, although the neighbour took a less serious view and planted it with Sitka Spruce! In practice, though, nothing much happens at Dendles Wood and nowadays there seems to be no great contradiction between dedicated woodland and 'minimal intervention'. Its future lies as a long-term monitoring site, whose scientific value depends on as little management as possible.

English Nature's management is further constrained by the law of the land. Parliamentary Acts that have a bearing on nature reserves are too numerous even to list, but the main ones include the Deer Act 1963 which prohibits the 'killing or taking' of deer outside the open season, and specifies the weapons and ammunition that must be used; the Agricultural Pests Acts of 1947 and 1954 which oblige the owner to control pests (which in some cases happen to be native wild animals—until fairly recently the rare Wild Cat and Polecat were among the wildlife on nature reserves which could legally be shot); and the Forestry Act 1967 which prevents the felling 'of any significant amount of timber' without a felling licence. Perhaps the most onerous of all are the safety laws. The Occupiers Liability Acts of 1957 and 1984 oblige the Conservancy to maintain 'safe conditions' for the public, whether or not the latter have any rights of access. The Reserve manager is responsible for inspecting footbridges, stiles, hand-rails and 'dangerous trees' to ensure that they do not present a public danger. At Castle Eden Dene NNR, fitting hand rails to bridges and other safety precautions cost English Nature £13,000 in 1992 alone. The manager must erect warning signs whenever potentially hazardous operations like tree-felling are taking place, and against dangerous places, such as diseased elms or quaking bogs. The Health and Safety at Work Act 1974 requires the Conservancy to produce a detailed site safety plan, including a map of the Reserve depicting all hazardous areas. I remember some discussion at the time on whether these included wasps' nests, wood-ant mounds or places noted for Adders. Under the Act, the Conservancy is responsible for providing 'a safe place of work' for contractors, as well as its own staff. Those who drafted the Act were not, of course, thinking primarily of nature reserves. There is a limit to how safe some nature reserves can be made without reducing the wildness that is an inherent part of their quality, to say nothing of the resource implications of making wild nature 'safe'. In practice, the Conservancy's safety record is good. No one has yet been killed or suffered lasting injury while working on an English National Nature Reserve, with the exception of poor Keith Park who was drowned in the River Tees in 1960. Perhaps the closest 'near miss' was the estate worker who sunk a metal post onto a 1000-V underground cable, but fortunately realised what he had done just in time!

MANAGEMENT PLANNING

The basis of work for each and every National Nature Reserve is the management plan. A good plan will contain a clear statement of what the Conservancy hopes to achieve at a particular Reserve, and then go on to itemise the necessary main tasks, formulate work programmes and in general see to it that money and manpower are being used in the most efficient and cost-effective way possible. In addition, the Conservancy's plans have usually contained a lengthy descriptive section, summarising everything that is known about the Reserve. In some cases this is a great deal, and two or three volumes may be necessary to write it all down. The descriptive section usually includes details of the local climate, hydrology and soils and lists all the wildlife from birds and mammals down to weird and wonderful things like rotifers and water-bears. The management plan is written for contemporary use, but it is also an important historical record. What seems obvious and inevitable to us today will almost certainly appear strange and unfathomable to a future generation of managers, just as some of the fashions and assumptions of the 1950s seem dogmatic and purblind now. A clear statement of aims, and a reasoned justification for them—what management planners term a rationale—is a vital part of the plan's long-term usefulness.

Since 1983, Reserve management plans have been produced to a common pattern under the guidance of a detailed handbook. The stated advantages of this are that it helps the less experienced to prepare plans, that recognised standards and procedures will prevail and that continuity of purpose is ensured, whoever is in charge. Unfortunately such standardisation does tend to reduce the plan's readability and can lead to tedious repetition. The handbook tacitly recognises the dangers of over-bureaucratisation when it recommends that for each Reserve the management plan should be written by a single person closely involved with running of the Reserve, 'consulting as necessary'. In practice this usually means the warden or chief warden, although in a few, usually rather specialised, cases the plan has been prepared by an external contractor.

Management plans fall into three main sections. The first, and usually the longest, consists mainly of description, and includes details of tenure, aerial photograph coverage and bibliography as well as physical, ecological and 'cultural' data. The second section attempts to evaluate the relative importance of the Reserve, both in general terms and in the more detailed aspects of its flora, fauna and physiology. It also specifies what would be desirable in an ideal world, and then goes on to list the obligations and constraints that limit what can be done in practice. This section forms the intellectual and scientific justification for what happens on the Reserve. It includes a reasoned review of options: does the habitat really need management? If so, should the latter be limited in extent or thorough-going? Are there special species which need individual attention? And how does one cater for a range of different habitats, all of them in the process of perpetual change? If it achieves nothing else, this crucial part of the plan does at least force managers to think carefully about their aims. In inexperienced hands, it can however lead to wholly illusory notions of control. Management plans ask the manager to 'specify the limits of change', that is to state how much of a particular habitat it is desirable to retain. The example given by the handbook is of 'woodland cover [which] should not fall below 85% with 60% of the canopy derived from oak'.

In practice it would be difficult to achieve such control in a garden, let alone a wild wood. The danger of such statements is that the uncautious may mistake them for reality. In practice, however, natural phenomena, financial limitations, changing fashions and perspectives and the attitude of the person in charge will govern what happens on nature reserves. For example, the thinning and singling of overgrown coppice to produce high forest has been one of the objectives for Monks Wood NNR for the past forty years. In practice, however, virtually no such work was ever done, although gales and disease have to some extent succeeded in doing the same job. The *de facto* management of much of Monks Wood, therefore, was not high forest management but non-intervention, and the management plan gave a false impression of the wood. David Massen, the present manager of Monks Wood, sensibly suggests that the next management plan 'ought to accept reality and formally reassign all woodland compartments from active management to non-intervention'.

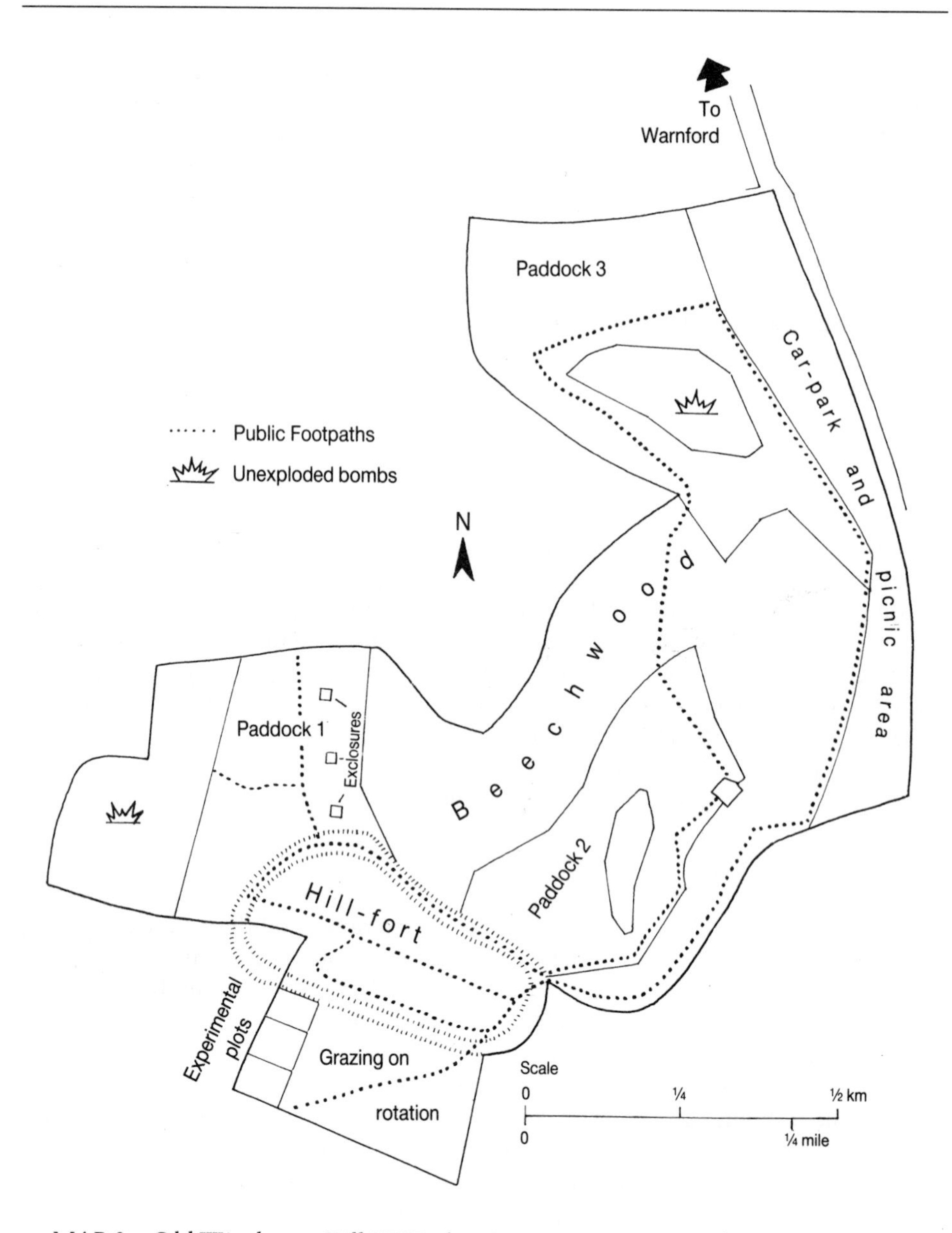

MAP 3 *Old Winchester Hill NNR showing compartments and picnic area*

The third and final section of the plan is known as the Prescription (an interesting pharmaceutical analogy: the cure for ills, perhaps?). The Prescription provides a logical framework for undertaking the various tasks over a fixed period, often of 5 years, and relates them to the objectives. Since the NCC acquired its present computing capabilities in the mid-1980s, each project has been allotted its own code and is entered on the Conservancy's Project Recording System. This record, which covers all the Reserves, helps managers in planning and budgeting, and provides a computer link with the Conservancy's scientific database, COREDATA. One important consequence of computerisation is that progress on one Reserve can be compared with that on another, so that work on the Reserves can be integrated into unified management policies more closely than in the past. In later chapters we will see how 'schools' of management have been built up in recent years—bog hydrology, stock-grazing, wetland irrigation and so on. Such experience also enables habitat manuals to be compiled, which in turn have a strong influence on future management. Lest the reader worry where all this standardisation may be leading, it should be added that planning can only go so far. Each Reserve is unique, the product of local particularities and long and subtle interactions between man and nature. There is no danger that any one of them will end up looking much the same as another.

One serious drawback to the present form of management plans is now widely acknowledged. They take far too long to compile. Serious attention is presently being given to the formulation of snappy short-term working plans of only 10 pages or so, leaving all the description and evaluation essentially as a library record.

Management planning has evolved into a fairly advanced art. The recording and monitoring of what actually happens on National Nature Reserves has tended to lag behind. Until the late 1960s, the main Reserve record was the warden's own reports, written at quarter-year intervals, with a more detailed report at the year's end. In 1967, a more standardised system of recording was introduced known as Event Records. The warden was supposed to record all 'events' which he thought significant on a punch-card, which would build up into a kind of chronology of the Reserve. 'Events' dealt mainly with matters under the warden's direct control—so many sheep at such and such a time, so much coppice cleared in a season and so on—with an occasional spicing of disasters like gales, droughts and vandalism. This system provides the only systematic record for Reserves for the 1970s and early 1980s, a rather staccato one I suspect. A personal memoir from each warden at the end of his tenure at a Reserve might have proved of more lasting value.

In 1984, the management and control systems of National Nature Reserves were reviewed in the light of the new computer age. The event record card was replaced with a project recording form of formidable complexity, designed as far as possible for the delivery of numerical information to the computer. The relatively arbitrary choice of 'events' has been replaced by coded projects firmly linking the record with the prescriptive section of the management plan. The nature of the record remains much the same, however: a computer memory of codes and statistics, requiring considerable computer numeracy to understand. As a workaday record it presumably justifies the time and boredom expended on completing the forms.

From 1991, an overview of all the English Nature Reserves is being compiled each year by English Nature's operations director, Eddie Idle. The report provides a useful factual record, as well as a means of judging progress towards the objectives for each Reserve. It assembles for the first time a comprehensive summary of costs, signing and access provisions and research projects within the National Nature Reserves of England. This information is now being stored on a computer database for use within the organisation and for interested parties (including other nature reserve managers) outside it. A sample page from the 1991/92 report is reproduced as Table 3. In general the record seems to point to a healthy state of affairs, with good or satisfactory progress reported for all but a handful of National Nature Reserves.

TABLE 3 *A page from English Nature's annual report on National Nature Reserves (1991/92)*

NNR	*Progress towards meeting management objectives*	*Research/monitoring*	*Visitors*	*Costs*	*Staffing (SM = site manager EW = estate worker)*	*Comments*
Castor Hanglands	Successful	ITE—Scrub dynamics. Lancaster University—long-term climate and air pollution studies. M Hillier—*Macrolepidoptera* list EN monitoring rare plants, butterfly transects, CBC, deer transects.	Approx 8000	£4650	SM x 1 also EW x 1 cover Barnack & Collyweston Summer warden 15 voluntary wardens	
Collyweston Great Wood	Successful	None	Permits 50	£1129	SM—See above EW	Declared February 1992
Barnack Hills & Holes	Successful	EN—species monitoring (rare plants, butterflies, CBC) Lancaster University—long-term climatic change	Approx 12,000	?	Summer warden 36 weeks SM—See Castor EW Hanglands	
Woodwalton Fen	All programmed work on. Management plan achieved	University of Sheffield—colonisation of newly dug peat pool University of Keele—ecology of Large Copper BBCS—observations on breeding success of Large Copper ITE—Ecology of Tawny Owls EN—Chinese Water Deer Breeding biology of Long-eared Owls	Permits 420 Conducted tours 10 Special groups 5	£30,642	SM 60% 4 x EWs 75%	
Holme Fen	All programmed work achieved. Mere levels very low after prolonged drought	EN (Cooke) Muntjac and Chinese Water Deer	Permits 420 500 casual visitors	?	SM 25% EWs 8%	
Saltfleetby Dunes	Reasonably successful. No stock grazing due to drought and very high rabbit numbers	Newcastle University—Invertebrate communities in freshwater marsh under different forms of management EN—Long-term monitoring projects	No accurate surveys *c.* 100,000	£4500	SM 55% EW 12 months 80%	

CHAPTER 4

Tread Softly for you Tread on my Orchids

THE new design of Reserve sign introduced by English Nature in 1991 differs in at least one important respect from its predecessors. It incorporates the word 'welcome'. The degree to which the estimated 3 million visitors to National Nature Reserves annually were welcome on National Nature Reserves up till then is debatable. On rights of way they are a fact of life. On a handful of Reserves, the Conservancy provides a fairly basic range of public facilities, such as display signs and nature trails, but these are without exception situated in places that are already much visited. They are not intended to turn the Reserve into a popular 'honeypot'. No Reserve was ever chosen for its recreational possibilities. On roughly half the English National Nature Reserves, access has been by permission only. Permits to visit Reserves are usually given fairly freely, except in a few cases where, largely for reasons of tenure, access is confined to bona fide researchers and escorted parties. Permits are also needed for specimen collecting. Compared with some of the properties owned by charitable bodies such as the RSPB, the National Trust and more recently the Woodland Trust, the reception at most National Nature Reserves was distinctly downbeat.

If the reader has already read the first and second chapters of this book, he or she may not be altogether surprised that this is so. The development of nature conservation in

Britain was science-led, and although the founders considered that Reserves should be available for 'quiet enjoyment' and nature study, so long as that did not inconvenience anything else, they were not intended to be primary functions of National Nature Reserves. It was hoped that local authorities would shoulder the burden by establishing Local Nature Reserves for use by schools, colleges and the general public. But the local authorities had other priorities (as usual, local politics ignored national politics) and the number of Local Nature Reserves remained miserably small until the 'green revolution' of the 1980s.

Responsibility for outdoor recreation and education remained with the National Park authorities in England and Wales. In 1968, the Countryside Commission took over that burden and also responsibility for the promotion of recreation in the countryside generally. But they were not allowed to influence National Nature Reserve management. In retrospect it might seem extraordinary that the Conservancy failed to co-operate more closely with its fellow countryside agencies. The Conservancy's own strategy, published in 1984, seemed to regret the fact: 'It is strange to many people that organisations with such closely related objectives are so distanced from each other when their interests would seem to have benefited from closer alignment'. It is true that nature conservation and scenic amenity do not invariably coincide, and that the Conservancy's way of doing things was radically different from the Commission's. But the extraordinary disparity between scientific nature conservation on the one hand and the public's enjoyment of the countryside on the other is a peculiarly British development. It is perhaps the consequence of the early start made in nature conservation, well ahead of public opinion. If the Conservancy had been born 20 years later, the two might well have been combined under the same umbrella.

The law has never been very clear on this matter. The Nature Conservancy Council Act of 1973 bade the Conservancy provide 'advice and the dissemination of knowledge about nature conservation'—not the most precise of remits, and the Wildlife and Countryside Act of 1981 did little to elucidate further. The functions of National Nature Reserves have otherwise remained unchanged in law since 1949. The 'dissemination of knowledge' has never been a high priority: a recent document on NNRs places it fourth, after management, 'the development of management expertise' and scientific research. In practice the provision of facilities on Reserves has been the responsibility of a small team at Headquarters working in concert with the local offices. Many of the more imaginative initiatives have come from the people on the spot, especially the Reserve managers.

At present, English Nature is liberalising its public access policy on the Reserves where it has full control, and, except where there are pressing reasons to the contrary, many hitherto restricted access Reserves are scheduled to become open to the public, on waymarked paths. Moreover every National Nature Reserve in England will be marked on the next generation of the Ordnance Survey's 1:50,000 Landranger maps. English Nature have decided to accept the principle of public access to Reserves, while not actively advertising the fact.

THE NATURE OF THE RESOURCE

National Nature Reserves in England are usually small, often privately owned and are sometimes not easily distinguishable from the surrounding landscape. They are not, as are some of the American and East European National Parks, genuine wilderness, scarcely, if at all, exploited by civilisation. Many of our Reserves have a history of management extending back hundreds, or in some cases possibly thousands, of years. Until technology changed the face of the landscape, many of today's National Nature Reserves were part of the fabric of rural life, generally occupying the least fertile land. Most of them are little known (how many English National Nature Reserves can *you* list?). Some were—a few still are—part of a working farm or estate. The larger animals on England's National Nature Reserves will be cows, sheep and the occasional wild deer, not bears or bison.

It is a common misconception that nature in England is shy or fragile, and will suffer if people are allowed access to Reserves. While it is true that some birds will not tolerate much disturbance at nesting time, and that wet or excessively dry places are easily damaged by treading, the evidence suggests that our wildlife is on the whole fairly resilient. It is, after all, used to people. In certain circumstances, a degree of disturbance can be positively beneficial. At Braunton Burrows, for example, the site manager John Breeds 'does not discourage' children from sliding down the dunes from time to time, for their fun helps to maintain sandy hollows among the dense marram grass where Sea Stock and other rare plants can find a roothold. In Dorset, the place to find the rare Early Spider Orchid is not among the wilder herbage but along the well-trampled public footpaths. The reason why access to so many National Nature Reserves is restricted is less to do with wildlife as with the wishes of their private owners. An Englishman's home is his castle, and conservationists are bound to respect his rights of property.

One of the things we take for granted in England is our remarkably *non-lethal* wildlife. Even our Adders and mosquitoes are better behaved than their congeners across the Channel. The worst that can befall you here is a swarm of midges or an unusually aggressive sheep (though sheep ticks may be an exception, as transmitters of Lyme disease). Our weather is much more treacherous than the landscape. Most of the dangers on English nature reserves are physical or man-made. Intertidal areas are, of course, potentially dangerous on the inflowing tide, but 'mud-wandering' is not the popular pastime here that it is in Holland. Just occasionally someone is buried by a collapsing dune, or is struck by lightning while crossing a bare heath, or breaks an ankle slipping on limestone pavement. There are remarkably few mountain crags and precipices on English National Nature Reserves, and not many towering sea-cliffs either. Many English Reserves are very beautiful, but few are undisputedly grand in the nineteenth century Romantic sense. In general one's sense of wilderness is very limited. There is often a nuclear power station or gas cylinder poking up on the horizon of even the remotest estuary, and there are few lowland Reserves where you cannot see fields (and, in season, combine harvesters) in the distance. At least two Reserves, however, are dangerous by any standards. Chartley Moss and Wybunbury Moss in the West Midlands are 'floating bogs' or *Schwingmoors*, a thin crust of peat over the deep impenetrable waters of a lake. They are no places to take the dog for a walk, and access is, understandably enough, restricted to permit holders. And even they are not encouraged to go there alone.

Another occasional danger is unexploded bombs and other wartime debris. At Studland you can still sometimes find glistening pellets of phosphorus on the beach which give a nasty burn if you pick them up. Old Winchester Hill is littered with rusting mortar shells left over from the days when it was an army range. Bomb disposal teams cleared hundreds of shells from the site after a bonfire built by a scrub clearance contractor suddenly exploded. Since it is virtually impossible to make safe the whole area, parts of this popular Reserve have had to be fenced off and warning notices erected. Kingley Vale is much the same. In 1991, bomb disposal experts removed some 6000 'items' from this Reserve, including 280 live shells which were blown up on-site. Unwelcome reminders of the war surface elsewhere from time to time. Someone rotovating the ground at Thetford Heath recently was understandably disconcerted to see a live grenade fly out from beneath his feet! In general, however, English nature reserves are no more challenging than the countryside around them. They offer a 'walk', rather than the New World reserves on which you 'hike'.

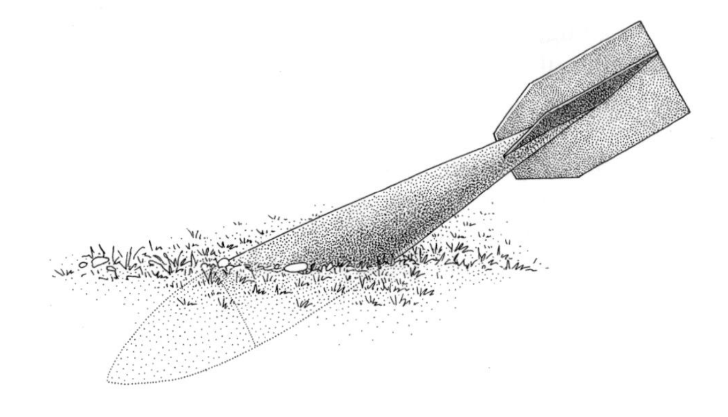

THE NATURE OF THE CUSTOMER

Some years ago there was a vogue for 'recreation ecology' in which the habits of human visitors were studied as though they, too, were wild animals. The conclusions reached by the researchers were rarely very surprising; they tended to confirm that the average person is uninformed, unadventurous and unlikely to move far from his or her car. At Old Winchester Hill, for example, the attraction lies in the view, which is well enough on a clear day, but many admire it as though it were two-dimensional, like a painting, without that extra dimension that allows us to walk into it. On coastal Reserves the aim of almost everyone is to reach the beach by the quickest and easiest route possible. Even the hardy walkers crossing Moor House or Ingleborough rarely stray from the footpath.

A sizeable minority, though, are interested in wildlife. A recent study of the people using nature trails in the Lake District and Scotland found that the majority were of the professional or middle classes and members of at least one conservation charity. The researchers doubted whether these people were benefiting very much from the kindergarten leaflets on offer. It is noticeable that educationalists and amenity experts tend to class anyone with some knowledge of natural history as a 'specialist', and hence someone beyond their remit. Certainly such people are potentially the most difficult to cater for and control. As one researcher put it, 'they feel that they have a right to go where they like, and they often know just where to go'. Some would argue that this is the very constituency to which National Nature Reserves should be catering, since they are clearly not fit places for mass entertainment.

One reason why the Conservancy has sometimes seemed less than enthusiastic about promoting its Reserves is that, while the benefits of visitors are intangible, the problems they can cause may be all too obvious. The early Annual Reports are full of examples of casual vandalism. The Conservancy was particularly proud of its original signs, which were surmounted by a heavy cast iron crown, a frequent target for the anarchists and republicans in our midst. The later board signs made excellent toboggans at Lathkill Dale, and a few of the more attractive ones were stolen, presumably for quieter contemplation in private. At present, English Nature has produced what it hopes is a vandal-proof sign for use at the main trouble spots. Ainsdale Sand Dunes on the Merseyside coast not far from Liverpool perhaps holds the record for the number of 'incidents'. According to Keith Payne, warden at Ainsdale during the 1970s, it can present quite a sight on summer weekends, nudists on the beach and in the sandy hollows, and clothed men 'climbing the dunes to peer at the man on the next peak who is peering back'. Elsewhere there were often roaming bands of young 'scallies' who 'display the sort of resilience that allows them to swim fully clothed in our ponds in mid-winter and then return on the train to Kirkby or Bootle, dripping from head to foot'. Another recent warden, David Wheeler, recalls an occasion when, in the space of an hour, his field office was looted, the police were chasing criminals across the dunes and part of the Reserve was on fire, all against the background crackle of the annual Wood Pigeon shoot!

Fires are perhaps the greatest hazard to Reserves, especially on lowland heaths. While it is seldom possible to trace the precise cause of a fire, it is noticeable that a few members of the public are breathtakingly careless when it comes to camping stoves, glowing cigarette ends and matches. At Old Winchester Hill, the warden once found two dozen stoves in use at a time of maximum fire risk, one of them within a few yards of a (vandalised) sign asking visitors to refrain from lighting fires! The Purbeck site managers, Mike Tuck and Rees Cox, have special authority from the Chief Constable of the Dorset police to mount blue lights and klaxons on their Land Rovers to enable them to rush, blaring, to the source of the blaze. Fortunately better preparation and fire service training has so far prevented a recurrence of the disastrous fires in the hot summers of 1959 and 1976.

The amount of petty larceny and break-ins to Reserve offices is, unfortunately, increasing. On my travels around England's Reserves in 1992, I made a sizeable list of separate incidents, in which the theft from the middle of a secluded wood of a carefully camouflaged generator, complete with its security cage, and of a Land Rover not 46 m from where the warden was at work, are among the highlights. Reserves close to large cities are especially vulnerable to such raids. The losses can mount up to an expensive replacement sum, since the Conservancy does not have comprehensive insurance cover for its technical equipment and vehicles. The warden himself may have to pay up if negligence is proved. Valuable tools now have to be locked up in security cages. Burglar alarms are also a regrettable necessity. At the Reserve office at the Lizard, a series of break-ins stripped the place bare—portable telephones, chain saws, stores of fencing wire, everything. Since then, the installation of a fairly elaborate alarm system has so far deterred the thieves.

Assault and physical violence on wardens is, mercifully, still rare. All warden/

managers are now equipped with portable telephones, and sometimes also two-way radios, which can be very useful in a tight corner, even when not switched on. A greater problem, especially on downland reserves with grazing flocks, is loose dogs. This can be a considerable constraint on the way the Reserve is managed, since it may be necessary to keep the sheep well away from the public footpath. On a few Reserves, like the Lizard and Finglandrigg Wood in Cumbria, the Conservancy uses breeds of sheep like the Soay or the Hebridean that are remarkably adept at dealing with dogs. Occasionally the boot is on the other foot. One reason why Parsonage Down is a restricted-access Reserve is the uncertain temper of its Longhorn bulls.

In the larger National Parks in America, elaborate planning has allowed the authorities to increase the Park's 'carrying capacity' without further damaging the environment. By the thoughtful siting of visitor centres and the replacement of private cars with public transport, it has become possible 'to handle three times the traffic of 10 years ago, with less than half the ecological stress'. Similar techniques have been used within National Parks and Country Parks in England, but on the generally smaller scale of National Nature Reserves, such planning is usually restricted to the siting of hides, small car parks and strengthened walkways across sensitive habitats. At Thursley Common in Surrey a well-made board walk allows people to inspect bog plants and watch dragonflies without damage. At Upper Teesdale the same purpose is served by the tarmac road to the dam at Cauldron Snout. Nature trails and way-marked walks are generally designed to take people through relatively robust parts of the Reserve, while enabling them to see a representative slice of the wildlife, landforms and management activities. On the majority of English National Nature Reserves, however, the public use is so small that no such plans are necessary.

EXPLAINING NATURE

The founding fathers envisaged a significant role for the Conservancy in 'furthering' environmental education (which in those days meant nature study). In practice, the latter had more urgent priorities, and the advent of Country Parks and the phenomenal growth of local and private sector nature reserves in the 1970s and 1980s, have created a varied platform for those engaged in 'explaining nature'. The Conservancy's attitude towards education has always been somewhat ambiguous: 'good in theory, but preferably in someone else's backyard' sums it up. Its published conservation strategy of 1984 was strongly advocatory: 'More field and interpretative centres should be established and such places better supplied with books, leaflets and other literature on local natural history and nature conservation'. So they were, but not on Conservancy land. Many National Nature Reserves offer great potential for field study and 'interpretation', but there are often better facilities and more robust land nearby where it makes better sense to concentrate one's efforts. Walberswick NNR, for example, has a wonderful range of wildlife habitats, but it is private land, and the existing facilities of the RSPB Reserve at Minsmere lie just round the corner. Ainsdale Sand Dunes NNR used to have a field centre and education facilities, but the burden of education is now shouldered by the local authorities and directed towards less sensitive sites along the Merseyside coast.

There are, in fact, reasonable grounds in almost every individual case for not using

National Nature Reserves for educational purposes. Nevertheless, the Conservancy recognised the need to show some form of leadership in the field. English Nature's present education adviser, Adam Cade, has produced a database of 880 sites considered suitable for nature study. In the 1980s the Conservancy decided to promote one National Nature Reserve in each of its 15 regions in Great Britain as an educational flagship, designed to cater for school parties, university courses and visitors generally. The Reserves selected were those which were already popular, and where some facilities already existed: Ainsdale, Old Winchester Hill, Studland Heath, Lathkill Dale in the Peak District, Kingley Vale in West Sussex. These plans have not so far amounted to very much. A proposal to build a Reserve centre for Lathkill Dale has been deferred through 'lack of resources'. Another, at the Wren's Nest in Dudley, is currently in abeyance. At Ainsdale, Old Winchester Hill and Aston Rowant English Nature is not putting up visitor centres but pulling them down. It all amounts to an obvious lack of enthusiasm, especially when compared with the efforts of bodies like the RSPB and the National Trust.

Through lack of resources and any strong central direction, education on Reserves has developed along strictly local lines or in partnership with other bodies. Some site managers, like Rees Cox at Studland, John Breeds at Braunton Burrows or Richard Williamson at Kingley Vale, have a talent for conveying their knowledge and love of nature to others, especially children. When all is said and done, this is the basis of learning. To a child, a 'nature warden' must seem close to a magician, a wonderful person who knows all there is to be known about the songs of birds and the secrets of a pond, and who can tell stories about them at the drop of a stick. At Avon Gorge, Tony Robinson runs an imaginative 'dawn till dusk' programme of natural history, during which mini-courses on flowers, bird songs, moths and bats are held at appropriate moments of the day or night. This extravaganza proved a popular success at its trial run in May 1992, though it tested the stamina both of guides and participants to the limit. Altogether some 23,800 people took part in organised walks and educational groups on National Nature Reserves in 1992.

The Wren's Nest NNR in the middle of Dudley is one of the best examples of a long-running partnership project that began in the 1960s. In such an area, environmental education is not so much an option as a necessity. The Reserve itself is suitably dramatic, a great whaleback of limestone that was once the floor of a sea, and which has yielded fossils of trilobites so perfectly preserved that they look as though they might wake up and crawl out of the rock. The slopes have been quarried and mined extensively and are full of interest both for geologists and for students of our industrial past. And, as if to emphasise the educational possibilities of the site, a school sits squarely on top of it. For the past 30 years, the Conservancy and the Borough of Dudley have jointly managed an educational project which includes geological trails, a Reserve handbook and, in Dudley Museum, an exhibition including a fine collection of fossils chipped from the Wren's Nest rocks during the past 200 years. The latest version of the handbook, aimed principally at 'A' level and undergraduate students, provides a well-illustrated and comprehensive account of the area's fossils, rock strata and mining history. And geologists have dug sections and trenches to display the numerous rocks and fossil beds to best advantage. The trail requires constant maintenance, because of rock slips and erosion, and the main cavern has been fenced off for fear of collapse, though it can be viewed from a specially built observation platform.

What is presently missing is an on-site visitor centre with classroom facilities. At the time of writing, English Nature have agreed to part-fund such a centre at the nearby Bluebell Park. Its completion will make the Wren's Nest Britain's premier site for the teaching of geology to schools and colleges.

An alternative approach is offered by Lathkill Dale, the largest and most heavily visited of the limestone dales within the Derbyshire Dales NNR. More than 7000 students from schools and the Peak District's three Field Centres use the Dale each year, and its beauties are admired by visitors who arrive in their tens of thousands. In the early 1980s, the Reserve warden was able to make good use of the opportunities provided by the Manpower Services Commission to establish a small educational team for taking parties around the Reserve. He developed slide packs, videos, students worksheets, and leaflets on every imaginable subject from lead mines to river restoration. Unfortunately the Conservancy lacked the resources to continue to support educational activities at this level after the demise of Manpower Services in 1985, and at the time of writing, the project is in limbo.

On the whole, education is not an important function of National Nature Reserves. The Reserves are acquired not for their potential as outdoor classrooms but to fulfil nature conservation priorities. Whether or not they should play a more positive role in environmental education is debatable. If their role does expand, however, it will almost certainly be on a low-key basis, and as part of a wider programme. The NNRs are unlikely to set the agenda.

THE RESERVES ON DISPLAY

I devote the remainder of this chapter to a consideration of the information and public facilities that are available on National Nature Reserves. This is of course a rolling picture, and at the time of writing English Nature has no firm policy on the public use of its Reserves. Many of the Reserve centres have become dilapidated, and the old nature trail leaflets are being replaced by waymarked paths and signboards. In keeping with the themes explored elsewhere in this book, I shall focus less on what might happen in the future and more on how things came to be the way they are (for experience teaches one to be chary of plans and policy papers, especially grandiose ones). There are five main ways in which information about Reserves can be conveyed to the visitor: signs, centres, self-guided trails, leaflets and 'live' conducted tours. The first thing you will see on a Reserve is the sign. Let us start with that.

'A WORD BEFORE YOU ENTER . . .'

Putting up a sign is an act of possession. At its most basic level, it is a way of saying 'this place is mine', and if you enter you do so on my terms. Signs are inseparable from the idea of nature reserves as sanctuaries, as places where wild animals and birds can live free of outside disturbance. The popular idea of a nature reserve sign is a big red 'no-entry' traffic warning (as on the cover of Dudley Stamp's *Nature Conservation in Britain*). In practice, of course, signs can be made considerably more welcoming and informative. It is an opportunity to tell the visitor something about the Reserve and why it is special. Many of those used in the past by the Conservancy included a map displaying the layout of the Reserve, with its footpaths and facilities. Unfortunately some of these have been removed in the belief that, because many people cannot read a map, maps are not necessary.

A sign is also a convenient place to display by-laws and appeals for the visitor's co-operation. For some Reserves there are only one or two signs, and for the most private ones none at all, but for others there may be dozens. The present record is held by the Lizard NNR with 56 signs at the boundaries of scattered holdings throughout that peninsula's miles of coastline and heath. Quite possibly some Reserves are 'over-signed', but the legislation requires that they be placed at all points of public access to the Reserve.

The Conservancy has always taken a great deal of care over the design of its signs, and has tried (not always successfully) to avoid anything avoidably ugly or out of place. The first generation of signs were simple pressed metal shields, but these were soon replaced by a more elaborate signpost designed by the Royal College of Art. Each consisted of a single piece of hardware attached to a reinforced concrete post. A simple metal frame was topped by a bold cast iron crown similar to that of the Conservancy's letter heads. The crown symbolised the Reserve's Crown Land status; but, with characteristic thrift, the Conservancy also intended its bold silhouette to act as a permanent marker for surveying on featureless moors. A map and a brief description of the Reserve were produced separately on a sheet of durable plastic, which was then secured to the frame by screws. All in all, it was a neat piece of work, dignified, informative and stylish.

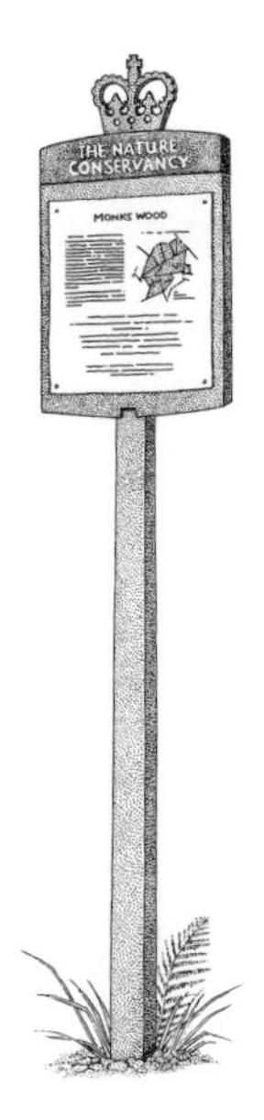

One of the practical consequences of the reorganisation of the old Nature Conservancy into a Nature Conservancy Council in 1973 was that all 135 Reserves had to be re-signed, a task which had only just come within sight of completion when the NCC was reorganised and renamed yet again. The opportunity was taken to develop a more flexible format, in which the sign could be placed in a wall or cairn, or on the bar of a gate. The imposing iron crowns were dispensed with (many of them ended their working life as door stops). This time the crown and name were cast on the surroundings of a rectangular aluminium frame, while text and map were printed on a single sheet of adhesive plastic which could be stuck onto the recessed interior. The maps were drawn to a large scale and included a considerable amount of detail. For reasons lost in the mists of time, it was decided to colour the whole sign brown.

With the passing of the NCC in 1991, a third generation of Reserve signs became necessary. This time English Nature decided to try to make them more 'user-friendly' and to tailor the design to the known level of public use. Each English Reserve was graded into those with 'high-use' (defined as more than 20,000 people per year), 'medium-use' (between 5000 and 20,000 people) and 'low-use' (5000 or fewer people). The first sort are to receive a multicolour poster combining a graphic impression of the Reserve with pictures of three or four representative species and a brief reference to other 'key' aspects of the Reserve. Some of the 'medium-use' Reserves will also receive illustrated signs, but those of the majority 'low-use' category will be confined to a short list of do's and don'ts and a line or two of description. Each sign is being produced as a self-adhesive silk-screen vinyl print, which is fixed to an aluminium backplate. The new signs undoubtedly look more up-to-date than the old, especially when combined with English Nature's distinctive headplate. They have been criticised for their lack of detail, and they are clearly aimed at the notional person on the No. 14 bus who, it is believed, knows little or nothing about maps, nature reserves or wildlife. But they are smart, cheap to make and reasonably durable. And, as I mentioned at the beginning of this chapter, they do at least contain the word 'welcome'.

'THE RESERVE IS RICH IN PLANT AND ANIMAL LIFE . . .'

There are remarkably few books about England's National Nature Reserves, individually or collectively. Max Nicholson's *Britain's Nature Reserves* (1957) is a detailed overview of the first few years, written at a time when the Conservancy considered it desirable to trumpet its wares. *Monks Wood. A Nature Reserve Record* (1973) was the homage of the Monks Wood Experimental Station staff to the old

Nature Conservancy, published on the convenient tenth anniversary of that well-known Reserve. *The Great Yew Forest. The Natural History of Kingley Vale* by Richard Williamson (1978) is a readable and interesting account by the man who has been in charge of the Vale for more than 30 years and recently it has been joined by *Island of Terns* (1993) by Bob Chestney, who was warden at Scolt Head Island for 30 years. There are also books about Hickling Broad and the Axmouth–Lyme Regis landslip. That is about all. Various 'Where-to-go-and-what-to-find' books, most notably MacMillan's blockbuster *Guide to Britain's Nature Reserves* (1984), list some of the National Nature Reserves, but they tend to be lost in the crowd of other nature reserves, country parks, picnic sites, open-air zoos and assorted heritage properties. The Conservancy, since 1957, has been far too modest.

The main sources of published information about the Reserves are the leaflets, which have been published at one time or another for all but the most private sites. Placed together, a full set would amount to several hundred pages, almost rival the MacMillan guide in size, and certainly outstrip it in detail. The leaflets are normally written by the warden/site manager responsible for that particular Reserve. The standard one, published between 1974 and 1989, consisted of a simple folded A4 sheet with a page or two of text, a map, and sometimes a view of the Reserve in monochrome. A few of the most popular Reserves, like Kingley Vale and Braunton Burrows, received full colour leaflets of eight or more pages. They were designed by the Conservancy's Interpretive Branch in that curious block lettering on shiny paper that became the 'house style'. The colour leaflets are illustrated by excellent photographs, but the others make do with line drawings in a variety of styles. The latter were selected from a central bank of material, evidently a small one for some drawings were used repeatedly and at some risk of becoming the visual equivalent of a cliché. Generally useful and informative, the leaflets are written in the earnest, slightly clipped style of someone who knows volumes about the Reserve in question but has to compress it all within 700 words. You would need at least 10 minutes of quiet contemplation to absorb their message.

The earliest leaflets date from the late 1950s. Contemporary records suggest that, *pace* the Nicholson book, the Nature Conservancy was initially against any publicity about the Reserves in case it encouraged the hordes and the charabancs. This policy was liberalised after National Nature Week in 1963, and the slow stream of leaflets became a flood after 1974, when several were translated into French, German, Spanish and Russian. The present policy is to confine leaflet production to the well-visited Reserves. Like the older style of leaflet, the new ones are printed on a single piece of A4 paper, but they are now folded into three so that you can slip them into a pocket. The maps have been much simplified and efforts are being made to introduce a more 'user-friendly' style.

Effective distribution has long been a problem since the leaflets are mostly in-house productions, and the Conservancy has no shops and few display areas. Leaflets are available on request from its main Regional offices (most are free) and are listed in its publications catalogue. They are also available from Reserve centres, where they still exist, and sometimes from Tourist Board caravans and 'honesty boxes' on the Reserve. They were never promoted very vigorously. The mountain was expected to go to Mohamet. At present many of the older leaflets are still available, but they will gradually be phased out and replaced by English Nature ones.

'YOU DIDN'T SEE A DORMOUSE, BUT HERE'S A PICTURE OF ONE'

Reserve centres come under many names and guises. In general they are a place in which material can be placed on display, talks held during wet weather, and where equipment and clothing can be stored and toilets and other basic facilities provided. They vary in size and elaboration from something not much grander than a garden shed to custom-designed permanent buildings containing a coffee bar, a shop, projection facilities and the very latest in hi-tech audio-visual presentation. We need not concern ourselves with the latter, however; there are none on the National Nature Reserves.

During the 1950s and 1960s, the Conservancy thought more in terms of scientific field stations than visitor centres. But some members of staff saw merit in putting aspects of the Reserves on public display and saying something about their management and about nature conservation in general. Most of these efforts were done on a shoestring budget and had an endearingly homemade quality. One example dating back to the mid-1960s was a series of display cases mounted along the trail at Yarner Wood in association with the Devon Education Authority's Schools Museum Service and designed for school parties. The cases, designed by the schools writer, Les Jackman, were a great success in their day, although they proved the very devil to weatherproof. Another was the papier-mâché model of Kingley Vale in Chichester Museum, built by Richard Williamson from 30 old copies of the *Sunday Times*. At the same time, prefabricated information centres were being knocked up at Old Winchester Hill, Kingley Vale and Ainsdale Sand Dunes, and others followed at Aston Rowant, Wye and Ebbor Gorge in the early 1970s. They were modest constructions —that at Old Winchester Hill cost precisely £120—and were stocked with whatever exhibits came to hand—skins, shells, bird's nests and pebbles, augmented with photographs and printed material. Of all the Reserve centres, perhaps the 'field museum' at Kingley Vale comes closest to what one might expect to find in the depths of a nature reserve—stuffed birds hanging from the rafters, a great table-top section of polished yew, hand-drawn charts detailing that season's records and a logbook (though the stuffed birds hang there no longer—the RSPB disapproved of them). The museum takes a 'hands-on' approach—children are encouraged to touch the exhibits—and its home-made rusticity is a world away from the slick professionalism of some recent visitor centres. Most of the thousands of people who visit the place each year seem to like it.

The Reserve centre at Aston Rowant was among the most elaborate to be built, for it was designed to commemorate the European Year of the Environment and the Conservancy's own 21st anniversary. While the earlier centres were built close to a car park, this one lay in the heart of the Reserve and commanded a wonderful view across the Chiltern escarpment. It was consequently a fiend to build: materials had to be carried to the site by hand or bumped across in the back of a Land Rover, and the ground preparation alone took the combined resources of the Conservancy's South Region, volunteers from its headquarters and a team of Royal Engineers. The building was designed to defeat the vandal: a squat prefabricated octagon with a projecting flat roof, it enclosed a series of display panels, each of which could be opened in the morning, and then turned round to be locked shut at night. Inside was a storage space and a chemical toilet. The formal opening of the centre on 11 March 1970, to which guests and the press were invited, seems to have been one of those occasions when nothing went right. The heavens opened. The speech by Sir Ralph Verney was punctuated by growls of thunder and frantic hammering from within the centre where the buildings officer was still making last minute adjustments to the display. The specially printed leaflets for the nature trail failed to arrive on time, not that the by now cold and bedraggled party showed much enthusiasm for walking anywhere; and after hot soup and sherry had temporarily restored their drooping spirits, their departing cars became stuck in the mud.

Many are the stories, apocryphal or not, that have been woven around the Reserve centres. My particular favourite is an overheard conversation between a lady and her daughter on discovering the garden of wild flowers on the chalky bank below the centre at Old Winchester Hill. The blooms were very seasonal and for much of the year all that you could see was the name-tag. Such was the scene on this occasion. After a pause, the little girl asked:

> 'What are those, mummy?'
> 'I think it's a graveyard dear. It is where they bury their sheep when they die.'
> 'Ooh—and look mummy, they've all got names.'
> 'Hard-heads. Basil. Rock-rose. Now isn't that nice. They really *do* love their animals here, don't they.'

The Conservancy's limited enthusiasm for public display centres eventually began to wane, and the buildings grew increasingly dilapidated and vandal-prone. The one at Wye was broken into and the contents burned on a bonfire outside. At Aston Rowant, the wooden panels started to rot, while the centre at Old Winchester Hill became infested with rats. There was little doubt that in their decaying state the old centres were far from an image-enhancing asset when English Nature took them over in 1991. They would also cost a great deal to repair to a professional standard. At the time of writing, some of the old centres have been pulled down, and the others are likely to follow. The question is: what will replace them? A modernised visitor centre run by English Nature alone is, at present, the least likely option. They are extremely expensive to design and construct, and a major commitment to maintain; they are one thing for a charity with a membership to cater for, quite another for a body funded by the taxpayer and answerable to the Treasury. It is much more likely that the old centres will be replaced by information panels, situated at car parks, in hides and along footpaths. Another possibility, if the right 'partners' can be found, might lie in co-operative ventures, with English Nature providing financial assistance for a centre, but leaving others to take charge of its design and day-to-day running. English Nature, then, will probably decide to take a 'back seat', providing resources and advice where it is needed, but otherwise concentrating on its traditional strengths of science and land management. There is, however, another view held within the organisation that National Nature Reserves should not be promoted at all. At present it seems torn between its broad policy to 'establish an identity and increase the public's awareness and understanding of, and support for, National Nature Reserves', and of having to convince the Treasury that it has taken the most cost-effective option available. The overall approach might be summed up in a phrase used in a recent policy statement and obviously based on bitter experience: 'Beware of consultants bearing gifts'.

'AT THE SEVENTH POST YOU MAY NOTICE A REDSTART'

Nature trails are good fun. They introduce you to things you might not have noticed, and they are as painless a way of learning about nature and wildlife as has ever been devised. They are cheap to run and maintain, they 'channel' large numbers of people away from sensitive areas and they earn the Reserve good-will. On the other hand they are no longer fashionable.

Nature trails were an American idea that was introduced to Britain in the early 1960s. It was not so much a failing of the British imagination as the 'no entry' policy on nature reserves that had prevented them from taking root before. In America, self-guided trails had been widely used in the 1950s by the National Parks Service and by the National Audubon Society (the US equivalent of the RSPB) as a basis for field studies, and they were often backed up by classroom facilities and field museums. In Britain the idea took root during the planning for National Nature Week in May 1963. Since the idea of the Nature Week was to draw public attention to wildlife conservation, it encouraged bodies like the Nature Conservancy to think about using some of its Reserves in pursuit of this laudable aim. Having helped to organise Nature Week, the Conservancy went on to celebrate the event with open days at its field stations, and by setting up temporary nature trails at Castor Hanglands and Studland Heath. With two others at Mousehold Heath near Norwich and Alvecote Pools in Warwickshire, these were the first nature trails in Britain. They were considered sufficiently successful for more, and more permanent, nature trails to be set up after a second National Nature Week in 1966. By the end of that year, eight English Reserves had nature trails, with a further eight in Scotland and five in Wales. Most of the impetus behind the trails and related educational projects on Reserves was due to the enthusiasm of the Conservancy's then information officer, Philip Oswald, and to Dr Tom Pritchard, who had seen some of the American trails at first hand. The two went on to write a popular pamphlet, *Nature Trails*, published in 1968. The Nature Conservancy can thus fairly claim to have pioneered the development of the nature trail in Britain.

By no means every nature reserve is suitable for a nature trail. What the latter needs is not so much habitat quality as diversity, physical robustness and the possibility of concealment. Trails are at their best when they pass through a succession of landscapes, or take the user to places where the opportunities to see wildlife are particularly good. Excellent trails have been devised in places as initially unpromising as coal bings and subsidence ponds. The nature trails on England's National Nature Reserves are generally devised with the family or a school party in mind, and they rarely extend more than a mile or two (unlike the strenuous mountain trail at Beinn Eighe, which takes you into real wilderness). Those at Ainsdale and Yarner Wood cater specifically for school biology classes and include worksheets and printed notes for the teacher. The geological trail at Wren's Nest and the landforms trail at Fyfield Down are aimed at 'A' level or undergraduate students, and are backed up by fairly technical handbooks. At the latter Reserve, the student is set some pretty tough geological exercises, and is recommended to read the handbook *before* setting out. Some of the more generalised trails also encourage the visitor to think by asking questions at stages along the route. Some of these are fairly challenging. The one at Kingley Vale asks: 'What are dangers of a reserve becoming an 'island'?' [ie isolated by agricultural land] and 'why does the Speckled Wood butterfly have yellow spots on its wings?'

Nature trails have various inherent drawbacks. Most native mammals are shy or nocturnal, and noisy and excited gatherings are not the best circumstances for birdwatching. The presence of wild beasts is best demonstrated by semi-permanent features such as wood-ant nests or badger setts, or by the surreptitious use of 'props'—bones, gnawed nut shells and pine cones, droppings, pellets and foot prints. Plastic badgers were briefly considered for Yarner Wood, but local staff understandably objected. The vegetable kingdom is more obliging in this respect, but there is no guarantee that a plant will reappear at a particular place or even that the landscape itself will remain unchanged—the nature trail at Hoveton Great Broad was laid down in open fen 20 years ago, but today most of that fen is now dense woodland. Partly for these reasons, most of the Conservancy's nature trails are less concerned with pointing out particular animals and plants than with presenting a 'holistic' view of the Reserve, which takes in landscape features, soil sections, archaeology and management. They are at least as much about *man's* use of the land, in the past and in the present, as about the other species that happen to live there.

Another limitation of the trails is that few people are aware of them. An appraisal of self-guided trails, carried out by the Dartington Amenity Research Trust at the request of the Countryside Commission in 1978, found that many trails were the product of past enthusiasms which had since grown faint; paths were overgrown and leaflets out of print. Only the 'key' trails, such as Ainsdale or Studland, are advertised in the teaching press, and in practice most of the users are local residents and nearby schools. The Trust also detected a certain ambivalence on matter of presentation. Who are nature trails for? Educationalists used to recommend that you write with 'the intelligent 11-year-old', or, by implication, the unintelligent adult, in mind. But at least a quarter of those interviewed by the Trust were dissatisfied with that level of interpretation. Furthermore, since naturalists are, almost by definition, seekers of wilderness, a formal trail can to some extent become self defeating, as so much of the pleasure of natural history depends on the unexpected, on *spontaneity*. Many people in the 'interpretation' business now regard nature trails, with their inbuilt inflexibility, as rather *passé*, as an idea whose time has run out. Certainly there are a diminishing number of formal nature trails on National Nature Reserves (I list those that survive in Table 5), and some of these are now run by educational interests rather than by English Nature directly.

Alternatives to the traditional post-and-leaflet trails are now appearing on Reserves. At Ham Street Woods in Kent, for example, the visitor is offered a choice of walks marked out by posts with colour-coded bands, a technique developed on Forest trails. In the place of a leaflet, sign panels interpret some of the themes of the Reserve—coppicing, ride management, pond life, butterflies and moths. In keeping with English Nature's ideal of involving the community in such projects, the cost of the signs was met by a local cosmetics firm, while the panels were designed by art students at Canterbury. Panels do not of course contain as much detail as leaflets, and they are vulnerable to the whims of vandals. But they do at least provide a foundation on which the visitor can build from his or her own observations and experiences.

'QUIET PLEASE, LOVE, LET'S GIVE THE BIRD A CHANCE'

The best way to see wildlife is to watch and wait. Most wild animals and birds regard human beings, with ample justification, as lethally dangerous. Hides and observatories of various kinds represent ways in which we can see them without their being aware of us. Hides occasionally form the focal point of a nature trail, as at Hoveton Great Broad, and large hides can double as a display centre, like the splendid Observation Hide at Studland. A luxury hide built by James Venner at the North Solent Reserve includes a small office and even a 'loo with a view'. They come in all shapes and sizes. There is one at Roudsea Wood which is mounted on a tower of scaffolding, which makes for a nervous climb whenever there is any wind. The Swale NNR has no fewer than six large hides, mounted high on the walls of clay bunds like prison watch towers. Some have complained, justifiably, that these prominent walls and hides have 'taken the wilderness out of the marshes', but they make birdwatching at the Swale among the best in England, at close quarters in perfect light. It is one of the ironies of the English way of conservation that improvements for wildlife are often made at the expense of wildness.

A great many National Nature Reserves contain well-built hides. They are useful to site managers for detecting and counting birds as well as the public. Hides are normally designed to overlook a place where birds congregate, especially lakes or 'scrapes', or a stretch of foreshore. A properly sited hide will avoid looking directly into the sun, should command a good breadth of view and stand well back from the viewing area. Many are screened by fences, often made of reed thatch (though thick hedges have better sound absorption qualities). Public hides need to be quite roomy—otherwise there will be a queue. They are fairly expensive to make: a standard 3.6-m hide housing eight birdwatchers will cost several thousand pounds.

One of the most popular hides in England is at Weeting Heath, where a large hide overlooks a patch of open grassland where Stone Curlews nest and display regularly. Some 5000 people visit the hide each season, sometimes in coachloads. It is a large enough enterprise to occupy two summer wardens employed by the Norfolk Naturalists Trust for much of the time. Another good 'rare bird' hide is the Observation Hide at Studland, in the midst of Dartford Warbler breeding territories. Sometimes these attractive birds nest almost under the watchers' binoculars, and in 1991 one of them actually flew *into* the hide, startling a group of naturalists watching ducks on Little Sea mere.

The use of most Reserve hides is free, although sometimes a permit is required for hides in a restricted area, such as those on Fenning Island at Bridgwater Bay. Those at North Solent, built along the shingly Solent shore and the reedbeds of the Beaulieu River, are available under a permit system operated by Beaulieu Estate Office. One of them is designed for use by wheelchair users, and won an award during the 1981 Year of the Disabled.

Hides are, unfortunately, a ready target for vandals, which constrains their potential usefulness as display centres. The most common form of hide abuse is to rip the door from its hinges. Last year, the absence of the door of the hide at Benacre NNR was noted by a passing queen hornet, and so within days there was an enormous buzzing nest, poised above the door like a Chinese lantern. The hornets didn't seem to mind human company, but it certainly lent spice to my visit with the site manager, Cliff Waller. We crawled in on hands and knees while the great wasps buzzed and settled and inspected us from above, eventually deciding that we were harmless. Later that day Cliff gave battle with the hornets armed with a beekeeper's mask and smoker. I hope he is all right. (Someone ought to research the natural history of hides. The

16. Above left: *Avon Gorge, the 'Somerset' bank of the river*. 17. Above right: *The dunes at Ainsdale*.
18. Below: *The small pond near the former Reserve centre at Aston Rowant*.

19. Left: *Lady Park Wood*.
20. Below: *The Bovey Valley Woodlands*.

21. Top: *The Wren's Nest at Dudley.*
22. Above right: *April Pasque Flowers in their bumpy habitat at Barnack Hills and Holes, an ancient quarry near Stamford.*
23. Left: *Leeward side of Scolt Head Island.*

24. Top: *Roudsea Wood.*
25. Above left: *Shrubby Cinquefoil below the High Force waterfall in Upper Teesdale.*
26. Right: *A rich ungrazed chalk flora on the southern slopes of Mount Caburn, Lewes Downs.*

Studland hide is the home of a large spider, *Pholcus*, the size and shape of a Daddy-long-legs. And a dormouse once made its nest in the medicine box in the hut at Old Winchester Hill.)

Some hides include a birdwatching logbook, which is always useful and interesting. They are presumably of small value to the burglar although that failed to prevent the disappearance of the North Solent hide logbook, a vast leather-bound ledger. Fortunately, from our point of view, the thief went on to break into a nearby house owned by a High Court judge, and left the logbook there on his retreat. It was returned to the hide by the police, who had presumably first checked to see if the burglar had left his name in the logbook, along with his ornithological observations. Unfortunately (for it would have made a good story) he hadn't.

TABLE 4 *Educational facilities on NNRs*

Ainsdale Sand Dunes	Education officer, guided walks (summer), school programmes, teachers guide, display panels, nature trail. Co-operation with Sefton Coast managers
Avon Gorge	Guided walks (summer), A-level study pack. Co-operation with Bristol City museum service
Braunton Burrows	Children's trail and workbook, guided walks, display panels
Castle Eden Dene	Education officer, schools education programmes, community-based projects
Fyfield Down	Students handbook
Ham Street Woods	Display panels, walks
Kingley Vale	Nature trail, worksheets, guided walks, field museum
Lathkill Dale	Teachers pack, schools project leaflets, slide pack, video. Visitor centre proposed, but plans currently in abeyance
North Solent	Woodland Centre, resource material, nature trails and hides, run by charitable trust
Old Winchester Hill	Nature trail, guided walks (summer)
Rostherne Mere	Observatory, hides, guided walks (permit only)
Stodmarsh	Hide, display panels, walks, trail for disabled
Studland	Teachers guide, nature trails, hides, observation hut with display. Large visitor centre run by National Trust
Wren's Nest	Geological handbook and trail. Visitor centre proposed, but plans currently in abeyance
Yarner Wood	Teachers guide, worksheets, nature trails, display panels

TABLE 5 *Current self-guiding trails on National Nature Reserves in England*

NNR	*Date of establishment*	*Length (km)*	*Type*	*Features interpreted*
Ainsdale Sand Dunes	1963	2.5	Numbered posts, leaflet, teachers' guide	Dune formation and history, dune slacks and heath, woodland, management
Aston Rowant	1970	2.5	Numbered posts, leaflet	Soil profile, scrub, beechwood, downland, management, viewpoint
Bure Marshes (Hoveton Great Broad)	1967	1	Numbered posts, leaflet	Fen carr, reedbed, open broad, succession, birds
Chaddesley Woods	1977	2	Waymarked, leaflet	Ancient and planted woodland, badgers, rides, pond
Ebbor Gorge	1962	2	Display panels, colour-coded paths, trail for disabled	Geology, woodland flowers, birds and butterflies, coppicing.
Fyfield Down	1976	5	Handbook, students' work sheets	Landforms, strata, sarsen stones, dew pond, archaeology
Ham Street Woods	1992	1–4	Three colour-coded walks, display panels	Coppicing, high forest, rides, ponds
Kingley Vale	1966	2.5	Two waymarked walks, numbered posts, leaflet	Yew forest, mixed woodland, downland, soil profiles, archaeology, management
Old Winchester Hill	1967	2	Numbered posts, leaflet. Guided walks	Downland, scrub, butterflies, management, viewpoint
Scolt Head Island	1966	1	Waymarked, leaflet	Shorebirds, saltmarsh and sand dune plants, strand-line
Stodmarsh		1	Panels, hide, trail for disabled	Management, birds, reedbeds
Studland Heath	1962	2–3	Numbered posts, leaflet	Two trails: sand dunes and woodland, both covering range of wildlife
Upper Teesdale (Widdybank Fell)	1969	3	Leaflet	Mountain plants, geology, history, management
Wren's Nest	1967	2	Technical handbook, numbered posts	Geological trail: strata, fossils, landforms
Wye	1966	1.5	Numbered posts, leaflet	Downland and scrub, management, viewpoint
Yarner Wood	1963	2.5–4.5	Two walks. Numbered posts, leaflets, display cases	Woodland management, copper mine and tramway, wood-ants, birds

The former nature trails at Braunton Burrows, Castor Hanglands, Holme Fen, Monks Wood and Tring Reservoirs no longer function.

CHAPTER 5

Outdoor Laboratories

AT Hartland Moor they pursued the cycle of minerals in dry heathland; at Woodwalton Fen they observed how a recently dug pool gradually became a pond ecosystem; at Moor House they produced a scientific dossier the length of the *Encyclopaedia Britannica*; and at Barton Hills they found out why Pasque Flowers are rare. By simply being there, National Nature Reserves have provided the 'outdoor laboratories' for many outstanding ecological studies at all levels from the 10-year international biological programme at Moor House to the recording of flowers and birds by amateur naturalists. In the first place, they were the workplaces of the Nature Conservancy's own scientists based at the field stations of Furzebrook near Wareham, Merlewood near Grange-over-Sands in the Lake District and the famous Monks Wood Experimental Station (now Monks Wood Scientific Station) on the edge of the Fens. The locations of the field stations were chosen partly for their proximity to National Nature Reserves: Hartland Moor and Studland in the case of Furzebrook, and Moor House and Roudsea Wood for Merlewood, while the Monks Wood station was custom-built in a field next door to its eponymous nature reserve, with Woodwalton Fen not far away. Not unnaturally these Reserves have received more intensive study than most, though the nature of that study has varied from place to place.

The field stations developed along different lines: Furzebrook specialised in invertebrate ecology, Merlewood in soil ecology and mathematical modelling, and Monks Wood became the centre for management studies, especially on semi-natural grasslands. What governed the work of the field stations in the 1950s and 1960s was the Nature Conservancy's statutory function of providing advice on environmental problems. Among those that dominated the period were the impact of myxomatosis on grasslands, the restoration of sand-dunes and coastal marshes and, above all, the impact of herbicides and pesticides on wildlife. Other nature reserve owners, including local authorities, not unnaturally turned to the Conservancy for advice on management. At the same time, scientists were also interested in using Reserves for fundamental research into nutrient cycling and the transfer of energy within the ecosystem.

The story of many of these early projects has already been told, most notably in

John Sheail's book about pesticide research at Monk's Wood and in *Grassland Ecology and Wildlife Management*, written by that station's grassland team. What has never been assessed is the contribution of all this work to Reserve management as practised today. In a few cases one can trace a progression of ideas which have led to fruitful results. One of the Nature Conservancy's first studentship awards went to Duncan Poore, later to succeed Max Nicholson as director, who used the vegetation of Woodwalton Fen to assess techniques of vegetation classification developed on the European mainland. He later extended this work to the Scottish Highlands, which led to the first of the Conservancy's three scientific monographs, *Plant Communities of the Scottish Highlands* (1962), by Donald McVean and Derek Ratcliffe. The further development and refinement of phytosociology as a means of defining and describing wild vegetation led in turn to the massive National Vegetation Classification project, funded by the NCC in the 1970s and which is at last in the process of publication in five fat volumes. The methods described in this work will doubtless be used by ecologists and conservationists for decades to come when classifying and mapping wild vegetation and assessing the adequacy of the present nature reserve network in protecting wild plant communities.

It was perhaps not surprising that, given the nature of the Conservancy's research projects, there was some overlap with those of the agricultural research council or with the Forestry Commission. All were looking at animal populations, grazing regimes and woodland productivity. Nor were their aims at first dissimilar. The Conservancy was expected to show scientific impartiality when advising other land users; a more forthright advocacy of nature conservation was, in the early days at least, largely restricted to the regional and field staff. A few of the Conservancy scientists were in fact vehemently anti-conservation: A S Thomas, for example, who later wrote a forgotten book called *The Follies of Conservation*, deriding conservationists as Luddites and sentimentalists who let their hearts rule their heads. Scientists, more than almost any other profession, are expected to abide by their codes of intellectual discipline and scientific rectitude. This is one of the qualities that tends to set academic minds apart from those seeking simple answers to day-to-day problems, and sadly often limits their potential contributions to practical land management. Another is the way in which scientific papers are written: reading some journals it is hard to avoid the conclusion that they are being made deliberately inaccessible to 'the man in the field'. Few scientists seem to feel the need to express themselves clearly in simple language. Much of the scientific edifice that was won from National Nature Reserves 30 years ago was probably useless in practical terms. Of greater influence were the usually low-budget studies with immediate practical aims: Ian Prestt's studies of heathland reptiles, for example, or Jeremy Thomas' work on butterflies, which combine modern ecological techniques with traditional observational and field skills.

The great exception was the work of Monks Wood Experimental Station in the days when it was part of the Nature Conservancy. Perhaps because Monks Wood specialised in *applied* research on land management, its researches on sheep grazing, hedges, scrub management and individual species have influenced nature reserve management ever since. The proximity of so much well-directed scientific talent to Monks Wood NNR and Woodwalton Fen ensured that these were among the first Reserves to be, in the contemporary phrase, 'taken in hand'.

The story of the Woodwalton ponds is a good example of the unexpected directions which ecological study can take. In 1961, Norman Moore had some 20 small circular ponds dug in a corner of the Reserve as an outdoor laboratory for pesticide research. The idea was to investigate the effects of certain aquatic herbicides on the growth of algae, and whether they also interfered with the growth of water fleas, the main 'grazers' of the pond ecosystem. At the same time it was an opportunity to observe which animals and plants would colonise the pools, and the order in which they did so. While the results of the pesticide work were not unexpected (the water fleas did indeed suffer), the simple natural history experiment surprised the researchers by revealing that no two ponds developed in quite the same way. In the 1970s, Norman Moore and the warden, Gordon Mason, dug three more ponds in an area of acid water for the purposes of dragonfly monitoring. Since these were known to be the only acid-water pools for miles around, they provided useful information on the ranges of different species of dragonfly. This in turn has helped to influence the selection of SSSIs by determining the size of the 'mesh' needed by the SSSI network to protect dragonflies. At the same time, the digging of ponds underlined the paramount need to keep the Fen as wet as possible, and that if one could not raise the water level one could at least lower the surface.

Monks Wood's interest in grazing experiments resulted in the introduction of livestock to several Reserves, notably the cattle at Woodwalton and the sheep at Aston Rowant and other downland Reserves. It was in order to control the grazing for scientific purposes that the Nature Conservancy first purchased its own stock. At Aston Rowant a series of fenced paddocks went up, each of which was grazed by different numbers of sheep. Such work established the kinds of grazing regimes which maintained stable plant communities and those which were most effective in reducing scrub and unwanted coarse grasses. The 'ideal' pattern of grazing depended of course on what you wanted to achieve. Short turf favoured many of the attractive wild flowers of chalk, but, as the entomologist M G Morris discovered, it was disastrous for most invertebrates, which thrive much better on a rotation of grazed and ungrazed plots. The Monks Wood grassland team also pioneered the concept of scrub management on grassland nature reserves. On downland Reserves today, scrub is no longer seen as a mere intrusive nuisance but as an important part of the downland ecosystem, supplying shelter, nectar and nesting cover to a large range of animals, birds and invertebrates. Lena Ward's now overgrown plots at Castor Hanglands NNR helped to establish rotational cutting regimes on Reserves, where some scrub is now treated as pseudo-coppice, and cut at intervals of 10–20 years to produce a range of young and older growth.

Monks Wood Experimental Station's golden decade was not the result of state generosity. Part of the appeal of experimental management studies was precisely that they were inexpensive and 'low-tech', often requiring no more than a tape measure and a quadrat frame. Only occasionally did events unleash a sudden flood of money, as did the row over the building of Cow Green reservoir at Upper Teesdale in the mid-1960s. In that particular case, the largesse of 'blood money' was so great that a research fund was established to decide what to do with it all. The result was a series of studentships and projects that made the unspectacular slopes of heather and grass on Widdybank Fell one of the most closely studied botanical sites in the world. Much of the fund concentrated on the ecology of plant communities and individual species, enabling students to map much of the area in minute detail, and to discover, among other things, that small populations of Spring Gentians may be thousands of years old. The value of such research is mainly subliminal and long-term, as its implications gradually filter into the consciousness of naturalists and land managers. It is sad that benefices of the Teesdale sort are generally the consequence of the destruction of wild places (as are the 'nature reserves' offered by developers *after* they have dug a quarry or built a superstore).

The way of science on nature reserves has seldom been plain. Some projects have established a baseline of knowledge that can be repeated and so incorporated into a monitoring programme, whether or not this had been envisaged at the start. Some were based on practices now outdated, such as the experimental plantings of Cord-grass, Marram and Cotton-grass at Bridgwater Bay, Braunton Burrows, Moor House and other Reserves in the early days. Whether or not the huge investment of resources on the International Biological Programme in the 1960s was worthwhile is debatable, but its contemporary value seems to be as base-line knowledge for long-term environmental monitoring rather than in the obsession with weights and measures that characterised production ecology in the 1960s. What is of lasting value in science is often quite unrelated to the original aims.

Perhaps the use of Reserves as outdoor laboratories can best be illuminated by looking at two that have received more attention than most, and which, in their different ways, say as much about scientists as about science: Yarner Wood and Moor House.

THE MOOR HOUSE EXPERIENCE

Moor House was purchased on the advice of W H Pearsall in November 1951 as a study area for moorland ecology and management. The Reserve takes its name from the remote Victorian shooting lodge high above the infant River Tees commanding a view as breathtaking as it is bleak. The eastern two-thirds of the Reserve is blanket bog, dissected by streams called burns or sikes. To the west, the Pennine Way crosses a series of windswept summits, each no more than a gravelly hump in the dun patchwork of grass and heather. On one of them stands a Civil Aviation Authority radar station; on another a rough track leads to an old lead mine, with its associated reservoirs and 'hushes'—channels where the stored water was released to wash away the soil and peat, and expose the lead-bearing rock beneath. Today the pickaxes and carts (and the gunfire on the grouse moor on August 12th) have been replaced by the lonely calls of Curlew and Golden Plover, the sound of falling water and the mid-summer midge. The moor seems as empty of human aspiration as anywhere in England. But appearances are deceptive: this is, in fact, the most thoroughly studied National Nature Reserve we have. Moor House is world famous. Ecologists in Finland or Japan may never have heard of English Nature or National Nature Reserves but they have almost certainly read a paper about Moor House.

The 40-year occupation of Moor House as an outdoor laboratory can be divided into three main phases: detailed surveys and what might (rather unkindly) be termed environmental tinkering (1952–65), the years of intensive scientific study under the International Biological Programme (1967–74), and the winding down of much of the scientific work after the closure of the field station in 1979. Today it is beginning to see a scientific revival as a 'flagship' site for research on environmental change under the NERC's banner (see below). The key to the Reserve's scientific future was the establishment of a field station with basic laboratory facilities at the lonely house on the moors in 1952. More advanced facilities were available not far away at Merlewood Research Station at Grange-over-Sands. The Conservancy also co-operated closely with scientists and students from Durham University under Professor J B Cragg. Much of the work of the first 10 years contributed towards a base-line knowledge of every conceivable '-ology' represented at the Reserve. It was collected together in a series of loose-leaf documents known as the Reserve Record. By 1963, this occupied eight thick volumes covering all aspects of the moorland environment from climate to craneflies. The geological material was published in 1963 as the second of the Nature Conservancy's three scientific monographs (the others were about Scottish mountain vegetation and wildfowl recording), and this detailed published database makes the Reserve an ideal training area for student geologists. Part of the value of these basic surveys lies in their interdisciplinary nature: studying an entire nature reserve broke down the barriers of specialisation and helped scientists to share experiences and to see things in the round. It made Moor House perhaps the most intensively and extensively studied moorland in the world.

In the 1950s and 1960s, the Nature Conservancy also carried out a great deal of experimental management. In the belief that Moor House represented a degraded landscape, various attempts were made to restore the trees and other plants which scientists considered had been lost through centuries of overgrazing and burning. The first management plan, completed in 1959, set out as its grandiose main aim the restoration of 'natural highland ecosystems'. With its limited means, the Conservancy travelled but a short distance down this particular road. A motley collection of sapling trees were planted inside fenced enclosures around the field station. The first batch of rowan, birch and Scots pine was promptly eaten by 'small herbivores'. Of later plantings, the native trees all did very poorly, partly because on frosty nights the rime grew heavy enough to break the young branches. The only species that showed any signs of vigour were two coniferous imports: Lodgepole Pine from Canada and Mountain Pine from the Alps. If the experiment proved anything, it was that acid peaty soil at 578 m above sea level is a hostile environment for trees—something that Gordon Manley's climatic studies had surely already indicated. Various arctic-alpine flowers, ferns and sedges from Scotland were planted on limestone knolls and stream flushes, having been selected as species that *ought* to have been present were it not for the marauding sheep. Most of these were eaten by rabbits. Cotton-grass was also planted on eroded peat, looking exactly like contemporary plantings of Marram on eroding coastal dunes. Part of the problem with such experiments was that the whole moor was heavily grazed, and fences could be erected only with the agreement of the commoners. Permission was in fact given for a number of small enclosures in the 1950s and 1960s to monitor the impact of rabbits and sheep, but with the exception of 10 long-term monitoring plots, these have since been abandoned.

The most intensive period of fundamental scientific research on any English Reserve began in 1965 with the selection of Moor House as an outdoor laboratory for the International Biological Programme (IBP) under the aegis of the newly formed Natural Environment Research Council (NERC). The Nature Conservancy had recently become a component of this Council, and its Reserves were obliged to 'pay their way'. The IBP was concerned principally with productivity studies, that is, the measurement of energy flow and nutrient recycling within the ecosystem. It was therefore more closely concerned with fundamental and laboratory-based science than the kind of empirical management-based studies that had hitherto been the Conservancy's forte. The IBP represented the high water mark of the use of nature reserves as outdoor laboratories. It was embraced with enthusiasm by those, like the Conservancy's woodlands scientist, Derek Ovington, whose interests leaned towards the more mathematical aspects of ecology. Production ecology meant, in effect, taking parts of the ecosystem to pieces, separating the various components of standing vegetation, litter and soil, and extracting the animal life from each. Moor House was large and robust enough to absorb the onslaught easily. For the necessarily more destructive work in woodlands, the NERC purchased a new site near Grange-over-Sands called Meathop Wood, since such work was judged to be incompatible with the conservation aims at the original site, Roudsea Wood NNR. Meathop Wood was quite a sight at the height of the IBP: I can remember the glint of plastic through the boughs, as we approached a litter of churns, bins, funnels and pipes, all busy measuring the leaf fall, rainwater, root respiration and a dozen other things. The whole wood was being wired like a volunteer in a psychological test to lay bare the largely invisible processes in which woods live, breathe and recycle nitrogen and phosphorus.

At Moor House, most of this work went on indoors, inside a custom-built laboratory attached to the field station. The programme concentrated on the productivity of moorland soils at different altitudes and the equivalent rate of decomposition. It measured the different amounts of the 'standing crop' eaten by sheep, grouse and psyllid bugs, and the role of various worms, insects and microfungi in breaking it down. The overall results were quite interesting. In these chilly uplands, ecosystems are dominated by just a few species, as Charles Elton had discovered in Spitzbergen in the 1920s. At Moor House, 90% of the plant and animal production is provided by no more than five species: heather, Cotton-grass, *Sphagnum* moss, a cranefly and an Enchytraeid worm. The utilisation of grass was surprisingly low, considering that the Reserve is supposed to be overgrazed. It is essentially an ecosystem in low gear, with a low nutrient budget, a slow turnover of nutrients, few species and simple flow diagrams. How all this information was processed and put to good use is part of the history of natural science rather than that of National Nature Reserves. Its application lay more in the fields of crop biology and international environmental monitoring than in any immediate gain for nature conservation.

It was a touch ironic that the designation in 1974 of Moor House and Upper Teesdale as the first UK Biosphere Reserve, dedicated to studying the impact of man on the natural environment, came at the end of the IBP and the beginning of a winding down of the science effort. By this time, the Conservancy's links with fundamental science had been severed in the reorganisation of 1973 which produced the Nature Conservancy Council. In the new circumstances it was inevitable that the field station would have to close. Its maintenance was a major commitment. The then warden, Tom Hodgson, spent more time looking after the house and its access road than the Reserve itself. The heating bills were enormous, and whenever the oil tanks froze Tom and his estate worker, Phil Holms, had to spend hours going over the fuel lines with a blowpipe and lighted rag. Even so, it was a losing battle. In 1979, the NCC decided to cut its losses and close the centre. By then the laboratory had already been demolished and its remaining equipment transferred to Merlewood Research Station at Grange-over-Sands. The house was stripped of its radiators, generator and old boiler, the windows boarded up and then 'left to the elements'. It was, in a way, the end of an era. It stands there still, with its marble fire places and bell pushes for the servants. One day, perhaps, it will be reclaimed by someone, for although the wood and plaster must by now be rotten, the house was built to last and the basic fabric is still sound.

The Reserve still has a scientific future. It is the only large example of an unshot and unmanaged grouse moor in Britain. And its scientific pedigree has ensured that few places have greater potential as monitoring stations for climatic change or atmospheric pollution. Much of the data collected over the past 40 years is now available to researchers through computer databases and English Nature's Geographic Information System. In 1991, Moor House was chosen as a 'lead site' for the Environmental Change Network, organised by the Merlewood Research Station to co-ordinate studies on the effects of global warming, pollution and land-use changes. Part of the data will come from the automatic weather station on Great Dun Fell, which is linked by telephone to the old research station. Data from the monitoring plots are also proving useful to study the long-term influence of grazing at different altitudes, and of pollution on sensitive plants like mosses and lichens. English Nature's main contribution has been to provide funds for a weatherproof laboratory at Moor House, a portable steel structure with its own bed and breakfast accommodation and work space. It was installed in May 1993, and ceremoniously handed over to the Network scientists. The projects planned for 1993 and beyond vary from the study of atmospheric chemistry, using nitrogen dioxide diffusion tubes, to the rate of development of frog spawn at different altitudes. The vegetation is already showing marked signs of air pollution. The purpose of Moor House for the foreseeable future will be to measure the results of pollution and global warming on a remote area relatively unaffected by other forms of land-use, and whose physical and biological characteristics have been studied in depth.

THE YARNER WOOD EXPERIENCE

Today, a new National Nature Reserve generally starts its life with a flurry of activity, replacing rusty fences and fallen gates, repairing sluices and improving access routes. Thirty years ago, something close to the opposite approach existed. The Conservancy took very seriously the need for an initial period of research and survey before committing itself to a particular management approach. The scientific work might vary from a census of nesting birds to the establishment of a fixed transect line for recording vegetation or the fencing of small experimental plots to assess the influence of grazing animals or to protect planted trees. This phase could go on for years, especially since the Conservancy scientists often disagreed among themselves as to what was desirable. It was only in the late 1960s that anything like the present level of management activity on Reserves began to develop. In the days of the original Nature Conservancy, science ruled.

An amusing account of the survey phase of one of the earliest Reserves, Yarner Wood in Devon, survives in the NCC's 'unofficial' staff magazine *Natural Selection*. In 1951, the Conservancy had recruited R M Fenton, a trained forester, to make a rapid assessment of the then unknown wood and its potential as an outdoor laboratory. The vertically challenged Fenton disappeared into the bracken and bramble thickets with a machete in one hand and a compass in the other, emerging eventually with what was described as 'a fairly inaccurate report'. Fenton's was in the nature of a broad brush vegetation survey. Three years later, the Conservancy's local officer James Archibald ('Archie') and Head Forester Eric Roberts ('Robbie') proceeded to make a much more detailed survey of the wood and defined management compartments in so far as they could be defined in a place where the brambles grew at neck height. In the meantime, Bruce Campbell made a survey of the breeding birds (which led to the introduction of nest boxes for Pied Flycatchers) and zoology students from the University College of Exeter under Professor L A Harvey had a look at the invertebrates. According to Archie, the latter report was filed away in a cupboard at the Conservancy's London Headquarters, and did not see the light of day again until 20 years later, during a search for archival material on Yarner Wood.

Someone decided that all these surveys would be more scientific if they could be related to fixed transect lines within the wood. Two young ecologists, Max Hooper (later to become Director of Monks Wood Field Station) and Dickie Clymo, were commissioned for the work. Their base was an ant-ridden wooden hut, and their only link with the outside world was 'Robbie' with his now legendary 'fast but erratic' BSA motorbike. The plan was to put in a line of posts against the grain of the land, up hill and down swampy dale, recording the vegetation as they went. The steepness and dense bracken meant that there was only one means of movement: 'on all fours—forward up and backwards down. We got to know the wood ants and they us—intimately'.

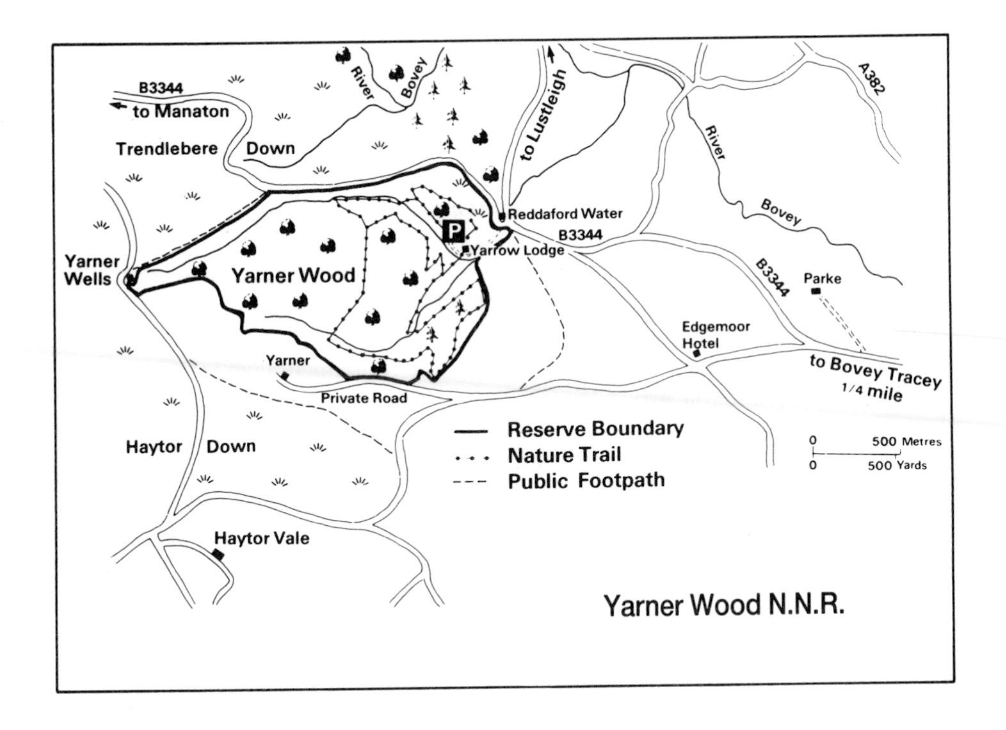

MAP 4 *Yarner Wood NNR*

One day their progress was interrupted by a party of scientists from Headquarters, who had come to see the wood and make some decisions about its future. An argument broke out between Archie and Gilbert Sale on the one hand, and Derek Ovington and J G Skellam on the other. The former were experienced woodland managers and they were confident that they already knew enough, in terms of general principles and local particulars, to make a start at Yarner Wood. Ovington, the woodland scientist, demurred. In his view there should be no action until all possible methods had been tested scientifically in a series of plot-by-plot experiments. Skellam, the statistician and, in effect, the Conservancy's 'scientific conscience', agreed in principle, but then the two proceeded to fall out over how many plots were needed, Ovington opting for relatively few, Skellam for many, on statistical grounds. And so 'it developed into a three-cornered fight, Sale and Archie on the one hand versus Skellam and Ovington on the other, and then between Skellam and Ovington, with Norman Moore (who also happened to be present) all the time trying to see fair play'. 'How it all ended,' added Max Hooper, 30 years later, 'I don't know but I believe Derek Ovington eventually got his way, set up the plots and then never looked at them again.'

It seems to have been a classic confrontation between scientific principle and conservation pragmatism. The plots were certainly set up, by clear felling 0.2-ha glades all over a 20-ha stretch of relatively level ground in which were planted various mixtures of oak, beech, alder and Scots pine in the belief that 'the establishment of a varied tree cover of mixed species [is] more akin to the natural pattern than the present stand of oak'. Firebreaks were cleared, ploughed and planted through the wood, using Japanese

Larch and beech as 'a very necessary precaution'. The experiments were clearly more concerned with silviculture than with nature conservation. The contemporary Annual Report hoped that 'these experiments will contribute something of future use to silvicultural practice'.

Some wider management was in fact done at this time, but not of a kind that would meet approval nowadays. As George Peterken put it after a visit to Yarner Wood in 1984, 'David Rogers [the then warden] is engaged in removing conifers planted by the Nature Conservancy in open heathy spaces, and beech planted (also by the NC) beneath a closed oak canopy. It's experiences like this that make me ease up when criticising modern forestry'.

James Archibald pointed to another flaw in the fundamental scientific approach. Suppose all of the suitable ground in the Reserve had been clothed with experimental plots, and that they all failed. Where then did you find more places on which to base the next round of experiments? It was considerations of this sort that led the Conservancy, *pace* the scientists and statisticians, to adopt the more pragmatic approach of trial and error. In Archie's opinion, 'with the benefit of a quarter-century of hindsight, we have learned a great deal about the management of woodlands by suck-it-and-see, and precious little from systematic experiment'.

SURVEYS AND MONITORING

In recent years, the majority of scientific work on National Nature Reserves has become concerned with survey and monitoring. An analysis of the 68 registered scientific projects at Castle Hill in East Sussex, for example, broke down as follows:

Fundamental science	: 3
Applied science	: 5
Survey and monitoring	: 60

Basic survey work has always been a high priority on National Nature Reserves. Some sites, like Wybunbury Moss, Rostherne Mere, Studland and Woodwalton Fen, had been studied by naturalists for decades before they became Reserves and there therefore already existed a large core of scientific work on which the Conservancy could draw. The sites which received most study in the 1950s and 1960s were, as we have seen, those closest to the scientific field stations. Today the most intensively studied sites are probably peat bogs, not for the sake of fundamental science so much as to gain a detailed understanding of their hydrology and thus enable the Conservancy to control the water regime.

A survey has been defined as 'a standard observation made at one point in time to furnish qualitative or quantitative descriptive data'. As such it can vary from counting ducks on a pond to recording vegetation numerically using quadrat frames or transect lines, or measuring relief using surveying instruments. Monitoring means a series of repeated surveys made in order to discover trends, and their extent and direction. Surveys usually become more meaningful when they are repeated in this way. For example, a survey of ditches in the Norfolk Broads made in the early 1970s became really useful only when a repeat survey 20 years later showed that the water quality and biological interest had declined severely during the interim. One problem with long-term monitoring of this sort is that the original data are often filed away and forgotten about. George Peterken spent a considerable amount of time in the 1980s digging out old woodland transect surveys whose true value lay in their being repeated a quarter-century later. The more rapid the turnover of staff, the less likely is it that such information will survive. It is only human, after all, to hang on to the material that interests you and consign the rest to the rubbish bin.

Monitoring is perhaps most useful when it is geared to some firm management objective, or else is part of an organised national scheme. Monitoring the results of a management project is now a routine part of nature reserve management. We will meet many examples later in this book. It is particularly valuable when assessing habitat restoration techniques, such as raising water levels (Chapter 8), clearing bracken and other invasive vegetation (Chapter 7) or retreating in the face of rising sea level (Chapter 9). It is, in fact, difficult to think of a major management project in recent years that has not included follow-up monitoring as part of its remit.

National recording schemes are part of the small-change of life on the nature reserve. National Nature Reserves are ideal for species monitoring since they are staffed by expert naturalists and any changes in species numbers can be compared with known changes to the environment. The BTO Common Bird Census takes place on many Reserves, though some are too small or the wrong shape to be really useful in this respect. Many of the coastal Reserves as well as wetland ones inland take part in the National Wildfowl and Wader Survey, in which monthly counts are made. The Butterfly Transect Scheme, founded by Ernie Pollard of Monks Wood Experimental Station in the 1970s, has been a notable success, providing a record of fluctuating butterfly numbers from sites across the whole of Britain. More than 30 English National Nature Reserves take part in the scheme (see Table 6), out of only 80 sites nationally, and supply many of the records for rare species like Silver-spotted Skipper, Adonis Blue and Swallowtail. The scheme is fairly demanding: the regular walk of a couple of miles must take place in warm and windless conditions, and at times counting butterflies is, as Dick Williamson says, 'like counting the pigeons in

TABLE 6 *Butterfly transects on National Nature Reserves* (from Pollard *et al.*, 1986, updated 1992)

Aston Rowant	Martin Down
Avon Gorge	Monks Wood
Barnack Hills and Holes	Old Winchester Hill
Bure Marshes (Woodbastwick Fen)	Pewsey Downs
Castor Hanglands	Rostherne Mere
Chippenham Fen	Roudsea Wood and Mosses
Derbyshire Dales (Lathkill Dale)	Saltfleetby and Theddlethorpe Dunes
Ebbor Gorge	Studland
Gibraltar Point	Thorne Moors
Ham Street Woods	Upper Teesdale (High Force)
Holkham	Walberswick
Holme Fen	Waterperry Wood FNR
Kingley Vale	Wicken Fen
Leigh	Woodwalton Fen
Lewes Down (Castle Hill)	Wye
Lullington Heath	Wyre Forest
	Yarner Wood

Trafalgar Square'. Like many wardens, Dick combines butterfly counting with Common Bird Censusing and picking up litter. It can be hard work!

The Conservancy's in-house field unit has been developing various ways of making rapid environmental 'health checks' in recent years, and although they are aimed chiefly at SSSIs, they also have their uses on nature reserves, especially those managed by agreements. At the simplest level, called 'Site Integrity Monitoring', the surveyor does little more than peer over the hedge to make sure that the habitat is still there. Although one hopes that this can be taken for granted on nature reserves, I can remember occasions in the past when seldom-visited corners have been surreptitiously reclaimed by the farmer or fenced for planting trees. Of more general use is 'Site Quality Monitoring' in which the surveyor walks over the area noting things like sward height, overall colour and the presence of 'indicator species'. The Unit of Comparative Plant Ecology at Sheffield University is looking into the biology of individual species of flowers whose presence tells us something about the environmental quality of the site, and their work is helping to refine these rapid assessment techniques.

Monitoring sometimes has a bearing on how the Reserve as a whole is managed, notably in woodland habitats where a series of long-term scientific studies has been established by George Peterken in places that are deliberately left unmanaged. Lady Park Wood NNR in the Wye Valley is unusual among English woodlands in that most of it has not been managed at all since 1945 (other than the felling of the odd sycamore or sick beech) and possibly not very much before that either, apart from the usual wartime vandalism. The combination of little or no management and intensive scientific recording over the past 50 years makes this a uniquely valuable site. It is an extraordinary place in other ways too. Lady Park is one of the few woods in Britain that contains almost all of our native trees and shrubs in a wild state (the main exception is Scots Pine), including both Large and Small-leaved Lime. Even among all the fine woods that line the valley of the lower Wye, this one stands out in its diversity and the vigour of its underwood. Lady Park Wood is, in fact, the ideal long-term research site: it is relatively inaccessible, undisturbed, healthy (apart from the gathering scourge of deer), has a detailed record database and is the subject of a 99-year agreement with its owner, the Forestry Commission. If the latter is privatised, English Nature will almost certainly purchase the site.

Long-term studies of woodland are important because very little is known about how temperate woods fare in their unmanaged state. This is because there are very few, if any, primeval woods in western Europe, and virtually every large wood has been managed for domestic or commercial purposes. The dearth of such knowledge may be why the results of long-term monitoring at Lady Park Wood have been such a surprise. It presents not the stately progression to a 'steady state' as described by Tansley and other theoreticians but a record of considerable violence. Gales, drought, disease and herbivores have produced unstable conditions in which the young and old growths are nicely balanced. Ecological theory predicted that beech would gradually shade out its competitors and dominate the wood. In practice, beech is now about the least healthy tree at Lady Park Wood. The unmanaged future seems to point to continued diversity, not monopoly. These results imply that leaving large areas of woodland unmanaged is not such a bad idea after all, even if it goes against the grain of English tradition. The great gale of 1987 (and the fear of more to follow) was

instrumental in changing existing perceptions of 'how woods work'. Since that cataclysmic, but on the whole beneficial, event, the Conservancy has set aside larger areas of woodland Reserves within its control—in some instances whole Reserves—as non-intervention zones for the purpose of long-term scientific study. The Bovey Valley Woods and Dendles Wood in Devon, Horsleyhope Ravine in Durham, Holme Fen in Cambridgeshire and Colt Park Wood in North Yorkshire are among the woodland Reserves which are now managed with only the lightest touch.

Long-term environmental monitoring is now assuming a much more prominent role on National Nature Reserves generally, especially those on the coast, in upland areas and on the Chalk. Many National Nature Reserves are once more becoming useful outdoor laboratories for universities and scientific institutes concerned with atmospheric pollution and other man-made disasters. The University of Lancaster, for example, is monitoring the effects of air pollution and climatic change on the vegetation of several Reserves in the Pennines and on the Chalk of southern England. In a related project, the University of Cambridge is studying the effects of pollution on the plants and soils on chalk grassland. Some Reserves, like the Derbyshire Dales and Upper Teesdale, have acid rain collection points operated by the Reserve manager. The University of Nottingham uses remote sensing techniques to monitor environmental change at Wybunbury Moss and Scolt Head Island. The latter Reserve is also used by geomorphologists from Birkbeck College, London, to learn more about the processes of sediment accretion on soft shores. Such work has often led to fruitful associations between English Nature field staff and university scientists. Long-term environmental monitoring is, as George Peterken has pointed out, one of the roles for which NNRs are uniquely well-suited—and indeed one for which they were expressly designed.

INTERNATIONAL SCIENTIFIC DESIGNATIONS

In Appendix 3 of this book I list the Reserves which are designated as places especially suitable for international environmental research. In Britain, and England in particular,

National Nature Reserves have a major limitation for research purposes: most of them are too small and isolated from other semi-natural habitats. The UK was among the signatories of the Man and Biosphere programme of UNESCO, formed in the 1970s to create a network of 'Biosphere Reserves' 'to conserve for present and future use the diversity and integrity of communities of plants and animals within natural ecosystems, and to safeguard the genetic diversity of species'. On the chosen sites the responsible body was supposed to provide areas and facilities for research, education and 'training'.

To English ears, such programmes may have stronger connotations with elephants and jungles than with the English countryside. It did in fact prove difficult to find suitable candidate areas in England. Of the 13 areas submitted to UNESCO by the UK government in 1976, only three were in England: the large chunk of the north Pennines represented by the Moor House and Upper Teesdale NNRs; the North Norfolk coast, which has an almost continuous string of nature reserves and other protected sites, including the Scolt Head and Holkham NNRs; and, on a more modest scale, Braunton Burrows NNR on the coast of north Devon. Designation provided no extra protection or resources, nor did it influence management in any way. Indeed Biosphere Reserves amounted to nothing very much at all in this country until the end of the 1980s, when their latent value for environmental monitoring was recognised. In 1989, the UK Committee, under English Nature's present chief executive, Dr Derek Langslow, set up a working party to look into their use as long-term monitoring stations for global warming. The party concluded that the Norfolk Coast Biosphere Reserve was particularly well-placed to monitor the rising sea level. A training seminar for Biosphere Reserve managers soon followed. Moor House, too, has seen a sudden resurgence of scientific effort. Perhaps such action would have been taken in any case, but the Biosphere concept has at last come into its own, both as a justification and as a catalyst, as a new role for National Nature Reserves. With the increased 'twinning' of Reserves with other EEC countries, and other symbolic weakenings of our island insularity, it seems likely that English National Nature Reserves will play a much greater international role in the future.

CHAPTER 6

Last Chances: Reserves as Sanctuaries for Rare Species

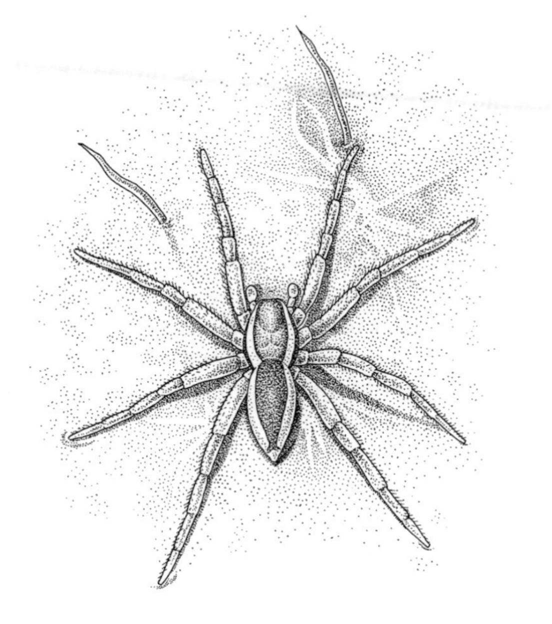

The Fen Raft Spider confined in Britain to National Nature Reserves in Suffolk and East Sussex

SAFEGUARDING rare species on nature reserves (and particularly on National Nature Reserves) used to be a surprisingly controversial subject. While most ordinary people visit nature reserves in the hope of seeing something scarce and unusual, English scientists have traditionally focused on habitat management alone. The species must fend for themselves. While the scientific community's widespread antipathy towards rarities doubtless had a psychological cause, there was some practical substance to it in that rare beasts can divert resources away from more vital tasks and encourage over-management. This view was aired recently at a conference on nature reserves by Brian Wood of University College London, who suggested that Reserve managers are exerting far too much control over nature in the hope of preventing rare species from disappearing. Why not let nature itself take charge, by re-introducing large herbivores or just allowing things to take their course? Other writers have poured scorn on the idea of preserving rare flowers and butterflies. Curiously enough these strictures rarely extended to Giant Pandas or rhinoceroses. Behind the arguments may have been a belief that most rare species in England are common somewhere else, and that in any case science should not get mixed up in sentimental nonsense.

At the moment, the very opposite point of view is in the ascendancy, as demonstrated by English Nature's Species Recovery Programme, aimed at restoring the fortunes of a variety of endangered wild animals and plants. People generally have personal reasons for wanting to preserve rarities. In everyday parlance it is what nature reserves are all about. Many rare animals and plants are beautiful, or have fascinating, often highly specialised life-histories, or tell us something about the environment. Some species are 'naturally' rare because of their special needs or limited range, but a very large number are rare simply because their habitat is disappearing. It so happens that a great many rarities, especially among wild plants and the often ignored invertebrates, are more or less confined to nature reserves. Many of them are characteristic of early seral stages that used to be maintained by cutting underwood, reeds, turf and bracken, but for which nature reserve management is now about the only hope. One of the great mysteries of English wildlife is the survival of so many sun-loving species in a land that was once covered from coast to coast by dense forest. No doubt Brian Wood is right about the role of wild cattle, beavers and deer. In practice, however, the needs of rare species have helped field staff to become better habitat managers. The present grazing regimes on downland Reserves or cutting rotations in woods owe a great deal to the carefully researched needs of butterflies. Much of the present efforts to improve the wetness of grazing marsh and reedbeds has the requirements of birds like the Bittern or the Snipe in mind. While the accusation of over-management and over-regulation is one that I think English Nature should take seriously, there is little doubt that rarities have been a useful catalyst in getting people to think about the detail of a site and not just its generalities. The resources lavished on rarities means that due attention is being paid to the principles of biodiversity. Someone, somewhere, has to 'hold the line', and if not on National Nature Reserves, then where?

This chapter will look at five species or groups of species that have influenced the ways in which Reserves are being looked after, and which between them illustrate a number of approaches to rare species conservation: the Natterjack Toad, the spider orchids, butterflies, two obscure insects and the Little Tern. I hope I can leave any ethical values they invoke to the conscience of the reader.

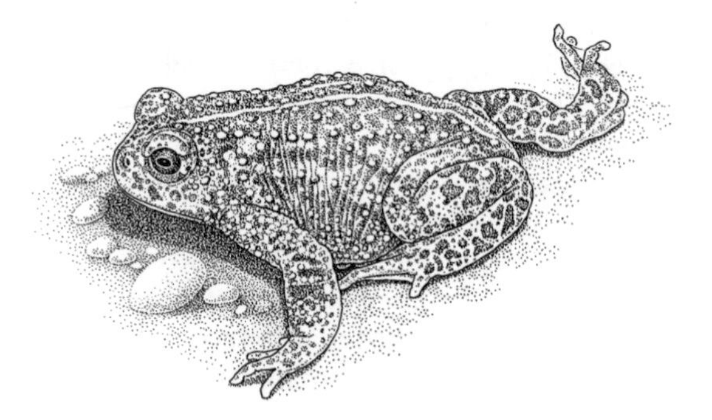

ANIMAL FARMS: THE RESCUE OF THE NATTERJACK TOAD

Modern times have not been kind to the Natterjack Toad. It has suffered more than most animals from habitat reclamation; it doesn't like tall vegetation or permanent deep ponds and soon disappears when, as they so often are, its pools are invaded by vulgar common frogs and toads; moreover, the Natterjack is vulnerable to acid rain. It is an all-European toad, not found in other continents, but throughout the continental mainland its numbers have dwindled with gathering speed, and today the only countries where it could still be regarded as common are Portugal and Spain. With its comic name and slightly lubberly appearance and habits, it has become, for some people, the epitome of a declining, possibly doomed, animal. Most unfairly, of course.

Despite appearances, the Natterjack is, like most rare species, beautifully adapted to its particular way of life, and were it not for the onslaught on its breeding places by mankind and its by-products, the toad would need no help from us. It is a burrowing animal, and lives in sandy places, mainly on coastal dunes or on open heaths. It can run quite fast—unlike the more ponderous Common Toad, the Natterjack chases its invertebrate prey—it has been recorded as scattering 'like mice' at the sound of a human footfall. The Natterjack's principal need is for warm, shallow pools with little dense vegetation and no predatory fish or insects, a place where its tadpoles can eat without being eaten. Such pools are often seasonal; and if they dry out too early, that is tough luck on the tadpoles: they will all perish. This does not matter particularly, since the Natterjack enjoys several years of sexual maturity, and to offset the bad years a good year will produce thousands of toadlets from a single pool. The temptation to well-meaning conservationists is to counter seasonal droughts by deepening the pond. That will be fatal for not only is the Natterjack a poor swimmer but the deeper water will soon attract its quota of dragonfly larvae, diving beetles and other predators, against which its tadpoles are helpless. Like so many of today's rarities, the Natterjack relies on what we might regard (anthropomorphically) as ascetic conditions. The instinct of many land managers is to smooth over the rugged contours of nature, to reduce its innate variety to garden-like proportions. Rare beasts do not live in gardens.

The Natterjack once shared the inland heaths of southern England with the Sand Lizard and the Smooth Snake, but of 50 or so heathland strongholds known at the turn of the century, only one remains. In many, the ponds are still present, but research has shown that many of these have become acidified. The Natterjack's home is now in the coastal sand dunes and dune hollows of northern and eastern England. England's National Nature Reserves have made an important contribution to the survival of the Natterjack. English Nature is directly responsible for looking after Natterjack colonies on five Reserves—Cabin Hill and Ainsdale on the Lancashire coast, Saltfleetby–Theddlethorpe Dunes on the Lincolnshire coast, and Holkham and Winterton Dunes in Norfolk. Local Wildlife Trusts manage the Natterjack colonies on two more National Nature Reserves: North Walney in Cumbria and Gibraltar Point in Lincolnshire, where a small colony has been established recently from nearby Saltfleetby stock. Together these amount to at least a quarter of Britain's Natterjack toads, and offer what should be among its safest sanctuaries. Left entirely to themselves, the toads would in some places probably decline inexorably towards extinction: some of their sanctuaries may be too small, or the pools in the dune slacks may dry out or the sandhills erode away by the tides or become covered in scrub. Management, it might be argued, may perpetuate unnatural numbers of toads by unnatural means, but, then, it is directed against unnatural influences. Arguments about the protection of rare species often present spiralling semantics of this sort. Perhaps we should agree with Bill McGibben, the author of *The End of Nature*, that nature conservation has ceased to be concerned with wild nature. What these specialised animals need is not a return to a notional wildness, which has never been witnessed, but a return to stability, that is, to what was there *before*. In most of England's countryside stability is maintained by hard work.

Natterjack conservation is largely directed towards the construction and maintenance of shallow ponds in places where the water table lies close to the surface. The results can be very effective. At the Winterton Dunes NNR the excavation of 12 shallow pools inside the dune slacks in 1971 transformed a failing colony to what was, by 1987, the seventh largest Natterjack colony in Britain. Granulated chalk was used to counter the acidified water (itself the result of chemical pollutants in the atmosphere) and bring the pH to an ideal 5.5–5.7.

The National Nature Reserve at Cabin Hill, a few kilometres south of Ainsdale Sand Dunes NNR, was established with the main purpose of giving better protection to a large but declining Natterjack colony. The Natterjack's problems were the familiar ones of this part of the coast: rank vegetation and scrub had invaded the former open dunes, and the old Natterjack ponds, once shallow sandy pools, had become choked with weeds and were teeming with the wrong kinds of amphibians, as well as a variety of predators with a taste for Natterjack tadpoles. To tilt the odds back in the favour of the Natterjack, some of the pools have been infilled with sand, a process known as 'shallowing', to make them more seasonal. Frogs and toads are being unceremoniously fished out with pond nets and transported to ponds inland, where they are wanted. At the same time, Michael Gee and his helpers are also working *with* nature to combat dune erosion and encourage the natural accretion of sand, thus producing the kind of undulating environment that Natterjacks like, with small sand hills and moist slacks. Relatively elaborate schemes of this sort are possible here and at Ainsdale because this coastline is managed as a unity, in concert with Sefton Borough Council, the National Trust and other conservation bodies.

Natterjack protection can be conservation at its most intensive, comparable almost with farmed deer. But the important difference in emphasis between this and farm management is that on nature reserves the stress is on habitat management, not the direct manipulation of the toad itself. At Cabin Hill and most other colonies on National Nature Reserves, the creation of artificial ponds may have achieved an unnatural concentration of Natterjacks, but in their design and location the ponds resemble natural pools as closely as possible. The rest is up to the toad. Some of the earlier interventions were much cruder: at Holkham, where the Natterjack ponds are rectangular and brick-lined, the line between nature reserves and outdoor zoos might have become blurred. At Gibraltar Point, where the recently (1992) introduced tadpoles are offered supplementary feeding, and at Saltfleetby–Theddlethorpe Dunes NNR, where the spawn is removed and reared through before release, we are close to a concept of animal farming. The procedure is justified as a short-term means of ensuring the 'sustainability' of the species in places where their numbers are so low that extinction is a possibility. To those who ask whether all this fuss is really justifiable, two replies are possible. Trevor Beebee, who has done more than anyone to encourage an interest in Natterjacks, has pointed out the unexpected spin-off from studying this particular rarity—it has drawn attention to the acidification of ponds in southern England, which might otherwise have escaped notice; and it has pointed the way towards the proper management of the habitat as a whole. To appreciate the other argument you have to visit Cabin Hill or North Walney or the Winterton Dunes on a calm warm night in April to listen to the eerie reeling chorus of the male Natterjacks, the sound of the Stone Age swamp. And many people do just that: the North Walney Natterjacks are now a considerable local attraction. The toads have become four-legged ambassadors for nature, having assumed a fame previously reserved for Ospreys and rare butterflies.

A TALE OF TWO SPIDERS

When National Nature Reserves were first established, the assumption of many people, including the politicians most closely concerned, was that nature reserves were essentially there to preserve rare species of animals and plants. In practice, the Conservancy, anxious to demonstrate that it was a serious scientific body and not obsessed with such trivial matters, reacted against any such idea. Virtually all of its Reserves were prime examples of habitats, but if, as they often did, they happened to contain rare species, that was largely incidental. This was one important difference between the National Nature Reserves and the local Trust reserves or, especially, the nature reserves belonging to the RSPB. (I say 'was' because that distinction has lessened in the course of time.) At least two early Reserves, Monks Wood and Blean Woods, were established partly to protect rare butterflies, but I cannot think of a single rare plant counterpart, except where the rare flower also happens to be a major component of the vegetation, as at the North Meadow near Cricklade, or the Lizard heaths. Nevertheless, some Reserves are of major importance for their assemblages of rare plant species. Upper Teesdale is undoubtedly the most famous example. Many other Reserves are very rewarding if you like searching for rare flowers. In terms of spectacle, the highlights might include the Pasque Flowers at Barnack, the Blue Flaxes at Thrislington Plantation, the fritillaries at North Meadow and the Jacob's Ladders at Lathkill Dale. More significant in international terms are some of the bryophyte and lichen-rich woods of the west coast. The best examples are in North Wales and West Scotland, but the Golitha Falls, Lizard and Downton Gorge Reserves are notable English counterparts.

Rare wild orchids are the showcase flowers; they are to the Plant Kingdom what butterflies and dragonflies are to that of the invertebrates. English Nature plays a leading part in the conservation of the Lady's Slipper Orchid at its sole remaining British site, and Lynne Farrell, its long-standing species protection person, is the authority on the Military Orchid. Certain orchids are better represented on Reserves than one might otherwise have expected, probably because they are useful indicators of top quality habitats, notably the Green-winged Orchid of ancient meadows and the very attractive Dwarf or Burnt-tip Orchid of limestone pastures. English National Nature Reserves contain a substantial proportion of England's Red, Dark-red and Dune Helleborines, Early and Late Spider Orchids, Coral-roots and the pale *ochroleuca* variety of the Early Marsh-orchid.

The way in which the attention lavished on rare plants can influence the management of a Reserve is exemplified by our two native Spider Orchids, the Early and the Late ('Late Spider Orchid' is a poor name; it flowers in June and is only 'late' in comparison with its earlier cousin; nor is it particularly spider-like). Together with the much commoner Fly and Bee Orchids, these flowers represent the cold weather rump of a remarkable array of insect mimics which flourish best on the islands and shores of the Mediterranean. In Britain, the Spiders are both plants of sunny, mainly south-facing, chalk banks and scarps, where the vegetation is kept cropped and relatively open by grazing. Both are very variable, and on the Continent the various forms have been dignified with Latin names; in England no one has bothered, but their variety here would seem to hint at a reasonably sound genetic health.

Recent demographic studies by Mike Hutchings of Sussex University helped, by John Duffield and Bob Russell at Wye NNR, and Alan Bowley and Malcolm Emery at Castle Hill NNR, indicate that these closely related plants have very different survival strategies. The Late Spider is a long-lived perennial—one plant at Wye has been monitored continuously for the past 30 years. By no means all the plants flower in a given year, and those that do rarely set seed, probably because English insects show no interest whatever in its gaudy blooms. On the Continent it is said to be pollinated by sex-starved male wasps, but on this side of the Channel the cunning stratagem has failed, for some unknown reason (our Bee Orchids avoid the same problem by giving up on insects altogether and pollinating themselves). It is not altogether surprising, therefore, that the Late Spider, always confined to Kent, is a plant of small, long-established colonies which rarely colonise new ground. Less than a dozen populations survive, of which the largest consists of no more than 50 plants. In one place it has flowered regularly since its original discovery 165 years ago.

The Late Spider's earlier and less conspicuous cousin is more of an opportunist. In Mediterranean countries it readily colonises new ground, spreading weed-like into fallow fields and wasteland. Monitoring has shown that, in Britain too, it can be short-lived but fast-moving. At Wye NNR, most plants flower and set seed every year. The flowers, though dingier than the Late Spider and appearing in April and early May when fewer insects are on the wing, attract good numbers of ants, honey bees, wasps and hoverflies, most of which are presumably in search of nectar rather than a mate. Successful fruiting consumes much of the plant's store of energy and the fertile plants die after only two flowering seasons. They may last considerably longer, though, if prevented from seeding by grazing, or by mowing as at one site in Sussex.

Without suitable management, however, neither species would last very long. They have declined sharply over the past 50 years, mainly through habitat destruction (the Wye NNR represents only a fraction of the extensive downland that existed in that district until the 1950s), but also through the mismanagement of what remains of the chalk downland habitat. Between 1975 and 1979, the Castle Hill Reserve was used for cattle grazing in winter. It was as well that Mike Hutchings had begun to monitor the Early Spider Orchid population at that time, for the plant declined rapidly under this regime, with the annual mortality far exceeding the recruitment of young plants. Partly for that reason, summer-grazing sheep were introduced in 1981 to maintain a much shorter sward, the orchids being protected from grazing during their short period of flowering and setting seed. Recovery was immediate and continuous. Since 1986, the orchid's population has increased from 1760 plants to more than 20,000—perhaps a quarter of the national total. The tight control of grazing possible only on managed nature reserves has been very successful in conserving this once endangered species. It is now doing well on several other National Nature Reserves as well as on Trust reserves in Kent, Sussex and Dorset. Indeed, the Early Spider Orchid has become a good example of a species that can put on a spectacular show on a handful of nature reserves, but which has all but died out from 'the wider countryside'. Without nature reserves its prospects would be far from secure.

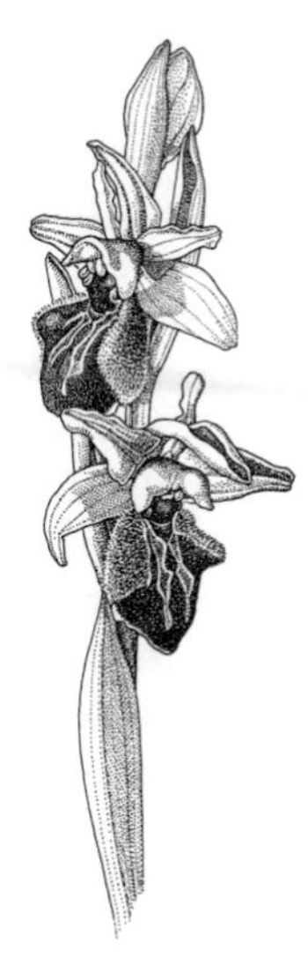

The Late Spider Orchid's biology makes it less likely to increase rapidly even when conditions are right. Yet, despite its extreme rarity, this plant withstands rough treatment quite well. One of the colonies at Wye is centred on a tumulus that was bulldozed in 1956. It can put up with fairly heavy cattle grazing even at flowering time. One reason for this is that it evidently tastes nasty. Bob Russell has watched calves biting off the flowers and then spitting them out in disgust. Experienced cattle avoid them. Hence, whereas the Early Spider is, *par excellence*, a plant of close-cropped downland, the Late Spider can grow among the ragged turf of cattle-chewed grass, and is less reliant on sheep grazing. No one expects this plant to increase its numbers rapidly, even under ideal management conditions. Its survival depends on preserving all the remaining sites; and it is pure luck that several of these are on National Nature Reserves.

The significance of plants like these is that they help to focus management from the generalised and vague to the particular and precise. Many other rare species have benefited from the nudge given to nature reserve managers by the study of Spider Orchids. It is a peculiarity of nature conservation that rare species become more closely studied than common ones, and this is as true of the orchids as it is of any other group. The attention given to individual species can yield wider truths about competition and the factors that regulate numbers, whether it is a short-lived opportunist, like the Early Spider Orchid, or a long-term survivalist, like the Late.

THE HELPFUL INFLUENCE OF BUTTERFLIES

Many National Nature Reserves are, or were, of great importance for our small but much-loved butterfly fauna. One of the reasons for the early acquisition of Monks

Wood, Castor Hanglands, Blean Woods and several other Reserves was that they were famous localities for rare butterflies. The introduction of the Dutch race of the Large Copper to Woodwalton Fen was an early and well-known ecological experiment. And butterfly conservation received a tremendous boost when the last remaining colony of the Large Blue died out in 1979. This event was represented by the media as something of a national tragedy: 'Send not for whom the bell tolls . . .' People otherwise unacquainted with ecological science know that when Large Coppers and Large Blues die out, something has gone wrong with the environment.

Butterflies are sensitive to change. Like reptiles, they seek warmth and sunshine, which in our windy and cool oceanic climate means that many of them are very choosy insects, dependent on the chances of slope, aspect and sward height which make one area warmer than another. It ought not to have surprised anyone when the fritillaries disappeared from shady and tangled woodland, or that the blues deserted the downs as the grass grew taller. What was not well understood until the 1970s was that the immature stages of these insects need even more precise, and sometimes transient, conditions. It is not enough that the larval foodplant should be present; it has to be the right size of plant growing in the right place. In the pre-war countryside, ideal conditions could usually be found here and there among the large expanses of permanent pasture or coppiced woodland that existed then. But increased habitat fragmentation and the decline of traditional labour-intensive practices have resulted in such places becoming fewer and more isolated. This does not matter in the case of wide-ranging butterflies, like Brimstones and Small Tortoiseshells, but for the more localised and sedentary species it is very bad news indeed.

Unfortunately the early record of National Nature Reserves in saving rare butterflies was abysmal. The fortunes of rare butterflies on Reserves in eastern England did not differ markedly from those on private land: they died out on both. In the 1950s and 1960s Monks Wood and Castor Hanglands lost nearly all of their rare butterflies (the exception, the Black Hairstreak, is a remarkably undemanding insect). The Adonis Blue disappeared from Old Winchester Hill, the Heath Fritillary became commoner in the commercial coppice at Blean than in the relatively unmanaged nature reserve; and the entire brood of Large Coppers at Woodwalton Fen perished in a flood in 1968. These losses were not all the Conservancy's fault. The sudden extinction of the Chequered Skipper and the disappearance of the once common fritillaries from virtually all of eastern England are still mysterious. But on most National Nature Reserves the plight of the butterflies was the direct result of insufficient management, or the wrong kind of management. The Conservancy did not know how to save even these best known of English insects.

It was in order to learn something more about the behaviour of butterflies in the wild, and especially their immature stages, that Dr Jeremy Thomas was appointed by the Conservancy in the late 1960s. Jeremy has been successful in applying the principles of Charles Elton and A S Watt, with their concepts of the ecological 'niche' and 'key factor analysis', to the traditional natural history of British butterflies. His work has been taken up by others more recently, and its influence on Reserve management has been profound. By using the greatly improved understanding of butterflies, allied to their own experience in site management, wardens like John Bacon at Old Winchester Hill, David Maylam at Blean Woods and Tony Aldridge at Gait Barrows have successfully boosted failing butterfly populations and re-established suitable conditions for endangered species. And the techniques thus developed on National Nature Reserves are now being used more widely on other reserves and on land with management agreements.

The story of the Large Copper at Woodwalton Fen is too well known to be worth repeating in detail here (see for example Duffey, 1974). It is worth emphasising, however, that this project was based on both of the strategies commonly used to conserve butterflies: captive breeding and habitat management. The population here proved too small for the insect to maintain its numbers, and so the larvae were collected each spring to rear in cages. Part of the Fen, the famous 'Copper Fields', was planted with Water Docks in the 1920s in a network of ditches. Even so, the population has required constant 'topping up' and has died out altogether on two or three occasions. Very likely the Fen is simply too small, and probably too dry, to maintain the species. Successive naturalists have persevered with it partly because this is a breathtakingly beautiful insect, fascinating in its finicky egg-laying habits, and partly because no one wants to call a halt to so famous and long-running a project. Woodwalton Fen owes much of its fame to its coppers, and many people visit the Reserve in July in the hope of seeing one. Even so, this form of conservation is hardly different from a butterfly farm, and in this case the chances of ultimate success are faint. A similar method has been used, with greater success so far, to reintroduce a Swedish race of the Large Blue to some of its old sites in the West Country.

The Conservancy has rightly pinned more faith in habitat management on Reserves than on rearing butterflies in captivity, realising that by the time the latter becomes necessary it is probably already too late. One of the more surprising conclusions to be drawn from recent studies is the extent to which butterflies are reliant on *managed* habitats. Most species depend on the maintenance of early seral stages, and even the woodland ones need glades and sunny edges. Monks Wood was the first Reserve to be managed properly for butterflies. Some of the rides were broadened and maintained by scrub cutting and mowing to create a mixture of scrub and flower-rich swards of different height. This regime suits the Black Hairstreak which asks little from life apart from an abundance of old Blackthorn bushes in full sunshine. But it came too late to save some of the other choice butterflies, like the Chequered Skipper and Pearl-bordered Fritillary, for which this wood was once famous.

At the Blean Wood Reserve near Canterbury, the Conservancy intervened just in time to save the rare Heath Fritillary from going the same way. This was at one time considered to be our most endangered native butterfly, with no more than a scatter of colonies in the Kentish Blean and in the south-west, none of them safe. The danger, in Kent at least, was not so much habitat destruction as the neglect of old coppice woods. Despite its rarity, the Heath Fritillary has come to rely on the work of the woodman. It is a rather lackadaisical insect, with none of the elegant soaring and sudden turns of speed that characterises the other woodland fritillaries. Rather, it wanders slowly, with small flicks of its tawny wings followed by a short glide, a foot or so above the ground. Individuals are easy to follow, and, if you do, it soon becomes evident that they do not wander very far—the same glade or section of ride serves as the butterfly's home throughout its short life. Yet the population as a whole does move: the butterfly was said to 'follow the woodman' as he went about his business cutting chestnut poles on rotation and thus creating a constant supply of temporary glades. At Blean these glades often flood, a season or so after felling, with the yellow flowers of Cow-wheat,

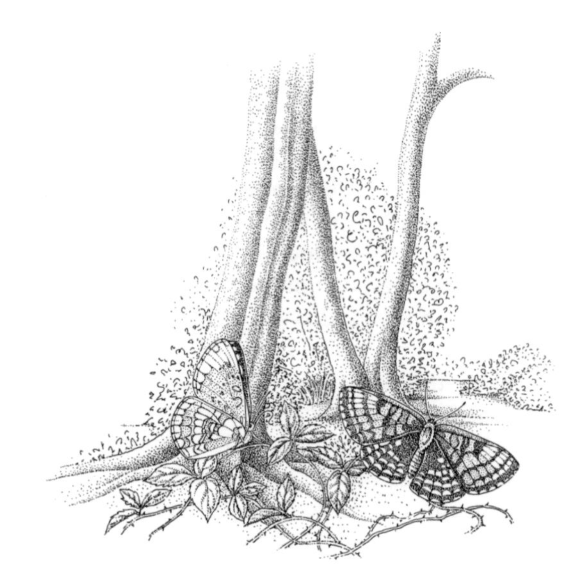

Health Fritillaries at Blean

the Heath Fritillary's main foodplant. But as the fast-growing chestnut stools become bushier and begin to shade the ground again, the fritillary has to move on or perish. Thus, to retain this butterfly, a wood must not only contain plenty of Cow-wheat, but must also be managed on a continuous and regular cycle of clearance and regeneration in such a way that the butterfly can always find a substantial area to lay its eggs. In the past this work was not of course done to oblige the Heath Fritillary: it was simply the most efficient method of harvesting chestnut poles and other small-bore timber. It was the butterfly that had adapted to the management. And since there is no need, under these circumstances, for powerful flight muscles for long questing journeys, the English Heath Fritillary has evolved into a sedentary, 'unadventurous' insect. What was not appreciated, until Martin Warren researched the species in the late 1970s, was just how critical warmth and sunshine are for species like this at the cool edge of their range. In warmer and sunnier climes on the European mainland, the Heath Fritillary is a much livelier butterfly and can tolerate light shade, but in chilly England it hangs on by the tips of its antennae; nothing except the warmest, most open form of woodland, with broad rides and big glades, will suffice.

While the needs of the Heath Fritillary have become reasonably clear, supplying them is another matter for the markets no longer favour coppice products. Many once suitable woods have been converted into shady high forest by planting or by singling the coppice stools, and, indeed, this was the original management aim for Blean Woods NNR. If carried out, it would have diminished the Reserve's importance for insect life considerably. The Heath Fritillary has helped us to a better solution. During the past decade, David Maylam has created and maintained a network of broad rides which he calls 'butterfly motorways', whose scrubby borders are cut every few years on the Monks Wood pattern—a form of linear coppice. Hazel and chestnut continue to be on a rotation, varying from 12 to 30 years, so that in any one year there are several glades in a suitable condition for the fritillary, which it can reach along the 'motorways'. So successful has this been that the Heath Fritillary has become the commonest butterfly in the wood: at its peak in late June you might count several hundred during the course of a walk. Its fortunes now look distinctly rosy, for most of the still extensive broadleaved woods of Blean are now owned by conservation bodies, and there are plans to extend the network of rides throughout the area. However this kind of management is expensive. The bushy side 'panels' at first had to be cut laboriously with handheld brush cutters, although, now that the numerous stumps have been cut level with the ground, this is likely to be superseded by the use of a tractor-mounted swipe. In the past some of this work could be financed by timber sales, but after the main pulpwood factory in Kent switched to recycling in 1990 it has become much harder to find commercial markets. David Maylam found no buyers at all between 1989 and 1992. On the credit side, the Forestry Authority now offer grants for coppice management (though as yet there is no special grant to offset the initial high cost of reinstating derelict woodland). All this might sound an awful lot of fuss over one small brown butterfly. But the Heath Fritillary is not alone in its need for 'traditional' management: in broad terms, opening up dense woodland is the key to the rejuvenation of wildlife of ancient coppices, from Nightingales to Bonfire Beetles. The significance of the Heath Fritillary is as a catalyst, nudging nature reserve managers in the right direction. A case perhaps of the swallowtail wagging the dog.

Chalk downland has one of the most attractive butterfly faunas, particularly the succession of the brilliant-winged 'blues', Common, Chalkhill and Adonis, that counterpoint the miniature beauty of the chalk herbs. The Conservancy owns and manages more than a dozen downland Reserves in southern England, and has built up a sizeable body of experience in maintaining them in a suitable condition for butterflies. Much of this has been pooled and published in the form of a habitat manual, published in 1986. It is important to recognise that the different species of downland butterflies have widely differing needs, especially for their early stages. The Adonis Blue, for example, needs very short, sun-baked turf and small, depauperate plants of Horseshoe Vetch for egg-laying, whereas the Chalkhill prefers a luxurious mass of the same plant in a taller sward. Where many species are present, the secret is to avoid a uniform close-cropped turf (a common mistake of earlier years), and aim instead at a diversity of different sward conditions within the same downland habitat. The way in which the site is managed depends on which butterflies are present—and that in turn reflects to some extent the use of the land in previous decades. Most downland butterflies are relatively sedentary insects, and they are not adept at colonising new ground unless it happens to be close-by. In recent years excellent results have been obtained by sheep grazing in winter and light cattle grazing in summer, or by cattle grazing alone. The 'right' management is often the one that was in place before the Reserve was declared.

The sudden decline of the rabbit after the outbreak of myxomatosis in 1954 was a disaster for short sward butterflies like the Adonis Blue and Silver-spotted Skipper. At Old Winchester Hill both species disappeared, since the Conservancy was unable to compensate for the loss of the rabbits by increasing the stockage of sheep: there was too much yew on the Reserve, and local farmers believed it would poison their stock. Here, as on many other Reserves, the best ground for butterflies is very localised—just a few acres on the steepest and sunniest slopes. In the early 1980s, the then warden, John Bacon, frustrated in his attempts to maintain viable numbers of orchids, butter-flies and juniper bushes on the same small patch of ground, began to experiment with small, temporary paddocks of electrified flexi-netting. He could obtain a mosaic of different sward conditions at the right time of year by moving the sheep around on a rotation, and it proved a most effective means of boosting butterfly numbers. The Adonis Blue, reintroduced to the Reserve in 1981, thrived for several years on this regime. It is unlikely that any downland shepherd grazed his flocks in quite that way, but the 'Bacon experiment' in effect replicates the variety of habitat conditions once found on the open sheep ranges, but compresses them into the much smaller space available to a nature reserve manager. Like Reserve management generally, it is labour-intensive and requires experience and the full control of one's livestock. And it is no more 'natural', of course, than the butterfly motorways at Blean Wood. This form of management by the half-acre, the fine-tuning of the sward, has become a characteristically English form of conservation, reflecting the fragmented quality of most lowland habitats today, and the relatively cramped, isolated conditions on even our best chalk nature reserves. The techniques pioneered by John Bacon have since been applied successfully to other Reserves in southern England, and some of them have become among the best butterfly sanctuaries in the country. This is the least *laissez-faire* form of management: its art lies in watching the turf like a hawk. The confidently written 'prescriptions' of Reserve management plans, stipulating stock densities and stock movements, can only go so far. In the end the state of the grass depends as much on the weather and local site conditions as on the number of animals that are eating it. Especially if you are looking not at its economic pasture value, but at the far more demanding tastes of downland butterflies.

HOPELESS CASES? THE WART-BITER BUSH-CRICKET AND THE BLACK-VEINED MOTH

One of the problems of concentrating on one particular rare species is that there may be others living in the area that are equally rare but have quite different, and sometimes contradictory, needs. This may cause an interesting conflict of loyalty: who can say which is the most important, a Dartford Warbler or a Sand Lizard? The RSPB

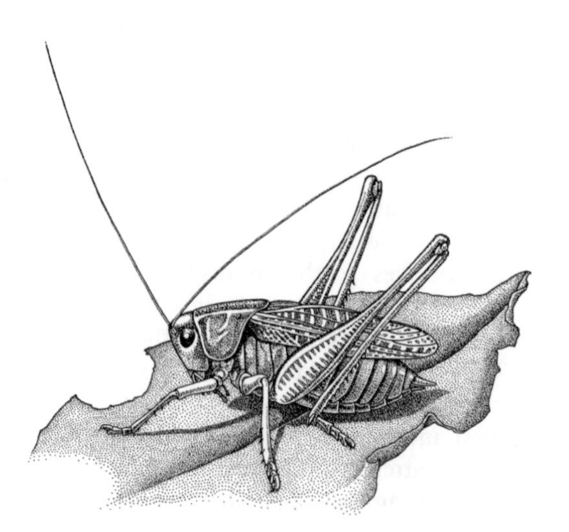

and the British Herpetological Society might well have their own views about this, but, as the national conservation body charged with protecting all species, the Conservancy is expected to be impartial. Such problems are multiplied when it comes to the Insect Kingdom, for there are some 30,000 species in Britain, which implies 30,000 different life-styles. Castle Hill National Nature Reserve provides an instance when three very attractive insects—the Adonis Blue butterfly, the Scarce Forester moth and the Wart-biter Bush-cricket—all occur on the same slope, and yet have conflicting habitat requirements. The Adonis Blue, as we have seen, is a short turf species, and management for it alone will greatly impoverish the naturally diverse insect fauna of limestone grassland. The Scarce Forester, on the other hand, is a member of a group of brightly coloured day-flying moths that need tall grass stems and plenty of flowers, and are sensitive to overgrazing. The food-plant of the Scarce Forester is knapweed, which thrives best in swards that are left ungrazed in summer. That most spectacular of 'grasshoppers', the Wart-biter, is known to have even more complex needs—a mosaic of habitats with bare ground for egg laying, short flowery grass for the nymph stage (youthful Wart-biters like to nibble dandelions and other flowers) and tussocky grass in which the fat-bodied late-stage nymphs and adults can hide from marauding magpies and kestrels. It is scarcely surprising that the Wart-biter is so rare—researchers looking for places to reintroduce it to found the right combination of conditions in only two out of a 100 sites visited. The Wart-biter would never reach them on its own, for not only are the sites isolated by farmland but it is, in any case, a most sedentary beast—it can jump well enough but it is a poor climber and virtually flightless. The reason why the Wart-biter does so well at Castle Hill, and why it can co-exist with the Adonis Blue and the Scarce Forester, is that both short and long grass, together with patches of bare ground, are found in close proximity along the narrow terraces of this steep south-facing escarpment. Here the land has long been grazed by cattle, which produce a ragged sward with more inherent variety than sheep-grazed downland.

A serious problem at Castle Hill, as at many semi-natural downs in the south-east, is the spread of tussock-forming grasses, especially Tor-grass (see Chapter 7). The traditional way of dealing with Tor-grass is to graze it hard in early spring, while the blades are comparatively tender, but at Castle Hill the presence of young Wart-biters among the grass rules out that option. Mowing and raking has been tried as a substitute, though so far not very successfully. Drought is another recurrent problem that is even less open to easy solutions. Monitoring indicates that the Wart-biter is still doing reasonably well under the current mixed regime of sheep and cattle, but the rotation of sheep pens which has proven a useful way of helping butterflies does not suit this species. Wart-biters seem to need a fine mosaic of vegetation that is more likely to be produced by free-range grazing over a large area. This may be a useful hint that we should, where possible, try to mimic traditional grazing regimes on nature reserves, especially when they have produced a rich flora and fauna.

Because it is the subject of a long-term study under English Nature's Species Recovery Programme (if you want funds and publicity, find a creature with a silly name!), it has been possible to learn a great deal about the Wart-biter. It is likely to go on receiving star treatment because it is one of our largest and rarest native insects, and attracts a certain amount of public interest. That option is not available to the vast majority of insects and invertebrates. Fortunately the Wart-biter is a useful 'star insect' since it reminds us that some invertebrates have unexpectedly complex requirements, and that their needs may change as they grow older and larger.

It is unlikely that the little piebald Black-veined Moth, *Sione lineata*, will ever receive comparable fame, though it too is an interesting insect, and equally attractive in its way. Like the Wart-biter, the Black-veined Moth is now drinking in the Last Chance saloon, in this case a small area on the Wye National Nature Reserve in Kent. Its recent history has been marked by terrible bad luck. Much of the formerly rough uncultivated grassland of the Wye district has been ploughed since the war, after early SSSI designation failed to save it. One good site, a chalk quarry, was obliterated by a council rubbish tip in 1976 and another, a railway cutting, scrubbed over after diesel locomotives replaced the old steam trains and the occasional useful fires they started. Further impediments to its conservation were an ignorance of the moth's habits and, frankly, a lack of interest in them; collectors aside, nobody cared about small moths and their ilk until the 1980s, when rare insects belatedly entered the conservation agenda.

The problem with the Black-veined Moth is that it likes Tor-grass, which is in other respects public enemy number one on chalk downland. It was thought that its caterpillar fed exclusively on Tor-grass, and that the species needed nothing but masses of this otherwise useless grass. Certainly it is on the blades of that grass that the moth usually chooses to lay its eggs. But Tor-grass is tough, unnutritive stuff, and it seemed strange that this delicate insect should be the only one of its tribe, the Geometridae, to feed on grass. The truth was discovered only in the late 1980s when the NCC employed a young moth specialist, Paul Waring, to look into the conservation of rare moths. At that time no one had ever succeeded in rearing this species in captivity. What usually happened was that the young larvae took one look at the piles of Tor-grass on offer, curled up and died. Paul decided it would be as well to offer them alternatives from the range of the herbs that grow among the tussocks of grass at Wye. The larvae jumped at one of them—Marjoram—and after that he experienced little difficulty in rearing them through to adulthood.

The implications of this discovery have a fundamental bearing on both the management for this species and the broader management of the Reserve, since it implies that the moth needs not a dense uniform mass of Tor-grass, as was once thought, but a varied and rather open turf of tussocks interspersed with herbs and flowers—the sort of conditions provided, in fact, by light cattle grazing in winter. Tor-grass, or other equally tussocky substitutes, are part of the moth's needs, but it uses them not for feeding but for shelter (after all, tussock grasses will look like a haystack to a small caterpillar). The Black-veined Moth is currently responding reasonably well to management geared at obtaining a small-scale patchwork of tussock and chalk flowers. The adults are showing particular interest in a sheltered field at the base of the downs, which has been managed for its benefit by light sheep grazing to encourage a herb-rich sward with plenty of Marjoram. The colonisation of new ground, tens of metres away, no doubt represents a big and unusual adventure for this species. It is when you have achieved this level of understanding, the result of hours and days in the field, allied to captive breeding programmes, that you have a realistic hope of conserving an insect whose numbers have declined to the red-light level. Guesswork, in this case, would probably have helped to propel the insect to extinction.

27. Top: *The Devil's Kneading-trough at Wye.*
28. Right: *Limestone pasture with crags and scattered rocks at the head of Lathkill Dale in the Peak District.*
29. Above: *Beulah sheep along Bokerley Dyke.*

30. *Heather, Bell-heather and Western Gorse at Holt Heath, Dorset.*

31. *Habitat restoration in progress at Holton Heath.*

32. *Shattered crags along the spine of the Stiperstones in Shropshire.*

33. Above: *The plateau heaths of The Lizard.*
34. Below right: *Holkham.* 35. Below left: *Ancient timbers of the Sweet Track to Glastonbury.*

36. Above: *A cleared rhyne at the Gordano Valley*. 37. Below: *Hay-making on the Bure Marshes*.

THE RESERVE AS BATTLEGROUND: THE TERNS OF SCOLT HEAD ISLAND

Terns are sociable birds and like to nest together in large numbers. Their colonies are usually situated on the least accessible extremities of the coast—on remote beaches, off-shore islands or spits of shingle. Nearly all the large colonies receive some protection during the nesting season, and National Nature Reserves play an important role in tern protection, especially at Scolt Head Island, Holkham and Winterton Dunes on the Norfolk coast and Gull Island on the Solent. Terns need all the protection they can get. Sudden storms in summer may blow sand over the eggs or wash them away with the tide, especially those of the Little Tern which often insists on nesting within a few metres of the high water mark. If there are insufficient fish, especially Sand Eels, in the sea nearby the young will starve. The nestlings have only their parents, sometimes aided by cohabitant Black-headed Gulls, to protect them from predators such as foxes, rats or Kestrels. And human beings passing too close will disturb these nervous, capricious birds, which can suddenly desert the site in a body, or switch to another site, sometimes for no apparent reason.

Terns are long-lived, and, other things being equal, a successful breeding season will compensate for a succession of poor ones. Sometimes, however, the same problem recurs, becomes a trend and eventually threatens the survival of the colony. On the East Anglian coast, predation by foxes has become a serious problem not only for terns but for other ground-nesting birds such as Avocet, Ringed Plover, Oystercatcher and Shelduck. The reserve manager is faced with an ethical choice: does he interfere in a 'natural' event and try to cull or even eliminate the fox or does he let nature take its course, even if that means the loss of much of the Reserve's conservation value? And if so, can he be sure that the birds will find somewhere else to nest along England's increasingly crowded coast? At Scolt Head Island, off the North Norfolk coast, the problem begs the question: if terns cannot raise young on an uninhabited offshore island, which also happens to be a National Nature Reserve, then where *can* they find peace?

Scolt Head Island is a natural ridge of sand and shingle about 6.4 km long, separated from the mainland by a kilometre or so of intertidal mud and saltmarsh. Unlike most islands along the East Anglian coast it is free of groynes, sea walls and other impediments to natural development, and its exceptional natural state has made it a centre for detailed studies into the natural processes of coastal accretion and erosion. People can visit the island, but as access is possible only around high tide and requires prior arrangements with a boat owner, many birdwatchers go instead to the more conveniently placed nature reserves at Titchwell or Holkham. The island's terns nest on the spit of shingle and sand that curves seawards from its western tip. Thanks to the patient efforts of Bob Chestney to secure the colony as a no-go area at nesting time, this colony is now one of the largest in Western Europe, numbering several thousands of pairs of Sandwich, Little and Common Terns in a good year. The Sandwich Tern colonies of Scolt Head and its neighbour Blakeney Point can alone number up to 4500 breeding pairs, a quarter of the UK population, making it one of the most important sites in the world for this species. This international significance is recognised in the designation of the island as a Ramsar site and a Special Protection

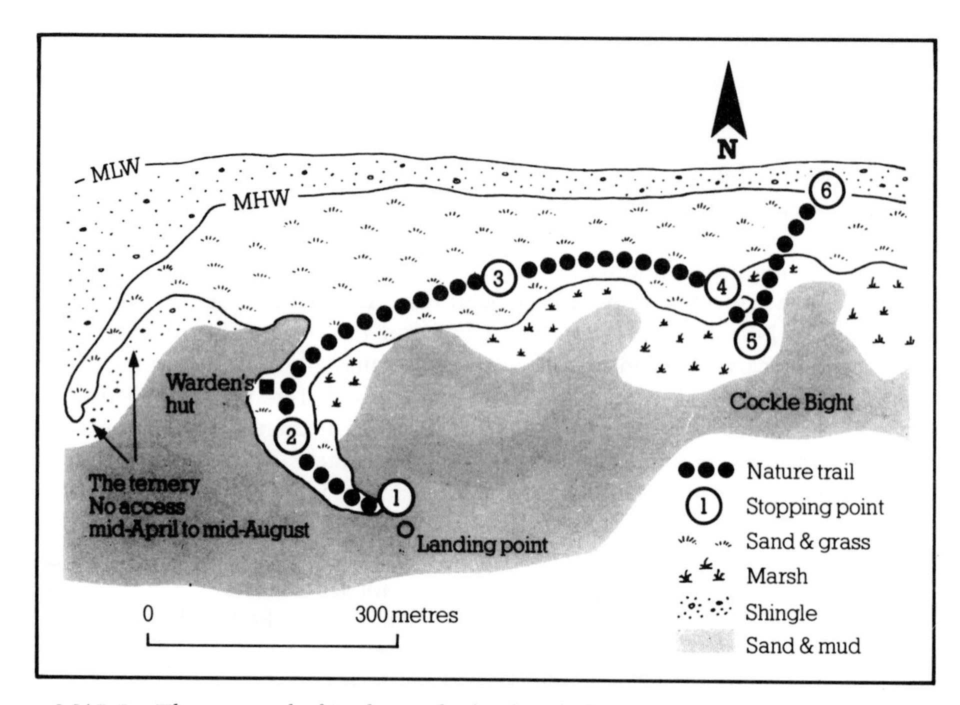

MAP 5 *The west end of Scolt Head Island with the ternery*

Area under the European Community Birds Directive. Not surprisingly, the protection of the terns is a principal aim of the Nature Reserve. Most of the conditions for success are in place—a protected site almost free from human disturbance, the right physical conditions and not too many sandblows or tidal surges. And yet, as Table 7, on p. 111 shows, the numbers of young raised here have recently suffered a complete collapse from a four-figure number to zero. There is no doubt at all about the cause of the catastrophe. Scolt Head Island is being invaded by foxes.

Foxes have increased dramatically on the mainland estates closest to Scolt. The cause is probably the diminished number of gamekeepers employed by these estates, and the increased availability of food in the form of rabbits and pheasants, not to mention the tasty scraps in the dustbins of suburban restaurants. In the past, foxes kept clear of Scolt Head, even in the days before myxomatosis when it swarmed with rabbits. From about 1985, however, they began to make regular forays to the island, crossing the intervening mud flats at night at low tide. A pair produced cubs on the island for the first time in spring 1988, and were it not for the constant vigilance of the Reserve's manager, Colin Campbell, and his assistants, there would undoubtedly be several resident families of foxes on the island by now.

The problem is how to stop foxes from raiding the tern colony during the breeding season (between April and July)—all those delicious eggs and tender young chicks. The dilemma is in this case unusually stark. There is no compatibility whatever between tern and fox: a contented fox means no young terns. Unfortunately the very factors which make the island so alluring to the fox also make it extremely difficult to get rid of them. There are miles and miles of cover, with unusually dense Marram, shoreline corridors of Seablite, and impenetrable thickets of brambles riddled with old rabbit workings. There are innumerable hollows and creeks in which the fox can lie up undetected. And an analysis of droppings suggests that the animal has no difficulty obtaining food there in any season, whether it is blackberries and rose hips in autumn, fresh crushed crabs from the trawlers, or the numerous rabbits, geese and duck on the Reserve. As Colin Campbell points out, 'Scolt Head is a paradise for foxes. Their only enemy is me!' Among all the other items on the menu, tern eggs and chicks are just a particular tasty *hors d'oeuvres*.

During the past 4 years, Scolt Head has seen an extraordinary battle of wits between the fox and Colin Campbell. Two main stratagems have been attempted, the first aimed at preventing the fox from reaching the ternery, the second at eliminating him altogether. Containment, the usual way of living with foxes, is not an option here, since bitter experience has shown that a single fox can undo months of carefully laid plans. Each March a 300-m electrified fence is laid across the narrow neck of the island just east of the ternery. The fence will not by itself prevent foxes from entering the ternery at low tide, but, so long as it is not short-circuited by blown sand or seaweed, it effectively channels the animals into corridors along the shoreline which can be covered by shooting butts. One suggestion to improve its effectiveness was to mount powerful gas lights at either end of the fence to frighten the foxes. That was ruled out after discussions with the coastguard confirmed that the lights might easily be mistaken by trawlermen for navigation lights. Another tack was to distribute polystyrene decoy gulls in the ternery to lure increased numbers of Black-headed Gulls into using the site. It was hoped that the gulls, which are larger and more aggressive than the terns, might help to drive off the foxes. For additional verisimilitude, nests were constructed for the decoys, complete with real gulls' eggs taken (under licence) from the nearby RSPB reserve at Titchwell. Some Black-heads were indeed 'gulled' by these props, but the experiment has unfortunately had little success in deterring the fox. Among the more bizarre suggestions not taken up were the distribution of lion dung, of which foxes are supposed to have an atavistic terror, coils of barbed wire, tethered dogs and a 'Maginot Line' of glittering stainless steel stretching across the island and out into the sea.

In the end mere deterrence has not worked. Short of abandoning the terns to their fate, there is no alternative to killing the foxes, to the warden taking on the role of a gamekeeper. How does he set about it? Snares and cage traps have been tried out, but to avoid problems with visitors' dogs, they have to be dismantled and removed early in the morning. They were not very successful anyway: the game wasn't worth the candle. Most foxes have been dispatched by shooting at night. This is no simple matter either. At nearby Holkham, 'lamping' for foxes is a relatively straightforward matter since the limited amount of cover there generally allows the marksman a clear shot. At Scolt Head Island, conditions are much more difficult, as Colin's own account of the fox campaign of early June 1991 will reveal. It had begun as quite a promising season: some 320 pairs of Sandwich Terns had laid eggs and others were still arriving and settling down. Fox control measures had been largely successful, and although one elusive adult and a cub remained at large, they had not so far dared to visit the ternery. Then a gale began to blow up from the sea . . . let Colin Campbell take up the story:

> From the 10–14 June strong westerly winds produced days of blowing sand over the whole western Ternery. Nests were buried and some terns deserted

> the site. On 12 June, the last adult fox entered the Ternery. The noisy calling of the Sandwich Terns at night, characteristic of the species, must have helped to lure the fox inexorably towards the colony. The prospect of eggs galore also possibly made it overcome its past wariness in approaching the electric fence. Thereafter, visits by both the adult and the cub continued on and off, despite all efforts to eliminate them. Access by these foxes, when it could be ascertained, was always on very dark nights at low water. A shingle bar had developed at the near edge of low water off the north Ternery shore. By running beneath this slope, foxes could not be seen from the ambush hide. During the rising moon period in the latter half of June, continual heavy clouds made night sight work largely impossible. The windy weather contributed to the problems by obscuring fox tracks in the sand and making it impossible to verify entry and exit points into and out of the Ternery. Planning the best next move, control-wise, to try to shoot these two foxes, became impossible. Truly frustration heaped upon frustration.
>
> By early July all the terns had deserted. . .

The night sight referred to is an advanced instrument that magnifies the available light so that the marksman can spot the shadowy form running silently along the foreshore. But even this technological wonder has its limitations. It is heavy, needs moonlit conditions to work well and can be put out of action by careless exposure to bright light. But let us rehearse a typical night. Colin and his companion (often a gamekeeper from one of the Norfolk estates) have crossed the water on the last ebb tide of the evening with all their heavy equipment, lamp, rifle, sights and food, and, avoiding the noisy crunch of the shingle, have taken up stations at the butt near the foreshore. Colin makes a passing imitation of the distress call of a rabbit by whistling through his knuckles. Tonight they are in luck. A dim shape appears in the sights, its eyes burning red for a second or two in the light of the lamp. The shape moves out of range, suspicious, trying to get downwind, seeking the scent of rabbit urine or blood. A gust of wind blows up from the shore, frustrating the marksman, for even a slight breeze can deflect a bullet at the maximum accurate range of 200 m. Sand gets everywhere, in the eyes, down your neck, on the rifle. The two of them stand absolutely still. They dare not risk firing and missing, for once shot at, a fox becomes lamp shy and more wary than ever. But we shall suppose that the wind has dropped and Colin is in luck—the fox has returned. Bang. A .222-calibre rifle bullet at about 50-m range kills the animal instantly. There is rarely any suffering involved—a mess, sometimes, but the fox knows nothing about it. Often there will be egg yolk on its muzzle, or a duck in its jaws. Colin crams the corpse down a rabbit hole. You have to remember that this is a good night—in practice only about one attempt in six is successful. Yet each attempt entails beaching the boat, shouldering heavy equipment over loose sand, hours of straining through the sights, and a long wait for the flood tide home. Over the past 4 years, Colin has killed 37 foxes at Scolt. At the end of every vigil, successful or not, both men are physically exhausted. As Colin wrote in his 1991 report:

> All the odds are loaded in favour of the foxes, most of the time. It needs a good deal of attendant luck to successfully eliminate the majority of them. The hardest obstacle of all to overcome is the extraordinary wariness and

> cunning of the remaining one or two animals. That these can ever be removed with the present combination of control methods remains to be proven.
>
> In the long term, the stark truth is that the pinnacle of success, the complete elimination of Scolt foxes each spring, will have to be repeated, year after year.

In 1992, the fox control measures seemed to be paying off: several hundred pairs of terns had raised young without undue disturbance. Then, in July, there was a violent thunderstorm and torrential rain. Only the 25 strongest chicks survived. The battle goes on, with an occasional reminder from nature that full control will always be an illusion.

TABLE 7 *Nesting and fledging numbers of terns and ringed plover at Scolt Head Island NNR 1986–92*

Year	Sandwich Tern		Common Tern		Little Tern		Ringed Plover
	Nests	Fledged	Nests	Fledged	Nests	Fledged	Nests
1986	2600	2200	200	110	70	35	150
1987	3089	3200	208	21	80	75	162
1988	2775	1200	208	45	65	31	119
1989	1052	0	159	10	63	12	90
1990	0	0	14	0	10	0	41
1991	320	0	41	0	22	0	38
1992	280	25			25		

STOP-PRESS!

The 1993 season at Scolt Head proved the most successful since 1988. All the methods of fox control described above continued, but in addition English Nature also enlisted the help of a gamekeeper during the critical time. Lanterns and baits of tinned dog food successfully diverted the foxes from their usual access routes into the ternery, and with their aid nine of the raiders were killed. The main breakthrough, however, was the killing of more than 50 foxes on the nearby mainland, which relieved the recruitment pressure on the island considerably. Meanwhile, the weather was unusually kind with no severe storms or floods during the breeding season, and plentiful shoals of fish nearby. The Sandwich Terns reared at least 1000 fledglings to flying stage from 853 nests. The Common and Little Terns also did quite well with 90 and 45 surviving fledglings respectively. For the moment, the tide has changed in favour of the terns.

CHAPTER 7

Down and Heath

THE next three chapters look at how National Nature Reserves are managed to provide the best set of conditions for wildlife. I have divided them into three main groups of habitats: 'dry' Reserves, namely chalk and limestone grassland and lowland heaths, and also the unique Breckland 'heaths' which are a sort of cross between the two, with a few sand dunes thrown in for good measure. Many Reserves of course contain more than one habitat: Barton Hills, for example, has an ancient wood as well as chalk hills. In keeping with the earlier chapters of this book I will not tell the story of each Reserve one by one, but instead will try to pull together common themes that may give the reader an insight into how National Nature Reserves are managed, and why. I have concentrated where possible on contemporary usage, a rapidly developing field, and on projects that have broader implications for the management of sites of high nature conservation interest. The following two chapters will look at the management of 'wet' habitats, like grazing marsh, peatlands and reedbeds, and then at woodlands, semi-natural pastures and coastal saltmarshes.

DOWNLAND AND LIVESTOCK GRAZING

Chalk grassland is one of the special habitats of England. There are downs and chalk cliffs along the Seine and elsewhere in northern France and in parts of the Netherlands, but nowhere do they compare with the grandeur of the White Cliffs of Dover or the Seven Sisters, which to many people are quintessential England. Recent surveys undertaken by the Conservancy's mobile field unit indicate that about 37,000 ha of unimproved chalk grassland remains in England; not much indeed, but even so enough to make southern England one of the most extensive chalk landscapes in

Western Europe. Nearly two-thirds of our downland is in Wiltshire, especially on Salisbury Plain and Porton Down, the last of the great unbroken chalk grassland landscapes in England. Elsewhere chalk grassland has become a mainly linear habitat, confined to scarp slopes whose steepness has deterred attempts to plough or reseed it. We have lost a great deal of our uncultivated downland to agriculture or the advance of woodland since 1945. Only 20 years ago, there were about 143 chalk grassland sites larger than 40 ha but nearly a quarter (21%) of these critically important large sites has since been lost. The continuing loss of chalk grassland vindicates the Conservancy's successful early efforts to build up a first-rate collection of nature reserves on the Chalk, representing some of the best examples and the full biogeographical range of that habitat in England. There are now about 20 National Nature Reserves composed partly or wholly of chalk grassland. They include sections of steep escarpments, like Aston Rowant in the Chilterns and Pewsey Downs in Wiltshire, isolated chalk hills like Mount Caburn in East Sussex and Barton Hills in Bedfordshire, and relatively flat, undulating panoramas of grass like Parsonage Down at the edge of Salisbury Plain and Martin Down on the border of Hampshire and Dorset.

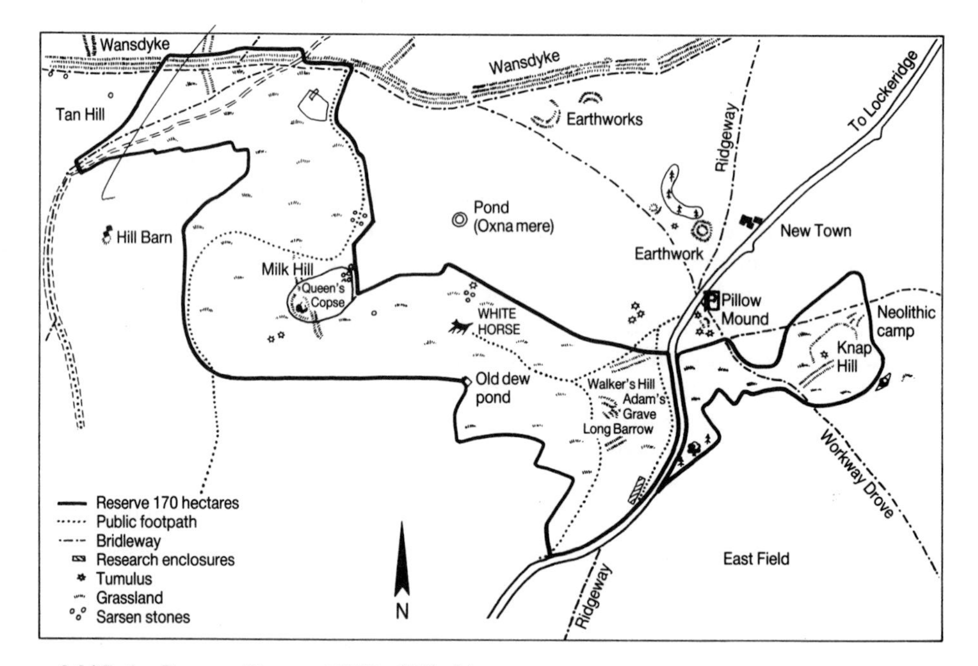

MAP 6 *Pewsey Downs NNR, Wiltshire*

Apart from its outstanding interest for wildlife, chalk grassland holds our most visible record of the ancient human past. Many chalk Reserves contain registered ancient monuments and elaborate field systems dating back to the Neolithic when they may have been the most cultivated parts of England. Kingley Vale, for example, contains one of the best-preserved bell barrows in the land. Legend has it that this is the grave of a king, hence Kingley Vale. Barrows of various shapes, sizes and periods indent the skyline at the Vale of Pewsey NNR in Wiltshire, which also boasts the early Saxon Wansdyke and a pond mentioned in a ninth century charter. Wylye Down NNR has medieval terraces superimposed on Celtic square field-banks. Fyfield Down near Marlborough contains one of the most extensive ancient field systems in Britain, a wonderful sight in low autumn light amid the scatter of sarsen stones. The value of these artefacts of the past is recognised and described at length in Reserve management plans as part of the historical and cultural context of the site. Archaeology and ecology are in many ways natural bed-fellows, especially in a country like England where even the wildest sites have been much modified by human use. On National Nature Reserves they have much to offer one another.

Chalk grassland is maintained by grazing, either by sheep and cattle or by wild rabbits. This does not, however, mean that they are necessarily of 'man-made' or recent origin. In many cases, downland turf is undoubtedly ancient, that is, its age is to be reckoned in thousands rather than in hundreds of years. Recent evidence suggests that in some areas chalk grassland existed even before the Neolithic farmers began to clear land for stock grazing. In more recent centuries, the main economic value of downland has been as out-pasture for sheep, and it is only in our own mad times that it has been relegated to the agricultural fringes or neglected altogether. In the 'classic' period of open-range sheep grazing on the downs, as remembered in W H Hudson's *A Shepherd's Life*, the flocks would be shepherded onto the down in the morning, and folded near the farm in the evening in a daily cycle, year in, year out. The point of the system was that, as sheep defecate mainly at night, they were effectively taking nutrients off the down and depositing them where they were needed—on the more productive 'in-bye' land around the farm. The chalk flowers benefited since the soils of the downs remained thin and impoverished—exactly what is needed to maintain the colourful, scented sward and deny a foothold to aggressive grasses and shrubs. Flower-rich grassland was, in turn, good for the hardy downland breeds of sheep, which prefer the flavour of flowers and herbs to plain grass, and which obtain all of their dietary needs from the array of plants on offer. The lonely shepherds no doubt appreciated the 'clouds' of blue butterflies and the songs of the Skylark and Corn Bunting, but these were no more than the incidental beneficiaries of what was then considered sound agriculture. This was a system of conservation only in the sense that it conserved soil nutrients via sheep dung.

That, of course, is history. Today's manager of a grassland nature reserve has to find a means both of preventing his fragment of old down from scrubbing over and of 'maximising its potential' as a nature reserve. His basic choices are grazing, mowing and burning. Many sites, especially rough grass in the Cotswolds, used to be burned regularly each winter to get rid of the litter of dead grass and provide an early 'bite' of sweet young grass in the spring. Conservationists rarely resort to burning, however, since it takes a very heavy toll of invertebrates and may kill plants like orchids or Pasque Flowers, whose tubers or growth buds lie close to the surface. Burning also adds unwelcome nutrients to the soil, encouraging the growth of coarse grasses such as Tor-grass. Much the same drawbacks apply to mowing, which, like burning, has the disadvantage of being an all-at-once operation, producing a lawn-like effect. Mowing has its uses in meadows that have always been harvested for hay, and along rides in fens and woods and other places where grazing is impracticable. But in general, grazing is by far the best option available, since animals crop the vegetation more gradually so that there are fewer invertebrate casualties and a much greater small-scale variety produced, from tussocky grass along the terraced sheep tracks to close-cropped turf and patches of bare ground.

Grazing, then, is the obvious choice, but how the site is grazed, by which and by whose livestock, in what season and at what intensity, are all matters of judgement which require experience and a knowledge of the site. The best known type of chalk vegetation, that of steep scarp slopes facing the sun, grows on a thin skin of blackish, drought-prone soil. This produces a sward of tough, water-retentive plants—narrow-leaved fescues and sedges, and mats of thyme and rock-rose. If rabbits are present in large numbers, such sites may look after themselves without much effort from us. But a greater degree of control is achievable by sheep grazing. In the past these escarpments were often grazed in the summer, but in conservation terms winter grazing only is preferable where the growth rate is slow, so that there will be lots of flowers and insects present in the summer.

Since the 1950s, rabbit numbers alone have rarely been sufficient to maintain a close-cropped sward—although on the present upward trend, they may well have a much greater role as cropping machines in the future, if the Ministry of Agriculture allows it. But rabbits cannot resist scratching and burrowing wherever they go and the result can be messy, with eroded banks and patches of nettles and thistles on the excavated soil. The scratchings have a beneficial side—the bare ground is used by insects for basking or egg laying or colonised by annuals and other short-lived plants like Ground Pine or English Gentian, which are often the 'missing component' of the chalk habitat. But rabbit numbers tend to go up and down, depending on the current virulence of the myxomatosis bug. At the moment, most downland reserves are experiencing a plague of them. At Martin Down, for example, rabbits have become a severe nuisance, eroding the soil and nibbling bark, and they have to be controlled by night-time shooting or gassing. All the same, I suspect that the main problem with wild rabbit grazing for the reserve manager is its unpredictability. Managers like to exert a strong degree of control over what happens on the nature reserve, to fit in with the aims of the Reserve management plan. They naturally prefer the 'safe deck' of livestock to the wild card of the rabbit. An exception to this rule is Weeting Heath NNR in the Breck, where the taller vegetation that followed the myxomatosis epidemic almost eliminated the breeding populations of Stone Curlew and Wheatear. Neither mowing nor rotovating the ground proved any kind of substitute, nor did the rather desperate expedient of sinking drainage pipes into the ground in the hope that Wheatears would mistake them for rabbit burrows and nest in them. In 1959, therefore, a 16-ha wire enclosure was erected to keep the remaining rabbits in. It has worked quite well. The rabbits increased and soon their numbers were restored to pre-myxomatosis numbers (they are still affected by the virus, but less so than the free-ranging rabbits outside). Both rare birds have returned, and the enclosure at Weeting Heath is now one of the best places to listen after dark to the eerie bubbling call of Stone Curlews.

In practice, every one of English Nature's chalk downland reserves is grazed by stock for at least part of the year, either by cattle or sheep, or both. With stock grazing the manager is in charge. The art of good grazing revolves around a complex equation of stocking units, time, season, turf and weather. An enormous amount of scientific research on downland stocking regimes has been done, partly on National Nature

Reserves, like Aston Rowant and Barton Hills. In practice, however, this theoretical information needs to be supplemented by an intimate knowledge of the site and what it will bear. Originally, most downland Reserves were grazed by sheep alone, but nowadays they are more likely to have mixed regimes of cattle and sheep, although not necessarily at the same time or in the same place. Ponies and tethered goats have been used to reinstate grassland from scrub and coarse grass at Kingley Vale and Lullington Heath, but they are less suitable for extant grassland sites. Goats prefer browsing leaves and twigs to grazing and are rarely winter hardy, while the pony's habit of selective grazing and dunging in the same place can lead to a terrible mess—nettles, ragged grass and poached mud, all mixed up. Sheep, particularly the hardy hill breeds, are more efficient all-round grazing machines. Sheep nibble the herbage, grazing it very short, often back to the rootstocks. We can only guess what goes through the sheep's mind as it chews its way across the down, but they evidently examine the sward carefully as they go, preferring some grasses to others and flowers to either. They are much more selective feeders than cattle, although some breeds can be persuaded to tackle ill-tasting stuff, even young rosettes of the noxious ragwort.

From the standpoint of modern farming, chalk nature reserves generally offer poor quality grazing in the sense that the grass grows slowly and has a short growing season—although in terms of nutritional quality wild chalk grass is every bit as good as sown grass, and can be particularly useful in winter when the downs are often drier than the farm fields (this is equally true of estuarine saltmarsh, where the grass is clean, tide-washed and succulent, and cattle depart fit and disease-free). Most modern breeds of lowland sheep are unsuitable for nature conservation purposes since they require supplementary feeding for their relatively high rates of lambing and fast growth. This is something to avoid on nature reserves, as the hay and other feed enriches the soil and encourages the spread of 'weeds' like Creeping Thistle and nettles. Through trial and error, the Conservancy found that the Beulah sheep, originally bred for the grassy hills of Wales, is almost ideal for the chalk. Beulahs have a range of virtues: they are small, they do not need much maintenance and, being relatively small and light, are easy to handle; they are reluctant to jump fences (though adept at wriggling under them); they can feed outside in all weathers and they make good mothers, lambing readily even on the open down. Their sharp little hooves help to prevent the build-up of coarse grassy litter. Like most of the 'wilder' breeds, they have their idiosyncrasies. Beulahs can affect not to notice wide open gates, and they prefer walking uphill to going down. And they seem to enjoy playing teasing games with the shepherd. Bob Russell, the warden at Wye NNR in Kent, tells me that a favourite is 'hide and seek': 'one second they are walking ahead, the next they put on a sudden burst of speed, and disappear into the scrub. Then before you know where you are, they reappear behind you, right back where you started!'. The downland turf provides virtually all the Beulah's nutritional needs, and they can even be persuaded to tackle scrub at a pinch, standing on their hind legs to do so, like deer. They have proved particularly useful for keeping down unwanted growth by nibbling thistle tops, old nettles, ivy and brambles. Their thick fleece can sometimes be a problem in scrubby, bramble-infested areas, for when a sheep becomes entangled in a bramble thicket it loses all reason in its frantic struggles to free itself. At Old Winchester Hill, Mick Finnemore is now experimenting with a cross between the Beulah and the Dorset Shorthorn called 'Easycare' (horrible modern name!) which has a much shorter coat.

The Beulah sheep, after some initial 'training', are comparatively 'biddable' and obliging. Not so the small goat-like Soay sheep, of which the Conservancy owns small flocks at the Lizard and Braunton Burrows. Soays are semi-wild. They thrive on natural vegetation, do not need shearing and are extremely agile and hardy. They are normally reasonably well behaved, running back from an open gate with their heads down like naughty children at the sound of the hooter, but they are much less co-operative when sheep-dipping time comes round. As the Reserve manager of the Lizard, Ray Lawman remarks 'they don't like the dip, and they know when it's dipping time. They haven't had intelligence bred out of them, like other sheep'. A full-grown Soay can leap over a five-bar gate from a standing start and outrun a dog. It takes Ray and his helpers an average of two and a half days to round up the sheep for dipping and clipping, and the former has scars to show for it.

Sheep can be used to reinstate species-rich turf from dense coarse grass, as Paul Toynton has effectively demonstrated at Martin Down NNR. When the Conservancy took over this site in the late 1970s, the grass was so tall that children disappeared in it and Paul's sheep dog had to stand on its hind legs to see where it was going. Mowing the stuff was like harvesting corn. Returning the sward to fine-leaved downland grass has taken 10 years of carefully regulated all-season sheep grazing. In general, however, sheep are at their most effective when the turf is in reasonable condition already. On more productive grassland, or where neglect has produced tall or rank vegetation, cattle come into their own. By wrapping their long tongues around tufts of grass and ripping them up (the 'wrap-around-and-pull' method), cattle produce a more ragged sward and their much greater weight can puncture and break up the turf. In moderation that is no bad thing. Butterflies, for example, often thrive on a cattle regime. Cattle, unlike sheep, prefer grass to flowers, and some butterflies, like the Wall and the Adonis Blue lay their eggs in the pockets of warm bare soil left by trampling cattle.

It was considerations of this sort that led to the introduction of cattle on many downland reserves in the early 1980s. Unfortunately beneficial treading can quickly turn into churned mud in wet weather, and that, combined with the great splodges of dung that cattle leave everywhere, is the cause of infestations of ragwort and other undesirable plants. Experience suggests that the most suitable animals for Reserves are healthy lightweight bullock calves up to 18 months old, and preferably of a hardy breed. Such animals are more excitable than sheep. One may decide to wander off for a drink. After watching it for a minute or two, the rest of the herd may then decide to follow at a gallop, sending divots of turf flying in all directions. Sometimes these 'spooky' bursts of activity have no obvious cause; perhaps they are sheer *joie de vivre*. So although cattle have their uses on nature reserves, the manager has to keep a close eye on the turf for incipient signs of erosion and poaching. Paul Toynton of Martin Down sums up their disadvantages as follows: 'it is easier for things to go wrong with cattle, and when they do, the results are worse than with sheep. And the problems happen more quickly'.

A judicious mixture of 'grazing styles' can give excellent results. A few sheep among the cattle, for instance, will help to remove the unsightly ring of tall grass around an old cow-pat, while a sprinkling of cattle among the sheep can prevent the dense matting of turf that may form with sheep alone. Alternating sheep and cattle in successive years, as the owner has done at Prescombe Down NNR, can produce a beautifully lush and colourful sward, and this method also has been effective at reducing parasitic worms as well as increasing meat production. At Castle Hill, sheep are used to 'fine tune' the sward left by cattle, while Pewsey Vale, which has ragwort problems, does well under a regime of mixed grazing in spring and early summer. On sites which have been carefully cattle-grazed for many decades, like Wylye Down, a sudden switch to sheep might do more harm than good. The 'right' solution is often the one that was there before.

Whether or not the Conservancy should own the stock or license a grazer to use the Reserve depends very much on local circumstances. There are arguments either way. The ownership of stock saddles the Conservancy with the responsibility for the animals' care and health, unless it bears the expense of a contractor. The Reserve must be equipped with a water supply and sometimes semi-improved lay-by fields for lambing. The Reserve manager has to learn the arts of the stockman and shepherd. The obvious advantage of letting the grazing under an annual licence—the Conservancy sometimes has informal arrangements with a neighbour but does not usually offer an agricultural tenancy—is that the financial outlay and all the stock husbandry tasks are undertaken by the farmer, while the Conservancy pays only for the fence and the cost of drinking water. Finding someone who is prepared to purchase a licence and abide by its restrictions is the job of the latter's land agents. It may not be easy. The restrictions need in some respects to be tighter than a grazier might find elsewhere: the stock must be strictly limited to an agreed number, and the licence usually contains a clause which requires their removal in wet weather or drought. Even so, licensing rarely provides the same degree of control that one obtains from owning livestock, and compromises may have to be made to make the offer more attractive to a farmer or grazier. Experience has shown that you cannot expect a grazier to pay an 'economic rent' *and* conform to a host of restrictions. An example of what can happen was at Knocking Hoe NNR in Bedfordshire in the mid-1980s after the regular grazier suddenly went out of stock. It proved difficult to find a replacement, and in the meantime the grass grew long. When sheep were finally found, they coincided with an increase in rabbits, so that 'in May, the turf looked like February'. Sudden swings of this sort are the antithesis of the stability which managers try to achieve on Reserves.

The argument in favour of owning sheep, at least, is therefore a strong one. Sometimes there is not much choice in any case. At Lullington Heath, there is little or no grazing of a sufficient quality to attract any farmer. Old Winchester Hill is full of yew trees, which were believed (mistakenly) to be dangerous to sheep. The first flock to be owned by the Conservancy was brought to Aston Rowant in 1964 to take part in controlled grazing experiments as part of the International Biological Programme. This proved a successful way of managing the Reserve, and English Nature now owns the flocks on many of the larger downland Reserves, notably at Wye, Parsonage Down, Old Winchester Hill, Lullington Heath, Martin Down, Castor Hanglands and Kingley Vale. In many cases initial trials were necessary to establish whether the animals could exist happily without a resident shepherd. In only one instance does English Nature own cattle: at Parsonage Down, where it inherited a working farm. With that exception, it lacks the more elaborate facilities required to raise cattle, and most of the animals seen on reserves will be owned by licensees or neighbours (the Nature Conservancy once owned cattle at Woodwalton Fen, but the animals there now belong to the licensee).

Owning a flock of sheep greatly improves a reserve manager's ability to carry out detailed conservation work. Sheep can be 'forced' to clear unpalatable herbage, for example. This might result in a slight loss of condition which is acceptable to unsentimental conservationists, but not to a farmer whose income depends on prime lamb. They can be moved about the reserve using temporary paddocks of flexi-netting to meet particular needs, or taken off at certain times to protect rare species. It is exactly this kind of control that distinguishes National Nature Reserves from SSSIs and most nature reserves owned by charities. Equally importantly, the ownership of the flock means that the putting-on and taking-off of stock will be independent of the ups and downs of the market, so that stock numbers can therefore be regulated and guaranteed.

The ownership of a herd requires a knowledge of stock breeding and maintenance, and to some extent it transforms the nature of the Reserve manager's job from a naturalist to a farmer. Most managers and estate workers seem to enjoy working with animals. And, with the advisory function that many Reserve managers are now providing for SSSIs, it is useful for them to be able to speak from direct experience; farmers and other landowners are more likely to respond to people who have personal experience of owning and managing stock. In the late 1980s, under the eye of Ridley, management plans often included a section on the economic potential of each Reserve. In most cases the conclusion was that attempts to make a profit from National Nature Reserves were certain to compromise their proper purpose of nature conservation, but raising lambs on grassland Reserves was at least a theoretical possibility. Calculations suggest however that the true profit, once the cost of labour is taken into account, is likely to be small and would divert the manager from more important tasks. Livestock on Reserves function as four-legged grazing machines for maintaining the desired quality of turf. Lambing usually requires extra feeding for the ewes and a great deal of care in the early spring, when the manager has enough on his plate already. At Wye, however, a lambing flock of Beulahs has been maintained successfully for several years, ever since a flock of wether ewes on grazing trials unexpectedly produced two lambs. But with a lambing enterprise, one complication can lead to another, and another. . . Let Bob Russell, the reserve manager at Wye, take up the story:

> When I contemplated a larger flock of Beulahs, I'd reckoned on a small breeding flock of about thirty-five head, which, with some retained ewe lambs to replace the ageing ewes, would give me a winter headage of about

fifty. Unfortunately this was misinterpreted, and instead I was given another fifty ewes. By taking in other grazing areas, and selling some of the surplus stock, I just about managed. But unfortunately a dry winter was followed by an even drier summer. No one wanted to buy what the Romney sheep men called our 'mobile brillo pads', not to mention our miserably small lambs (and in that year it was difficult to sell even good lambs). So we were stuck with the ewes *and* the lambs throughout the winter.

The last thing I wanted in these circumstances was another crop of lambs, and so 'Rambo', as our tup ram was inevitably called, was kept well away from the ewes behind a very secure fence. Picture then my horror when I discovered that someone passing through on Christmas Day had opened all the gates so that Rambo was now busy giving all the ewes a Christmas present. He resisted all my attempts to return him to his own field, and in the end it took three of us and a dog to round him up. By that time, of course, all the ewes were fertilised.

We normally aim to get lambing out of the way by mid-April. One or two lambs in May we can cope with. But a December tupping means lambs in June!—when we should be shearing, not lambing. Fortunately the story had an unexpected happy ending. Our May lambs didn't do very well that year, but the June lambs thrived. So we were able to market them successfully, and return our flock to a manageable size.

THE SPECIAL PROBLEM OF TOR-GRASS

Tor-grass is a big tufted grass with blades like emery paper and the sort of yellowish-green hue that is best described as 'bilious'. It is common on lightly grazed downland swards throughout the southern Chalk and Cotswold limestones, preferring the deeper, more fertile soils where it often shares the ground with Upright Brome. There are three main problems with Tor-grass, apart from its aesthetic disadvantages. It is an unneighbourly grass, preferring to grow on its own in a dense sward, crowding out the more delicate plants under a thick pile of undecayed straw. It is the most unnutritious of grasses, becoming dry and completely unpalatable by the time its austere flowers appear in July. And given half a chance it will spread out of control, and may threaten to take over the pasture altogether. Once well established it is the devil to get rid of. On some downland Reserves Tor-grass has become the greatest biological and economic problem after scrub invasion.

The cause of this spread, much of which is recent, has been much debated. Undoubtedly the sudden relaxation of grazing in the 1950s favoured the plant, as did the now largely defunct practice of burning downland (ironically this was generally done to get rid of the matt of dead grass, but it produced ideal conditions for new Tor-grass shoots). Dutch scientists have found evidence that Tor-grass is benefiting from atmospheric pollution. Grassland can 'capture' atmospheric pollutants just as canopies of trees do, and in the case of nitrogen transfer it to the soil. Chalk grassland in Holland receives a dosage of up to 50 kg per hectare per year of nitrogen compounds captured from the air—about as much as farmers once used as fertiliser.

Under laboratory conditions, a dosage not much more than this caused a 50–80% increase in Tor-grass. This may help to account for the apparent scarcity (to judge from contemporary floras) of the species before the nineteenth century. One legend has it that Tor-grass was carried to this country in the paliasses (mattress covers) of soldiers returning from the Napoleonic Wars. It certainly lacks the 'balanced community' good manners of most of our native plants.

Dealing with Tor-grass is a problem that most chalk Reserve managers have had to face. The worst affected Reserves are those in the south-east. Wye seems in places to be over-run with it (although the situation is not as bad as it may look from a distance), and the Lewes Downs Reserves have a great deal more than is desirable. At Martin Down in Hampshire, on the other hand, Tor-grass is present only very locally, and at Barton Hills in Bedfordshire there is only a solitary patch, high up on a chalk hill like a lime-green postage stamp. Grazing experiments carried out at Aston Rowant and elsewhere in the 1960s showed that cattle and sheep are most reluctant to touch mature Tor-grass—it must be like eating hacksaw blades—unless they are actually starving (although the Dutch claim to have a breed of sheep called Mergollen that will tackle it). To control Tor-grass you have to persuade animals to graze it in the early spring, while the leaves are still tender and there is less alternative herbage to choose from. Early mowing has some effect, but it comes at the expense of the invertebrate interest and is in any case difficult or impossible on steep escarpments. In most places cattle have proved better at controlling Tor-grass than sheep, and this is another reason for the use of mixed-grazing on nature reserves. After 20 years of an all-sheep regime at Wye, the standing dead stems of Tor-grass were knee-high in places over a dense layer of partly decomposed litter. It looked, in Bob Russell's words, 'like the remains of a hay stack'. Ten years of cattle grazing in winter, initially with some follow-up grazing by sheep, has since reinstated much of the former species-rich turf. Serious infestations need a greater density of wintering cattle than would otherwise be desirable to bash through the mat of dead grass and, by grazing it hard, weaken its appalling vigour. This approach, which has worked particularly well at Mount Caburn on the Lewes Downs Reserve, carries the risk of poaching and enrichment from droppings and supplementary feed. Careful grazing can keep Tor-grass in check but rarely eliminates it altogether (and in terms of its value as shelter for some invertebrates, that may not be desirable in any case). Where Tor-grass is still patchy, herbicides may be worth trying, although great care has to be taken to avoid any drift onto nearby grassland.

LOOKING AFTER HEATHER

Heath is an old word—the *hethin* of the Anglo-Saxons—and describes a landscape that was all too familiar to the peoples who lived around the shores of the North Sea and the English Channel: barren, uncultivated, sour land, dominated by a single plant, appropriately named after its habitat and called heather. There are similar heaths farther south, along the Atlantic seaboard of France (especially in Brittany) and the north coast of Spain and Portugal, but Britain, Ireland, Holland and Denmark are the only European countries in which heather-dominated landscapes could once be found on mineral-poor soils from coast to coast at all points of the compass. In Britain it is

customary to distinguish between the cool, wet heather moors of the north, which are generally on waterlogged, peaty soils, and the warm, dry lowland heaths of southern and eastern England, which lie on free-draining sand with boggy bits in the hollows and valleys. In terms of their wildlife, the two are distinct habitats which both happen to be covered in heather. Here I am concerned only with the lowland heaths, one of our most attractive natural landscapes, especially in August when the lilacs and pinks of heather and its relatives vie with the golden yellow cushions of Western Gorse, the grey feathering of lichens and the scarlet and dun patches of Bell Heather and Bristle Bent. There are many special plants, animals and invertebrates that in England are more or less confined to lowland heath—Sand Lizard, Smooth Snake, Dartford Warbler and the Silver-studded Blue butterfly are among the best known. Despite our disgraceful record of destruction and mismanagement, England has become, by default, one of the more important European countries for heathland, with perhaps a fifth of the European total. We may have got rid of nearly three-quarters (72%) of our heaths during the last 150 years, but we have at least shown greater restraint than Holland (95%) or Denmark (98%) which have destroyed nearly all of theirs.

Heaths survived not because they were of great value to anyone, but because they were impossible to cultivate. Their traditional use was celebrated, famously, by Thomas Hardy in *The Return of the Native*, which describes the scrimping, gypsyish life on the heaths in about 1840—the cutting of bracken, gorse and turf, the roughest possible grazing for hardy breeds of cattle and ponies. But in Hardy's own lifetime, 'Egdon Heath' was under reclamation, here an attempt at ploughland, there a struggling square of pines. Today, there are just a few places left—Studland is one—where you can stand in heath stretching to the horizon and see the 'eternal' heath as Hardy would have known it.

Heath has become a true wilderness. While most wildlife habitats in England have some economic worth, heath has none: it is completely wild. Unfortunately you can build houses on it, and the Dorset heaths all lie uncomfortably close to the housing sprawl of Bournemouth and Poole, where development pressures are intense. What this amounts to is that the *only* way to save substantial chunks of Dorset heathland is to manage them as nature reserves. An early start was made in Dorset, thanks to the prescience of the then Regional Officer, Norman Moore. Three of the largest heaths, Holt Heath, Studland and Hartland Moor, as well as several smaller ones, are now Reserves. But, as Moore points out in his book, *The Bird of Time*, the Conservancy arrived too late to save anything but fragments of the great expanses of heath which existed in Hardy's day. The continuing losses of modern times—about 20% of Dorset's and Hampshire's heaths have been destroyed *since* 1960, including SSSIs like Horton Common—suggest that without a system of National Nature Reserves, our heaths might have gone the same way as Denmark's. About one-third of the Dorset heathland is now protected in nature reserves. Virtually all of it is designated as Sites of Special Scientific Interest. Elsewhere, heathland is well represented in the NNR series: English Nature looks after Surrey's largest and wettest heath at Thursley Common, and two of the largest surviving portions of the Sandling heaths of Suffolk lie at Walberswick and Westleton Heath NNRs. In the Breckland district of Norfolk and Suffolk, there are four NNRs, though only Cavenham Heath has substantial areas of heather-covered ground. The Dersingham Reserve near Sandringham, managed by English Nature, is one of the last of the North Norfolk heaths. Fortunately at the other great expanse of English heath, in western Cornwall, the Conservancy did get there in time. The Lizard NNR is now the largest heathland reserve in England, built up with great patience and perseverance over the past 15 years by Brian Bradley, the local land agent. Much of that peninsula's natural cover of heath is still intact, particularly on the central plateau of Goonhilly Downs where the glorious blossoming of Cornish Heath in July would put most heather rock gardens to shame. Finally, there is the Stiperstones NNR in Shropshire, a ridge of heather and frost-shattered rock which lies on the indeterminate divide between lowland heath and upland moor (complete with grouse). The only major gap in the series is the New Forest, whose unique set of laws has effectively protected its heaths from the fate of so many of those across the Avon in neighbouring Dorset.

On heathland Reserves, nature conservation is not only the primary function of the land but often the only function. But there is not always a unanimity on how they should be managed. The main aims of the heathland manager are to prevent the encroachment of scrub, trees and bracken, and to maintain the full range of natural vegetation, including each of the stages of the 20-year growth cycle of heather. But whereas the botanist might wish to achieve these aims by burning the heather on rotation, the herpetologist might object, citing evidence to prove that burning regimes are very harmful to reptiles, especially highly territorial ones, like the Sand Lizard. And while the herpetologist might want to clear away all of the scrub, and some of the heather, too, to provide bare sand for basking and burrowing, an ornithologist would be less enthusiastic, pointing out that scrub, in moderation, is important for the characteristic birds of the heath, such as Dartford Warbler, Woodlark, Stonechat and Nightjar—though he, too, might have reservations about burning. Heathland, then, is a habitat in which several influential groups of conservationists have interests that are potentially conflicting. All parties agree that the uncontrolled fires that can sweep across the heaths in dry weather represent a comprehensive disaster to wildlife against which all possible preventive measures should be taken. The most harmonious form of management would be light grazing, but in Dorset there are practical difficulties in finding suitable grazers. In the longer term, English Nature hopes to reintroduce grazing to some of its larger heathland Reserves.

How heaths are managed depends on their location and local circumstances. In general, those that are important for rare reptiles are not deliberately burned. Controlled burning is employed at Westleton Heath in Suffolk and the Stiperstones in Shropshire where this is not a consideration. At the former, burning has been an effective means of controlling scrub birch, while the Stiperstones has traditionally been burned to maintain areas of young, nutritious heather for sheep and grouse and to prevent 'wild fires'. On the Dorset heaths, the emphasis is on scrub clearance and fire prevention. One of the Reserves, Morden Bog, cannot in any case be burned because of the risk to the nearby conifer plantations, and has therefore become a non-intervention area in which there is no management at all apart from the maintenance of firebreaks. One alternative to burning and grazing is to mow the heather close to the ground in winter, using a tractor and forage harvester. The RSPB uses this technique extensively on its large Reserve at Arne in Dorset, and the Conservancy has experimented with it in places where the ground is sufficiently level and free of large stones. It is a labour-intensive form of management, however—the RSPB reckons on mowing about 1 ha of heath in 4 hours. At the Dersingham Reserve, Phil Holms uses a small tractor with a rear-mounted flail mower to cut the heather. This breaks the cut material into small fragments, which will rot down reasonably quickly. This technique works best on relatively short rotations, whereas forage harvesters will work well in relatively old stands of heather.

The Lizard heaths are more akin to those of the New Forest than those in Dorset or Suffolk in that they are still used for rough grazing. Burning, of a drop-match-and-retire variety, is traditional here, and in the mild, maritime climate of west Cornwall, the vegetation generally recovers quickly amid spectacular bursts of orchids and other flowers. The Conservancy's main concern is for the beneficial grazing to continue, against the economic trend, and it has stepped in to help local farmers through investment in a major programme of stock fencing, and through participation in conservation schemes in which grants are paid to promote or maintain farming sympathetic to local conditions and wildlife.

Let us look more closely at the matter of fire. Heath is unusual among British vegetation in that it catches light easily in dry weather, especially the old, 'leggy' stands which contain a large proportion of dead or dry wood. Burning, in patches of 2 ha or less and aiming to cover the whole ground every 10–12 years, used to be a traditional means of improving the livestock grazing, and it also helps to make the land more fireproof by limiting the area of tinder-dry old heather. This can be beneficial to wildlife in that the rotation creates a series of stages of growth, analogous to coppice in woodland, from recently burned ground, through dense young heather to the more open bushes of mature heather. Many plants, including such local specialities as Dorset Heath and Marsh Gentian, take advantage of the bare ground and gaps in the heather to flower and set seed. It also seems to suit some invertebrates, including that pretty and hopelessly sedentary butterfly, the Silver-studded Blue. The best time to burn is in February or March, after frost and wind have dried the vegetation but before new growth has begun. Unlicensed burning is prohibited from 31 March (or 15 April in upland areas) to 1 November. The Conservancy generally prefers a longer rotation to that used by graziers. Westleton Heath is divided into compartments with different burn rotations, varying from 5 to 20 years. The site manager, Cliff Waller prefers to burn on frosty ground, which minimises any risk to the roots. Careful burning against the wind, known as back-burning, aims to clear away all the vegetation above ground while leaving the roots and the seed bank in the surface layers unscathed.

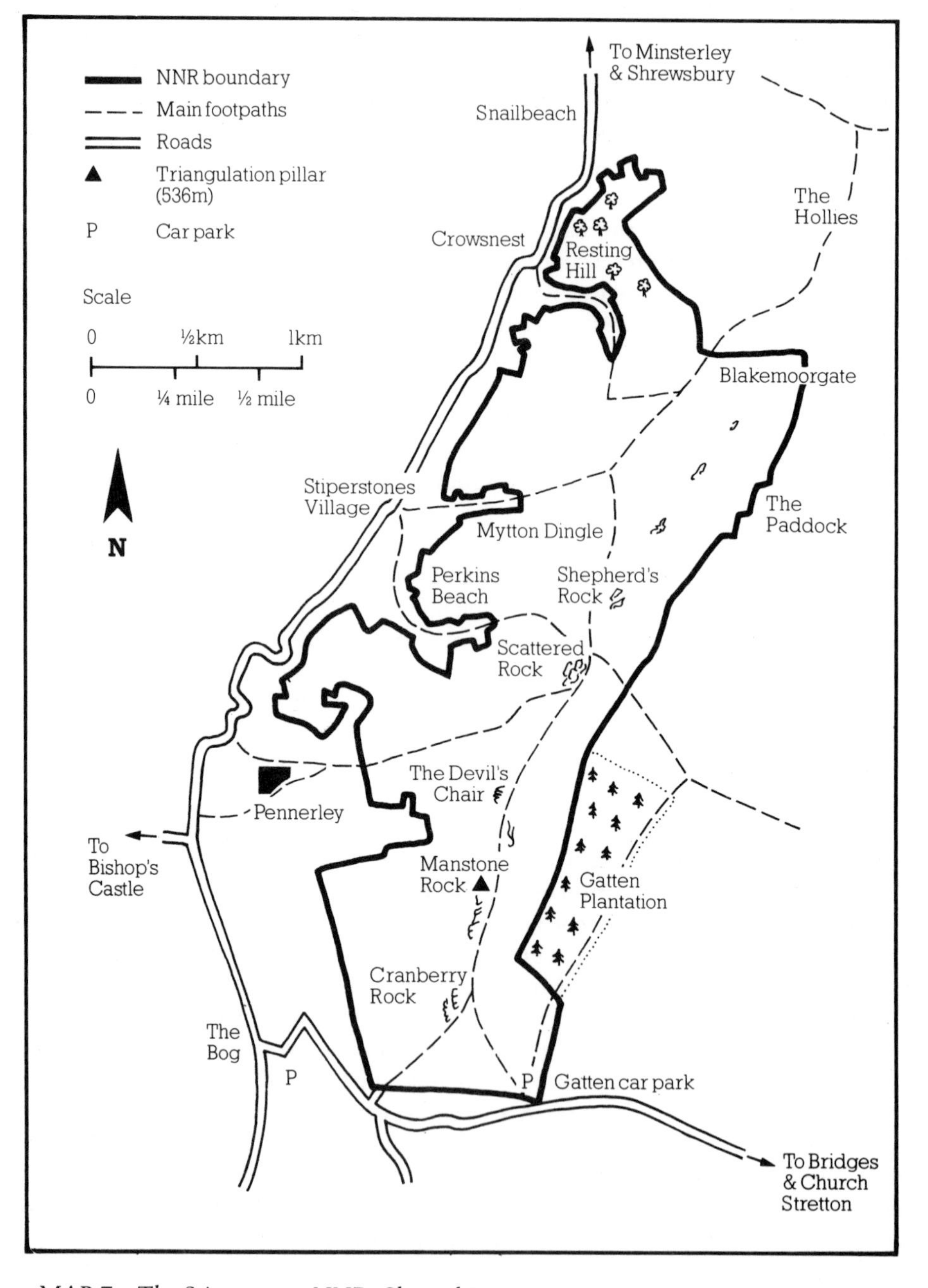

MAP 7 *The Stiperstones NNR, Shropshire*

At the Stiperstones, Tom Wall intends to burn each patch of heather once every 15 years. On the gentler slopes a tractor and swipe is used to mow the ground, but on the steep ground, or where heather and bracken hide an archipelago of boulders, wheeled vehicles are out of the question. Burning here is a most laborious task. First, he must give neighbours and other parties at least 24 hours written notice of his intention to burn: which means the dispatching of 40 or so letters. On the appointed day, the paraffin burner with its hose, spout and heavy fuel cylinder has to be unloaded from the Land Rover and hauled into position on the hillside while the beaters take up their positions. Back-burning is rarely possible, but Tom attempts to burn *up* the hill, in small patches to minimise the risk of soil erosion and bracken invasion. Good clean 'textbook' burns are difficult because of the broken nature of the ground. Regular burning helps, however, to maintain good public relations. Not only does it improve the grazing, but also results in vintage crops of whinberries, which flourish on the recently burned patches. Many end up inside delicious pies sold at the nearby Stiperstones Inn—one of the few culinary examples of 'nature reserve produce'.

One of the best reasons for burning is to prevent that scourge of the heaths, wild fires. Unlike most of us, heathland managers have good reason to dread a long, hot summer. There were numerous devastating fires in the dry summers of 1959, 1976 and 1984. During August and September 1976, Hartland Moor and Thursley Common blazed from end to end, 80 ha of Lizard heathland went up in flames and the Stiperstones smouldered for so long that the local fire brigade opened a fish and chip account at the local inn. At Studland, there is often a plume of smoke somewhere on warm summer weekends and Bank Holiday, when the Reserve is over-run by a tide of pleasure seekers. Large numbers of people can be helpful when it comes to putting out fires (Studland's nudist colony has an astonishing record of bravery in fire-fighting), but their parked cars all too often block the access routes to the heath, and careless picnic stoves, or cigarettes and matches thrown from car windows, are common causes of fires. Stolen cars, dumped and set alight by the thieves, have started fires at Holt Heath. The most bizarre incident was of a woman who set *herself* alight and succeeded in burning 3 ha of heath as well. It is small wonder that the Dorset wardens Mike Tuck and Rees Cox regularly 'get out our prayer mats on Friday afternoon and pray for a wet weekend'.

Fire precautions, greatly improved since 1976, have reduced the number and extent of uncontrolled blazes. The last big one was at Godlingstone Heath at Studland in 1984. Efficient fire-fighting means tackling the problem on three fronts. There must be an adequate provision of firebreaks, water holes and access tracks. Fire-fighting equipment is stored close to the Reserves, and maintained at full readiness. Essential equipment ranges from beaters on-site to land rovers equipped with radios, pumps and water tanks. Mike Tuck and Rees Cox have been authorised by the Chief Constable to mount emergency flashing blue lights and klaxons to their Land Rovers. And finally there has to be a good working relationship with the local fire brigade. One of the most significant advances of recent years is the willingness of fire brigades to treat heathland as an emergency on a par with burning buildings, and to train their crews accordingly. This was not always so in the past (see below) but fire crews, especially in Dorset, have become increasingly skilled in the special techniques needed for tackling fires on heaths.

Firebreaks can be created by rotovating the surface, or by regular mowing to keep the heather short, green and relatively fireproof. Their purpose is at least as much to provide access for vehicles as it is to 'break' fires (which, for the worst fires, they don't). Mike Tuck prefers the term 'access tracks' as it is less misleading. Whatever they are called, these gaps in the heather take up a lot of valuable space, so it is fortunate that they have some conservation value as well. Carefully sited breaks along sunny bankside 'hot spots' are often used by Sand Lizards and burrowing insects, although the presence of the former restricts the rotovating season to May, when the lizards are out of hibernation but have not yet laid their eggs. At Cavenham Heath, rotovated strips have proven so successful a means of regenerating heather that clearing strips on a fixed rotation has become a technique of management. Breckland heather seems to benefit from occasional disturbance: one of the few heather-dominated parts of Brettenham Heath NNR is along the route of a gas main, put in by the gas board 20 years ago. The effective width of a break can be reduced by regularly mowing the heather on either side, as at Westleton Heath, where the rotovated sand track is only 1.8 m wide. Much of the regular clearance is done by contractors, but the firebreaks at the Lizard have now become so intricate that the work has to be done in-house.

Managing gorse is another of the heath manager's arts. While the plant can be a pernicious nuisance, rapidly spreading over land on which grazing has suddenly been abandoned, few managers would wish to eradicate it completely. In the past it was considered quite a valuable plant, useful for fodder and for kindling-wood, and hence was tolerated. At the Stiperstones, commoners used to gather gorse in sacks and roll them downhill to their cottages; the dry brash was particularly useful for boiling water. There are several ways of throttling back the natural vigour of gorse. One is to trim and layer the plant as a roadside hedge, as at Holt Heath and Hartland Moor where it provides a useful barrier between the road and the Reserve. Another is to cut or burn the plant to the ground once in a while, as a form of coppice. Recovery is generally rapid, so long as the surface litter is removed, and the prickly regrowth helps to safeguard the more tender shoots of heather from rabbits and deer. Regular cutting helps to provide the small, compact bushes, about 1–1.5 m tall, that Dartford Warblers like to nest in. To clear the plant altogether, it is generally necessary to cut the regrowth by hand, as has been done at the Lizard in an attempt to restore natural grassland.

Clearing scrub is not so much a skill as a necessary steady plod, or rather a canter along a belt moving in the opposite direction in which one has to run hard to stand still. At the Suffolk Sandlings the main invader is birch, which has already turned many a former heath into a dull, damp wood. At Westleton Heath, 18,000 birches and other trees were removed in 1991 alone, which took two men, armed with mattocks and chain-saws, a total of 8 weeks. The stumps are generally treated with a herbicide, such as trichoryl, in a diesel oil emulsion. On the Dorset heaths, and at Dersingham in Norfolk, the main problems are pine and Rhododendron seeding in from nearby woods and plantations. A scatter of mature pines is generally tolerated by managers for their aesthetic beauty—old Scots Pines and heaths seem to belong together, regardless of whether or not the former is strictly native to the area. Groups of pines or birches can also enhance considerably the value of a heath for nesting birds, as can a screen of scrub between the heath and a neighbouring wood. At Dersingham, Phil Holms 'coppices' scrub birches to create dense foliage with shaded patches of bare ground beneath, where Nightjars like to nest. Much of the scrub clearance on heathland Reserves, as elsewhere, is carried out by conservation volunteers and, while they lasted, by Manpower Services teams, with contractors being hired for the heavier jobs.

One Reserve whose value has been transformed by scrub clearance from an ugly sister to a veritable Cinderella is Holton Heath in Dorset. On the face of it, this is one of the more surprising Reserves, a heath, true enough, but one which had become overgrown with pines and birches, pitted with the ruins of a munitions factory and its railway system and surrounded by an industrial estate, a busy road and a main railway line. But despite its unprepossessing location, Holton Heath holds good numbers of Sand Lizards and Smooth Snakes, has an excellent insect fauna, including rare dragonflies and burrowing wasps, and a number of rare plants. A noisome heap of fly ash, asbestos and waste vinyl from the Decca gramophone factory harbours perhaps the biggest population of the Jersey Cudweed in Britain. Even so, it is unlikely that the site would have been made a National Nature Reserve had it not been offered by the Rank Organisation on a tempting 1000-year lease in exchange for a mill of peppercorns. Having taken on responsibility for it, the Conservancy had to turn Holton Heath into a nature reserve. Mike Tuck's approach to the half-grown pines and other invasives that were threatening to choke the heath was to enlist others to help in the task of clearing by declaring: 'Here's cheap wood. Help yourself!' Many did so; the Water Authority took some of the brash to make into fascines for controlling riverbank erosion; locals cut up logs for firewood; and timber contractors paid up to £9 a tonne for it. By investing in a bark peeler and saw bench, Mike himself set about converting some of the logs into fence stakes for use on the Reserve. Indeed, if only the Treasury allowed the Conservancy to channel income into Reserve maintenance costs, Holton Heath would now run itself. After 10 years of hard work, much of the ground is now heath again, the heather having shown an amazing resilience and ability to spring back from the dead, once the overshading trees were removed.

THE GREAT FIRE AT HARTLAND MOOR

Between 14 and 21 August 1976, two-thirds of Hartland Moor was destroyed by fire, the worst single disaster ever suffered on a National Nature Reserve. Everything in the path of the flames perished, the soil was scorched to the depth of the heather roots and the vital bank of seeds in the surface layers was lost. What was the previous week a glorious patchwork of late summer colours had become a blackened, smoking desert. Anyone who saw Hartland Moor after the great fire might have been forgiven for writing-off the whole area. But other heaths have known catastrophic fires, and although the Moor took a long time to recover, and there were surprises along the way, today it bears no obvious scars of the events of August 1976. But the drama of that week is unlikely ever to be forgotten by the participants, two of whom came close to losing their lives. There are always lessons to be learned from disasters, and at least one legacy of this fire was that fire-fighting measures were greatly improved.

Before describing that memorable week, a few words about the Reserve. Hartland Moor was one of the earliest National Nature Reserves, having been established in 1954 to serve as an 'outdoor laboratory' for the nearby Furzebrook research station and 'to conserve one of the best remaining examples of southern lowland heath, with its associated wetland areas'. The Moor lies on gently undulating ground, rising to a 30-m knoll at one end, and enclosing a shallow Y-shaped valley, full of Sphagnum moss and bog plants. Among the more significant of the research projects carried out there was a long-term study of ant populations by Dr M V Brian, based on permanent plots near the knoll. Like all Dorset heathland Reserves, Hartland Moor's management plan included elaborate fire precautions, including a network of broad firebreaks and water holes, and access routes for Land Rovers and fire engines. At the time of the fire, the wardening team, based only a mile from the Reserve at Slepe Farm, could call on two long wheel-base Land Rovers, each with a 120-gallon water tank and spray pump with a reel hose, as well as a back-up short wheel-base Land Rover with a 60-gallon tank. The Reserve's workers that year included Mike Tuck and Rees Cox, two estate workers, Laurie Clark and Derick Rigg, Laurie's girlfriend, Sylvia, and a voluntary helper, Andrew Helford. In normal weather, there were enough people immediately available to tackle most fires, so long as the latter were reported in time. Unfortunately the conditions of weather and ground in August 1976 were exceptional. The preceding 12 months had been the driest on record, with below-average rain in all but 3 months. On top of already dry conditions came the famous drought of summer 1976, caused by a block of high pressure over Ireland which diverted the usual rainy westerlies well north of the British Isles. The heathland wardens were on alert for the inevitable fires. It was a question of 'when' rather than 'if'.

Mike Tuck takes up the story from a diary he made shortly afterwards:

> It was 1640 on Saturday, 14 August 1976. The task for all the staff that day was erecting the boundary fence at Slepe Farm, while I was putting in the hanging and hasp post for the front gate. I was just thinking that it was about time for a cup of tea when the first smoke was spotted. I stayed to telephone the fire service whilst the estate workers went off to the fire ground. I had considerable difficulty in explaining the exact location of the fire to the fire service. Having collected Sylvia, I contacted Rees [Rees Cox, the warden of the nearby Studland Heath NNR] by radio and then set off to the Moor myself.
>
> I arrived to find the flames travelling very fast indeed. Taking over the hose nozzle from Andrew, I asked Laurie to start filling the long wheel-base [Landrover's] water tank from the short wheel-base's tank. The smoke and heat were already becoming difficult to cope with, although, by now, the western flank of the fire was nearly extinguished. Andrew tried to beat out some of the flames flaring up again behind us. Derick took off in one Landrover to refill the tank, leaving Sylvia and myself training the hose at the front of the fire. We saw the fire service coming along the old tramway and hoped that they would make a start on the eastern flank. Derick returned with a full tank of water. We could still contain it.
>
> I sent Andrew off to find out what the fire service was doing.
>
> The smoke and heat were getting worse and the front of the fire widened. Andrew returned to say that the brigade was only looking on, and not fighting the fire. We were losing control and the fire crossed the fire break

behind us. We discovered at this point that we had used up all our water. We had lost it!

I went to see the officer-in-charge. He was from Portland, and said his brigade had never attended a heathland fire before. [By sheer bad luck, the local fire brigade was away fighting a fire in Bournemouth.] Their hoses had been burned before they had a chance to put water through them. I asked them to take a light pump to the front of the fire and set it in the water hole at the eastern end of Great Knoll. Derick and Laurie removed the water tank from the Landrover and lifted in the pump with several lengths of hose. I asked Derick to take a fireman with him and try and stop the fire attacking Great Knoll. Rees arrived from Studland and started to work on the western front, while I stayed on the east side, both of us filling our Landrovers from the fire engine. We were at last beginning to make an impression, but only by using a great deal of water. Suddenly Derick came through on the radio: he was completely surrounded by flames! I radioed to Rees that I was going to rescue Derick and set off. I could hardly see through the smoke in front of me and put on the klaxon to warn anyone in front that a vehicle was approaching. I found Derick under the Landrover in an island of unburnt heather. He was still using the hose to protect the Landrover and himself. He had been unable to get a fireman to come with him.

By now the flames were on top of the Knoll and I told Rees that there was no longer any point in our remaining here. We would go to the western side of the Knoll and attempt to hold the fire in the mown break surrounding it.

More helpers had arrived by now, mostly visitors and local farmers. They organised a back burn along the western fire break on Great Knoll. Many birds were overhead picking off insects fleeing from the flames. The main fire front now came upon us and we managed to hold it at the mown break with beaters and water. Flames had crossed Soldiers Road and were now burning through a field of rye.

It was now getting dark. One of the farmer's dogs had been lost in the smoke. Eventually both flanks were put out. Elizabeth Olivant arrived with coffee, the first drink we had had since lunchtime. We met up with the RSPB fire tender and crew who had been working on the southern end of the western flank, unbeknown to us. By 0230 everyone was searching their pockets for one pound notes in order to use Purbeck Motor Co's petrol vending machine for filling up the vehicles. After doing so, we returned to the fire ground to damp down and extinguish the isolated outbreaks of flames that continually erupted. At 0600 we went home to get some food, leaving Rees on the heath.

On returning at 0800, fire and fire engines were everywhere. I approached the officer-in-charge (yet another one with no experience of heathland fires) and discussed the possibility of setting one of their light pumps in the water hole on the south-western side. I stressed the importance of the ant research compartment which the flames were now approaching. Two tenders were called away to deal with another fire leaving the remaining two tenders and four Landrovers behind, plus our own tenders.

I also asked the Police Officer to inform the Ambulance HQ that we had a major incident, so that they could place a vehicle on standby. This was done through an exdirectory number previously arranged.

My Landrover and a fire service one met at the ploughed break and began wetting the heather on the south side. Rees positioned himself between the bog and the ant compartment to stop it crossing from that point. The fire came at us across the ridge of Hospital Heath. In a moment we were engulfed in flames and smoke. We quickly retreated to the ploughed break, but then realised that Laurie was nowhere to be seen. I went back into the smoke, dragged him out and bundled him into a vehicle. We cut the hoses and beat a hasty retreat up the break in our vehicles, the fire chasing us all the way. We managed to get out on to the road, where Laurie was taken to a police car. Luckily the ambulance arrived at this point and took him to hospital.

The fire was completely out of control again, consuming everything in its path, including the power lines crossing the Reserve. All traffic was halted on Soldiers Road since the power lines were now sagging dangerously. The fire jumped the road again, burning towards Mr Bacon's house. Two tenders went off to deal with this. I went back down the fire break to retrieve any nozzles and hoses that had not got burnt. I met one of the farmers who had helped on Saturday. He had lost his dog and asked if we could keep an eye open for it. I refilled my Landrover from a tender. Mr Bacon's partner was out on the Reserve with his tractor and scraper blade, trying to prevent any spread through the peat on the north side of Little Knoll.

Sunday roast lunch arrived on a plate for one of Wareham's fireman (courtesy of his wife) and my wife brought food for the NCC staff. Only isolated patches were burning now and Sunday night was spent dealing with these.

On Monday morning, 16 August, I met up with the Portland Officer who we dealt with on Saturday. He had not been off duty since and told me he now knew a little more about heathland fires . . .

The fire blazed on, more intermittently, for five more days. At one point the army was called in to form a makeshift firebreak using a pair of tanks equipped with bulldozer blades to shovel away the potentially flammable surface peat. The hydraulics of one of the tanks broke down, and it later became stuck fast in the bog for two days, partly blocking the road. The Fire Service remained on duty until Friday, damping the ground and extinguishing any sudden flaring of the fire. The vehicles had to keep moving, however, as the heat was such that rubber tyres started to smoulder after a few minutes. The body of the farmer's dog was recovered; it had been trapped by the flames. The last smouldering areas of peat were finally extinguished on Tuesday, 23 August, 10 days after the start of the fire. Some 180 ha—nearly two-thirds of the Reserve—was categorised as 'severely burnt'. Much of it, commented Mike Tuck, looked very like an industrial slag heap.

One of the lessons learned from the fire was to increase the number of water holes. Another was to have a permanent urn of tea standing by for the fire-fighting crew! The most important outcome, however, was a much improved liaison between the Fire Service and the Conservancy, and a much higher priority given to training servicemen in the techniques of heathland fire-fighting. Without more fire-fighting vehicles, and more water at the critical moment, it is unlikely that much more could have been done to control this particular fire.

Full recovery was clearly going to take a long time, especially since heavy rain that autumn had eroded great ruts in the blackened soil. Researchers from Furzebrook kept the precious ant colonies going with treats of sugar and cheese in plastic trays, much to the glee of the local press (and to the appreciation of the local badgers). The less severely burned areas began to regenerate almost immediately, especially on the wet heath, where fire-resistant plants like Cotton-grass and Moor-grass (*Molinia*) grow. By the following summer, much of the moor had become a mass of Rosebay Willowherb, a plant hitherto barely present at all, but which was living up to its old name of 'bonfire weed'. The Reserve staff tried swiping the plant with scythes, which was hopeless, or blasting it with flame guns, which only succeeded in bursting open the pods and letting forth a blizzard of fresh seed. They were becoming resigned to a long reign of the Willowherb when, in August 1978, small, shiny blue beetles were noted on the foliage, which turned out to be the Willowherb-eating Chrysomelid, *Haltica oleracea*. The following year, the beetles had increased to plague numbers, 30 or more per plant, all busy perforating and shredding the leaves and devouring the pods. By the close of the season the Willowherb jungle was a yellowing, wilted wreck. Next year, both the Willowherb and the beetle had gone. Gradually the moor regained its old form and variety, and Sand Lizards and other former residents began to recolonise the site. Today, Hartland Moor is much as it was before the fire, give or take a few stubbornly bare patches, a dark line in the soil and the clumps of Willowherb along the open sandy banks.

BRACKEN-BASHING

Brettenham Heath in the Breckland of south-west Norfolk, is one of the less dramatic National Nature Reserves. From the vantage point of the busy main road that forms its northern boundary one looks over several hundred hectares of pinkish-grey grass, varied only by a scatter of pines and birch trees, patches of bracken and greener stony ground where the underlying chalk reaches the surface. On a windy day in mid-summer, when the grass, whose strange colour is the result of the massed inflorescences of Wavy Hair-grass, is in constant motion, the effect is a rippling shimmer, like shot silk. There is little here to suggest that Brettenham Heath was the battleground of a 10-year struggle with bracken, which at one time all but engulfed the original heath. Yet it is on such relatively little known 'Cinderella' reserves that some of the most influential management techniques have been tried and tested.

The Conservancy took a lease on the heath in 1983, to save it from being turned into a pig farm. At the time, there were misgivings, not so much about the site's importance as about the management implications of its fallen state. But dry Breckland heath is no longer so widespread that conservationists could contemplate losing several hundred

hectares more. Although the bracken was in places so high that it could swallow up a Land Rover, its dominance was comparatively recent and partly the result of a fire. Experts considered that the heath was still recoverable, although the size of the task seemed awesome. Before starting on the bracken, it was first necessary to cut the invading hawthorn bushes down to the stumps to permit the use of tractor-drawn machinery. Then it was a question of repeated cutting, over and over again, to weaken the reservoirs of food, mainly starch, that the bracken can draw from its underground network of rhizomes. These contain considerably more food reserves than is needed for a single year's frond production. Finally, once the bracken is beaten, it becomes possible to reintroduce sheep to maintain the open heath and prevent the reinvasion of the fern from its stronghold in the surrounding woods.

Dense bracken is generally unwelcome on nature reserves. Although bracken has value as cover and shelter, as the host of a number of scarce insects, and as protection for plants in areas of heavy grazing, heavy infestations reduce the wildlife communities of heath or permanent grassland to sterile litter and deep shade. Having once established itself, bracken has a way of becoming permanent, for its accumulated litter, and, probably, inhibiting substances in the fronds, make this one of the most pernicious of wild plants.

Fortunately, for Brettenham Heath, there was a great deal of scientific research on bracken control to draw from. Rob Marrs and John Lowday, then of Monks Wood Field Station, had for several years been studying the problem of bracken on heathland. The short cut to bracken control is to spray the herbicide asulam onto the fully expanded fronds. Asulam is transported by the rhizome system to the underground buds, which it kills most effectively. Unfortunately a few buds always escape, and the bracken may bounce back from the dead. When using asulam it is as well to avoid half-measures. The bracken should be drenched in the stuff from a knapsack sprayer or, ground permitting, by tractor and boom. It can be softened up first by repeated cutting in the preceding 2–3 months, and by cutting it again the following winter. At the Dersingham Reserve, where much of the invading bracken clings to steep morainic slopes inaccessible to vehicles, the herbicide was even sprayed (on a windless day) from a helicopter. In most cases, however, the Conservancy prefers mechanical control to herbicides. At Brettenham, Marrs' advice was to cut the fronds at 4–6 week intervals between June and September to exhaust the underground food supply. His work suggested that this treatment would take at least 3 years to be effective: bracken control is not quick nor easy nor cheap.

The fight to reclaim Brettenham Heath was undertaken by the Reserve manager, Malcolm Wright, and his estate workers, using a tractor-drawn swipe armed with three rotating blades, held just above ground level by hydraulic linkage. In the early days, Malcolm used an old County Ford forestry tractor with big wheels, front and rear. Driving into dense bracken with this machine was somewhat hazardous, with the tractor lurching over bumps and hollows and occasionally threatening to overturn. If driven too fast over uneven ground it would start to bounce and make the driver wish he had worn a crash helmet. Fortunately a superior tractor was acquired in 1990 and with this machine swiping has become a relatively comfortable activity which goes well with the test match commentary on the fitted radio!

On the relatively level ground at Brettenham it was possible to cut about 80 ha a month. The open heart of the heath was tackled first, and the programme was later extended to some of the tree-invaded peripheral areas. The cut fronds were left to wither away. For the follow-up grazing the heath was enclosed by wire fences and divided into four compartments for stock control purposes. The unsightliness of such fences on the open ranges of the Breck is unfortunate, but so long as Breckland nature reserves remain isolated from the surrounding land, it is hard to find an alternative. After 9 years of work, Brettenham Heath has been transformed, and some of the pattern of the underlying soils has returned, including intriguing circles of green grass that may date back to the late Ice Age. The patches of sparse, low bracken that still appears can now be tackled by a single cut in late summer.

When the battle against bracken is won, there remains the job of removing the litter and persuading the heathland vegetation to regenerate. Bracken may leave a calling card in the form of semi-permanent soil enrichment, especially in naturally nutrient-poor soils. This is probably the reason why Brettenham Heath is now covered in grass rather than heather (although heather is now regenerating well on the eastern side of the reserve). At Thursley Common, Simon Nobes has got rid of the bracken litter by simply burning it, which seems to have had no harmful side-effects. Experiment there suggests that what hurts bracken more than repeated swiping is mechanical damage to the rhizomes. Rotovating the ground on a dry hot day in late summer exposes the rhizomes to dessication, and later to frost. Chisel ploughing has also proved a useful technique, especially on ground where surface disturbance is, for one reason or another, undesirable. In both cases it is important to remove the litter first to avoid 'manuring' the lower levels of the soil.

The Conservancy can usually afford to live with controllable quantities of bracken, and indeed some bracken can be desirable. Short swards among the shelter of low bracken, which is Cliff Waller's aim at Walberswick NNR in Suffolk, offer good nesting habitat for a number of declining ground-nesting birds, especially the Woodlark. Regular annual mowing there maintains the right mix. Cliff has also hired a forage harvester to remove the dry bracken litter mechanically. Some of it was sold to a commercial grower of Azaleas and Rhododendrons for use as bedding material. The main drawback of forage harvesters, apart from their expense, is that they are slow to operate and can be used only on comparatively level, rock-free ground. On the brackeny hillsides of the Bovey Valley Woods NNR in Devon, bracken is cut annually in plots about 10 m across, and the surface scratched to encourage flushes of violets, the foodplant of the now rare and endangered High Brown Fritillary. For this beautiful butterfly, the existence of a light canopy of bracken seems to be essential. As in most aspects of nature conservation management, bracken control is a question of balance. There are few native plants so pernicious that outright eradication forms the only sensible solution.

CHAPTER 8

Wilderness and Wet

HOLKHAM National Nature Reserve was until recently the largest in England, covering over 4000 ha of dune, saltmarsh and rough grassland along the North Norfolk shoreline between Burnham Norton and Blakeney Point. It is in effect several nature reserves rolled into one: the late summer acres of shimmering sea lavender on saltmarshes at Wells, the dunes of Holkham Bay with their crest of mature pines, and the miles of broad foreshore stretching eastwards towards Blakeney Point. The big sandy beaches of Holkham attract half a million visitors every year. Perhaps it is just as well that no more than a small fraction of them go there to watch wildlife.

English Nature owns none of this land. That such a large area could be declared a nature reserve is due to the generosity and co-operation of the Earl of Leicester, Lord Coke and the tenants of Holkham estate. Unusually, the Reserve 'package' happened to include 704 ha of improved farmland, whose interest for wildlife was confined largely to the network of drainage dykes that divide the fields. This area had been gradually reclaimed from the sea by successive Cokes of Holkham, a name made familiar to every schoolchild from the famous Thomas Coke of Holkham, one of the leading agricultural improvers of the eighteenth century. The belt of Corsican Pines, the most prominent landmark on this part of the coast, was planted to protect the reclaimed land from windblown sand—it represents one of the earliest attempts to stabilise sand dunes using the roots and shelter of trees. Until the Second World War these fields were permanent pasture. Modern farming practices led to the lowering of the water table and, by 1985, nearly half of the area had been ploughed and seeded with grass or cereal crops.

Under the terms of the 1967 Reserve agreement, the Conservancy had some influence on the management of these fields, but no say in the drainage regime. It was therefore unable to improve their value for wildlife. However, the Wildlife and Countryside Act 1981 provided better opportunities for concluding management agreements on areas in agricultural production. By the 1980s, interest in coastal grazing marsh was growing—partly because of Britain's growing international obligations on bird-rich wetlands, partly because the march of agriculture had placed the future of much of our remaining wet grassland in jeopardy. The Holkham estate agreed to allow the Conservancy to try to restore grazing marsh as an asset for the nature reserve. At the time this was a new venture for the NCC, although some results were available from experience on RSPB reserves, and from across the North Sea in Holland. The aim was to raise the water level to within 10 cm of the surface and regulate the system of dykes to prevent the fields from drying out in the summer. The lowest fields were to form winter floodland, and a small area would form a permanently flooded 'scrape'. The main beneficiaries were expected to be the Brent, White-fronted and Pink-footed Geese, together with nesting birds like Snipe and Redshank, which have declined over much of Britain because of field drainage and the loss of permanent pasture.

The task depended on the willingness of the Holkham tenants to change their farming practices voluntarily, and on the ability of the then warden, David Henshilwood, to put

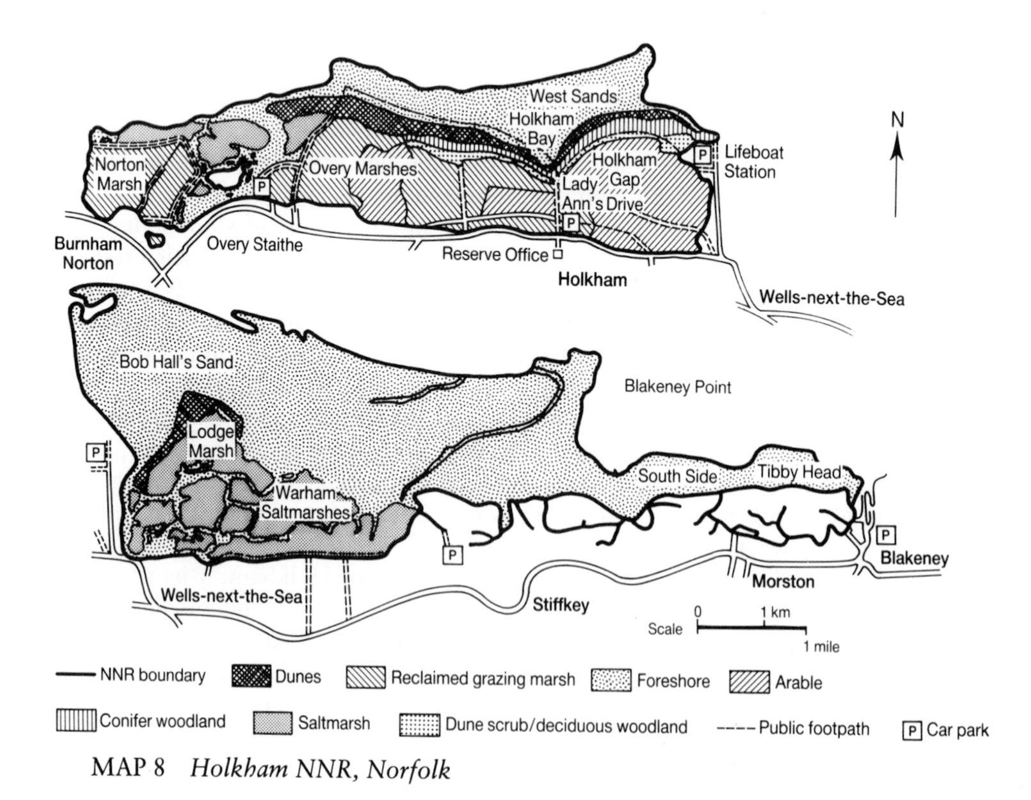

MAP 8 *Holkham NNR, Norfolk*

38. Above left: *Gowk Bank*. 39. Above right: *White Beak-sedge, Bog-bean and Pudnore Pool at Thursley Common.*
40. Below: *Small-leaved Lime with standard oaks at Swanton Novers.*

41. Top: *Monks Wood, Cambridgeshire.*
42. Left: *High Leys meadows.*
43. Above: *Collyweston Great Wood.*

44. Above: *Oxlip flowers at Hales Wood.*
45. Right: *Cotswold Commons and Beechwoods.*
46. Below: *The Holy Island causeway at Lindisfarne.*

47. Above: *Wyre Forest*. 48. Above right: *Pyefleet Channel at the Colne Estuary*.
49. Below: *Pevensey Levels*.

into practice a decidedly experimental field of conservation management. There were two main strands to the work. Firstly the water draining into the Reserve from spring-fed streams had to be retained by internal sluices, replacing the old system in which the water flowed straight through and out into the sea. Secondly the level of cattle grazing had to be reduced. Grazing was still necessary, however, to produce suitable sward conditions for geese and nesting waders. Research suggested that a density of only one or two cows per 0.4 ha in summer was the appropriate level.

Although it took several years to complete, the experiment at Holkham proved a remarkable success. The experience gained there has since been put to good use on other nature reserves on grazing marsh, such as Walberswick and the Pevensey Levels. The key to the work is to obtain a thorough understanding of the way in which water flows through the area, in order to establish the best water control points. The work was simplified by the use of flexible elbow-bend pipes which could be used to revitalise old defective culverts and sluices without the need to build new dams (though some of the original earth dams at Holkham have since been strengthened). Once these were in place, the right degree of flooding could be obtained without further ado. Not everything went according to plan, of course. Some water obstinately flowed the wrong way onto neighbouring land. And sorting out the grazing was fraught with problems, since the tenure was divided into 10 annual 'blocks'. Fortunately new arrangements were worked out in time and a cattle-less *interregnum* was avoided. The main job now is the annual 'bashing' of the ragwort and thistles that have inevitably increased with the change to lower rates of stocking.

There have been immediate and, in some cases, dramatic increases in visiting and nesting birds, including exciting ones like Marsh Harrier and Avocet. In 1993, the nesting density of Redshanks at Holkham—at around 15 pairs to the square kilometre—was as high as anywhere in Britain, and although Snipe still have a little catching up to do, they too are now nesting in good numbers. The greater depth of water in the dykes has benefited birds like Little Grebe and Coot. The biggest increases have been achieved by geese and Wigeon. In 1939, the area had been a well-known sanctuary for Pink-footed Goose, but the bird objected to wartime disturbances and deserted this part of the coast, not returning until the 1980s. Today around 6000 Pink-feet and as many Brent Geese graze the winter marshland of Holkham, using it as a refuge for inland feeding. The increase in Wigeon has also been spectacular: from about 250 to some 7000 birds each winter. It is possible to monitor breeding territories and nests in some detail at Holkham, since the extra staff needed in the summer months to warden this popular Reserve can spend much of the quieter mid-week days watching birds. The office of the present site manager, Ron Harold, rather resembles, I fancy, Montgomery's caravan at El Alamein: its walls are covered in charts and maps, with circles and little flags marking the territory of every known breeding pair of marsh birds, from Marsh Harriers down to the humblest Coot.

The Holkham experiment was one of the first successful attempts to transform a large, relatively dull area of land into one of high value to wildlife. At the same time it demonstrated that such land could still be of interest to graziers, even on a system of annual licences and within the restrictions of a nature reserve management plan. Although the original idea was to restore marshland habitat, the scheme in practice has focused mainly on the needs of birds, although other plants and animals have certainly benefited from the higher water levels. The experiment brought the management of a National Nature Reserve significantly closer to that of an RSPB reserve. It signalled the Conservancy's abandonment of the *status quo*, that balance of habitats which existed on the day the Reserve was declared, by introducing the notion of large-scale manipulation to create new habitats. It had enormous implications for the future of National Nature Reserves.

Wetland restoration was taken a step further at the Swale NNR in Kent. The Swale Reserve, along the eastern tip of the Isle of Sheppey, was declared in 1976, the year in which both the Ramsar Convention on wetland conservation came into force in the United Kingdom and the Council of Europe's annual crusade happened to be devoted to wetlands. Wilderness and wet were in many people's thoughts that year. It was high noon for agriculture, then engaged in an increasingly mindless quest to drain the last remaining corners of wetland England. The great drought of that year merely underlined the implications of existing agricultural practice. The Conservancy had little influence on the wider environment at the time, and so it was all the more important to safeguard the few areas within its control from the overall trend.

The Swale NNR is isolated by crop fields from other coastal marshlands on Sheppey. In its original form, the Reserve amounted to little more than an expanse of rather dry grazing marsh intersected by brackish ditches, with a narrow tidal fringe of saltmarsh. The bird fauna was unremarkable, apart from a colony of Little Terns on a spit made of cockle shells, called Shellness. Already too dry to interest wildfowl or waders, the Swale threatened to dry out even further with the drainage of the landward arable fields in winter and the abstraction of groundwater to irrigate the crops in summer. The solution adopted at the Swale was a great deal more radical than that at Holkham. At the latter there was already a sufficient supply of clean water flowing naturally downhill which could conveniently be diverted. But for the Swale, water would have to be pumped into the Reserve and prevented from leaving it. The only way this could be done was to build a series of waterproof earthen embankments or bunds, like giant field banks, to seal in the wet. They had a second useful purpose in ensuring that the birds inside would not be able to see the approach of the bird watchers outside. To ensure that the water is reasonably clear and free of nitrates, it is obtained from a 50-m borehole in the underlying shale beds and pumped out into the bunds along a network of feeder ditches. Pumping at intervals produces a mosaic of pools, 'flashes' and islands of drier grassland, which can be 'rotated' in such a way that no area is flooded for more than a year at a time. A nature trail with no fewer than six hides winds around the periphery of the bunded area. At present there are plans to extend the project by digging a second borehole to enable additional flooding during the summer.

As at Holkham, intervention has transformed the Swale from a rather dull site to some of the best close-range birdwatching in England. Virtually every species of wildfowl or wader has increased, and the Reserve has become a wonderful place to see passage birds like Avocet, Bar and Black-tailed Godwit, Ruff and Greenshank, often under ideal viewing conditions. A carefully regulated system of year-round grazing by sheep and cattle produces close-sward conditions suitable for Wigeon and White-fronted goose, and also tussocky pasture for breeding waders. Some 12 ha of tall grass and reeds has been set aside as a roost for wintering waders and harriers. That the work was completed in the nick of time can be demonstrated by the state of the land outside the bunded fields, after three drier-than-average years: parched yellowing grass and dusty, salt-bleached soil. Against that must be set the high cost of this project—some £140,000, met partly out of EC funds—which is likely to deter all but the richest conservation bodies from copying the idea. The bunds themselves have failed to grass over, as was hoped, partly because they have become a paradise for rabbits. Only the bottom 0.6 m of the bund acts as a clay dam; the rest is just top soil, and it now requires regular maintenance to prevent the much-burrowed steep sides from collapsing. The juxtaposition of a large rabbit warren and a wet marsh does at least produce some interesting variants of animal behaviour. On my visit to the Swale in 1992 I spent some time watching a heron 'fishing for rabbits' on the eroding sides of the bund, though how a heron would deal with a full-grown live rabbit I never found out.

The problem of isolating Reserves from the surrounding land, with its all-too-efficient drainage and a surface run-off of nitrate soup every time it rains, is a general one on English wetland Reserves. At the scatter of holdings that make up the small Somerset Levels NNR, for example, the main drain is lower than the field drains, so that the fields are gradually drying out, like flannel on a clothes-line. One early sign of this is that the field edge starts to crumble, first with clods of earth, but later metre-sized patches of turf, tumbling into the ditch. Small units of land are not really viable in such a situation, unless conservation bodies can influence the way the surrounding land is used. At the Levels the hope is to acquire land with main drains, and also flooded peat cuttings which act as reservoirs and allow some regulation of the water level. For Ludham Marshes NNR in the Norfolk Broads, English Nature plan to isolate the Reserve from the main drains by a system of sluice-gates, using the faithful elbow pipes that have proved so successful elsewhere. Isolating the Reserve altogether is something of a last-ditch(!) resort, expensive and uncertain of success, but in cases like this, when the wildlife interest is centred squarely on the dykes, there may be no satisfactory alternatives.

One alternative to The Swale solution of enclosed wetland oases is to devise a self-regulating system of irrigation. This has worked well at two Reserves at opposite ends of the country, Shapwick Heath in Somerset and Woodwalton Fen in Cambridgeshire (née Huntingdonshire). Shapwick Heath is the last substantial surviving portion of the great bog that once stretched from Glastonbury to the coast: King Arthur's Avalon and the retreat of Athelney where Alfred the Great held out against the Danes. It is an individual place, a small-scale representation of that long-lost landscape with its peat cuttings and hay meadows, damp woods and reedbeds, balmy

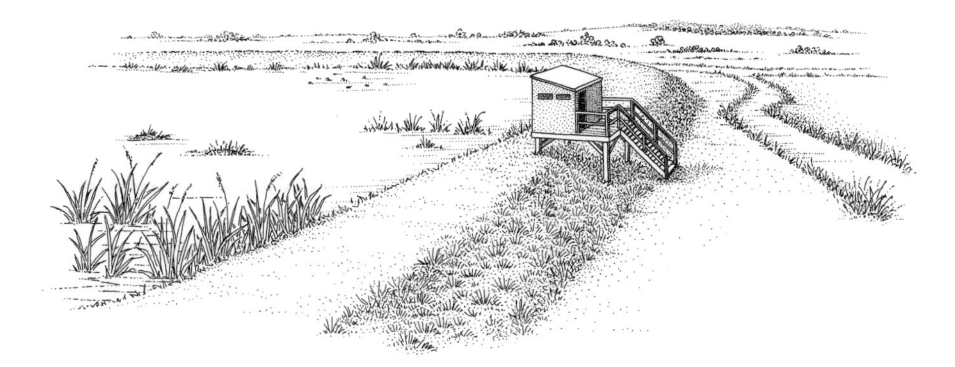

with the scent of Bog Myrtle. This is an area of great archaeological importance, for the wet peat has preserved many of the timbers of prehistoric dwellings and of the ancient trackways that passed through the swamp between the Polden Hills and the islands of the valley. One of these timber piers, called the Sweet Track, passes through Shapwick Heath. The Conservancy is responsible for maintaining this well-preserved section of the track, which means keeping the timbers wet at all times and cutting any tree roots that threaten to damage them. In the early days this seemed like a chore that the warden could well do without. It was no simple matter to irrigate a long section of track in a place that was becoming gradually drier as each year went by. But by happy chance, the Sweet Track has supplied the means for saving the whole Reserve. Because of its importance, sufficient funds became available from English Heritage for the Conservancy to purchase a powerful automatic pump to convey water to the Track; and in so doing it could irrigate the rest of Shapwick Heath as well.

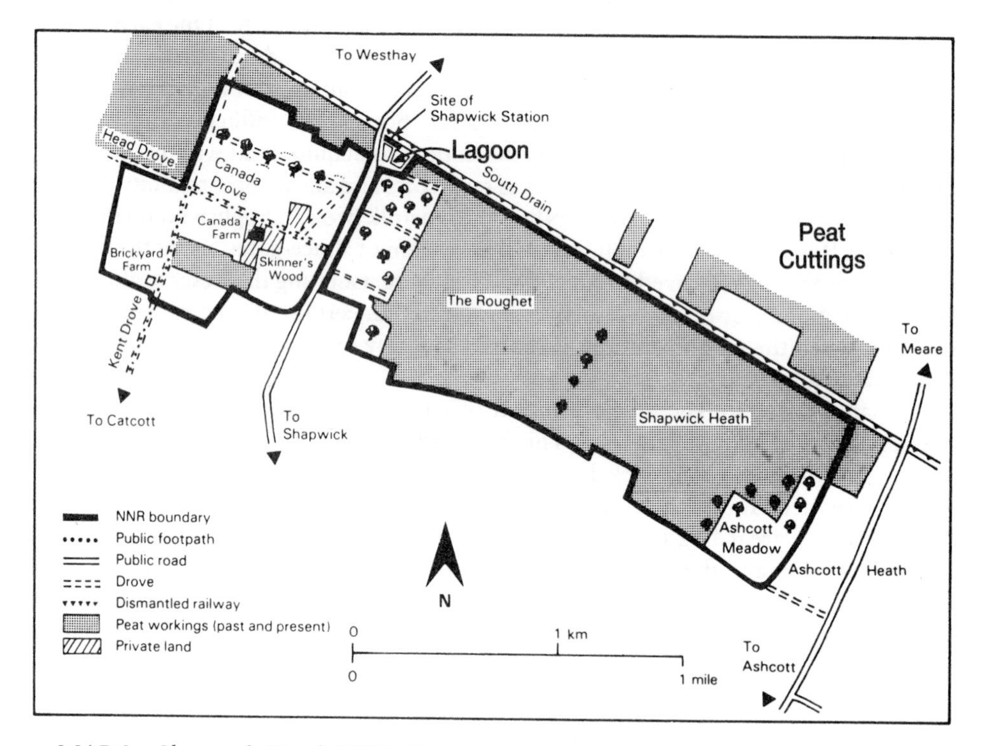

MAP 9 *Shapwick Heath NNR, Somerset*

The Reserve manager, Robin Prowse, has devised an ingenious system of water supply and control. On the northern boundary of the Reserve lie two large lagoons, constructed by the Wessex Water Authority as part of a scheme called Avalon Lakes that would have meant flooding an area of worked-out peat. Although this plan fell through, these conveniently situated lakes gave Robin an idea. A purpose-built lagoon was dug next door to the water authority ones with a sufficient capacity to supply water to distant parts of the Reserve, using a powerful pump to convey the flow through an intricate network of ditches. The water is purified 'naturally' by the reeds that quickly established. The water level is controlled by a series of sluices equipped with the ever-faithful elbow pipes. Robin has also persuaded Fisons, whose own pump is used to drain the nearby peatland, to help extend the irrigation system to a recently acquired extension of the Reserve, and to top-up the lagoon when required. The main constraint on this system is that the lagoon has become popular with nesting warblers, including the rare Cetti's Warbler, so that Robin is reluctant to raise and lower the water table too drastically.

For Woodwalton Fen, that rectangle of well-regulated wilderness amid the croplands of Cambridgeshire, efficient irrigation was achieved by a joint scheme between the Conservancy and the Middle Level Commissioners, responsible for the drainage of that part of the Fens. The Reserve is raised slightly above the surrounding farmland, thanks to the peat shrinkage so clearly demonstrated by the iron pillar at nearby Holme Fen. This poses problems for the Reserve's long-term future because Cambridgeshire has a low rainfall and Woodwalton Fen depends almost wholly on drainage water flowing in from the higher land to the west. By 1960, most of this water was failing to reach the Reserve since the water level of the main drain, the Great Raveley Drain, by then lay nearly a metre below the land surface. Shrinking peat, falling water—if this had gone on, the famous Reserve would have turned into another Holme Fen—a relatively dull place of dry, oxidised peat, birch trees and bracken. Fortunately the means to save it lay in a convergence of interests: the Conservancy and the drainage authority both saw merit in keeping the Fen wet, the former for wildlife reasons, the latter as a 'washland' to absorb floodwater in times of heavy rain. By 1969 (when, ironically, the Fen had just experienced the worst summer flood in its history) the details of a scheme had been worked out. It was ambitious. The Reserve itself would be sealed by a lining of clay around the entire perimeter to isolate its water regime from that of the surrounding farmland. A new catchment drain would bring relatively clean drainage water from the clay lands a few kilometres to the west into Great Raveley Drain, and so along the eastern boundary of the Reserve. A control sluice would close automatically in times of flood and divert the floodwater into the Reserve to soak into the peat, as if into a giant sponge. There were even fears, happily unfounded, that the scheme might turn out to be a bit too successful, with the Fen becoming swamped by rushes of floodwater.

The clay for coring the nearby drains came from the Reserve itself. Two big holes were dug in the middle of the Fen, which soon filled with water and have matured into natural-looking meres—providing the best bird-watching on the Reserve. At the time this was controversial. Some praised the meres as conservation at its most imaginative and pragmatic; others suggested that, as open fenland was among the scarcest and most endangered habitats in England, one ought not to reduce it further. Taken as a whole, however, the scheme has been very successful at preserving an island of wilderness and wet in one of the most intensively farmed landscapes in Europe.

At the opposite end of the Fens, Chippenham Fen NNR was threatened with drying out for other reasons. The character of Chippenham Fen is quite different from Woodwalton. It lies in a depression where fen meets chalk, and the latter often reaches the surface along the Fen's broad mown rides, so that Cowslips and Columbines can be found growing next to Meadow-sweet and Saw-sedge. This Fen is fed by springs from a chalk aquifer. The liminess of its hydrology is evident, especially in the luscious meadows of Chippenham, full of orchids, Black Bog-rush and Meadow Thistle. However, springs are notoriously susceptible to groundwater abstraction by water authority boreholes. In the late 1980s, the water authority decided to put no less than 10 new boreholes into the Cambridgeshire chalk to cater for the anticipated demand from new housing estates in and around Cambridge. The nearest of these lay only 3 km from the Reserve.

Once the borehole was in operation there was a strong risk that the springheads at Chippenham Fen would dry out just when the Fen needed them most, in late summer. The situation was exacerbated by the succession of warm, dry summers in the late 1980s that had turned into one of the longest droughts in living memory. In 1989, the new National Rivers Authority offered to fund a compensation scheme in which a new pipeline would connect the Fen to another borehole, formerly used as a public water supply. The pipe is capable, if need be, of discharging water at up to 30 litres per second into three outlets around the Reserve. There are control valves around the Reserve that can turn the water on and off like a tap. This is believed to be sufficient to guarantee the Reserve's two main priorities: the maintenance of a permanently high water table and, in consequence, of an open fen relatively free of encroaching scrub. The hydrology of the Fen is monitored constantly by means of 15 piezometers sunk into the ground at different points, as well as by a flow gauge on the outlet stream. In addition, Anglian Water are funding a 5-year survey of the flora and invertebrate fauna to see if any changes are occurring as a result of the change in the water regime.

It is an elaborate scheme, the first of its kind on a National Nature Reserve, and expensive far beyond the means of conservationists. Whether such schemes point the way for fenland conservation remains to be seen. But they are likely to be available only to the most highly graded fenland sites.

SLUBBING THE DYKES

Slubbing is a lovely word, with just the right onomatopoeic quality to suggest the unglamorous activity of shovelling out wet sloppy mud from the bottom of a ditch. Although I cannot find it in my dictionary, slubbing seems to be a widely used word in the Fens, perhaps borrowed from Dutch drainage engineers. The Conservancy certainly uses it frequently. Slubbing is the act of dredging a ditch of silt and reed rhizomes, and the spoil left on the bank afterwards is called the *slubbings*. It is a routine maintenance job on any land which is drained by open ditches. It becomes an art on nature reserves where much of the wildlife interest is centred on those very ditches. Routine dredging would strip them bare and perhaps reduce their interest permanently; but without regular maintenance they would eventually fill with silt and rotting vegetation, with much the same consequences. Wetland Reserve managers must needs become artful slubbers.

The best ditches lie in the shrinking number of places where clean and unpolluted water lies close to the surface all year round. In grazing marsh, both along the coast and in the broader river valleys inland, the ditches are there to hold the water which would otherwise flood into the fields and spoil the grazing. At the same time broad ditches or rhynes can also make useful 'wet fences', as at Gordano Valley near Bristol and the Pevensey Levels in East Sussex. In the Fens and Norfolk Broads, canal-sized ditches were used to transport barge-loads of reed-thatch, fen hay and turf. Past managers of wet meadows were masters of water regulation. Detailed control was obtained using sluice-gates, so that the water could be drawn from the pasture, or flooded back into it to fertilise the ground with silt and preserve the grass or reeds from frosts. On the water meadows of Wiltshire and Hampshire this used to be the task of the *drowner*, a person of some importance in the local farming community who was respected as a craftsman. It is, unfortunately, an extinct craft. One of the consequences of the ditch-deepening which characterised the rush to arable in the 1970s was that wet pastureland like this became threatened as never before. The Conservancy managed to acquire several key areas as National Nature Reserves, partly as a spin-off to broader negotiations over SSSIs. Among them are Ludham Marshes in the Norfolk Broads, the Gordano Valley near Bristol, the wettest remaining part of the Pevensey Levels and much of the remaining floodland of the River Derwent in Yorkshire. It also hopes one day to declare one of the last working water meadows, at Lower Woodford near Salisbury, as a National Nature Reserve.

The art of good slubbing can be summed up in a phrase which could apply to conservation management generally—little and often. By working round the network in short stretches at a time, so that each area is slubbed about once every 7–10 years, a manager can create a wealth of conditions, varying from open water with no more than a scatter of duckweed to well-vegetated dykes with a thick fringe of sedge, iris and aquatic grasses. In effect the ditch is replicating the pond-edge succession of plant communities from floating and underwater plants through marsh and reedbed to grassland.

As ditches go, those of the Pevensey Levels NNR are in a class of their own, partly because of their wonderfully clear water, and partly no doubt because of their great age—for the network of winding dykes at Pevensey was first developed in the early

Middle Ages. There are more than a dozen species of pondweeds (*Potamogeton*) here, all five of the native duckweeds, 20 species of dragonflies and an interesting assortment of exotic beasts, including the Fen Raft Spider and a bloodsucking leech, *Placobdella costata*. Here slubbing takes place in the autumn, once activity in the ditch begins to wind down, clearing only one half at a time. In one ditch where rare water beetles have been noted, only 30 m is cleaned at a stretch to make doubly sure that the habitat is not unduly disturbed. With 9.6 km of dykes to cover, manual slubbing would take an impossibly long time, and so the work is done by a contractor using a Hymac and hydraulic bucket. In skilled hands, such work can be done with remarkable sensitivity, and so far there seem to be no ill effects.

At Woodwalton Fen the nomenclature of ditch cleaning is more refined. In the 1950s, the Reserve's overgrown dykes were restored with great labour and new sluices installed to control the flow in one of the first large-scale management projects on any National Nature Reserve. The original practice was to clean out the ditches annually in a process known as *roding*, and to cut the overshading reeds by scythe in an operation known locally as *brinking*. It later dawned on the Reserve managers that such treatment was a trifle drastic, especially for floating and submerged plants like Frog-bit and Bladderwort that need several years to become well established. The traditional but damaging practice of roding was abandoned in the early 1980s and replaced by more judicious slubbing over a period of around 7–10 years. The beautiful displays of flowering Frog-bit and Bladderwort flourishing there now are one of the sights of the Reserve.

One of the problems with slubbing is that the mud excavated from the ditch and dumped on the bank can become an ideal seedbed for thistles, nettles, docks and other undesirable (because potentially invasive) plants. Different remedies have been adopted from place to place. Fen peat, as at Woodwalton or Walberswick NNRs, is relatively easy to disperse and the underlying vegetation often re-establishes itself in a season or two. Heavy clay is more difficult to deal with, and is very prone to thistle invasion. At the Gordano Valley NNR, Tony Robinson rotovates the clay once it is dry, which seems to avoid the worst of the problem. At the Swale, the mud is spread as thinly as possible with a bulldozer to deter rabbits from burrowing into it. Even so, regular swiping is needed to 'top' the thistles before they produce seed. The method evolved at Pevensey is to dump the clay at least 5 m away from the ditch, leave it for a year or so to dry out, and then to harrow and reseed it with grasses. This is evidently a traditional method, to judge from the banks that follow some of the dykes a short distance away.

DEALING WITH DIRTY WATER

Most wetlands are lower than their surroundings. In areas of intensive farming—most of eastern England, that is—this means that the inflowing water will be enriched from fertilisers and other chemicals, if not actually polluted. The worst-off sites, which include the Norfolk Broads, receive a kind of nutrient soup of nitrate fertiliser and phosphates from sewage works, spiced with the occasional offerings of a leaking silage clamp or rusting can of petrol. What happened in consequence to the Norfolk Broads is well known from the carefully documented research carried out in the

1970s. Within living memory the waters of the Broads were famous for their crystal clarity. A rich flora of submerged and floating plants characterised many of these sheltered waters—lush waterscapes of lilies, Water Soldiers, Frogbit and pondweeds, that recall Monet's famous lily pool in their shimmering colours and textures. Such scenes survive, alas, only in photographs and in some of the Broadland dykes that have suffered less than the open Broads from pollution and enrichment. What happened from the 1960s onwards was that dense plankton blooms became more frequent and lasted longer, so that light no longer filtered to the bottom of the Broads. The dead algae contributed to the silt which accumulated on the bottom, smothering the vegetation and becoming a deadly store of phosphates and other sewage products. Toxins released from algae and bacteria resulted in spectacular 'fish kills' and epidemics of avian botulism. The whole process could happen with disconcerting speed. While the Broads of the Bure had begun to lose their former glory as early as the 1950s, those of the Thurne system, like Hickling Broad, remained in a good condition until the late 1960s. Then, in the space of a single year, Hickling Broad grew turbid, dead fish floated on the surface, and the erstwhile underwater forest, which included acres of the rare Holly-leaved Naiad, was replaced by mud, midge larvae and blood-worms.

The Broadland National Nature Reserves—Hickling on the Thurne and the Broads of the Bure Marshes—are connected to their respective rivers and shared fully in the collapse of the Broadland ecosystem. It was hoped that little Cockshoot Broad on the Bure might prove an exception, since it was isolated from the river except for a narrow channel where the flow could be controlled. But it was not to be—by the mid-1970s, Cockshoot had become choked with mud from river and field drains and a mulch of decaying leaves from the encroaching alder carr. Perhaps the most lurid example of all was Calthorpe Broad, a small isolated Broad that had been presented to the Conservancy by deed of gift in 1953. In this case, the cause of its demise was not pollution (for Calthorpe Broad is not connected to a river) but drainage. The Nature Conservation Review describes the gruesome chain of chemical reactions which virtually sterilised the Broad as follows:

> In 1969 this was the only Broad known to contain the characteristic aquatic plant species which formerly occurred in all the freshwater Broads. . . In 1970, however, drastic changes occurred in the Broad which resulted in the loss of most of the submerged plants and invertebrates and a complete kill of the fish. In the summer of that year the water level in the inflow dykes was lowered so that the Broad became perched above the surrounding water table, and owing to seepage and a broken sluice the water level within the Broad itself, and in the surrounding carr, dropped. Under these conditions the usually waterlogged peat became oxidised and ferrous sulphide was converted to ferric sulphate. In the autumn there followed a period of heavy rain which leached the products of oxidation from the peat and hydrolysed the ferric sulphate to produce sulphuric acid and ferric hydroxide. The latter was precipitated on the bottom of the Broad, while in the absence of sufficient buffering cations in the rain water the acid reduced the pH of the water to 3.0.
>
> From: *A Nature Conservation Review*, Vol. 2, p. 172, edited by D. A. Ratcliffe (1977).

The death of Calthorpe Broad can be reproduced in a test tube; I would advise against drinking the resultant 'water'.

The NCC did its best to revive Calthorpe Broad. In 1978, Martyn Howat and Rick Southwood shovelled some 15 tonnes of powdered lime into the Broad—by hand—to restore its pH to about 6.5–7.0. But, although the Broad is again carpeted in water lilies, the former rich flora has not returned. And, despite dams, its dyke system still dries up in hot summers. With the removal of the Coypu, though, the marginal swamp is beginning to spread inwards, forming floating rafts of vegetation known as 'hover' which are of considerable biological interest.

Since it was impractical, as well as too late, to seal off the nature reserves from the rest of the Broadland system, their salvation lies in improvements to the water quality of the Broads as a whole. A slow but steady improvement has indeed taken place in recent years, thanks to the public money now available for conservation work through the offices of the Broads Authority and the National Rivers Authority. 'Phosphate-stripping' plants installed at sewage treatment works on the Bure in 1977 and 1986 have reduced the phosphate level in the discharge water. This does not of course remove the nutrient-rich mud at the bottom of the Broads, which has to be dredged. The Conservancy began a programme of suction dredging at the Bure Marshes in 1970 using a specially designed boat-mounted pump that squirts out mud and water at high pressure via a rotatable nozzle. Such work is expensive—that at Cockshoot Broad alone cost some £50,000. Fortunately dredging is now a service provided by the Broads Authority, using a more sophisticated type of pump.

On a more local scale, the Conservancy provided a site for the Broads Authority and National River Authority to experiment with a novel way of reducing algal blooms—by boosting the numbers of their main 'grazers', the water fleas. Water fleas like quiet water with a lot of shelter—and most of the latter was removed when the larger plants died. One way of encouraging them is to dump brushwood, cut from the invading alder and willow carr, into the shallows. This method would have won the approval of the late Charles Elton as a classic application of the principles of animal ecology to practical management. Unfortunately, as Elton would have been the first to point out, while water fleas feed on plankton, young fish feed on water fleas. If the water fleas increased, so would the fish. The theoretical solution—to blockade the food-chain by removing the fish—has proven a practical reality, at least on a small scale. In 1990, a recycled plastic stockboard barrier was built across the south-western arm of Hoveton Great Broad, with wire mesh windows to permit the flow of water while excluding mature fish. A local consultant, Dr Martin Perrow, was invited to go 'electro-fishing' behind the barrier, using an electronic stunning device and a narrow mesh net. The Roach, Tench, Eels and other fish thus captured are stored in buckets and released unharmed into the main body of the lake. Dr Perrow claims that the method is 100% effective in removing all the fish from behind the barrier, although small fry hiding among the tree roots are admittedly difficult to net. At the time of writing, this project is still in its early stage, but already the water is clearer than at any time since the 1960s, and some floating and submerged plants have increased. If it works, the method is likely to be extended to the rest of Hoveton Great Broad and also to other protected Broads like Cockshoot and Alderfen.

Unfortunately young aquatic plants are subjected to heavy grazing by waterfowl. The worst offenders are Coots, especially when they are feeding their young. A

number of chicken wire enclosures ranging from 1.5 to 15 m in diameter have therefore been erected at Hoveton Great, Ranworth and Cockshoot Broads on the Bure Marshes NNR to help the water lilies and other plants to become established. At the same time, plants which are unlikely to re-establish under their own steam, like Water Soldier, Frogbit and Hornwort, are being introduced to these Broads from other Broadland sites. Perhaps, in time, the damage wrought by decades of human misuse will be reversed, and at least a vestige of the former beauty of the Norfolk Broads restored to Broadland nature reserves.

Water quality control is at the heart of the management of a quite different National Nature Reserve at the opposite side of the country—Wybunbury Moss on the Cheshire plain. Wybunbury [pronounced Wim-bury] Moss is a quaking bog or *Schwingmoor*, whose surface wobbles like a blancmange if you are so unwise as to jump up and down on it. It lies in an area that is prone to subsidence when the underlying rock salt has been mined out or where the fissures have flooded and the salt has dissolved. The commercial extraction of brine for industrial use has exacerbated the situation. The church at Wybunbury has become a well-known victim of subsidence. The old church collapsed completely in 1832; it was rebuilt, but by the 1970s it was again in such a dangerous condition that the nave had to be demolished. Only the tower remains, and it has developed an ominous lean. As for the nearby Moss, it is a place of legendary danger: 'Old people tell of animals lost in the mire:

foxhounds, ponies, someone's horse and cart, and another's cow'. Attempts were made to drain it, none of them successful.

Wybunbury Moss is really a lake with a crust of peat and surface vegetation floating on top, like the skin on a bowl of custard. The crust is about 3 m thick on average while the black lake beneath is up to 15 m deep. It probably lies in a natural hollow made by a melting glacier at the end of the Ice Age, but the hollow has since deepened through subsidence. Around the edge is a belt of reedswamp called a lagg fen, growing through up to 4 m of semi-liquid mud. This is obviously no place for the unwary. It has, however, attracted scientists from all over the world for *Schwingmoors* like this are rare, and Wybunbury Moss may be one of the best examples there is. It has been well known to English naturalists for more than a century. The Reserve management plan contains details of fascinating and sometimes highly specialised studies made at the Moss, among which surveys of testate amoebae and sclerotinaceous fungi tend to catch the eye.

Wybunbury Moss became a National Nature Reserve as long ago as 1954. Purchasing the site, however, proved no defence against the insidious pressures on it from surrounding houses and roads. Over the years the moss has received a great deal of polluted water from overflowing septic tanks and road drains. The moss began to stink foully in hot weather, and its natural inhospitality was not improved by the clouds of midges and mosquitoes breeding in the enriched water. More importantly, the polluted water had started to erode the bog surface by inducing the chemical breakdown of the peat. Peat is sustained by nutrient-poor water. Once the water becomes sufficiently eutrophic, it begins to lose its cohesion, turning into black, porridge-like mud in which plants cannot root themselves. Early signs of this process at Wybunbury Moss included the increase in fen woodland at the expense of acid-loving *Sphagnum* bog, the appearance of bare patches of unstable, slushy peat and the death and collapse of the birch and pine trees that scatter the surface.

The deteriorating situation was studied in great detail by hydrological experts from Nottingham University. The means of saving the moss, put into effect on their recommendations from 1986 onwards, has been to prevent polluted water from entering the lake by using a powerful pump to divert it along the peripheral lagg ditch and into the outflowing stream, like traffic flowing round a road island. Most of the water entering the moss should now be the naturally nutrient-poor spring and rainwater that have sustained the moss for most of its life. The considerable capital outlay (£100,000) was borne partly by the NCC and partly by the local Water Authority. A temporary sluice on the lagg ditch allows the raising and lowering of the raft of peat, and this may have important implications for future management. At present the moss appears to be concave in shape, that is, it sinks towards the centre. This means that the surface water flows inwards rather than outwards, as in a raised bog. This has slightly enriched the peat with the result that Moor-grass is spreading at the expense of the *Sphagnum* moss. Once a permanent sluice has been installed it might be possible to lift the peat surface so that the centre balloons upwards to become a dome, like a raised bog, thus ensuring that the surface water will flow downhill out of the bog and into the lagg stream. Whether this can be achieved in practice remains to be seen. This form of experimental management does not seem to have been attempted anywhere else. In the meantime, the quality of the surface and subsurface water is being monitored every few days by the site manager, Martin Davey, using a conductivity meter, while more detailed sampling continues to be done on contract by scientists at Nottingham University. With a basin as large as Wybunbury's black lake, it will probably take years to return the water to the desired nutrient-poor condition, but there are already encouraging signs of improvement.

REVIVING THE BOG

It might be as well to define what is meant by a bog, since in popular parlance, marshes, mires and bogs are much the same thing. Bogs form when the drainage is so poor, or the rainfall so high, that the site is permanently waterlogged. These conditions favour the formation of peat. Botanists distinguish between fens, whose peat is made up of partially decomposed reeds, sedges and other fenny species, and bogs where the peat consists mainly of that remarkable plant, *Sphagnum* moss. *Sphagnum* has two unusual qualities. It grows to an indefinite length, like *Sargassum* seaweed, and because of its internal structure it can soak up water like a sponge. *Sphagnum* bogs are among the most colourful of wild habitats, although we seldom see them at their best because they put on their best show in winter or early spring. On mild days early in the year you find not the parched, faded bog of summer but a vivid Persian carpet of greens, reds, oranges and browns where the different species of *Sphagnum* mingle on the uneven ground. A really good wet bog is an entity made up of billions of strands of *Sphagnum* and nourished by little more than rainwater. The moss grows fastest when wettest, and so the wet centre of the bog is often higher than the margins and forms a low dome.

Textbooks always show beautiful dome-shaped 'raised bogs' with sloping sides or *rands* and a surrounding water course called a *lagg*. There are in fact a few classic bogs like that in Wales and Scotland. The best known is Cors Tregaron National Nature Reserve in Wales—land so wild and wet that the Nature Conservancy could find no one who claimed to own it. But few lowland bogs in England remain in such a pristine state. Over the years they have been nibbled around the edges by farmers and cut over by commoners and peat-producing companies, and the larger ones are criss-crossed with ditches where successive owners have tried to drain them. In recent times they have become perhaps the most threatened of all wild habitats. Some 60% of all lowland peat bogs in Britain were damaged or destroyed by cutting and drainage between 1948 and 1984. Cutting technology developed in the past 10 years has enabled peat producers to make an even more thorough job of demolishing the ecosystem by stripping away the peat layer by layer until the underlying clay is reached. This not only removes the habitat but denies any possibility of it returning. Today only 445 ha of undisturbed raised bog is left in England. On the present rate of loss, lowland peat bogs would in theory cease to exist in 30 years time.

There are only half a dozen extensive bogs in lowland England and of them Thorne and Hatfield Moors near Doncaster are as large as all the rest put together. Unlike the heaths, bogs are of considerable economic value (so long, of course, as they have mineral planning consent), and leading peat producers, notably Fisons plc, either own large parts of them or have rights to cut peat there. Until the 1980s, the Conservancy had managed to preserve only a few small, well-preserved bogs as National Nature Reserves. There was Glasson Moss on the Solway Plain, Rusland Moss in Cumbria, and the wet Mosses that surround Roudsea Wood by Morecambe Bay. Morden Bog in Dorset and Thursley Common in Surrey are also acid bogs, but they lie in wet basins and are not technically raised bogs, though they share much the same vegetation. Several of the upland raised bogs in the North Pennines were saved from drainage and planting with conifers by an agreement between the Conservancy and the Forestry Commission in the late 1950s, and one of them, Coom Rigg Moss, was leased by the former for scientific purposes and declared a National Nature Reserve. Most of these latter bogs are now inaccessible, appearing on the map as small oval 'eyes' swallowed up in the green vastnesses of Wark Forest.

These Reserves are not in themselves sufficient to save more than a minute fragment of the peat bog habitat. In the early days it was thought that portions of bogs could be preserved despite the effects of peripheral cutting and drainage. Experience has proven otherwise. A peat bog is sustained by its unique hydrology: it is less a lump of wet matter than a lake with cohesive properties. As Richard Lindsay, the former NCC's peatlands expert, has pointed out, the bog sits on the ground like a drop of water. In consequence, even minor disruptions to its hydrology can have profound effects on the whole bog. The nature of the bog makes the concept of protecting half a bog almost as useless as protecting half a lake. For that reason, and because of the alarming rate at which peat bogs are now disappearing, the Conservancy has made strenuous efforts in recent years to secure agreements with peat producers over the whole of the half dozen or so really large lowland bogs that remain.

In some cases, like Glasson Moss and Wedholme Flow it has also bought up 'stints' of land (long strips with peat-cutting rights attached to them) as they became available. The most substantial outright purchase so far has been at the complex of 'mosses' along the border between Shropshire and Powys known as Fenn's, Whixall and Bettisfield Mosses, where the NCC purchased 509 ha from a producer of horticultural peat in 1990. This action, taken to save the moss from further damaging exploitation, cost the NCC a cool £1.6 million, representing an investment almost on the scale of the Ribble Estuary and made possible only by grants from the National Heritage Memorial Fund, Shropshire County Council and (eventually, after a lot of hum-ing and ha-ing), by the Department of the Environment itself. Public concern over the future of 'Fenn's-Whixall' was instrumental in the decision of a consortium of conservation charities to launch their Peatlands Campaign in 1990, dedicated to 'increasing public awareness of the destruction of British and Irish peatlands and to encourage the use of alternatives to peat in horticulture'. The promotion of alternatives to commercial peat is an urgent necessity, since peat is a limited and dwindling resource. And, unlike traditional peat digging by hand, modern methods of peat extraction leave little or no room for compromise between production and conservation. Peat producing is no longer a harvest of a renewable resource but the obliteration of an ancient habitat. We are faced with the choice between nature reserves and deserts of milled peat between (figuratively speaking) white and black.

In 1992, peatland conservation became headline news with the announcement of a deal between Fisons plc, the leading peat producer, and the NCC's successor, English Nature. Under the agreement, Fisons are to hand over their entire holding of peatland Sites of Special Scientific Interest to English Nature. Much of this vast area, amounting to some 11,000 ha, lies at Thorne and Hatfield Moors, with smaller areas at Wedholme Flow in Cumbria and on the Somerset Levels. The part of the holding which is still relatively intact will thereby be preserved from further peat extraction. For the rest, Fisons will continue to extract peat until the last metre or so is reached. At the time of writing this agreement has not yet been signed. It proved controversial, partly because of the conditions of secrecy in which it was negotiated, and was condemned by the Peatlands Campaigners as a sell-out. English Nature defended the deal in pragmatic terms, as a considerable gain for nature conservation at relatively little cost compared with that expended over Fenn's and Whixall Mosses. And the principle of partnership and co-operation with other land-users, to which English Nature is committed, has other advantages. Restoration management can be integrated into the routine operations of commercial peat winning, and the experience of local operators is being lent to the process of blocking drains and sealing in the wet.

Whichever view one takes of it, the Fisons deal represents the first example in Britain of a conservation plan for an entire habitat. Not all the land will necessarily be declared as National Nature Reserves. But the centre of Thorne Moors, already owned by English Nature, has been an undeclared Reserve for many years, and it is here that the basic techniques of peatland are being tested. Thorne Moors is, in its way, a breathtaking place. On most lowland bogs you can see the surrounding land not far away on all sides of you, and are almost claustrophobically conscious of the smallness and frailty of the place. Not so on Thorne Moors—it *is* the landscape, a vast, empty no-man's-land known to few apart from naturalists and peat producers. Certainly I shall never forget my first view: mile after mile, stretching to the northern horizon, of nothing but flat dark brown peat, like a vast tarmacadam parade ground under a sky that seems twice its normal size. What you see there now is a moonscape of milled peat without a blade of grass, broken only by the spars of ancient timbers dug from the peat and cast aside like apple cores, and by the distant sounds of tractors and milling machinery on their steady trundle up and down, turning 5000 years of life into sackfuls of dust for gardeners to put on their flowerbeds. It is a vision of monumental sterility, a place of awesome silence. It was not always thus. Evidence of the past lies all around you. You can pick up lumps of peat made of the fibrous remains of *Scheuzeria*, now confined as a living plant to lonely Rannoch Moor. Inside the peat at Thorne are the perfectly preserved remains of plants, beetles and tree trunks thousands of years old, the best record in Britain of the flora and fauna of prehistory.

Happily, substantial areas of peat cut by older, less damaging methods still cover much of the southern end of Thorne Moors. In places it has produced a landscape striped like a tiger with tawny channels of Cotton-Grass alternating with the drier peat baulks. These areas may regenerate in time, especially if the water level can be raised. For the hundreds of hectares of milled peat the future is less certain. There are no pockets of wild vegetation to begin the slow process of recolonisation, once the machines have gone. Despite what the peat producers find it convenient to claim, there is no evidence that bogs can be restored to these dusky plains.

The last remnant of the old Thorne Moors lies on the south-western side, against the doleful backdrop of the derelict collieries of Thorne. It is on a rectangular block of land (the most geometrical Reserve in England) last cut over in 1922 and preserved from further exploitation by an agreement made in 1974 between the NCC and Fisons. The NCC purchased the 79-ha plot 11 years later. It is a singular place with its regular pattern of wet lanes full of *Sphagnum*, Bog Rosemary and Cotton-Grass running between banks of heather. It owes its appearance to the activities of the Dutch

Griendstveen Moss Litter Company, who purchased the site in 1894 and dug into it a network of canals to enable the peat to be removed from the Moor by horse-drawn barges. The clay lining of the canals survives in places and is probably responsible for the odd corner and tuft of fen in this otherwise acid ground (there are even plants of the chalk on the old clinker tramways that cross the Moor). By 1985, much of the 'Dutch canals' area had become dry enough for birch to invade and threaten to turn the bog into a wood. Like all bogs it was also vulnerable to fire. In August 1989, a stubble-burn near the edge of Thorne Moors set light to the heather and soon a large part of the bog was blazing out of control, producing an orange glow in the night sky that could be seen for miles around. Some 405 ha, including all of the Reserve, was burned and charred to a depth of several centimetres. The Reserve manager, Peter Roworth recalls the eerie silence that followed for several days, until it was broken by snatches of autumn bird song as the resident species began to return. The blaze did have at least one benefit: it killed much of the birch scrub that was sucking the water out of the centre of the moss.

With the help of Fisons operators and a specially adapted wide-tracked Hymac excavator, Peter Roworth has begun a major programme of post-fire dam-building, blocking all the exit ditches and drains with peat bulwarks designed to seal-off the Reserve from the rest of the moor. The big water-filled ditches that surround it are

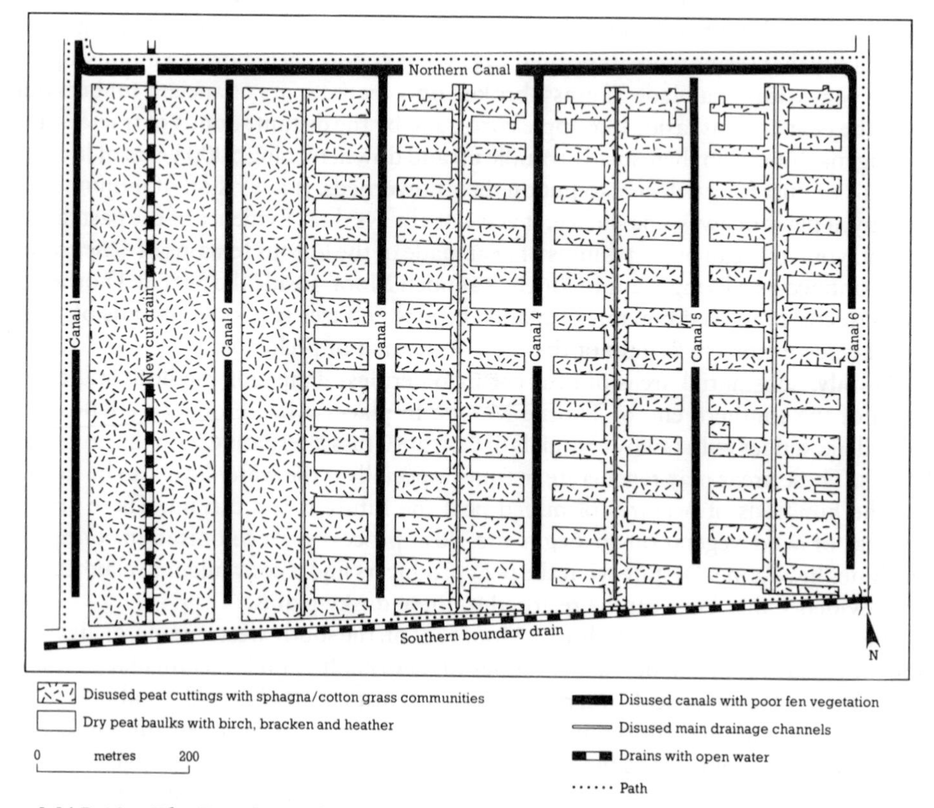

MAP 10 *The Dutch canals area at Thorne Moors, Humberside*

now as broad and deep as the Dutchmen's canals. That, however, is the relatively easy part in the hoped-for restoration of this vast, much-abused bog under the Fisons/ English Nature agreement. Peter has been busy plugging all the obvious outflows with dams of peat: about 1300 of them to date. More difficult to deal with is the loss of water through transpiration from the invading birch scrub. It might be possible to keep the birch at bay on small areas in the wet heart of the bog, but for the rest it has to be accepted as a fact of life. As for the large area that is to be worked to exhaustion by Fisons under the agreement, its future is likely to lie in the demonstration of the possibilities, and no doubt limitations, of habitat restoration. For much of the Moor, English Nature (or some successor body) will be starting with what might be, and will certainly look like, a blank slate.

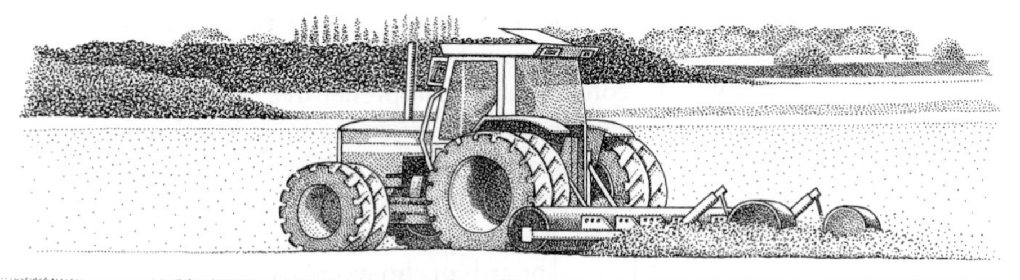

Such work is likely to be expensive. English Nature is already committed to managing more than 1000 ha of raised bog and intervening scrubby moor at Fenn's, Whixall and Bettisfield Mosses. As with Thorne Moors, virtually the whole of this area has been cut over at least once, most recently by large machines imported from Germany that created a construction-site landscape of bare peat and steep-sided water-filled channels. Restoration on this scale involves a large measure of experimental work, since previous experience is limited and confined mainly to the Netherlands. The larger drainage channels will need to be dammed immediately and a start made on clearing the dense scrub as soon as possible. The bog cannot be made too wet too suddenly, for flood water is likely to enrich the naturally acid ground and reduce the chances of peat regeneration. It may be preferable to maintain the water table just below the surface for as much of the year as possible, although this would require a great deal of regulation and constant monitoring. It is estimated that managing this site alone will cost some £500,000 over a 10-year period.

At the other end of the bog manager's scale is Glasson Moss NNR, a 93-ha hump of land on the road from Bowness to Kirkbride on the Solway plain. As a long-established National Nature Reserve, however, Glasson Moss provides a good case of changing approaches to peat-bog preservation. The original Reserve consisted of about a third—the least 'damaged' part—of this typically oval raised bog lying within a stone's throw of the westernmost fort of Hadrian's Wall. This part had not been cut over in living memory, although it had been affected by nineteenth century drainage. The rest had, like most bogs, been cut over extensively, the northern part at the turn of the century by the United Alkali and Manure Company, for the production of ammonia fertiliser and paraffin wax, and the southern part between 1948 and 1954 by the Cumberland Moss Litter Company for horticultural use (some of it finishing up inside American greenhouses). The borders of the Reserve consist mostly of dried-out peat baulks where the heather has grown old and 'leggy' and birch woodland is developing. The Conservancy did very little with any of it between the purchase of the Moss in 1967 and the hot summer of 1976, except to keep an eye on the place. Thus, there was little to prevent the fire of 1976, which began in old dry heather outside the Reserve, from racing across the parched surface of the moss and burning it from end to end.

There is nothing like a good blaze to stimulate action on a nature reserve. While the charred peat bog started on its long road to recovery in a magnificent display of White Beak-sedge, the Reserve warden, assisted by some of the first job creation scheme employees and by local schoolchildren, began a fire prevention programme by digging a series of lagoons along the contours of the dome-shaped bog, blocking the most actively flowing drains and cutting back the bracken. This not only lessened the risk of fires—it also helped to sustain the bog's water supply. More recently, the present manager, Frank Mawby, has completed a comprehensive programme of dam-building there, blocking all the main drains and reversing their function from one of taking water out of the bog to one of holding it in. Frank began fairly tentatively by blocking drains with heavy duty polythene sheets and shovelling peat on top. The smaller ones were blocked by sheets of tin off-cuts from builders' yards which he riveted together and sealed. Traditional boards of elm wood were also tried, but unless these are thoroughly weathered they tend to shrink and let the water through (although water-resistant plywood and elm boards have been used successfully at Grains Head Moss and Muckle Moss NNRs in Northumberland). But with the confidence that comes with experience, Frank found ways of bringing heavy machinery onto the bog without damaging the surface to block the biggest ditches with great bulwarks of peat up to 3 m across. By 1992, nearly 1000 dams and £15,000 later, the programme was complete. Glasson Moss has already become noticeably wetter; heather is in retreat from the centre of the bog and the beautiful orange *Sphagnum pulchrum*, almost wiped out in 1976, has recolonised large areas of the moss. In time the surface might even develop the classic hummock and pool topography which is thought to have been present before the moss was drained in the last century. Frank's dam-building expertise is now being used to raise the water levels over part of the nearby and much larger Wedholme Flow. As Robbie Bridson, for many years the Conservancy's chief warden in north-west England, points out, 'until the fire at Glasson Moss, no one gave much thought to blocking drains on peat bogs. Now we have the confidence to use large machines and are at last starting to look at bog management on a national level'.

The other half of a bog manager's job is scrub clearance. An increase in scrub and bracken is a sure sign of a drying bog. A scrubby edge, as at Thorne Moors, may provide excellent habitat for birds such as Nightjar, Whinchat and Nightingale, but on the living peat surface scrub is a double menace, smothering and changing the surface chemistry, and helping very effectively to dry out the site. Woodwalton Fen—always a pioneer Reserve in terms of habitat management—was one of the first National Nature Reserves to receive regular scrub removal to reclaim the open fen. Nowadays this work is done by machine—a Hymac tractor and shovel to pull out the bushes and pile them up for drying. Men armed with chain saws complete the clearance and chop up the material to manageable proportions. Once the wood is dry, generally a year later, the bonfires are burned. The work is always done in winter to avoid disturbance to wildlife. It creates what is initially a messy waterlogged surface of bare, churned-up peat, but after a season or two the natural vegetation reestablishes itself and can thereafter be maintained by cattle grazing or mowing. A bonus of surface disturbance is that long-dormant seeds may be brought to the surface and stimulated to germinate. At Woodwalton, scrub cutting and ditch clearance have resulted in temporary displays of two rare plants once thought of as lost—Fen Violet and Fen Woodrush.

In 1980, the NCC acquired some 200 ha of scrub-invaded raised bog in the eastern lee of Roudsea Wood in the Lake District. This was one of the first areas to be purchased as much for its potential as for its actual interest. The bog had been drained by a local ironworks using a series of parallel ditches half a chain apart—evidently a Lake District custom, for Glasson Moss has a very similar ditch network. The bog dried out very obligingly, but fortunately the ironworks went broke before much of the peat could be cut. A scrub of Rhododendron, birch and pine quickly spread over the dry bog surface. Getting rid of it all has taken the Reserve manager, Peter Singleton, the best part of 10 years. In Germany and in Scandinavia, similar landscapes can be kept open by burning the scrub when the ground is frozen, but on England's maritime bogs frosts are rarely hard enough to protect the surface from scorching. Instead Peter provided an artificial surface of corrugated iron sheets, and piled up the bonfire material on that. At first most of the work was done by hand, but the really tough scrub has been tackled more recently with the universal Hymac diggers. A boardwalk has been built along the edge of the bog to allow access for the Conservancy's indispensable Honda 'Big X' mini-tractor without damaging the bog surface.

Rhododendron is perhaps the most pernicious of all invaders on raised bogs. It is a more localised menace than birch or pine, but where it occurs it can be tremendously difficult to eradicate. The Dersingham Reserve in Norfolk was invaded by Rhododendron as a result of changes since the 1950s, including falling water levels and declining rabbit populations, but most notably and the loss of the steam railway—the cause of numerous accidental fires which kept the valley relatively free of scrub. To get rid of Rhododendron it is necessary not only to cut the iron-hard wood but also to spray the regrowth with a herbicide such as glyphosate until the roots are exhausted. During the first half of the 1980s, youth volunteers from the Manpower Services Commission made useful inroads into the scrub, but after the demise of the Youth Opportunities Programme in 1986, it became quite a struggle for the manager, Phil Holms and his assistant Chris Everitt, even aided by conservation volunteers, to maintain the status quo. The effect of herbicide use on the surrounding bog is little known, and it is important to apply the stuff in a way that restricts its effect to the target species as much as possible. An effective way to control cut Rhododendron is to spray glyphosate mixed with a wetting agent on a full season's regrowth in August. Clearing Rhododendron takes roughly 30 man days per hectare, compared with only 12 man days for the same area of birch or pine scrub. On the very acid bog at Dersingham, bonfire sites have been kept to a minimum and all the ash removed afterwards to avoid any accumulation of nutrients in the peaty ground. Needless to say great care has to be taken to avoid a peat fire. During the past 3 years, the worst of the scrub of

Rhododendron and birch—some 30 ha on the bog and another 40 ha on old heathland—has at last been removed, and it is now possible to contemplate removing the larger timber and reclaiming these endangered habitats from the advance of woodland. The Reserve has been restored to a state where the traditional grazers, rabbits, may well increase and where low density sheep grazing is now possible. Dersingham, like many of the bog and heath National Nature Reserves, is ready for a less intensive care and maintenance programme, the nature reserve ideal, after 10 year's hard work to undo the results of the previous 20 years.

REEDBEDS AND TURF PONDS

Large reedbeds are comparatively rare. A national survey conducted by the RSPB in 1980 found only 109 reedbeds of more than 2 ha in England and Wales, and only 33 that exceeded 20 ha. This fact alone explains why those birds that require large areas of reeds, notably the Bearded Tit and the Bittern, are relatively rare in Britain. Reedbeds and their associated habitats are relatively well represented on National Nature Reserves. Those at Walberswick NNR on the Suffolk coast are believed to be the most extensive in Britain, though most of them date from no earlier than 1940 when this part of the coast was flooded as a defence measure. There are also large coastal reedbeds at Benacre and the North Solent NNRs, and inland at Stodmarsh in Kent and in the Broadland and Fenland Reserves.

Reeds grow only in shallow water no more than a metre in depth. If reedbeds are left unmanaged they accumulate a litter of stem and leaf fragments mixed with trapped sediment that may in time raise the bed high and dry, allowing sallows and other woody plants to colonise the surface and begin the slow progression to woodland. Commercial reedbeds were maintained in a permanently wet condition by networks of dykes that allowed water to be taken out of the bed for harvesting, and poured back in again to protect the new shoots from frost and suppress the growth of other, unwanted plants. Most reed cutting was done in winter, after the blades have fallen from the dry stems. In the past the cutting was done by hand using a double-handed scythe. The traditional method still survives in a few places like the Norfolk Broads, but most cutting on National Nature Reserves is now done by machine.

Reed cutting is a valuable means of maintaining open fen and preventing the build-up of litter and the invasion of scrub. The speed at which sallows, alders and other trees can invade neglected reedbeds is a great problem for reserve managers. The board walk at Hoveton Great Broad, built through open reeds and sedges in 1967, is now a shaded tunnel through dense scrub. The demand for reed thatch is high enough locally for cutting to remain a commercially viable practice. However, the aims of reed cutters do not always coincide with those of naturalists, nor do botanists necessarily always agree with ornithologists over the right way to manage reedbeds. On National Nature Reserves the aim is to preserve as wide a habitat diversity as possible by cutting and mowing, whilst leaving older stands of reeds and reed litter for species like Bearded Tits and the Reed Leopard moth. One of the first Reserves to regularise reed cutting for management purposes was Stodmarsh NNR, an area of floodland by the River Stour in East Kent and well known for its wetland birds (Stodmarsh is a famous landfall for migratory birds and was the first place in England where Savi's and Cetti's

Warbler nested regularly). The Reserve is unusual in that its habitats have formed recently and mainly as a result of human activity on (and under) the surrounding land. The reedbeds developed in the 1930s as a result of coal mining subsidence. At the same time, Stodmarsh is vulnerable to drying and the water levels there have to be carefully controlled. It was with that in mind, and to prevent scrub from spreading, that the NCC began to experiment with a reed harvesting machine in the early 1970s. A rotating double scythe attached to a metal frame cuts a swathe through the bed and automatically binds each bundle of reeds for the baler to stack onto the trailer. Part of the reedbed is cut each winter, but in small patches only, to preserve the rest of the bed for nesting birds the following spring. At the same time the network of open dykes is maintained by regular brinking (weed cutting) and by occasional slubbing. In 1985 a Swale-style clay wall or bund was constructed along the Reserve's eastern boundary to enable the manipulation of the water level in the reedbeds and grazing marshes without affecting the neighbouring farmland.

At Walberswick NNR, the reedbeds continue to be managed commercially, and some 16,000 bundles of reeds are sold each year to thatchers. Under the owner's conditions of lease, most of the commercial reedbeds are cut annually (known as 'single wale') to produce a dense crop of high quality reeds. This is less than ideal for wildlife since it reduces the available habitat for birds like the Reed Warbler which likes to suspend its nest from the previous year's stems. From the point of view of wildlife management, it would be preferable to manage the reeds under a series of rotations varying from 2 years ('double wale') to 6 years or more. Maintaining a wide diversity in large reedbeds is important since each species of reedland birds has its own special needs. Bitterns, for example, like wet reedbeds with plenty of shallow open water in the dykes where they can fish for eels. Bearded Tits, on one hand, prefer older reeds with a deep dry litter in which to build their nests. The ideal conditions for the tits are a mixture of unmanaged or occasionally cut reeds next to regularly cut areas where these delightful birds have been known to follow the cutter 'like Robins' to feed on the abundant seeds and insects left in his wake.

Some reedbeds, especially at the Bure Marshes and Walberswick NNRs, are mown in the summer as 'marsh hay'. Until the turn of the century this was a valuable crop used as fodder and bedding for horses before the internal combustion engine changed everything. Many of the former hayfields now lie beneath a dense tangle of alders and willows. Rick Southwood and his helpers usually cut the hay in July and August, when the reeds are at their peak of growth. Since there is no longer much demand for this crop, the hay is stacked into piles which are either burned or left as 'habitat piles'. Removing the litter stunts the growth of the next year's reeds and makes them easier to harvest as well as more open and richer in other marshland plants. Because wet ground is easily damaged by heavy machinery, the Conservancy uses an 'Octad' tractor with eight broad-tyred wheels to spread the load as widely as possible. At the Bure Marshes, where the Conservancy has a relatively free hand, parts of 'mowing marsh' are cut annually while others are cut on a rotation of between 4 and 12 years to enable plants like Marsh Pea, Milk Parsley and Water Parsnip to colonise the bed and allow some accumulation of litter and the development of 'structure', so important to many invertebrates. Here an important consideration is the needs of the Swallowtail butterfly which is confined as a resident species to the Broads. The Swallowtail lays its eggs only on Milk Parsley of the right size and growing in the right place. Milk Parsley is a biennial plant, and therefore cannot grow in reedbeds harvested by single wale, nor does it occur in wet reedbeds. It is generally at the right size to interest Swallowtails 2 years after cutting. A mixture of winter-cut reedbeds and summer-mown meadows favours this resplendent insect, and a good place to look for its yellow eggs and bright green and orange-striped caterpillars is on robust plants of Milk Parsley at the edge of a recently mown block. As is usual with butterflies, it is management that maintains this species, and the presence of such a beast is a useful incentive for Reserve managers to sharpen their scythe blades.

Chippenham Fen is the home of another rarity that has some bearing on how the Reserve is managed—the attractive Cambridge Milk-parsley *Selinum carvifolia*. Like the 'common' Milk Parsley, *Selinum* favours relatively dry, rather open fen meadows, and in parts of Chippenham Fen it pushes out its delicately cut leaves and fleecy umbels as though it were an ordinary hogweed or hemlock. Because *Selinum* flowers late, and does not set seed until early autumn, mowing in July, the usual way of maintaining fen meadows, might damage the plant's future prospects. The Reserve manager, Malcolm Wright, therefore leaves the main *Selinum* meadows till last. Unfortunately, by the time these areas are cut (using a mower borrowed from a neighbour) the vegetation has grown so dry and tough that its fodder value is low. In one year, however, Malcolm found an unusual outlet for it: the llamas and alpacas of Kilverstone Zoo, which are used to tough semi-desert plants and need something challenging to grind their teeth against. This must be one of the least expected conjunctions in English nature conservation: one of our rarest plants being used to aid the digestion of a South American ruminant!

Another wetland plant found on nature reserves is still harvested for thatch: the Saw-sedge, which is most abundant in the Cambridgeshire and Broadland Fens. A Saw-sedge meadow is a distinctive sight with its bobbles of gingery flowers among the drying saw-toothed stems and leaves. Saw-sedge is more flexible than reed, and is used by the thatcher to strengthen the roof by combing the bundles over the ridge. Wicken Fen has a history of sedge-cutting going back to the Middle Ages, and the practice was resumed there by the National Trust in the 1960s, after several decades of neglect. At Chippenham Fen, where it dominates a large meadow in the middle of the Reserve, the sedge is cut by David Fransham from Great Yarmouth, using a converted rice-cutter which is steered like a plough. The meadow is divided into four blocks, one of which is cut each year, with David Fransham pushing the cutter and three others bundling up the viciously sharp stems and carting them away. (It is nice to see that a bush of Guelder Rose has been retained in the middle of this meadow, partly as a song-perch for Sedge Warblers, but mainly, one suspects, for its beauty.) Saw-sedge is usually cut in summer in such a way that the new growth will be above the winter flood level. Reinstating old sedge-beds and reedbeds can be expensive, since any invasive scrub has to be removed, the old growth cut and the litter raked out before a regular cycle of cutting can begin. In recent years, the results of sedge-cutting, both in terms of vigour and species-richness, have improved by cutting earlier, in April/May rather than July/September. Historical research by Terry Rowell has shown that early cutting had been the tradition at Wicken, and that our forebears used to cut sedge on a shorter cycle than do most Fenmen today.

In the 1950s, Joyce Lambert proved that the Broads were all man-made lakes, produced by medieval turf cutters and peat diggers. Much of Woodbastwick Fen in the Bure Marshes NNR is itself a dried-out turf pond, originally about 1.6 km long but no more than 1–2 m deep. Some of the more delicate wild plants of the Broads depend on such shallow peaty ponds, but they have become scarce through the present lack of suitable habitat. To do something about this, the Conservancy and the Broads Authority have dug a series of small experimental turf ponds on peaty ground on several Broadland SSSIs, monitoring the succession of plants as they colonised the shallow pools. The results were encouraging and so, in 1992, the Authority, in partnership with English Nature, purchased a powerful 20-tonne JCB excavator and employed a skilled driver to undertake conservation work on a much larger scale at Woodbastwick Fen and elsewhere in Broadland. The plants of turf ponds depend on pure peat and rainwater. The ponds therefore have to be isolated from the rivers and their dykes and dug into suitably moist acid peat. It is also desirable that the chosen ground is not already of high conservation interest! The digger helpfully enables the Reserve managers to solve two problems for the price of one, for the digger is powerful enough to remove scrub and small trees—stumps, roots and all. They are piled up around the experimental plots together with the spoil from the diggings and then levelled to form linear banks.

In skilled hands, this machine is able to dig out turf ponds in a couple of quick, clean scoops to a predetermined depth, varying between 25 and 100 cm. The technique can also be used to scrape the surface to create wet reedbeds for birds like the Bittern—on the principle that if you can't raise the water level, you might as well lower the land! The turf ponds effectively re-establish a distinctive plant community long thought lost to the Broads (though it would have been very familiar to the medieval peat-diggers). First to arrive on the bare peat are the stoneworts, those attractive, prickly little plants that appear from nowhere in newly dug clear water pools and ditches. In time—perhaps as much as a century in the case of the deeper pools—a floating 'hover' community dominated by mosses is likely to form. The prize which all anticipate with fingers crossed is the Fen Orchid, one of the rarest of Broadland plants which depended on a regular supply of shallow peat cuttings. There is every likelihood that it will return. There seems to be a large bank of living seed preserved in the surface peat, to judge from the plants that have appeared in the smaller experimental pools—including previously unrecorded ones like Fen Pondweed and Cotton-grass. In 1993, two large ponds covering a total of 3.6 ha at Woodbastwick were dug in an area recently reclaimed from dense alder and sallow scrub. These will be used as demonstration sites to encourage other Broadland landowners. With a proposed 10-year work programme for their 20-tonne JCB, English Nature and the Broads Authority have it in their gift to make a dramatic impact on the neglected and floristically impoverished parts of the Broads.

CHAPTER 9

Meadows, Woods and the Coast

BUOYING UP TRADITION

Mottey Meadows in the parish of Lapley, Staffordshire, is one of those delightful corners of old England which our forebears might still recognise. The scale is still designed for humans and beasts rather than for combine harvesters. A patchwork of wet meadows of different shapes and sizes follows the course of a brook, a winding, gurgling affair which floods on to the fields in winter. Some of the meadows are bounded by thick hedgerows with a venerable Black Poplar or two, and there are field ponds in the corners. Where water lies in the hollows the soil has grown black and peaty, and has provided the place-name, Mottey, from *motteaux*, meaning peaty earth. The place *has* changed of course. A tithe map of 1843 shows open drains, which have since been put underground, and an even more intricate jigsaw of fields, including an area known as the Dole Fields where the parish poor could cut hay from a strip of land, retaining some of the sale profits to supplement their miserable income. In this part of the Midlands, where suitable haymaking weather was by no means guaranteed, the cut hay was usually spread over the meadow in the morning in a process known as tedding and then left to dry before being raked together in 'win-rows' and bound into 'cobs' or 'grass-cocks'. The drying process might take a day or two to complete, before the hay was finally towed to the main stack. A populous place it must have been in early July, not at all like today's farmer alone in his tractor. The business of spreading the hay almost certainly helped to distribute wild flower seeds about the meadows and maintain their colourful richness.

The survival of traditional haymaking in this small corner of the West Midlands has ensured that, almost alone in the county, Mottey Meadows are still bright with wild flowers, among them marsh orchids, Meadow-rue, Pepper Saxifrage, Saw-wort and an abundance of the fuzzy purple balls of flowering Great Burnet, a plant that symbolises as well as any the past glories of the meadow. The flowers were appreciated by local people: a festival was held here once a year on the first Sunday in May when folk from the surrounding villages would meet to pick the pale purple bells of the Snakes-head Fritillary which gave its name to the festival: the Fritillary Wake or Folfalarum. These beautiful lilies must have been common then. With improved drainage they had declined almost to extinction at Mottey Meadows by the 1970s, but since the latter became a National Nature Reserve (the site was declared officially in 1982), the flowers have begun to recover their former numbers, probably because the grass is no longer grazed in the spring.

Places like Mottey Meadows are not only rich in wild flowers but also in types of wild vegetation. This Reserve has no fewer than nine recognisable types of grassland, which between them hold nearly all of the best mesotrophic (neutral) grassland in the entire county. What might seem at first sight to be a uniform area of grass and wild flowers turns out on close examination to be a mosaic of ridges and hollows, levels of peat and islands of drier sandier soil, each with a different flora. Once a meadow is drained and ploughed, these ancient and natural characteristics are lost, probably for ever. At Mottey Meadows some were indeed ploughed and reseeded, and have become the kind of uniformly green rye-grass swards that one finds from Cornwall to Kent. The botanical interest survives mainly on the fields which continue to grow hay in early summer, and which are 'after-grazed' by livestock in a thread of historical continuity that takes us back to the tithe map of 1843 and no doubt long before that, to the Norman landlord who gave us the name of Mottey.

The conservation pioneers paid little attention to uncultivated alluvial grassland which, in their day, was widespread in broad river valleys throughout England. Unfortunately it was all too easy, given government investment in drainage 'improvements', to convert meadowland to corn and treble the land's profitability. Most farmers did so with results that we see everywhere today. Less than 3% of the original area of permanent pasture survives. The Fritillary has become a rare wild flower, confined mainly to nature reserves and other protected sites. Because conservationists were slow to recognise the importance of wet meadows, it was only when the majority had already been drained and reseeded that the best of the rest became candidates for nature reserves. Since the 1970s, they have become a conservation priority. Between 1973 and 1992, the Conservancy acquired a dozen of the most interesting meadowlands in England as National Nature Reserves, ranging from the limestone dales of northern England to the floodplain of the Thames. Each Reserve has its own distinctive quality, and sometimes its own rare wild flower. Barrington Hill Meadows NNR in Somerset is made up of four fields on a gentle slope, one of which has thousands of Green-winged Orchids and another a good sprinkling of the local speciality, the Corky-fruited Water-dropwort, *Oenanthe pimpinelloides*. Muston Meadows in Rutland and Upwood Meadows in Cambridgeshire contain ridge-and-furrow fields, ploughed during some long-forgotten famine but later allowed to revert to wild grass. The furrows at Bentley Meadow in the latter site are unusually broad and have 'S-bends', evidently made by powerful plough-teams of eight oxen, yoked in pairs. About 150 species of flowering plants have been recorded from this single field, including 15 kinds of grass. Local people go there to remind themselves what cowslip meadows used to look like. In north-west England, High Leys and Gowk Bank NNRs are islands of traditionally managed grassland, the former on a gentle slope with seepage lines, the latter on the watery confluence of the River Irthing and the Butterburn. Here the vegetation has a pronounced northern flavour, with tall plants of cool, wet grass, like Globeflower, Melancholy Thistle and Wood Cranesbill.

Reserves on a much larger scale are Upper Teesdale in Durham and the Lower Derwent Valley in Yorkshire. Teesdale is best known for the alpine flowers of the sugar limestone turf above Cow Green Reservoir, but much of the nature reserve lies further down the valley, in the narrow fields leading from the white-washed houses on the hillside down to the boggy bottomland of the Tees. Here the severe climate has preserved a traditional way of mixed farming in which quantities of hay are needed to feed the livestock during the long cold winters of the dale. The Teesdale hay meadows, which are among the most beautiful in the country, are set in a wonderfully varied landscape of small woods, the fast-flowing river with its shingle beds and rocky gorges, the scrub of juniper and whin and the surrounding curlew-haunted moor. Here are perhaps the finest subalpine meadows in England, where in places you can find familiar buttercups, clovers and dandelions rubbing shoulders with northern delights like Spring Gentian, Bird's-eye Primrose, Alpine Bartsia and a bewildering variety of Lady's-mantles.

The Lower Derwent Valley (better known as The Derwent Ings) is among the most important National Nature Reserves to have been declared in recent years. The Derwent is one of the cleanest of English rivers, rising on the North Yorkshire Moors and soon swelling into a broad waterway winding across the lowlands of the Vale of York. It is notoriously prone to flooding in winter, especially after heavy snow on the Moors. Between Sutton upon Derwent and Bubwith, the river effectively acts as the main drains for the surrounding wet fields and meadows. A network of gravity-fed ditches drains into the river via a one-way flap valve known as a clew or clough. The water from the fields can normally enter the river by pushing open the flap, but during a flood the pressure of river water keeps the flap firmly closed, thus preventing the flood-water from flowing onto the fields. Different degrees of flooding have preserved a variety of wet grassland that is unusual even for natural meadowland. The flora of these meadows, swamps and ditches may be the richest of their kind in England, with 395 recorded species of flowering plants, including rarities like Marsh Pea, Loose Silky-bent, Mousetail and Narrow-leaved Water-dropwort. The area is large enough to form a valuable refuge for breeding duck and waders, and the large flocks of ducks, swans and Golden Plover that over-winter on the washlands of the Derwent Valley are one of the sights of northern England. The survival of this exceptionally rich flora and fauna was in doubt in the late 1970s, when a proposed pump drainage scheme would have enabled farmers to lower the water table below the critical summer level and convert the fields to grass leys or even arable. Fortunately the Conservancy was able to safeguard the viability of these precious wetlands in partnership with the Yorkshire Wildlife Trust, who already looked after a corner of them at Wheldrake Ings. In 1990 it was able to declare some 420 ha of the Derwent Valley as a National Nature Reserve.

The best known hayfield in all England is undoubtedly the North Meadow at Cricklade in Wiltshire, with its wonderful vista of Fritillaries around May Day. This

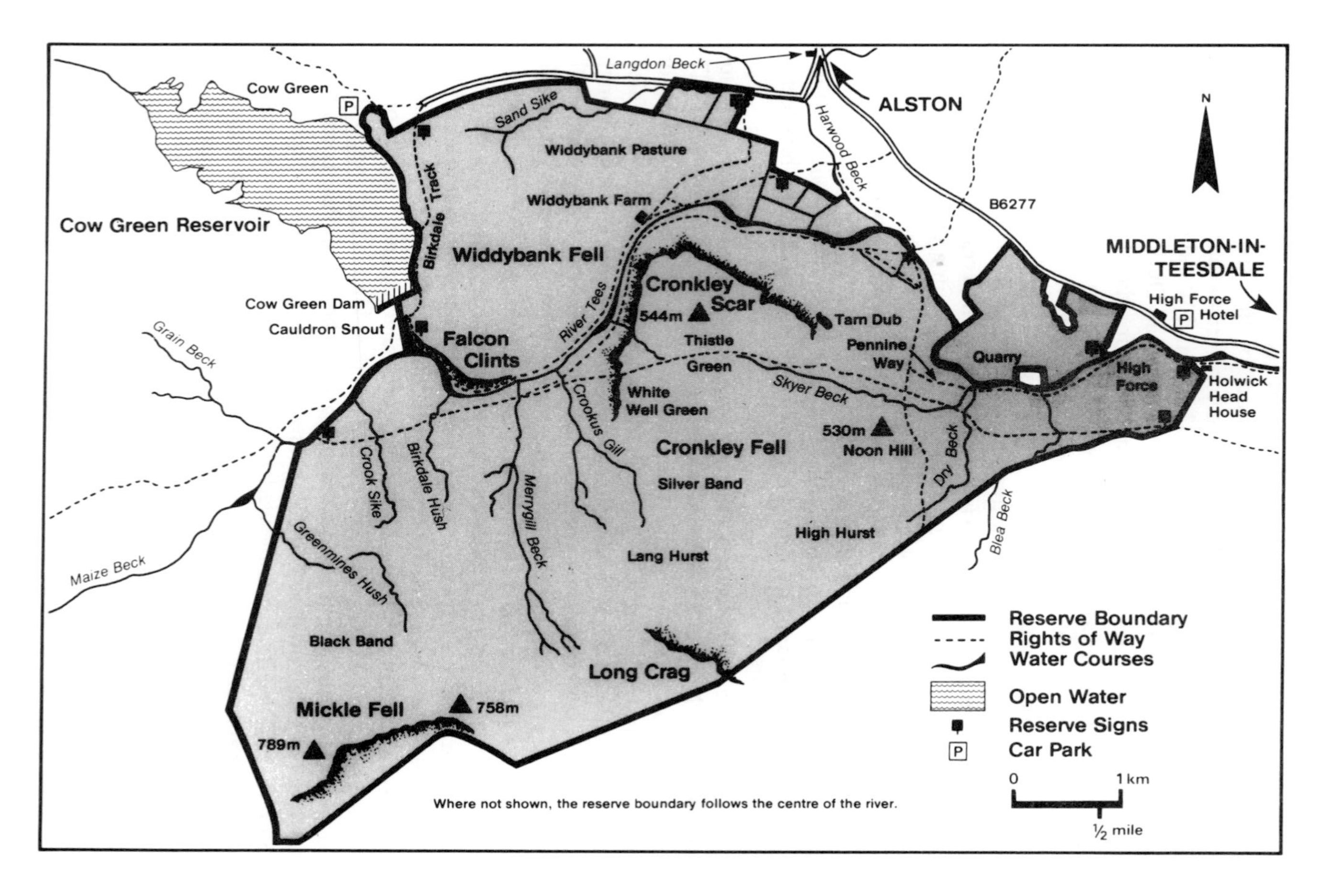

MAP 11 *Upper Teesdale NNR, Durham*

level field bounded by the young Thames and its tributary the Churn, survives because of a carefully regulated system of land tenure which has changed little in 800 years. By custom (which was enshrined in law in 1814), the residents of that ancient borough are entitled to pasture a maximum of 10 head of horses or cattle between Lammas Day (12 August) and Lady Day (12 February), or 20 head of sheep between 12 September and 12 February. For the rest of the year, the meadow reverts to private ownership and is 'shut up' for growing hay. This is a deeply seasonal place, becoming open common-land, hay meadow, floodland and cattle range by turns at different times of the year. Jeremy Purseglove describes memorably the important occasion on 12 August when Jim Marley, the hayward and postman of Cricklade, opens the meadow gate to let in the horses and cattle on Lammas Day:

> Seventy-five head of horses and cattle thunder into the field with a lack of sense of ancient ritual which would do justice to a rodeo. Their tails whisk, and they stampede off into the wide open spaces of their new-found freedom. One year, thirty horses galloped away into the meadow, charging straight up to the end of its 100 acres and vanishing into the willow-shrouded distance.

One of the most satisfying aspects of nature reserve management on old meadows is that many of them are still looked after on the Conservancy's behalf by people who have farmed the land for decades. Muston Meadows, for example, was farmed until 1988 by the Levesley family, who have preserved these beautiful meadows for more than 60 years and managed to save them from the Ministry ploughman during the wartime emergency. The Conservancy's main obligations on such sites are to maintain stock-proof hedges and fences, and sometimes also the drainage system. At North Meadow it pollards the Crack Willows by the Thames and rents up to 8 ha of the meadow at a time to a wild flower seed merchant. At the Upper Teesdale NNR, it operates field-by-field management agreements with the farmers of the dale, all but one of whom are tenants of one of two large upland estates. Here, the main problem is that despite the harshness of the climate, with its short growing season and late-lying snow, the use of chemical fertilisers and grant-aided drainage have made it possible to increase the productivity of the meadows by switching from the traditional system of hay and after-grazing to one of bale silage. Silage regimes increase the proportion of grass at the expense of wild flowers, and also involve fixed feeding areas which soon become muddy and trampled. The Conservancy offers financial compensation to farmers for sticking to old-fashioned haymaking. Virtually every field on the Reserve has a different 'management prescription', since some areas need a degree of cattle poaching to create open spaces for rare flowers, while others require fencing in summer to protect nesting birds, and others still need just the right amount of grazing to maintain wet grassland without producing an invasion of rushes. The management plan depends of course on the ability and willingness of the farming tenants to co-operate with the Conservancy within their overall conditions of tenancy. Fortunately more than half of the farmers of the dale now operate under the Ministry of Agriculture's Environmentally Sensitive Areas scheme which provides grants for less intensive and more 'environment-friendly' methods of farming. It is proving a useful inducement for farmers to resist the blandishments of tile drains, soluble nitrates and big bale silage. The Conservancy's role is increasingly one of 'fine-tuning' the system so that each field is farmed in such a way that its wildlife is protected or even (in the fashionable word) 'enhanced'.

The management of hayfield nature reserves sometimes poses a difficult dilemma. While hayfields are undoubtedly beautiful, the farming system that brought them into being was concerned with fodder for horses and farm animals, not pretty wild flowers; these simply came with the technique. It is quite possible to increase the species diversity of meadows, by varying the dates of cutting for example, or by ceasing to manure the meadow, but this may also mean reducing their value as pasture. High Leys NNR in the limestone hills of West Cumbria is a case in point. The higher of the five fields making up this small Reserve are a delight to the eye in June, a mass of Ox-eye Daisies, Yellow Rattles, Lady's-mantles and orchids, of exactly the kind that wild flower seed merchants try to emulate. To some local farmers, however, the field is 'a bloody disgrace'. In particular, they note that Yellow Rattle and eyebright have increased dramatically while the pasture grasses have declined. In agricultural terms it is crying out for quantities of the well-rotted farm manure that were traditionally spread on such fields in the early spring to maintain their productivity. (In the north hay-fields were sometimes grazed as well, and hence not cropped until late July.) The choice is between a traditional meadow of reasonable pasture value or an area of stressed herb-rich grass which may delight a botanist but make a farmer groan. In purist nature conservation terms we may prefer the latter, but if the Conservancy wishes to find a stock grazer it might have to compromise between the two.

Changing farming methods are in any case something that the manager of a nature reserve whose interest depends on livestock grazing has to come to terms with. On some of the larger chalk downland Reserves, the Conservancy controls the stock grazing by owning the flock or herd (see Chapter 7), but this is rarely a practical option on smaller sites. The Derbyshire Dales NNR is a case in point. This Reserve consists of a scatter of limestone dales many kilometres apart, and operates under a complex tenure of leases and freehold ownership. Each dale depends on grazing at different intensities, and by cattle as well as sheep, to maintain the varied swards that characterise and enrich the Dales landscape. The Conservancy is directly responsible for the maintenance of walls, fences and paths—a considerable commitment in this area. All the grazing is licensed. Unfortunately the traditional system of grazing that maintained the rich flora of the dales is in decline. Improvements in the quality of the pasture on the level ground above the dales, and the increased usage of indoor wintering for cattle and sheep, have meant that the dales are no longer grazed as heavily as they were. Moreover the breeds of sheep that are currently in favour—Suffolks, Leicesters and various French imports—tend to be frightened of steep slopes and, if possible, will keep to level ground. The result has been an increase in hawthorn, brambles and coarse grassland in places that used to be full of beautiful and uncommon limestone flowers. Fortunately scrub spreads relatively slowly in these upland dales, and it is usually possible to spot the danger signs and take appropriate action in time. At present, sufficient stock grazers still take advantage of the various perks offered by the Conservancy—stock proof walls, piped water supplies and electric fencing by dangerous cliffs—to maintain the Reserve's overall objective as a traditional Dales landscape of grassland, scrub and woodland. The system depends on good relations with local graziers and the Conservancy's reputation as a provider of a good farming service. Many of the present graziers are of an older generation, and whether the farmers that one day will replace them will wish to go on farming the dales in the manner of their fathers and grandfathers remains to be seen. In the long-term, a home-owned flock of hill sheep offers the main alternative, though an expensive one in terms of shepherding, trailers, dipping equipment and other capital costs.

THE WOOD BEHIND THE TREES

Of all our managed natural habitats, woodlands have seen perhaps the greatest change in attitudes since the 1950s. While many early nature reserves on grassland, wetland or heath suffered from too little management, some woodland ones suffered from too much, or at any rate, from the wrong kind. The main reason was a confusion between what is good for the individual trees and what is good for the ecological health of the broader woodland community. Conserving woods for wildlife is at least as much a matter of looking after the gaps—rides, ponds and glades—as about silviculture. Unfortunately, in 1950 most of the available expertise lay in the commercial cultivation of trees. And trees were generally regarded, in Oliver Rackham's memorable phrase, as 'gateposts with leaves'. They were supposed to grow fast, straight and close together. Wild, twisty, spreading, burr-ridden specimens were regarded as, at best, unsightly, and quite possibly diseased, a blemish on the forester's art. Unlike any other wild plant, trees are supposed to grow the way we want them to grow.

When the first woodland National Nature Reserves were established in the early 1950s, many of our long-established woods were in a bad state of repair, silviculturally speaking. The best timber had been stripped from the woods during the wartime emergency, and the surviving low-grade, mainly young, growth had become a tangle of regenerating stumps and brambles on poorly drained boggy ground. The system of coppicing, which had maintained the majority of our woods between the early Middle Ages and the late nineteenth century, was by then in terminal decline. By the 1950s, commercial coppice was confined mainly to south-eastern England where there was still a thriving market for chestnut palings, poles for various uses and pulp wood. Elsewhere our once valuable woods had reached a nadir of profitability. Their future purpose seemed to lie in timber production, which meant mainly softwood conifers or, in a few cases, in 'amenity' management (which meant conifers plus picnic sites).

Curiously enough, few knowledgeable people disagreed. The Conservancy preferred native hardwood trees to coniferous imports, but it too thought more in terms of silviculture than in wildlife management—not altogether surprisingly since most of its woodland specialists had been trained as foresters. The British school of forestry had turned its back on traditional methods of woodland management. It thought futuristically, and the future lay in fast-growing trees that could be harvested after 60 years in one fell swoop. It believed that conifers, especially the ubiquitous Sitka Spruce, would grow well on the sites of old English woods. It was not much interested in continental techniques of selection forestry and shelterwood systems which promote mixed-aged woods, nor in the cultivation of specialised markets for native timber and underwood. Native woods were, by and large, a hindrance to forestry and were best replaced with commercially viable crops of timber. Such attitudes were to remain engrained until the 1980s.

The rediscovery of how wild woods work (for it *was* a rediscovery; medieval woodmen clearly knew all about tree management but their knowledge died with them) began in the late 1960s, with the now well-known books and papers about woodland history and biogeography by Dr Oliver Rackham of Corpus Christi College, in Cambridge, and Dr George Peterken, then of Monks Wood Experimental Station and later the Conservancy's woodlands officer. Perhaps the most significant conclusion they came to was that many of our woods are extremely ancient, and some of them are almost certainly direct descendants of the 'Wildwood', the aboriginal forest which, for a few thousand years, covered most of lowland England before man began to settle down and clear the land. Woods known from historical evidence to be hundreds of years old have special characteristics, such as rare species, complex soils, curved borders and ancient banks. Woodland plants like Bluebells, Primroses and Wood Anemones are adapted to stable conditions or, at least, regular cycles of growth and regrowth. Some, but not all, woodland trees can reach a tremendous age, especially if they are cut regularly as coppice or pollards. Our oldest woodland trees are probably the large stools of Small and Large-leaved Lime, which may be 1000 years-old and only a few generations removed from the Stone Age.

Using information from old maps and documents coupled with surveys on the ground, the Conservancy has recently completed a grand survey of Britain's ancient and semi-natural woods, and this information is being used by the Forestry Commission and by local authorities to decide levels of grant-aid and planning protection. Securing this recognition of the special characteristics of ancient woodland and the consensus that it is something worth preserving is, arguably, the greatest achievement of nature conservation during the past quarter century. It might be noted that it was one made by a few individuals who managed to impress their ideas and discoveries on others. Committees had nothing to do with it. Certainly the preservation of our older woods seems to have struck a chord with the British people, to judge from the support given to campaigns to preserve woods and the successful appeals of charities like the Woodland Trust.

50. *Lower Derwent Valley.*

51. Above left: *The Ribble Marshes*. 52. Above right: *Lullington Heath in East Sussex*. 53. Below: *Finglandrigg Wood*.

54. Above: *The dramatic shingle desert at Orfordness.* 55. Below: *Skoska Wood, North Yorkshire.*

56. Above left: *Dunsdon Farm*. 57. Above right: *Chartley Moss in Staffordshire*. 58. Below: *Scar Close, Ingleborough*.

Much of the impetus behind this remarkable Renaissance has come from techniques pioneered in individual woods. A handful of places—Monks Wood, Bradfield Woods in Suffolk, Hayley Wood near Cambridge and the Shabbington Woods near Oxford, to name four prominent ones—have become well enough known to inspire the subsequent management of scores of woodland nature reserves elsewhere. Of the National Nature Reserves, Monks Wood has perhaps had the greatest influence. It was one of the first Reserves to be taken fully in hand, thanks to the influence of the nearby intellectual powerhouse of Monks Wood Experimental Station, and it occupies an important place in the conservation history of English woodland. Monks Wood is one of the largest ancient woods on the Cambridgeshire boulder clay. Its fame dates from 1828 when the first British specimens of the Black Hairstreak butterfly were noted there. Like many of our ancient coppice woods Monks Wood has few old trees, for virtually the whole wood was felled and 'left a desert' by Canadian lumberjacks during and after the First World War. Almost all the present trees have grown up during the past 70 years. Nevertheless it has developed into a fairly varied wood with an unusually large number of ponds where the streams have been dammed, and areas of young and older growth. Because of this innate variety, the Reserve management plan embraces virtually all of the options open to the Conservancy when managing ancient woods. Part has been allowed to grow up as high forest of oak and ash by singling the coppice stools and thinning the canopy to enable the best trees to grow well. But most of the wood has simply been left alone to develop in a natural way. In the original management plan, these 'non-intervention zones' were there to provide a 'control' for comparing managed and unmanaged woodland, but scientists now recognise that there is merit, not to say due humility, in leaving certain areas to nature, especially on nature reserves.

Where hazel grows well at Monks Wood, the growth is cut in a regular cycle as coppice. This work began in 1954 and was supplemented by the planting of saplings and by 'layering' the cut shoots by bending them over and pegging them into the ground. Nowadays there is more emphasis on mixed coppice, and hazel is no longer layered or planted. By the mid-1980s, the future of coppice at Monks Wood was in doubt, since the Muntjac deer using the wood had greatly increased in number and were browsing the life out of the coppice, threatening to reduce natural regeneration to zero. Fortunately, electric fencing erected in 1988 succeeded in protecting the new shoots, allowing some 14 ha of the wood to continue to be cut over as hazel or mixed coppice by the estate worker team.

The pioneering aspect of the Monks Wood's experience, however, lay not in coppicing but in the management of its permanent glades and 18 km network of rides. The open spaces and borders of a wood are generally its richest areas for wildlife, especially for wild flowers and nectar-seeking insects like butterflies, hoverflies and bees. Monks Wood used to enjoy the reputation of being one of the best butterfly sites in the East Midlands, and it was the needs of the Black Hairstreak in particular that encouraged people to pay due attention to the long rides and borders of the wood. To counter the growing shade, the main rides were at first restored and later widened by felling trees along the sides, and thereafter were maintained by cutting and mowing to produce a gradation from the woodland canopy through scrub and tall flowery grass to the closer mown grass of the ride itself. The technique has been improved and elaborated over the years, and the main rides have been broadened even further.

Present research suggests that in mature woodland a ride will need to be at least 30–45 m wide to cater for the most sun-demanding woodland insects, like some of the fritillaries. Rides of at least that size were not uncommon in large coppiced woods in the past. The essence of the Monks Wood-pioneered technique of ride management is to compress the natural variety of woodland edges and open spaces into zones along the rides, which thereupon become arterial routes for wildlife as well as people and machines. The spring flushes of Primroses and Bugles, and the sudden access of sunshine and light to the interior of the wood make them more pleasurable for people, too.

In the northern half of Monks Wood are two large permanent glades, the result of a futile wartime attempt to grow potatoes. For many years these have been mown each autumn by a tractor and swipe to keep the encroaching scrub at bay. In recent years management has been refined to create a mixture of short swards, favoured by insects like the Grizzled Skipper butterfly, and areas of longer grass together with patches of scrub. The gain in habitat diversity has been increased further by allowing scrub and tall grass to develop at intervals along the margins to create a scalloping of bushy headlands and grassy bays. This broadening of the ecologically rich border between woodland and open spaces is now a widespread form of management on woodland Reserves. It reflects the trend we have noted in other habitats: of management in detail, aided by advances in technology. Perhaps the high degree of habitat management on English nature reserves owes something to the Englishman's traditional love of gardening. But it is fundamentally a reaction to the desperately small and isolated nature of our remaining wild habitats, especially in East Anglia. Some 370 species of flowering plants and ferns, more than 1000 species of beetles and 100 species of hoverflies have been recorded from the 157 ha of Monks Wood. The only chance of keeping them all is to go all out for diversity.

The recent remarkable revival of traditional coppice management in woodland nature reserves has been achieved in spite of the falling market for coppice products. The great gale of 1987 provided small timber in plenty and killed the firewood market stone dead. More recently, the pulpwood outlet has also dried up after the mills switched to recycling. At Monks Wood relatively little coppice wood finds a market. David Massen has received the occasional call for hazel rods to make thatching spars, and one contractor used the wood for fencing stakes, hedge-binders and, on one occasion, to restore the wattles of a timber-framed house. Before the electric fence was erected, some of the 'brash' was piled onto freshly cut stools to protect them from deer damage, but now most of it ends up on the bonfire. Several other Reserves have more regular commercial outlets for coppiced underwood. Swanton Novers NNR in Norfolk sells wood to the local river and coastal defence authorities to make fascines used for shoring up crumbling river banks and for trapping drifting sand. It helps that in this case the underwood is of unusually high quality, having been harvested continuously and by the same man, Mr Jesse Leeder, since 1946. In the past there was a much more varied demand for underwood from Swanton Novers to make hurdles, pea sticks and faggots for the nearby brick kilns. Repeated cropping over many years has produced the extraordinary natural architecture of that Reserve—vast lime stools, like rugged barrels, cut high because of the wet ground, and long-disused Sessile Oak coppice, twisting and flaring from the woody pedestals, like bouquets. Underwood at Highbury Wood NNR in the Wye Valley is also cut regularly, by a contractor who pays £300 a tonne for it, although the Conservancy first had to put in a hard access track. The Reserve manager, Malcolm Whitmore, still does the more fiddly work himself, notably where the coppice shoots are hopelessly tangled by clematis.

Tom Wall hit on a novel way of reinstating old oak coppice at the Stiperstones NNR and involving local people in the management of the Reserve at the same time. Here oak grows on the lower slopes of the steep hillside, and was probably cut regularly in former years for fuelling the local lead mining industry (though in later years they used coal). Tom divided the coppice into a number of hectare-sized coups, each of which was to be felled in turn on a long rotation. The first coup went smoothly enough after the standing timber was sold to a local man to cut for firewood. For the second, however, no buyer could be found. Instead, Tom arranged for a contractor to do the felling. As six people had expressed an interest in purchasing the fallen timber as firewood, he divided the plot into as many strips running up the hillside. A ballot was drawn for the strips, so that each purchaser had an equal chance to buy the better quality strips. The purchasers then collected the fallen wood themselves, having paid as much as £45 for the easiest slope or as little as £25 for the hardest. The Tom Wall method of wood sale echoes the age-old practice of blind lots frequently used on hay meadows where the quality of the crop was naturally uneven.

The Wyre Forest and Roudsea Wood NNRs still provide small quantities of the traditional products of western oakwoods, charcoal and bark. Both woods were once cut over regularly to supply underwood to the leather industry, and the iron smelters of the West Midlands and the Furness district. They are rich in relicts of the industrial past, Roudsea Wood quite extraordinarily so. In little more than a mile of walking there you can find circles of stones, the remains of huts where bark peelers used to live, funnel-shaped pits where the wood was baked to make potash, hearths where charcoal was cooked in large turf-covered mounds, lime kilns fuelled by wooden faggots and a well-preserved stone barn where the cut bark was stored and seasoned. It is a vivid reminder of how thoroughly worked were many of our ancient woods, and the historical evidence seems at first sight to be at odds with the scientist's belief that Roudsea Wood has not changed significantly in 3000 years. The resolution of intensive use and apparently natural composition comes in the management of the wood as a *harvest*, taking advantage of natural cycles of growth and renewal. By keeping out grazing animals at critical times, and by minor modifications to the drainage, the woodman could remove quantities of small-bore timber from Roudsea Wood without changing its overall character. The conifers and other trees planted in Roudsea Wood in more recent times represent something quite different: the removal of the natural vegetation and its replacement with trees chosen by the forester. In view of its history, it is fitting that a few Lake District craftsmen still use underwood from Roudsea Wood and its neighbours to make charcoal for barbecues, tanbark for leather goods, and poles for tent pegs and rustic tool handles. It is equally encouraging that the Sitka Spruce planted there in the 1950s is being removed.

Over much of lowland England the most valuable coppice product was hazel with its amazing springiness and pliability, especially when split. At the Wyre Forest in Worcestershire, however, the main 'crop' was oak of about 20-years-old, the best raw material to make high quality industrial charcoal. By the mid-seventeenth century, virtually the whole of this 3000-ha forest had been harnessed for the iron smelting industry, and organised into compartments of 12–40 ha on a cutting rotation of 20 years or so. Very few large standard trees were spared, and the requirement for good charcoal and bark meant that trees other than oak were weeded out. The oak, however, remained wild Sessile Oak. If the Forest had been managed for timber it would probably have been planted with Pedunculate Oak and beech, but for charcoal purposes the native, scrubby hill oaks were quite good enough. Wildlife adapted to the change—woodpeckers and hawks might have lost their favourite perches and nesting sites, but this was more than compensated for by the gain in open clearings and broad rides, together with sheltered pastures and hay fields to supply fodder for the horses. Such was its usefulness that this medieval Forest has survived to the present day more or less intact. For the past 80 years or so, however, the oak woods of Wyre have been neglected or converted to high forest by singling the stools, while the Forestry Commission has replaced some of the old woods with conifers. This was the position in 1978 when the NCC took over the management of 600 ha of neglected but semi-natural forest as a National Nature Reserve.

For a decade, the Wyre Forest Reserve was managed mainly as high forest of mixed age and as many broad rides and glades as the manager, John Robinson, had time to maintain. In 1988, however, John began something altogether more ambitious: a programme of works to change the Forest from its present rather uniform aspect to a much more varied and interesting series of woodlands with areas of pure coppice, coppice-with-standards and oak high forest. Over the next 30 years, it is hoped to restore some 120 ha of coppice at a rate of 4 ha per year. It will involve the felling of hundreds of 60–80-year-old oaks, which are sold as firewood logs or used as fencing stakes on the Reserve (their quality is too poor for the saw-mill). At the same time, the high forest is being diversified further by the clearance of 0.4 acre-sized 'coups' which English Nature plans to thin every 30 years and fell after 90 years. The remainder of the trees will remain untouched to live out their natural life-span. Scattered about the Reserve, often in the least accessible places, are 'limited intervention areas' where management will be confined to removing invasive trees like sycamore. The project is still only 5-years-old, and although it remains on target, 30 years is a long time in conservation . . . But the Wyre Forest has the potential, at least, to become one of the most impressive nature reserves of the twenty-first century, a demonstration area of woodland management for conservation, and—who knows?—one that may hold lessons for commercial foresters as well as nature reserve managers.

Downton Gorge NNR in Herefordshire presents a different sort of management challenge. The woods that line the rocky banks overlooking the clear waters of the Teme as it flows over limestones, siltstones and sandstones in a series of rocky dells and gurgling hollows, contain big standard oaks, low pollarded limes and large coppice stools that hint at a complex history. Taverner records that in the sixteenth century trees from the Gorge were 'lopped and shredd to make Cole for the Council at Ludlowe'. Later on the natural beauty of the Gorge so inspired its owner, the connoisseur and aesthete Richard Payne Knight (1751–1824), that he used it as his perfect illustration of the ideals of the Picturesque landscape. In his championship of the rough and the natural, Knight anticipated the Romantic poets and painters. In his long 'didactic poem' he inveighed against the formalism represented by Capability Brown and his followers who:

. . . . alike lay waste
The forms of nature, and the works of taste!
T'improve, adorn, and polish, they profess;
But shave the goddess, whom they come to dress;
Level each broken bank and shaggy mound,
And fashion all to one unvaried round!'

(from *The Landscape: a Didactic Poem* (1794) by Richard Payne Knight)

Knight developed the point at Downton Gorge by laying out walks designed to show off the scenery and viewpoints where the visitor could admire the rocky defile and the river with the peaceful scene of cattle and sheep grazing in the fields beyond. He also enhanced the dramatic appeal of the Gorge in characteristic eighteenth century fashion by excavating caverns and building a bath house which, since he was a classics scholar, inevitably became known as the Roman Baths.

Knight's subtle design is now somewhat overgrown but his ideas chime rather nicely with English Nature's own management principles, a point made by the site manager Tom Wall in the Reserve management plan. Knight had maintained what amounted to a nature reserve, carefully preserving the Gorge's essential wildness, but varying it here and there by coppicing the underwood and creating glades. 'It would be fitting,' suggests Tom, 'if English Nature were to reciprocate by encouraging the restoration of his designed landscape.'

The main threat to the future of woods managed by natural regeneration techniques is a four-legged one—deer. The increase in our largest wild animals is as mysterious as it is troublesome for foresters. The present numbers of deer far exceed the 'carrying capacity' of woodland over large areas of eastern England, and unless young coppice is protected by expensive fences and/or deep piles of brash, it will be devoured, every last shoot and leaf. Some woods, like those of Castor Hanglands NNR near Peterborough, now have a prominent browse line at antler height, below which the vegetation is stripped bare. Deer are also fond of flowers. Hales Wood NNR in Essex used to be famous for its displays of Oxlips, but, as in so many woods in Oxlip country, the flowers now grow mainly behind tall fences or under the protection of piles of brushwood. The Conservancy has had some success there with 'dead hedges'—dense thickets of brushwood piled around the periphery of the coppiced plot to deter the deer. Unfortunately the problem is spreading to areas hitherto untroubled by excessive browsing. Deer fencing is now necessary at the Wyre Forest to protect the young coppice from damage, which of course increases the bill for conservation work by hundreds of pounds a hectare. At Wyre the Conservancy co-operates with neighbouring landowners in a regular deer cull, but in most areas occasional shooting has made little impact on deer numbers. Deer are at present a problem without a solution, meat without a predator. This situation is probably new to history.

The other environmental 'disasters' that have visited English woodlands in recent decades—gales and Dutch Elm disease—have proven much more benign. Dutch Elm disease certainly changed the character of woods containing large stands of elm, especially the limestone woods of the north and west where Wych Elm is an important component of the canopy. At the Avon Gorge NNR near Bristol and Ebbor Gorge in the Mendips, Dutch Elm disease set in with a vengeance in the late 1970s, causing a great deal of extra work removing some of the dead standing timber, a task which has to be approached cautiously for safety reasons. The temporary muddy mess that resulted caused a public outcry. In the longer term, the death of the elms removed most of the need for thinning, created some excellent glades and allowed the Conservancy to pay more attention to coppicing. Much of the 'dead' elm has recently sprung back from the roots, though we may have to regard elm in future as underwood rather than standard trees. The hurricanes of 1987 and 1990 have had much the same effect on a more limited number of woods (poor Avon Gorge received a heavy dose of both winds). The Reserves most badly hit in 1987 were Ham Street Woods in Kent and Benacre in Suffolk. In these cases much of the timber has been left where it fell to form *ipso facto* non-intervention zones, once the rides and main access ways were cleared. Most conservationists now regard these occasional powerful winds as a Good Thing, not least because they are a strong argument against even-aged monocultures and for more traditional, mixed-aged management.

A woodland Reserve manager spends much of his time 'weeding out' unwanted trees, notably sycamore, which is an unmannerly tree and likes to take over the wood, and conifers which were generally planted there by a previous owner (though in the case of Yarner Wood it was the Conservancy itself that planted them!—see Chapter 5). Whether or not such trees are a problem varies from site to site. At Castle Eden Dene in Durham, sycamore control is a major task but the small blocks of conifers are tolerated since they support a small population of red squirrels. Sometimes the aims of management have changed with shifting perceptions. Chaddesley Wood NNR in Worcestershire was originally set up with the aim of reconciling modern methods of forestry with nature conservation. For that reason, and because the wood was under a dedication agreement, the half of it that was under conifers was retained but given a modest face-lift with nest boxes, broader rides and a pond or two. With the Forestry Commission's Damascene conversion to broadleaved management in the mid-1980s, the original point of Chaddesley Woods was overtaken by events. The new management plan acknowledges that conifers have no business being there at all, and proposes to replace them with broadleaved trees native to the site. Perhaps confidence has increased too.

Coppice management receives the lion's share of publicity on woodland National Nature Reserves, especially when it is designed to benefit a rare species like the Heath Fritillary at Blean Woods (see Chapter 6) or the High Brown Fritillary at Gait Barrows. The management of mature woodland and high forest is generally of a more routine nature, though with refinements like the clearance of small coups to encourage natural regeneration and open up the woodland floor. Workman's Wood, part of the Cotswold Commons and Beechwoods NNR, is unusual in that it is managed commercially by its owner, John Workman, using methods entirely in sympathy with the character of these beautiful escarpment woods and their wildlife. For more than a century, Workman's Wood has yielded high quality timber using a system of small-scale felling on regular rotations that vary between 30 and 180 years. Most of the replacement trees come from natural regeneration in the gaps, although some planting has taken place where the former proves inadequate. The result is an attractive beechwood, much more varied in age structure and composition than most such woods, and rich in the many rare and local wild flowers of the Cotswolds area. The

Conservancy's main involvement is to compensate John Workman for any expected revenue from trees that have been spared to live out their natural lives. Over-mature trees are especially important in this wood since most of the dead wood has been removed by the commoners with estover rights. If only more woods had been looked after as well during the past century we might have less need for woodland nature reserves.

GUARDING METHUSELAH: WOOD-PASTURE RESERVES

Most really old trees, that is those aged 500 years or more, do not occur in woods (except as large coppice stools) but in the more open landscapes of ancient parks and commons. Places like this which combine old trees with extensive grasslands for grazing animals—deer, cattle, sheep or horses—are known by ecologists as wood-pasture. England has an unrivalled heritage of wood-pastures in the 'ancient and ornamental' woods of the New Forest, the royal Great Park at Windsor and the private parks of country houses, such as Duncombe, Moccas, Staverton and Boconnoc. Old trees of vast girth, partly rotten inside and with raggle-taggle crowns represent an ecosystem in themselves, with a large dependent flora and fauna, including lichens and bryophytes on the bark, fungi as rotting agents and beetles and other insects that subsist on the products of the crumbling tree—sap, sawdust, leaf mulch and decomposing bodies. By the nature of their situation, wood-pastures often lie on the most private of private land: where the country gentry have rode, hunted and generally enjoyed themselves in generations dating back to the Conquest (one tottering oak at Windsor is traditionally associated with William the Conqueror). It is perhaps not surprising that this habitat is poorly represented on National Nature Reserves. None the less, the two largest sites do have protective covenants. Windsor's Great Park and Forest is managed by the Crown Estate Commissioners under an informal 'minute of intent' with English Nature, and the trees of the New Forest have been preserved by laws that long predate all nature conservation legislation, and are none the worse for that.

The only private park to be declared a National Nature Reserve under private agreement is Moccas Park in Herefordshire, although it is likely that Duncombe Park near Helmsley in North Yorkshire will soon join it. Fine old trees are also present at Benacre, Ashford Hill, Buckingham Thick Copse, Cotswold Commons and Beechwoods, Downton Gorge and the Wyre Forest NNRs.

Old trees require very little management in themselves. We are sometimes sentimental about particular trees, giving them names, and propping up their tottering masses with wires supports so that they resemble sick giants on crutches. In the United States, park rangers sometimes hasten the process of decay by blowing off bark with explosives, gouging out holes with chainsaws and even inoculating the tree with the spores of wood-rotting fungi, with the aim of providing better habitats for insects, woodpeckers and racoons. From a conservation viewpoint there is no reason why an old tree should not be left alone to fall slowly to pieces. The important thing is that the hulks are left to rot where they are and are not removed or burned. Many of these 'sick' trees will, of course, be living still when we are all gone. In English nature reserves, the 'management' of large old trees is generally confined to looking after their immediate surroundings and ensuring that a new generation of trees will be in place when eventually the old ones die.

An example of the former approach is Buckingham Thick Copse, part of Whittlewood Forest on the Bucks/Northants border, which was formally declared a National Nature Reserve in 1990, though the Conservancy had already managed it for several years, having purchasing the standing timber. Much of the interest of this well-preserved wood is centred on 44 ancient oaks, whose gnarled and embossed hulks grace the woodland rides. Unfortunately half of the hulks are dead, including one great tree straight out of a horror film, with a bee's nest in its midst, called 'Fred'. Only 12 trees are still reasonably vital. No one knows why these trees are dying. The Reserve manager, Graham Bellamy, believes that the best trees of the wood were selectively felled in the past leaving only the lame and the knock-kneed. Even so, the die-back has been greater here than in other woods in the region. Competition from other trees and air pollution may be responsible. To give the survivors a chance, Graham has cut down some of the surrounding younger growth to allow more space and light for the crowns. He has also selected suitable replacement trees for pollarding by choosing oaks in prominent positions, preferably near the rides. At the same time, some low ash pollards, presently marooned in a thicket of scrub, will be rescued and cropped regularly to preserve their form and prolong their life.

Moccas Park NNR, where the Conservancy has a short-term agreement with the estate trustees, has 40 times as many ancient trees as Buckingham Thick Copse, set in one of the most impressive medieval parks in the country. Many of the trees are pollards with characteristic massive trunks and small but spreading crowns. The park is well known to entomologists for its fauna of rare beetles, and it is also a notable place for the lichens of old bark—a surviving remnant of the flora and fauna of prehistoric woodland. As in many parks, there is little or no regeneration. The estate put cages round some of the old trees in the 1950s to protect them from browsing and bark nibbling. They otherwise seem secure—indeed the famous diarist Francis Kilvert thought they would last until Judgement Day. The same cannot be said, unfortunately, for their bark lichens which are in deep decline. The reasons for this are obscure. The present air pollution load is surprisingly high, probably because of the frequent mists and low cloud in this hilly district. Much of the Park was ploughed, limed and fertilised in the 1960s (before it became a National Nature Reserve) and the stocking levels were increased. The drift of fertiliser may have produced an enrichment of the bark, as shown by the green algae now growing on the lichens. It is also possible that ammonia released from animal dung may have contributed to the effect. Many bark lichens are extremely sensitive to air pollutants, especially sulphur dioxide from coal, and are increasingly confined to western and upland districts farthest from industrial areas.

With a view to providing a new generation of pollarded trees at Moccas, English Nature are pollarding a number of 150-year maiden oaks and have also planted about 1000 trees from locally gathered seed, including oak, beech, maple, lime, ash and Sweet Chestnut—perhaps the most long-term investment on any Reserve (rare beetles prefer oaks at least 300 years old, but the average Reserve management agreement runs for only 21 years!). Tree planting is nowadays comparatively rare on National Nature Reserves, and done only when there is little chance of trees colonising naturally, for example, along the upland gills of Ingleborough, or in places badly stricken by Dutch Elm disease.

CANUTE REVISITED: DEFENDING THE COAST

Nature reserves below the high water mark differ from their landward equivalents in at least one important respect: they have no fixed size or shape, for while some intertidal zones may grow in size year after year, others may wash away during a storm or disappear beneath the rising sea. In the natural course of events, some 'soft' shores are accreting, such as the saltmarshes of the Wash and North Norfolk coast, whilst others, like those of Essex, are in retreat. In part this is an entirely natural event: our whole island behaves rather like a raft. Scotland sank slightly under the extra

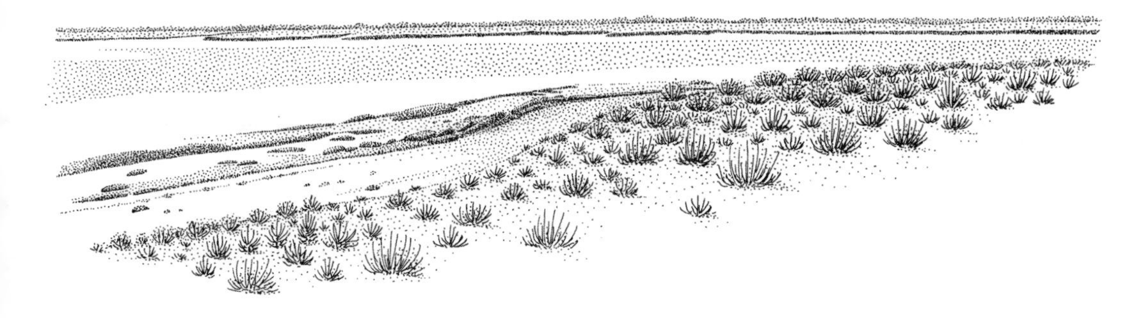

burden of ice during the Pleistocene, but as the land adjusted to ice-free conditions it was southern England's turn to dip into the sea. Civilisation has complicated these natural rises and falls in two important ways. Firstly we have built sea walls along the most vulnerable shorelines to turn back the tide. Secondly our by-products have increased the level of carbon dioxide in the atmosphere so that we seem to be experiencing a mild greenhouse effect, the notorious global warming. As the poles melt, the sea rises. In the past century the sea is estimated to have risen by an average of 10–20 cm. On current predictions it will rise by another 20 cm by 2030 and by 65 cm by the end of the twenty-first century.

If these figures are right, then the implications for some of our estuaries and other soft shores are far-reaching. The intertidal zone in which saltmarsh forms is already being 'squeezed' between the rising tide and the sea walls. To make matters worse, many marshes are being eroded immediately in front of the walls, since the energy of the tide is no longer being absorbed naturally through a system of creeks. In these circumstances, the sea walls themselves become undermined, and the material to patch them up comes, as often as not, from the saltmarsh immediately in front. And, since the saltmarsh acts as an effective buffer of tidal energy, its loss means that sea walls have to be built ever higher and stronger. The logical end result may be, in English Nature's uncharacteristically apocalyptic words, 'a vision of solid concreted cliffs and barren sea walls'.

The erosion of saltmarsh is most acute in Suffolk and Essex, just where the habitat is at its most extensive. In the Blackwater Estuary, a National Nature Reserve since 1983, some 16% of its saltmarsh has been lost over the past 20 years, representing a rate of 7 ha a year. This proportion seems to be about normal for that part of the coast. The National Nature Reserves most threatened by 'coastal squeeze' are the five Reserves on the Essex coast (which effectively form a near-continuous stretch of intertidal habitat) and the Walberswick and Benacre Reserves in Suffolk. At Dengie and Hamford Water in Essex, coastal defences have been strengthened by sinking Thames barges laden with silt and gravel in a line 500 m offshore to form makeshift breakwaters. The idea is that sediment will accrete in the calm water behind the wrecks and restore the saltmarsh where it is most needed. These expedients have an air of desperation about them. A long-term solution demands a rather more subtle approach.

A new idea that is gaining ground is the notion of 'managed retreat'. As part of its Living Coast campaign, English Nature has argued that it is more intelligent—and less expensive—to work with natural forces to absorb the energy of waves and tides, rather than by building higher and higher walls. For undeveloped parts of the coast it advocates abandoning the present line of coastal defences and shifting them landwards as the sea rises, in the manner of a General with limited troops faced with the prospect of a massive enemy onslaught. With the right kind of 'soft engineering', marine sediments could be encouraged to accrete in front of the new walls and form a new saltmarsh zone, while freshwater grazing marsh could be created behind the barrier through a system of water control. Such ideas conform well with geomorphological theory, but they go against the grain of agricultural tradition: the farmers of the Wash, for example, are used to regarding the saltings as 'the next generation's cabbages'. To convince others of the practicality of managed retreat, demonstration areas will be needed. This is another instance where National Nature Reserves, notably the Wash and the Essex Coast Reserves, may have an important part to play.

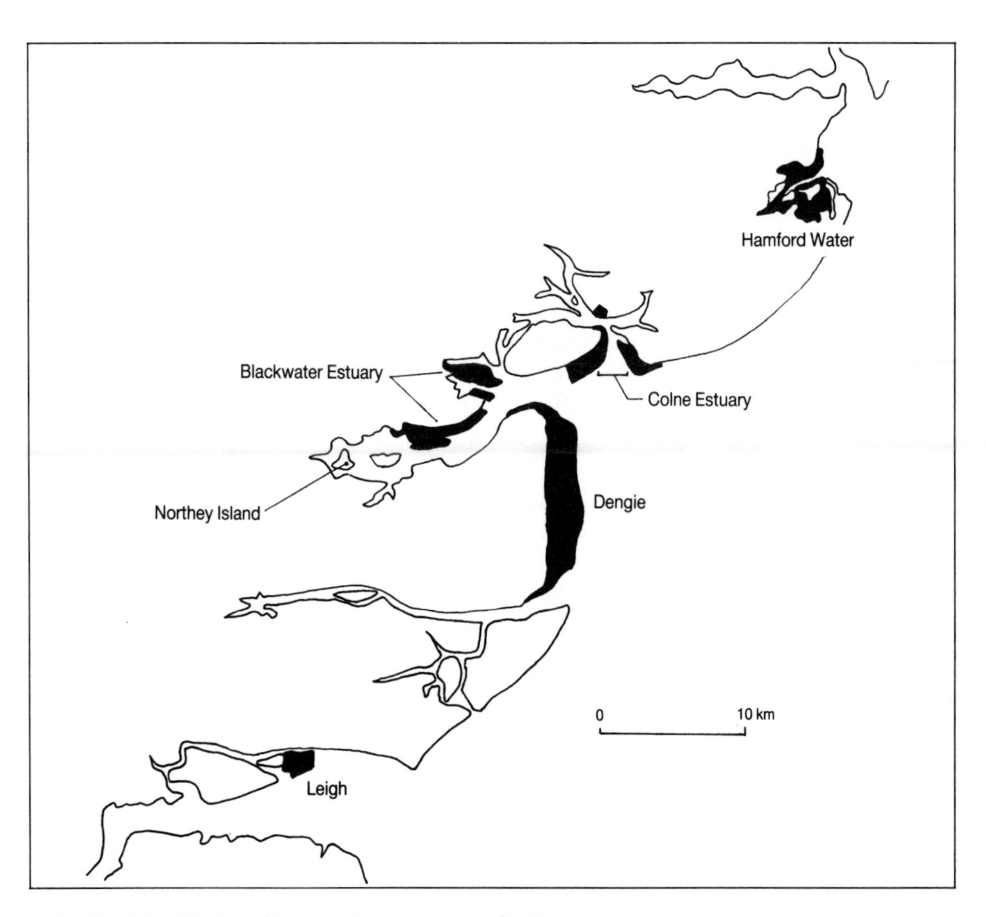

MAP 12 *National Nature Reserves on the Essex coast*

A small-scale experiment to test the possibilities of managed retreat is presently underway at Northey Island, a National Trust property near the upper end of the Blackwater Estuary NNR, as a co-operative venture funded by the Trust, English Nature and the National Rivers Authority. Much of the island is already a *de facto* example of managed retreat, since its extensive marshland is less than 100 years old, having formed after the old sea wall was breached at the turn of the century. Creating new saltmarsh quickly, and within the constraints of a budget, requires careful design. The idea is not simply to lower the sea wall and wait for the sea to rush in, but to control the tide in such a way that its scouring action is minimised and marine sediment is able to accumulate over erstwhile farmland. To achieve this at Northey Island, the sea wall was lowered just enough to allow overtopping at high tide. Meanwhile a 20-m spillway was made along a gentle slope just above sea level to allow the ebb tide to flow seawards. An inner embankment slightly higher than the original one was raised 50 m inland. The design allows the 0.8-ha site to be flooded for about one day in three, which, it is believed, will encourage the widest diversity of saltmarsh plants. The follow-up monitoring by English Nature staff suggests that we are correct in believing that saltmarshes can form remarkably quickly, given the right conditions. After 2 years, parts of the former fields are already a glistening carpet of glasswort, one of the main saltmarsh pioneers, and a creek system is beginning to develop. The experiment, including the consultant's report, cost some £25,000, which compares favourably with the estimated £55,000 needed to repair the sea wall. It is likely to hold implications for the future of much of the 260 km of sea walls in Essex.

At Benacre Broad, part of the Benacre NNR on the Suffolk coast, managed retreat has been used to postpone what may be its inevitable fate of inundation. This Broad is a most unusual habitat, not an ancient peat digging like the Norfolk Broads but a natural brackish lagoon in a peat-lined basin and separated from the sea only by a low and narrow shingle bar. The bar is frequently breached or overtopped at high tide, and a particularly high spring tide in 1993 surged into the Broad, washing away the steps of the hide and depositing all kinds of rubbish in its wake. The first signs of the rising sea and increased salinity within the lagoon were noticed by the Reserve manager, Cliff Waller, as long ago as 1984, when the reeds at the landward end of the Broad began to die back. An engineered solution involving strengthening the bar was far too expensive to contemplate, and Cliff's eventual answer was much more in keeping with traditional nature reserve management under the maxim of 'low cost, low key; low impact, low input'. Using diggers and dump trucks to transport material, he built a series of low bunds across the Broad to protect the places which still held good stands of reed, using peat and reed rhizomes from an overgrown dyke and a capping of clay obtained from nearby land. These cheap and relatively lightweight barriers have proven sufficient to withstand the tide, so long as its main force continues to be absorbed by the shingle bar. Building them has also been an exercise in habitat creation, for the pools left by the excavations have proved attractive to ducks and other birds, while sluices placed in the bunds to raise the water level have created excellent natural scrapes for passage waders, as well as a range of different salinities from mildly brackish to heavily saline. Cliff has used similar techniques to protect other broads and reedbeds at Benacre and Walberswick, with the difference that, by taking action at an early stage, it may be possible to protect these areas for longer than is likely at Benacre Broad. The type of managed retreat envisaged at Northey Island and the Wash is, unfortunately, impracticable here since the land rises immediately behind the narrow coastal zone. The accent has to be on buying time, time which can be used to refine habitat creation techniques, demonstrate the practicality of managed retreat and to convince others of the need to come to terms with the rising sea.

Countering the destructive effects of tides on nature reserves is not, of course, new. Most coastal Reserves have experienced occasional tidal surges of enormous power—natural events to be sure, but ones which can put back years of work. Gibraltar Point, for example, lost its colonies of Natterjacks and Crested Newts in 1978 when the tide breached the dunes and flooded the freshwater marsh. The high seaward dunes at Braunton Burrows and Ainsdale have been undercut by storm tides and the sand blown hundreds of metres inland. There is a limit to what any Reserve manager can do to prevent violent events of this sort. The chestnut paling used at Ainsdale and North Walney NNRs can help to trap sand and build small dunes. Marram-grass was also planted at Braunton Burrows and elsewhere in the early days, but it has now been virtually abandoned as a conservation technique, partly on the grounds of limited success, partly because planting on nature reserves is no longer in vogue. The Conservancy now accepts blow-outs and dune erosion as part of the dynamic that continues to mould our coastline. One of the biggest and most onerous tasks of duneland managers in the 1970s and 1980s was in fact to remove the Sea Buckthorn planted in the best King Canute spirit by the Ministry of Defence and others in an attempt to restore those parts of the coast that were damaged by military training.

Nowhere was the latent power of the sea demonstrated more forcefully in recent years than on the Solent in the late 1980s. The manager of the North Solent NNR, James Venner, remembers the gales of December 1989, which caused the worst flooding on the south coast since 1912, as the first time in his life that he had been afraid of the English weather. By day on 16 December the Solent looked 'as if it was on fire', with clouds of spray sweeping up the estuary in the screaming wind. At the time, James was marooned on the shore at the end of a shingle spit inside a half-built hide. To prevent the loose 2.4 × 1.2 m sterling boards from blowing away he was obliged to drive his truck over them. The greatest surge, the sting in the tail of a high spring tide, came later that night when most people were cowering in their beds. The atmospheric pressure dropped like a stone, the storm blew in the sea, and by dawn much of Lymington and the low-lying land around the Solent had been flooded. Some 160 ha of the Reserve above the high tide mark was under water. Once the weather had grown calmer, James made a tour of the Reserve by boat. A large hide, once firmly rooted in drums of concrete, was floating intact but upside down on the sea, 0.8 km inland, with its steps pointing to the sky. Everywhere fences had been lifted out bodily, strainers, stakes and all, and washed away on the tide. No fewer than 14 foot-bridges had gone, some never to be seen again. It took 3 days to clear one side of the river bank of its strand line of broken groynes, fish crates, splintered gates and railway sleepers.

The one place that did withstand the gale was Gull Island at the mouth of the Beaulieu River, part of the North Solent NNR and the focus, a few years before, of one of England's more elaborate conservation schemes. Where the Beaulieu River reaches the sea, a shingle spit has formed. In 1727, one Charles Bull was paid £5 to cut a narrow navigation channel through it called the Swatchway. Over the years the Swatchway has grown wider and wider, and by the 1980s, the detached part, now known as Gull Island, had become separated from the rest by a waterway more than 200 m wide. The tidal scour now running through the Swatchway was rapidly

removing shingle from Gull Island and threatening the island's very survival. This was undesirable for two reasons. First, Gull Island fully lives up to its name as the home of the largest Black-headed Gull colony in England, as well as three species of tern. Secondly, its loss would expose the Beaulieu River, with its hundreds of yachts and numerous moorings, to the full force of wind and water. A survey of erosion rates undertaken by the Conservancy between 1979 and 1984 confirmed that the island would soon disappear. The solution was clear enough: to reunite the shingle spit by blocking the Swatchway, thus allowing shingle to drift eastwards with the current to rebuild the island. To do so, however, required an Act of Parliament, since the Swatchway was a navigable waterway. Moreover, no government funding was available since private ownership on this part of the coast extends down to low water, a legacy dating from 1204 when King John made a gift of the land to the Cistercians, including the rights of wreck and salvage, and to 'royal fish'.

These considerations being overcome by autumn 1986, the physical work was completed in only 19 days. James Venner was on site for much of the time during those days and nights of frantic activity that temporarily transformed the lonely spit to a building site, with huge Moxey dumper trucks trundling 11,000 tonnes of shingle from the low water mark to the point where an even larger bulldozer-cum-excavator was busy building a great barrier across the Swatchway. Once the barrier had settled down, James and a local contractor dug in 6000 groyne timbers, from softwood logs cut on the Beaulieu estate, along the barrier front. The work started at dawn each day and went on until dark, breaking only during high tide. The barrier stood up well to its first severe test, the great hurricane of 1987, which shrieked across southern England—though fortunately not at high tide. An estimated 10,000 tonnes of shingle have shifted to the shore of the island since then, and the western end of the new bank has already doubled in width. The success of the project was sealed by the Solent Protection Society's annual conservation award on its co-sponsors, the Beaulieu Estate and the NCC.

WILDFOWL AND WILDFOWLING

Nature reserves are meant to protect wildlife. Wildfowlers brave considerable discomforts to shoot ducks and geese. Are the two compatible? While many hold strong opinions on either side, the unsentimental scientific answer is to test the situation by monitoring wildfowl numbers in an area where regular shooting is taking place. If the birds are decreasing, then something is wrong and wildfowling may be the cause. If not, we are forced to concede that ducks and geese seem to accept shooting along with all the other natural and man-made hazards of their lives—as something with which, within limits, they are prepared to live. And since many quarry species have not only increased in recent years, but have in many instances increased spectacularly, the Conservancy is usually prepared to accommodate the wildfowlers on large Reserves, especially when the latter were there first. Besides, there are still naturalists who enjoy shooting—and vice versa: many wildfowlers enjoy watching birds as well as shooting them. And both share a common interest in ensuring that our estuaries and coasts continue to teem with birds.

Wildfowl conservation is an international concern. Most of the vast flocks of Wigeon and wild geese that visit our shores in winter breed not in Britain but in the Arctic. Conservation also impinges on the livelihood and sport of many people. Wildfowl, especially geese, have the potential to reduce a farmer's income, especially since the direct drilling of barley in autumn has encouraged the birds to stay for longer. The Conservancy's attitude towards wildfowl has always been the pragmatic one of live and let live, summed up in a lecture in 1963 by its then Scottish Director, W J Eggeling: 'We take a harvest of the wild geese, which yield both food and sport; food and recreation for man. If we didn't, there might well be larger "clanging battalions" [geese, that is] but there would be equally loud outcries from the farming population'. His point was that in a crowded and intensively farmed island like ours, no animal with the consumer capacity of a large flock of Barnacles or Pink-feet can avoid conflict with human interests, and we are perfectly entitled to shoot some of them. The key word is *harvest*. Harvests imply sustainability, which must mean controls on the marksman as well as the bird. Thus most wildfowl conservation is not about straight protection, *per se*, but about resource management, an unsentimental matter of numbers, balance sheets and codes of practice, in which the aim is the maintenance of a healthy population, not necessarily happy contented individuals. But here I am less concerned with the wider aspects of wildfowl management, which are very thoroughly documented for the British Isles, as with the specific contribution of English National Nature Reserves.

Wildfowl refuges have existed through private agreements for more than a century, but it was not until 1954, when the Protection of Birds Act became law, that such arrangements were formalised under statute. The first formal wildfowl sanctuary—the Humber—followed a year later and since then a national system of refuges has been established in our larger estuaries and sheltered bays, such as Bridgwater Bay, Caerlaverock, the Ribble and Lindisfarne. The Nature Conservancy's Wildfowl Conservation Committee under Max Nicholson played a leading role in this, and some refuges, including all the above-mentioned, have since become National Nature Reserves. The first to be declared was Bridgwater Bay in Somerset, but no attempt was made to control the shooting there for several years. The earliest agreement signed by the Conservancy and the Wildfowlers' Association (now the British Association of Shooting and Conservation) was over the flats and marshes of Caerlaverock in Dumfriesshire in 1957. Caerlaverock was famous for wild geese, especially the protected Barnacle Goose, whose wintering flocks there are among the largest in the world. Wildfowlers had long converged on Caerlaverock from all over Britain every winter, and as the bulk of the shooting took place above high water mark, on land whose owners intended it to continue, some compromise was needed to achieve the Conservancy's aims while allowing the fowlers their sport. Simply banning all shooting was never an option. The Conservancy did not have the power to do so, nor did it believe it to be necessary.

The problem here, as elsewhere, was not shooting, but bad shooting. The effective killing range of a shotgun is no more than 32 m or so, and it takes skill and patience to get that close to a wary wild duck. In fact even experienced shoulder-gunners (as opposed to punt-gunners) shoot remarkably few birds, we are told—about one for every 2 days shooting. Problems arise not from wildfowlers who have mastered their craft and who respect its codes, but from the 'cowboy' element, who come to the estuaries to make a great deal of noise and let off their guns at everything in sight. Bad shooting creates far more disturbance than good, and this is the nub of the problem: if wildfowl are unable to find places where they can roost and feed in peace they will desert the area. Effective wildfowl conservation relies on co-operation with the wildfowlers' representatives to establish sanctuaries where access is strictly controlled and shooting not allowed, and to exert control over the extent of shooting elsewhere.

The solution worked out at Caerlaverock in 1957, with remarkable speed and absence of friction, was to give the Conservancy effective control over the shooting by acquiring the rights and applying for bye-laws to make shooting illegal without its permission. As a body of the Crown, the Conservancy is in a position, with the co-operation of the landowners, to enforce local laws. In exchange, the wildfowlers are offered a stake in the management of the Reserve. At Caerlaverock, the shooting is supervised by a panel of three, representing the Conservancy, the owners and the wildfowlers, which arbitrates over any disputes that may arise. Only the central part of the Reserve is shot over; the remainder, including the foreshore, is a sanctuary to which access is prohibited, except by permit. The Barnacle Geese are completely protected. The other hinge of the agreement rests on good relations and regular contact between the Reserve manager and the individual wildfowlers and local people. The system works well in practice, and is often cited as a model compromise between conservation and sport. Its main disadvantage is to the Conservancy's administrative staff who have the boring and unglamorous task of issuing permits. But one useful spin-off from a well-administered permit system is that a great deal of information on wildfowl numbers and behaviour can be gathered thereby. By the end of the 1960s, some 2000 individual wildfowlers had been issued with permits at Caerlaverock, although no more than 600 birds were being shot each year. As the then Regional Officer, Tom Huxley, put it, 'shooting about one bird in a couple of days on a marsh to get to which one may have motored several hundred miles, may be an adequate prize for one's efforts'. It should be added that the Conservancy does go out of its way to stress that admitting what one has legally shot will not prejudice one's chances of obtaining a permit next year.

Bridgwater Bay was the first English Reserve to operate a permit system for wildfowling, although in this case local opposition necessitated a public inquiry before the Secretary of State decided to confirm the Nature Conservancy's draft byelaws. The permit system here is relatively straightforward to operate since, not only are there fewer wildfowlers than at Caerlaverock, but all are members of two clubs, the Bridgwater Bay Wildfowlers and the Highbridge, Huntspill and Burnham District Club, which use different sectors of the bay. As at Caerlaverock, the Conservancy is concerned not so much about the shooting itself, which amounts to no more than a couple of hundred birds each year, than with the degree of disturbance that such shooting might cause to roosting and feeding birds. In 1959, a warden, Jim Morley, was appointed, part of whose job was to liaise with the clubs and establish the facts about bird numbers and movements. Thanks to these studies, and to the returns from the shooting permits, this has become one of the best documented Reserves in the country. Morley's research confirmed that in allowing wildfowling to continue along a 1.6-km strip of sea wall by the Huntspill River and on the east bank of the River Parrett, the Conservancy had achieved an effective compromise which was not causing the birds undue alarm. Permits are limited to three species of duck and two of waders. A maximum of 45 permits used to be issued every July to each club and returned the following February. In recent years, however, the level of shooting has been well below that level. As at Caerlaverock, relations have been good, with remarkably few conflicts of interest; indeed some shooting club members help to look after the Reserve as voluntary wardens.

Absence of incident could hardly be said to characterise Lindisfarne NNR, which was established in 1964 to conserve the large numbers of wildfowl and waders from the Arctic that overwinter on the flats and marshes of that part of the Northumberland coast. This is the only regular wintering ground in Britain for the pale-bellied race of Brent Goose, which breeds in Spitzbergen, and there are also relatively large regular flocks of Wigeon and Whooper Swan. As everyone who knows this part of the coast will agree, this is a wild and beautiful area, unusual in that, although it is classed as an estuary, there is no large inflowing river, and so its waters are almost entirely marine. The Reserve was established at the instigation of landowners and the Wildfowlers Association who, concerned at the deteriorating standards of sportsmanship since the war, approached the Nature Conservancy with an offer of the shooting rights. The outcome was a plan along the Caerlaverock model to declare the coast, from Cheswick Black Rock in the north to Budle Bay in the south, as a National Nature Reserve, in which shooting would continue under Conservancy control. Budle Bay was to be a true sanctuary, a non-shooting zone. Some 500 permits are currently issued each season both to individuals and, as a block, to the Northumberland and Durham Wildfowling Association. The less common birds of Lindisfarne, including the pale-bellied Brents, are fully protected. Compared with Bridgwater Bay, the area is still very popular: some 2993 birds were shot in the 1991/92 winter, most of them Wigeon.

Because there are numerous interests involved, Lindisfarne has a two-tier administrative system: a Joint Advisory Committee, consisting of local councillors, landowners and naturalists, which deals with the broader issues of the Reserve, and the Lindisfarne Wildfowl Panel, which advises on matters specifically affecting wildfowling. While the arrangement has worked well enough over the past quarter century, it is somewhat cumbersome, and issuing permits has become a major administrative burden on the Conservancy's north-eastern office. English Nature proposes to involve the wildfowlers more directly in the supervision of their sport by transferring the responsibility for regulating and issuing permits, setting and collecting fees and other administrative matters, to the Lindisfarne panel. In effect, this would create a self-regulating wildfowling club for Lindisfarne that would be formally responsible to English Nature.

At Lindisfarne, two traditional activities have been at the fore in recent years—punt-gunning and bait-digging. Punt-gunning seems to have started here in the middle of the last century, and among the regular visitors was the great hunter-collector, Abel Chapman, who wrote an evocative account of the excitements and privations of the sport in his *Bird Life of the Borders* (1889). The punts with their huge guns were kept on Holy Island, and when not in use by their generally well-to-do owners would be appropriated by local fishermen who used them to supplement their income (a convenient railway station nearby took baskets of duck and geese to markets in Newcastle and London). Punts became a way of life. Most of those at Lindisfarne are operated by two men, a steersman and the gunner. The guns, which weigh about 64 kg and take a 15–20 cm long black powder cartridge, are mounted along the bow. The punts are launched on the ebb tide, preferably in the early morning mist, and glide with as little noise as possible towards a large 'raft' of duck. Once the punt is in range, the steersman strikes the side of the boat, the duck rise and the gunner, prone in the bottom of the boat, pulls a lanyard; a great roar and a cloud of smoke sends some 2500 lead pellets on their way. A well-aimed punt gun can down 80 or more wild duck in one shot. Those on the periphery of the shot spread are likely to be injured rather than killed outright, so the next job for the puntsmen is to leap out of the boat, gather up the corpses and finish off any wounded birds with a 12-bore 'cripple stopper'. The picking-up operation can take up to 30–40 min, and causes at least as much disturbance as the shot itself. Such powerful weapons require careful handling; two people have been killed at Lindisfarne during the past 16 years when their weapons misfired.

Punting at Lindisfarne is restricted to the hours of daylight. English Nature authorise eight punting outfits at present, four of them owned by local residents and four by visitors. The former tend to launch a punt only if they see the potential for a good shot, and are active mostly at the start of the shooting season. Visitors often spend much longer paddling about in search of a shot, and as they tend to launch the punts on the ebb tide and return with the incoming tide, the boats are often afloat for several hours, whether or not a shot is fired. That punt-gunning was having an adverse impact on the main quarry species, the Wigeon, became apparent in the mid-1980s, when the average winter population declined by more than half, and that at a time when numbers were on the upturn elsewhere in Britain. Moreover, the Wigeon were leaving Lindisfarne much earlier in the season than formerly. A study by the then Reserve manager, David O'Connor, and his colleague David Townshend established a strong connection between intensive punting, especially early in winter, and Wigeon departing. Most were being scared away, not shot. The evidence suggested that more than 15 periods, or 30 consecutive days, of punt-gunning would cause nearly all the Wigeon to desert Lindisfarne. As a result of this analysis, punt-gunning is now restricted to alternate days of the week.

It would be unfair to blame the fall in Wigeon numbers on punt-gunning alone. The unusually low numbers of Wigeon present during the winters of 1985/86 and 1986/87 coincided with the highest use of the sanctuary area in Budle Bay by bait-diggers. Like punting, the digging of lugworms for angling bait has been a popular activity at Lindisfarne for many years. Budle Bay is the favourite area, partly because of the abundance of lugworm there, partly because it is accessible by road. The activity became a serious problem when bait-digging increased 10-fold in the early 1980s, when up to 120 people could be seen at any one time, busily piling the worms into their buckets. The NCC responded by using the Reserve bye-laws to close the Bay to bait-digging for 2 years, to allow the worms to recover. Their numbers were monitored by an independent expert. Unfortunately the reopening of the southern shore coincided with the 1984 miners' strike, when many people from the north-eastern coalfields with time on their hands homed in on the Bay with the result that almost the entire population of lugworms, estimated at some 4 million, was dug up and removed from the permitted area. And so bait-digging was again prohibited in the Bay, while an alternative area, along either side of the causeway to Holy Island, was offered to the diggers. Some refused to co-operate, citing rights under the Magna Carta to dig where they pleased, and, in a well-publicised court case, three men were convicted under the bye-laws and fined. Bait-digging on this scale is completely at odds with nature conservation. Not only is there depletion of an important food source and considerable disturbance to wildfowl, there are also more insidious side-effects, notably the release of toxic pollutants, such as cadmium and mercury, from the disturbed mud.

The reimposition of the ban on digging at Budle Bay produced immediate benefits, especially for Wigeon, Bar-tailed Godwit and Redshank (see Table 8, based on the figures published by O'Connor and Townshend). Other wildfowl also increased in the year after the ban, a three-fold increase for Mallard, seven-fold for Teal.

At the cost of a considerable administrative burden, ways and means have been found to reconcile the presence of people and wildfowl at Lindisfarne. But perhaps the most spectacular example in all Britain of the benefits to wildfowl of a well-managed Reserve is at the Ribble Marshes NNR on the Lancashire coast, just north of Southport. Like Lindisfarne, this area became a Reserve not by design but by circumstance—as we saw in Chapter 2, it happened to be the only means available to safeguard the estuary from agricultural development. At roughly 4000 ha, the Reserve is of impressive enough proportions, but when you add the vast intertidal sand flats of the Southport Sanctuary, established in 1956 to protect the low water roosting grounds of wild geese, and further areas of grazing marsh leased by the RSPB or owned by the Lytham and District Wildfowlers Association, you have one of the wildest and best protected estuaries in north-west Europe—and furthermore one that is unusually free from industrial pollution and unsightly development. At the Ribble it is possible to plan for the whole natural ecosystem rather than one isolated part of it.

The Ribble forms one link in the chain of large estuaries on the coast of north-west England, along which tens of thousands of waders and wildfowl move between autumn and spring. The 'carrying capacity' of the Ribble is altogether exceptional, however: it has some of the most extensive sand and mudflats in Britain, with a 10 km tidal range and an enormous expanse of saltmarsh. In the summer, at least, it resembles a huge open-range meadow, dotted with hundreds of cows. Each winter, birds congregate there in staggering numbers: the estuary is an internationally important area for Pink-footed Goose, Wigeon, Knot, Dunlin and both godwits, all of which have increased in recent years. Detailed monthly counts of waders and wildfowl are maintained by more than 30 ornithologists. The Redshanks of the Ribble are among the best studied in the world, having been under continuous observation since 1975 by Professor W G Hale and his students at Liverpool Polytechnic.

The Conservancy's involvement with the Ribble Estuary predates the Reserve. It had administered the Southport Sanctuary Committee and used to pay someone to count the birds using the sanctuary each winter. With the sudden broadening of its responsibilities as a result of the 1979 Reserve purchase, the NCC set up a liaison committee, consisting of wildfowlers' representatives, local naturalists and, more recently, the RSPB, the Wildfowl and Wetlands Trust and local authorities, who form a regular 'talking shop' to ensure that everyone is moving in the same direction. Wildfowling on the Reserve is managed by one of the oldest such clubs in the country, the Southport and District Wildfowlers Association, which has recently celebrated its centenary. Until the 1960s, access difficulties meant that shooting here remained in skilled hands and at a relatively low level. Moreover the club has long been a believer in sanctuaries, with a proportion of their own land being set aside as a non-shooting area. However, increasing numbers of wildfowlers, attracted by the relatively easy shooting and large game bags, meant that something had to be done to safeguard the main quarry species. The crux came in 1985 when 1800 Wigeon were shot in a single month, more than even the Ribble could sustain. The traditional practice of shooting at night under the full moon was banned, much to the relief of those who had to undergo regular night time patrols in the dead of winter, and goose shooting was restricted to the morning and evening flights. Since then, the increase in some birds has been spectacular. The short-grazed sward of the Ribble marshes is ideal for geese and Wigeon, and, with the creation of a large sanctuary at Banks Marsh in 1980 and the cessation of moonlight shooting, the true potential of the estuary is now being realised. Pink-footed Geese have increased from a peak of 5000 in 1979/80 to the 20,000–30,000 birds of recent years, while the Wigeon have increased even more spectacularly from around 5000 to an incredible 90,000 birds in 1991/92 (the highest count in Europe); indeed they have become very difficult to count accurately. Other wildfowl, notably Teal, have shown proportionately similar increases, and the number of waders using the estuary have roughly doubled since the late 1970s, with a recent peak count of 146,000 birds. The Ribble has become one of the most important wildfowl sanctuaries in the country: a major success story. Clearly the Conservancy's policy of combining shooting control with habitat management has paid off, so much so that the Ribble's present manager, Dick Lambert, is beginning to wonder whether it is really in the best interests of the Wigeon to have so many individuals in the same place. Perhaps there should be some upper limit on species numbers, a point at which protection objectives could be said to have succeeded fully. But if so, how do you hold the line? And at what point does the conservation of wild nature blend with the stock management and careful regulation of a well-run farming enterprise?

TABLE 8 *Average peak numbers of three species of waterfowl in early winter (October–December) using the sanctuary area of Budle Bay, Lindisfarne before, during and after periods when bait-digging was permitted*

Years	1980/81 & 1981/82	1982/83 & 1983/84	1984/85, 85/86 & 1986/87	1987/88
Bait-digging	Unrestricted	None permitted	Permitted in restricted zone	None permitted
Wigeon	1535	6900	497	5400
Bar-tailed Godwit	210	480	353	2010
Redshank	222	385	201	1750

CHAPTER 10

Signposts for the Future

ON 19 May 1992, English Nature celebrated the 40th birthday of one of the oldest National Nature Reserves, Yarner Wood in Devon. Those who had been closely involved in the running of this famous wood—a surprisingly large number—congregated in a glade on one of the hottest, sunniest days of that rain-lashed year. To mark the occasion, a charcoal mound made of billets of oak and covered by a layer of turf was fired, recreating a scene once familiar at Yarner in the distant days when oak underwood was regularly cut to smelt the ore from a nearby copper mine. The thin column of bluish-grey smoke that curled above the canopied oaks and up into the cloudless sky was a symbol of historic continuity at Yarner, of the balance of exploitation and renewal which has shaped and preserved the wood over the decades. By coincidence, the numbers of those present on that occasion were roughly the same as the miners and colliers (charcoal-burners) that used to work the wood in mid-Victorian times. Our values and priorities change, but each generation has had its reasons for preserving this near-natural oakwood *as an oak-wood*. For many years after the mining ceased, Yarner Wood served as a pheasant covert. The gamekeeper later became the Nature Conservancy's first warden. At first the Conservancy used the wood for silvicultural experiments, with the aim of developing techniques of woodland management that could be used more widely on nature reserves elsewhere. Later on, the wood became a popular venue for field study by Devon schools, based on the two nature trails constructed there in the 1960s. In recent years management has focused on maintaining the rides and glades on which so many of Yarner Wood's flowers and insects rely. But the wood also plays a wider role in environmental protection. One of the site manager's daily jobs is to take recordings at a weather station in the wood to monitor the levels of atmospheric pollution and ozone depletion. At the same time, Yarner Wood is no longer an isolated nature reserve. A second National Nature Reserve, the Bovey Valley Woodlands, lies close by and the Woodland Trust also own property in the valley. Yarner Wood and the Bovey Valley are likely to become a 'natural biodiversity area', managed as a unity, and in close co-operation with neighbouring owners and tenants, and with the Dartmoor National Park ranger service. Human priorities seem to change every decade or so. But, with luck, Yarner Wood will remain recognisably Yarner Wood.

The legal and scientific basis of National Nature Reserves has not changed significantly over the past 40 years. They continue to be selected as the best-known examples of particular wild habitats, and managed to benefit their constituent animal and plant communities. But England is not the place it was in 1952 when Yarner Wood was 'declared'. The countryside has changed enormously: much marginal land has been pressed into production, only to be taken out again in recent years; the ribbon development of bungalows in the 1930s has become a ribbon development of motorways and bypasses; and concern about our environment has grown as our wildlife and its habitats have suffered and diminished. Yarner Wood was not regarded as particularly special or outstanding in 1952 when oakwoods were still extensive around the fringes of Dartmoor. It certainly is so regarded now when non-coniferised upland woods are in short supply.

As I have tried to demonstrate in this book, the management of National Nature Reserves in England has experienced a quiet revolution during the past decade. Technology and growing experience have allowed Reserve wardens and managers to tackle problems that would have been regarded as impossible in 1952—the restoration of hundreds of hectares of heath, the raising of water levels on grazing marsh and peat bogs, and the management in fine detail of complex kaleidoscopes of related landscapes. Yet, impressive as the results have been, they remain little known to the wider public, and have not influenced other land-users in the way that conservationists must have hoped. The newspaper headlines are not about English downs and heaths but about rain forests, ozone layers and invisible pollutants. Most people seem to care more about animals they have never seen wild, like tigers and whales, than about the Sand Lizards and Field Crickets in our own back garden. Ignorance of ecology and landscape history is such that developers and local politicians can offer to replace ancient habitats with resown fields in the apparently sincere belief that the exchange is a fair one. The loss of SSSIs has been justified at the highest level with the consoling thought that the official bodies can always designate a few new ones! In the end we are all losers when cynics move the goal posts.

The government's recent reorganisation of nature conservation in Britain, and the creation of English Nature from the rump of the former NCC, provided an opportunity for reflection about the future role of National Nature Reserves. One of the last acts of the NCC was to host a two-day conference on nature reserves under the provocative title: '*Nature reserves: who needs them?*'. The question displays an interesting choice of pronoun—who, not what—perhaps a tacit recognition that nature reserves are a response to human needs as much as those of flora and fauna. Nature reserves become increasingly important as the quality of our environment is degraded. Chapter 6 of this book gave examples of a growing number of species that survive mainly on nature reserves, and which would probably be extinct without the concentration of effort possible on protected land. In practice the conference tacitly accepted that nature reserves are indeed needed and focused on the limitations and even downright failures of nature reserve-based conservation in practice. One speaker pointed to the polarisation of landscape quality and the artificial divides inherent in the nature reserve ideal: 'we can no longer afford to speak of human domination over nature [but] equally we can no longer afford to describe nature as existing separately from human endeavour'. Another speaker deplored the failure of nature reserves to make any impact on the agenda of green issues: 'Nature reserves have made nature inaccessible—conceptually, socially, geographically and ultimately politically. How is it that we have failed to persuade people that nature is the ultimate victim of environmental abuse?'

Such criticisms seem to point to the failure of conservationists to sell the case for nature reserves, not the failure of the Reserves themselves. The techniques worked out through experiment and experience on nature reserves have in fact been notably successful in their primary aim of conserving wildlife. Some of the National Nature Reserves of England have helped to revive traditional rural crafts and practices like coppicing, open-range grazing and ditching, as well as inventing a few new ones like wild-seed harvesting and the sculpting of wood-edge profiles. Nature reserve management has become one of the distinctive arts of the late twentieth century. It has in some cases created a new kind of landscape, the Habitat Mosaic, in which the maximum number of habitats are crammed within the confines of a small, isolated Reserve. Such places can be maintained only by relatively intensive work, aided by the machines. At least one speaker at the conference was critical of this approach. Why not, he asked, give nature a chance to look after herself for a change? Have we become so arrogant that we think we can improve on nature in the name of nature conservation? In practice, of course, there are plenty of National Nature Reserves, particularly in woodland, in which nature is indeed pretty well left to take its course which, as we have been reminded recently, includes gales, drought, landslides and floods. National Nature Reserves are so diverse, both in terms of natural phenomena and management strategies, that it is difficult to generalise about them. But taken as a whole, they surely have something to offer to the era of agricultural surpluses and popular environmental concern. At the least, they point to ways of wise co-existence between man and nature, with all that that implies about our need for spiritual refreshment and natural beauty.

In the meantime, whether or not anyone is taking any notice, nature reserve management is becoming ever more adventurous as the bounds of the possible continue to expand. For most of this book, I have concentrated on the 'traditional' uses of National Nature Reserves: science, habitat maintenance, species protection and the public enjoyment of nature. I have reserved for this last chapter four areas which seem to point in new directions. The first, habitat creation, is rooted in the Conservancy's experience of restoring grassland and heath from scrub. The second, habitat *translocation*, is newer and more controversial. The third could be summed up as 'co-operative conservation', which, if not new, is at least increasing in scale. And the last is, at present, not much more than an idea: nature reserves as a contribution to human culture.

NEW HABITATS FOR OLD

Nature reserves not uncommonly include parcels of land that came with the purchase or agreement deal, but which are not in themselves of much interest for wildlife. Conversely there may be other areas which were once of considerable interest but which have become overgrown by scrub or have in other ways declined greatly in value. In both cases it is often possible to create or restore good wildlife habitat, and some of the techniques for doing so have been forged on National Nature Reserves. Perhaps the first major essay in habitat restoration was at Lullington Heath in East

Sussex. Lullington Heath was one of the early National Nature Reserves, chosen as the best known example of a chalk heath, that is, an area where acid soils overlie much of the chalk, producing a curious mixture of heather and other acid-loving species side-by-side with typical chalk plants like Wild Thyme, Salad Burnet and Rough Hawkbit. Such places are rare, and, like the chalk downs, used to be maintained by sheep and rabbits. It was bad luck, therefore, that the lease of Lullington Heath coincided with the outbreak of myxomatosis. Worse, the Conservancy was not at first allowed to introduce sheep to the Reserve in case they contaminated the ground water—for the Heath was owned by a water company as an important catchment area for Eastbourne. The immediate consequence was that coarse grass, gorse, hawthorn and brambles leapt across the erstwhile heath, threatening its very survival. What was once an open expanse on which you could play a game of cricket became, in the space of a few years, a jungle in which gorse thickets towered up to 14′ high, and the Stone Curlews and Skylarks of old were replaced by robins, thrushes and, for a while at least, Dartford Warblers. Lullington Heath had become the classic illustration of the instability of grassland and heath in the absence of grazing.

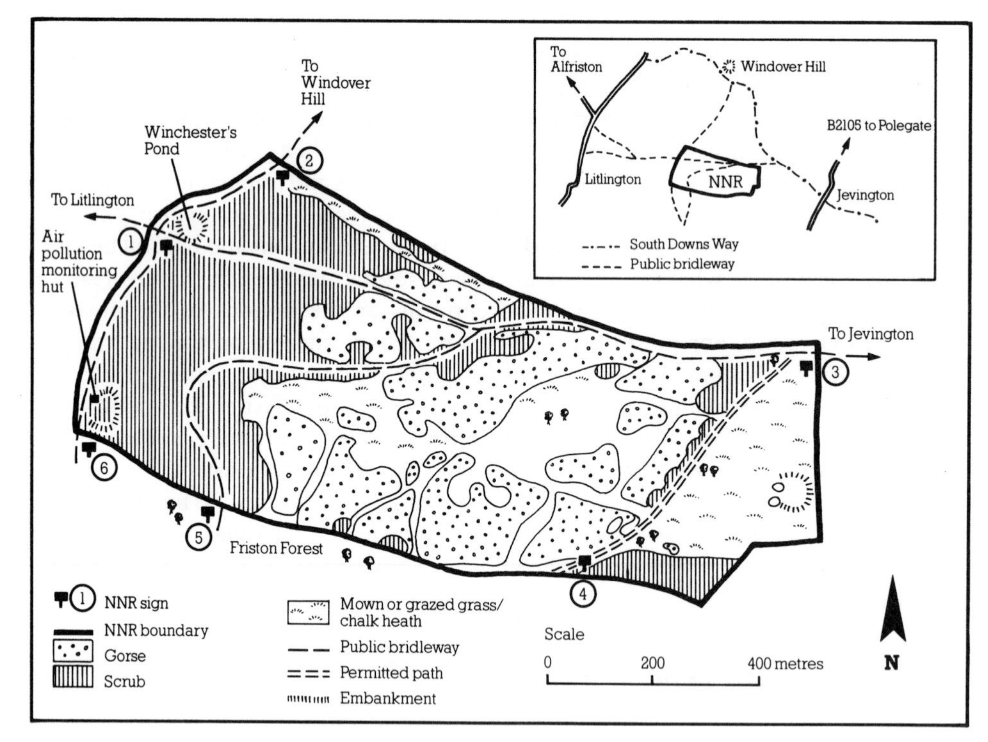

MAP 13 *Lullington Heath NNR, East Sussex*

The only option left to the Nature Conservancy was mowing. During the 1960s rides were hacked through the gorse thickets and a series of trials, using tractor-drawn mowers, were made to see if heathland could be returned. There were two main problems. The first was that litter from gorse and other shrubs had already begun to change the soil chemistry, making it at once more acid and more nutrient-rich than the original soils. And mowing produced a uniform, less diverse structure to the vegetation, without the inherent patterns and irregularities produced in the sward by rabbit grazing. Moreover, mowing was hazardous on the steeper slopes. Nevertheless a great deal was learned from these trials and the techniques forged at Lullington Heath have been put to good use on other public open spaces where scrub invasion is a problem. This was one of the first direct applications of nature reserve management experience to the wider public domain.

In 1972, the Conservancy at last obtained permission to introduce grazing animals to the Heath. Aided by a partial recovery of the rabbit population, the Conservancy's four New Forest ponies and flock of Beulah sheep have since then restored much of the former heathland. The area where a pony was photographed up to its hocks in thick grass, thistles and hawthorn sprouts 10 years ago is today a short sward of fine grass. Recently, the Reserve manager has also attacked some of the densest areas of gorse with a tracked vehicle and hinged bucket which can remove mouthfuls of gorse without disturbing the soil. Once the accumulated litter of gorse needles was removed, the heathland plants returned with encouraging speed (although there is doubt as to whether the chalk flora will return in anything like its former glory). Even so, this will always be one of the more back-breaking Reserves. As Alan Bowley remarked in his 1989 report for the Reserve, 'I cannot foresee a time when grazing alone will maintain the chalk heath. There is too much gorse and bramble . . . I see a combination of mowing and grazing as the correct way to manage the cleared area'.

On the light, free-draining soils of lowland heaths, arable land can revert to semi-natural habitat remarkably quickly. Indeed it is likely that the whole of the Breckland of Norfolk and Suffolk was under arable cultivation at one time or another during the past 200 years, the farmer moving on to a new patch once the old one had lost its meagre supply of nutrients. The reversion is likely to take a little longer today, when unending fertility is available from sackfuls of nitrate, but at Cavenham Heath NNR in Suffolk an ingenious method has been devised to hasten the process. In 1979, the NCC had seized an opportunity to purchase Roper's Heath, part of the original Cmd 7122 site, which had been under cultivation since the 1950s. To strip the soil of its accumulated load of nitrogen, the Reserve's managers, Malcolm Wright and Martin Musgrave, simply had it sown with barley—but without using any fertiliser. The barley crop was followed by two seasons of rye, after which the area was fenced and sheep were put in. The method proved a great success. The heath grew fabulously 'weedy', a mass of Shepherd's Cress and other Breckland plants, and, by the late-1980s, heather was spreading over much of the erstwhile barley fields. Part of the area has since been fenced against sheep and rabbits to assess the effect of grazing animals on the restoration process. The designation of much of the Breck as an Environmentally Sensitive Area (ESA) means that such methods might be used widely to replace third-rate cropland with rough grassland and heath.

A similar exercise in the restoration of semi-natural land from arable is taking place at Stoborough Heath NNR in Dorset, where former cereal fields have reverted to grass heath of high wildlife interest within a decade. Fields like these, whose conversion to arable lasted only a few years, continue to harbour a seed-bank of wild plants in the surface layers of the soil. Once the agricultural fertilisers have disappeared into the thirsty soil, even heather can return within a few years. In the case of Stoborough

Heath, Mike Tuck, English Nature's manager, is in two minds as to whether he wants the heather back at all. There is very little grass heath on the acid sands of Purbeck, and that little is much favoured by Hobbies and bats because of the wealth of cockchafers and other large insects that live among the grass. Moreover, Stoborough Heath has a small colony of the rare Wart-biter grasshopper, which provides a strong incentive to maintain at least some lightly grazed grassland.

Good damage limitation and restoration techniques are needed when an oil company decides to build a pipeline across a sensitive National Nature Reserve, as they do from time to time. In 'the wider countryside' oil companies have become adept at healing the scars left by subterranean pipes, but on nature reserves where much depends on undisturbed soil profiles and natural patterns of drainage, ordinary pipemanship is unlikely to be sufficient to avoid lasting damage. By an unfortunate happenstance, Hartland Moor NNR in Dorset happens to lie between the wells of England's main onshore oil field and its railhead. In 1974, British Petroleum told the NCC that they could not avoid a route that would take the pipeline straight through the most sensitive part of the Reserve—the wet valley fen which winds between the drier slopes of the heath. The next 18 months were spent arguing and deliberating about how the pipe might be installed without turning the fen into a quagmire. No one really knew how. Some experimental work at a practice site produced an appalling mess. The NCC was offered two concessions: only turves along the actual trench line would be removed, and they would be replaced in exactly the same spot once the pipe had been laid. The excavated soil and subsoil would be similarly preserved, using a special waterproof membrane, and returned by hand in the same order. Vehicular access was to be minimised, and in the wettest parts of the site vehicles were to travel only on wooden mats.

Which was all very well, but, according to Mike Tuck, rule number one in these circumstances is that the best laid plans gang aft a' gley. In practice, success depended on close daily contact between Mike and the contractor. The plan worked because the parties involved talked about the inevitable unforeseen problems as they arose and worked out solutions before proceeding. In the end the pipe was *pulled* under the fen by welding one end to a mole plough and winching it through the ground without disturbing the surface: apparently a technological 'first'. Such techniques proved valuable when pipes had to be laid across Thursley Common NNR and on equally sensitive sites elsewhere. As a result of experiences like the Hartland Moor pipeline it was possible to produce a handbook to the techniques of heathland restoration, published by British Gas in 1988. The key to the successful outcome in this particular case, however, was the constant presence at the pipeface of Mike Tuck. As Mike puts it, you can't just agree things in the office and then go off birdwatching: the only way is to 'chuck your bins (binoculars) away and join in!'.

TRANSPLANTING NATURE: THE THRISLINGTON STORY

Thrislington Plantation is not at first sight the most exciting of landscapes. To non-botanists it looks little more than a patch of scrubby grassland with a steep bank at one end, tucked out of sight behind quarry workings and a village football pitch. The name 'plantation' commemorates an unsuccessful nineteenth century attempt to grow larches. Neither is there any longer a village called Thrislington. The name is a memory of a 'lost village' whose inhabitants long ago either died of the plague or sensibly moved somewhere else. Doubtless it mattered no more to them than the Victorian larch-grower that their patch of rough grazing happened to be the best example of magnesian limestone grassland in Britain. Prime nature sites do not always lie among dramatic scenery. This one can boast, among other things, the best colony of blue flax, one of the biggest populations of the Castle Eden Argus butterfly and numerous glow-worms. But if anyone outside the county has heard of Thrislington Plantation today it is less because of its biological glories than because this 26-ha site has become famous as 'the nature reserve that moved'.

The rock on which Thrislington Plantation stood was commercially valuable, and had been reserved in the County's mineral plan for quarrying. After conservationists had fought and lost a public inquiry to save the site in 1980, local naturalists backed by the NCC came to an agreement with the owners, Steetley Minerals Ltd (now Redland Aggregates), to transplant some 5 ha worth of turves from the path of the advancing quarry to prepared ground at a safe site a few hundred metres away. The work took 8 years to complete, using a specially designed hydraulic bucket to excavate and transport huge 9-m^2 turves weighing 5 tonnes or more, along with their complete soil profile and a portion of bedrock. In effect the whole site was scooped up in sections and slewed by some 90° so that by the end of the project it had much the same shape as before except that it was now aligned from west to east, rather than north to south. The turves were packed together in the right order, like a big green chessboard and everyone involved hoped for the best.

The turves required a great deal of aftercare, since they had a tendency to shrink in dry weather creating channels of crumbling soil that are an open invitation for aggressive weeds to establish. Patiently, conservation volunteers, under the guidance of Steetley's ecologist David Park, watered and weeded the turves by hand, and gave the area a good mowing in early autumn once all the wild flower seeds had dispersed. Earth bunds were built around the area, making it look more like a chessboard than ever. As the quarry grew ever nearer, those monitoring the progress of plants and insects were advised to wear hard hats and put their fingers in their ears during blasting, when bits of magnesite would blow high into the air only yards away. Although a Nature Reserve Agreement had been signed between the quarry company and the NCC as long ago as 1982, the latter decided to wait until the transplant showed clear signs of success before declaring the site as a National Nature Reserve. The moment finally came on 3 July 1992, when the new Reserve was opened by the local MP, Mr Tony Blair, on a day of unseasonable cold wind and rain.

There was cause for celebration. Most of the rare plants and insects transported along with their habitat seem to have survived the change. The glow-worms still glow happily in mid-summer and the blue flaxes are as spectacular as ever. David Sheppard, monitoring the invertebrate fauna, noted that quite a number of invertebrates had in fact disappeared, but they were not species that a non-specialist would notice or miss. All in all, the scheme had exceeded most people's expectations. English Nature have now piped water to the site and erected fences so that livestock can be introduced. The 'donor' site is still a great deal starker than the original, but a regime of low intensity grazing should gradually heal the scars left by the transplant operation.

It is natural for those closely involved to get caught up in the excitement of a major pioneering project, and enthuse about the wonders of technology that enabled 5 ha of ancient turf to be lifted from one place and dumped on another. Mutual congratulations are also in order whenever industry and conservation co-operate in a positive fashion. The danger of such projects is that the euphoria thus generated may encourage developers to promote habitat translocation as a solution whenever they wish to build a road or a quarry or a superstore on an SSSI. The Thrislington experiment enjoyed greater success than most such schemes are likely to achieve for a number of reasons. The project was supervised at all stages and in detail by a trained ecologist; a method for excavating large turves was perfected; being a dry site, there were no hydrological problems to consider; and by fortunate chance a geologically similar site lay nearby. Even so, it proved extremely expensive and time-consuming. English Nature was at pains to emphasise that grassland translocation should not be considered as an acceptable form of habitat conservation: 'The scheme at Thrislington should be viewed as an experiment and not as an alternative to conventional *in situ* habitat management'. In other words, it considered the Thrislington experiment to be a one-off, last-ditch type of operation and not as a precedent for future transplant operations of this type. Whether others will accept it as such remains to be seen. Thrislington NNR may prove all too successful as a demonstration site.

NATURE RESERVES AND THE WIDER LANDSCAPE

Foreign visitors often remark on the small size of so many of England's National Nature Reserves when compared with similar habitats abroad. A sparrow could fly across Cothill Fen in less than a minute, and in the majority of Reserves in eastern England you can see from one end to the other. This is, to some extent, the nature of the English landscape, but many Reserves are much smaller than those recommended by the conservation pioneers back in the 1940s. And because of their limited size they are vulnerable to actions taking place outside their boundaries. It is all the more desirable, therefore, for English Reserves to have surroundings that are managed in a benign way, and for English Nature to co-operate with its neighbours wherever possible. The outstanding example of such co-operation is along the Sefton Coast between Liverpool and Southport, where the National Nature Reserves of Ainsdale and Cabin Hill form part of a wider conservation area to which local naturalists, the local authority and the National Trust also contribute. The effect has been to lift some of the burden of education and public access from the shoulders of the hard-pressed Reserve managers, and to divert those seeking only sunshine and playgrounds to more robust sites.

In several cases, the protection of National Nature Reserves has improved as a result of the various recent schemes to take land out of agricultural production or to encourage farmers to adopt environmentally friendly ways of working the land. This has radically changed the surroundings of Knocking Hoe NNR in the north Chilterns from mainly arable to abandoned farmland and grass leys. The Cambridge and Bedford Wildlife Trust have acquired 81 ha of semi-natural downland and former farm fields close to the Barton Hills NNR nearby, and the opportunity is there to transform the landscape from life rafts of natural vegetation in an ocean of wheat to one of the largest wildlife areas in the Chilterns. The different Reserves could be managed in common, using the same flocks, and there is spare land enough to allow considerable flexibility in running a sheep enterprise and perhaps even allow lambing, if that is thought desirable. The Reserves themselves could function as wildlife reservoirs and sources of wild seed for restoring the former arable land to semi-natural grassland. And 'buffer land' itself improves the conservation value of the Reserves, preserving them from spray drift and other harmful influences and, probably, boosting the populations of birds like Corn Bunting and Barn Owl. In all this, English Nature's experienced site managers will have a considerable part to play. At the time of writing, an unofficial forum comprising the nature reserve managers and representatives from Bedfordshire County Council and the National Trust are making recommendations for the unified management of the Barton Hills area. From being something of a conservation backwater, this once intensively farmed corner of England is all set to become a working demonstration of the reconciliation of farming and wildlife needs in 'set-aside' areas. Recent failures and disappointments over the application of set-aside land show that working demonstration areas like this are badly needed.

The Pevensey Levels in East Sussex is another area where golden opportunities have suddenly arisen. Until 1945, the Levels were a vast area of wild grass, scored like a jigsaw puzzle with winding freshwater dykes, bordered by hawthorn bushes, sedges and pond-side flowers. It is one of our more recently formed natural landscapes: William the Conqueror knew it as a tidal lagoon, but drifting shingle eventually severed the influence of Channel tides and the area became landlocked. By the time the medieval drainage engineers had finished with it, the Levels were soon fattening thousands of head of fine, healthy cattle each summer. And so the situation remained: grazing in summer, flooding in winter, until modern times when pump-drainage at last enabled water to be withdrawn even in winter, and allow the farmers to reseed the grass and even grow crops. The wettest remaining area was the Pevensey Bridge Level, the lowest level and the one closest to the sea. And the wettest part of this wettest area—some 12 fields over 52 ha—was purchased by the NCC in 1985 to save it from drying out further.

Some 52 ha among marshlands that once extended over 4300 ha is not a very

substantial amount of land (though it cost the NCC a substantial amount of money—£141,500—because of its agricultural potential). Fortunately a large proportion (3501 ha) of the Pevensey Levels is scheduled as a Site of Special Scientific Interest, which enables the Conservancy to restrict certain harmful practices such as the use of nitrate fertilisers and the further deepening of drains. More recently, this limited protection has been improved by English Nature's successful Wildlife Enhancement Scheme which promotes more positive ways of managing the land to benefit wildlife by, for example, adjusting the time of grazing and hay-cropping. Under these circumstances, the National Nature Reserve has a useful wider role to play as a working example of good management practice. It can demonstrate grazing regimes which are compatible with the needs of nesting waders like Snipe, Lapwing and Redshank. It can also provide a valuable test-bed for ditch management. A 6-year cycle of ditch cleaning developed on the Reserve is now in use over a wide part of the Levels, and has, among other things, resulted in a spectacular increase in that attractive floating lily, Frog-bit. There is already a much greater variety of ditch conditions on the Levels than in the recent past, including a network of broader pools where two or more ditches meet. The ditch flora and fauna is monitored each summer by English Nature's local officer, Basil Lindsay, aided by volunteers. At present the fields are still too dry in winter to encourage large numbers of wildfowl and waders, and so a series of scrapes is being dug on a neighbouring nature reserve owned by the Sussex Wildlife Trust as a means of increasing the winter and all-year floodland. All of this good work is demonstrated to a wider public through guided tours organised by Basil and the site manager, Malcolm Emery. All in all, there is an air of goodwill and optimism on the Pevensey Levels today, which bodes well for the future.

NATURE RESERVES AND THE ARTS

I have seen few memorable paintings or graphic interpretations of National Nature Reserves, at least as *reserves* rather than as wild and attractive parts of the landscape. The *Shell Bird Book* (1966) contained some attractively painted panoramas of bird reserves, including one of Rostherne Mere by S R Badmin. But virtually all publications about nature reserves since then have preferred the medium of photography. There are few Reserve portraits even in the local offices of English Nature: a couple of watercolours by W H Pearsall at Blackwell and a rather empty painting of the Swale 'wetland project' at Wye are the only paintings of note that I can recall. Possibly a trawl of local art galleries and private collections would give a different impression, but on present evidence the contribution of National Nature Reserves to contemporary art seems close to zero.

Until recently, the Conservancy did little to promote the arts, as opposed to the sciences, on National Nature Reserves. In 1992, however, English Nature funded an 'artist-in-residence' Lionel Playford, to produce a series of paintings of Castle Eden Dene NNR that captured something of the spirit and atmosphere of that dramatic limestone defile near the Durham coast. Some 500 local people also took part in art 'workshops' and the project attracted a fair amount of attention from the media, intrigued by the novelty of the idea. The 24 paintings were put on public display. Sinuous dead boughs in semi-abstract patterns, bark flaking from rotting elm stumps, croziers of young bracken uncurling in a deep green haze: these would not necessarily be everyone's idea of Castle Eden Dene, but as an artist's interpretation of the objects and images you encounter as you walk through a Reserve they form a fascinating and unique collection. The exercise was judged successful, suggesting that 'participation in art can be used to encourage the public appreciation of National Nature Reserves and to develop an interest in nature conservation'. If so, I hope English Nature will develop the idea. It seems full of attractive possibilities.

The promotion of the arts in wild and natural places would certainly have won the approval of Richard Payne Knight, the eighteenth-century proprietor of what is now Downton Gorge NNR and the sworn enemy of formalism in landscape gardening. As we saw in Chapter 9, Knight's subtle modifications to the gorge were designed not to tame its rugged character but to enhance its dramatic appeal through the creation of artificial caves, woodland glades and precipitous footpaths. He was so well pleased with the result that he commissioned Thomas Hearne to paint a series of 12 watercolours of the gorge and its surrounds. Hearne's paintings appear to be very accurate and are of great historic value (one of his other Herefordshire subjects, a mighty oak at Moccas Park, still stands, hardly changed in 200 years). This collaboration of landscaper and artist reminds us that Georgian ideas of landscape beautification can be entirely compatible with scientific principles of nature reserve management.

Many landscapes which happen to be nature reserves today form the backcloth to novels about country life, often full of beautifully observed detail. Indeed, one could probably compile a lengthy anthology from *Gawain and the Green Knight* to Malcolm Saville. It might be difficult to decide whether this or that Reserve in Dorset was part of Hardy's Egdon Heath, but Braunton Burrows and its neighbouring estuary appear prominently and unambiguously in several of Henry Williamson's books, including *Tarka the Otter*. The Stiperstones forms the jagged background to two of the agonised romances of Mary Webb, *The Golden Arrow* (1916) and *Gone to Earth* (1917), and more recently of children's stories by Malcolm Saville (who also wrote *The Secret of the Gorge*, based at Downton Gorge), not to mention a light opera, *Wild Edric*, concerned with local legend. Yarner Wood is the subject of two other romantic novels, *The Forest on the Hill* (1912) by Eden Phillpots and Brian Carter's animal story, *A Black Fox Running* (1981). The Axmouth–Lyme Regis landslip was, of course, the setting for *The French Lieutenant's Woman* by John Fowles. I am eagerly awaiting the arrival of a latterday James Herriot to write about the life and times of a National Nature Reserve warden. There must be enough good stories to stuff a whole shelf of books.

Whether or not the experimental earthwork at Fyfield Down counts as art or science I am not sure, but it certainly ranks prominently among the more imaginative projects on National Nature Reserves. Fyfield Down lies close to the Ridgeway, high above the Kennet Valley and overlooks the ancient wonders of Avebury with its stone circles, avenues and neighbouring tombs. The eastern half of the down is itself of archaeological interest as a well-preserved ancient field system, a series of square-banked fields interspersed with shallow vales, and swarming with pale grey sarsen stones that from a distance look like sleeping sheep. It is a fitting place for Britain's longest-running archaeological project, an attempt to find out how the prehistoric earthworks and ditches, so abundant in this part of England, would have looked in their prime. In 1960 a bank and ditch some 30 m long and 7 m wide was dug on Fyfield Down by a party of archaeologists and earth scientists using replicas of the bone tools employed by the original architects of Avebury. The idea is to cut through the dyke at intervals to observe the changes brought about by natural erosion and deposition, and thereby calculate to what degree the ancient earthworks have slumped and worn away during the past 4000 years or so. One unexpected spin-off for the nature reserve is that, because the dyke has been fenced to exclude rabbits (there were, of course, no rabbits in prehistoric England), the chalk flora has gained at least 11 new species. Perhaps ancient Avebury was beautifully coloured and scented by banks of thyme, rock-rose and Fragrant Orchids. The experiment is due to run until the year 2088. As Professor Fowler, one of the originators of the experiment, points out, 'we do not expect to write the final report'. In the meantime, the dyke is now old enough to qualify as an Ancient Monument or Listed Building.

Although this is far from being the only collaboration between archaeologists and nature reserve managers, it is one of the most accessible in its appeal to the imagination. Such projects can lend a more positive image to nature reserves and build bridges to the wider landscapes and rural communities of which nature reserves were once a part.

THE FUTURE LANDSCAPE

English Nature's second annual report, covering the financial year ending on 31 March 1993, lists 140 National Nature Reserves covering some 57,000 ha. This book has been concerned mainly with their history, especially their recent history, with the purposes these special places serve and with how they are looked after on behalf of the nation. Here we must consider, more briefly, the future of National Nature Reserves, in so far as it is possible to do so. We are currently living through considerable changes in government policy in the fields of agriculture, forestry and country planning. Various schemes to encourage 'environmentally sensitive' farming in areas of scenic beauty and high wildlife interest are being tried and tested. Land is being taken out of production, either temporarily or semi-permanently. Acronyms and grant-schemes are multiplying in ever-increasing profusion and complexity. At the same time, the 'private sector' of nature conservation, as represented by bodies like the RSPB, Woodland Trust and the county naturalists trusts, has grown stronger. And public landowners like the National Trust, the Forestry Commission and the Ministry of Defence have changed their policies and attitudes for the better, so far as nature is concerned.

Within these greatly changed circumstances, the role of National Nature Reserves is ripe for re-evaluation. Some have gone so far as to question whether they any longer serve a useful function. Surely limited resources, it has been argued, might with greater benefit be used to enable local authorities to plant more trees around cities, or to enable country landowners to be even more environmentally friendly. Such arguments tend to ignore the basic facts of biogeography. For at least 80 years, British naturalists have realised that wildlife is not distributed at random throughout the countryside but concentrated in particular localities where, through a combination of physical and historical circumstances, the needs of species are met. National Nature Reserves are not normally artificial constructs but areas of land which, for whatever reason,

59. Right: *Ebbor Gorge.*

60. Below left: *Downton Gorge. Inside the Roman Bath.*

61. Below right: *Downton Gorge, white water, Hereford and Worcestershire.*

62. *Some long-serving Reserve wardens.*
Top row, left to right: *Phil Page (Yarner Wood), Rees Cox (Studland), Mike Tuck (Dorset heaths), Richard Williamson (Kingley Vale), Cliff Waller (Walberswick), Paul Toynton (Martin Down),*
Bottom row, left to right: *Ron Harold (Holkham), Tom Wall (Stiperstones), John Robinson (Wyre Forest). Ian Findlay (Upper Teesdale), James Venner (North Solent), Bill Elliot (Parsonage Down).*

contain outstanding populations of wild plants and animals. It is perfectly possible to improve 'ordinary land' for wildlife, but a field of sown grass or crops will never become a Parsonage Down; planted woods of beech or sycamores may be used by badgers and nesting birds but they will never acquire the characteristics of a Ham Street Wood or a Moccas Park, which have evolved over hundreds, if not thousands, of years, and largely naturally. Some Reserves contain pockets of unusually mild microclimate, which have more in common with central France than with our own cool, cloudy country. Others are lucky enough to have escaped the clear fellings, underground drainage and nitrate blitzes of recent times, and are a reminder of the 'traditional' countryside of mixed farming and rural crafts that only old people can now remember. Others still are habitats that are no longer found in 'ordinary countryside'—acid bogs, open heaths, grazing marsh and flowery meads. If we neglect such places, we stand to lose much of our remaining wildlife.

Whatever objections idealists might make about the exclusive philosophy underlying the concept of nature reserves, it is unlikely that a satisfactory substitute will be found for them. Grants and amenity schemes are no substitute, for they are based on the man-centred idea of creating habitats, which benefits only migratory or opportunistic species and, even then, only if they are left undisturbed. And we are not yet clever enough to reproduce the conditions that created ancient woodland, raised bogs or the chalk downs. The challenge today is to ensure that the irreplaceable places of greatest wildlife value do not become marginalised at a time when it is fashionable to be 'green' but when (bird watchers apart) field naturalists are thinner on the ground than they were.

When, in the 1940s, the concept of National Nature Reserves first became enshrined in the legislation, their original purpose was to preserve flora and fauna, or (in a few cases) geological and physiographic features. They would also serve as 'outdoor laboratories' where ecologists could study the living environment and learn how to 'manage' wild habitats. In those days, National Nature Reserves were the lynch-pin of nature conservation in Britain. Since then, charitable bodies like the RSPB have become wealthy enough to acquire land of equivalent size and importance, especially after 1981 when grant-aid for land-purchase became widely available. The protective mechanism of Sites of Special Scientific Interest (SSSIs) has been greatly improved, and some SSSIs are now managed under private agreements that resemble those of privately owned National Nature Reserves. With the break-up of the NCC and the formation of a new body, English Nature, representing England alone, it is doubly likely that the old assumptions and practices are due for a radical overview. At the time of writing, English Nature is in the middle of a policy review designed to integrate National Nature Reserves within the organisation's broader conservation objectives. Can the experience gained on National Nature Reserves be used more widely, especially on SSSIs of equivalent quality? Should English Nature seek to manage all of the NNRs directly, or is there a case for farming some of them out to other wildlife bodies? And, since resources are very limited, which natural habitats form the highest priority for the Reserves of the future?

The integration of National Nature Reserves within a broader conservation framework is already well underway. In earlier chapters of this book we met many examples of work on Reserves that is helping in a more general way to refine the management of land for nature conservation. The development of management handbooks and of English Nature's annual Reserve Review, as well as the colour magazine *Enact*, are helping to make such information easily available, almost for the first time. Furthermore, the Reserves themselves are in certain areas becoming part of a broader strategy for nature conservation. Like most rare species, the distribution of National Nature Reserves is clumped, with the highest density within places that have a high natural biodiversity, such as the Purbeck heaths, the Breckland and the East Anglian coast. In the near future, Reserve managers in such areas will be working more closely with other conservation bodies, sharing experience and a common agenda. The Sefton Coast management scheme, incorporating the Ainsdale and Cabin Hill NNRs is already up and running. It is likely that we shall soon see a similar arrangement on the Purbeck heaths, with the long-term goal of reintroducing the much-needed stock-grazing in place of the present forage-harvesting and burning regimes. The restoration of heath from farmland will also be a conservation priority in places where the land has gone out of agricultural production. In other areas of 'natural biodiversity' the emphasis may be different. The Upper Teesdale NNR will help to steer the broader SSSI and Environmentally Sensitive Area of the dale. The experience of Reserve managers in stock handling will become useful if grazing is reintroduced to the Cotswold Commons. In some areas, such as the Wash, English Nature will take the lead. In others, it intends to work in partnership with other conservation and local government agencies. The central idea is teamwork to ensure that the diverse but highly experienced conservation world is pulling on the same rope, and in the same direction.

In future it is probable that a much higher proportion of National Nature Reserves will be managed by bodies other than English Nature. We have seen a shoal of recent examples: Malham Tarn and Slapton Lea being looked after by the Field Studies Council, Wicken Fen, the Farne Islands and Bassenthwaite by the National Trust and Duncombe Park by a private trust. Such Reserves will continue to be of the highest quality in nature conservation terms and managed to the highest standards. Semantically, they perhaps represent a shift in the meaning of the word 'national' from direct stewardship by a body of the Crown to a benchmark of scientific quality. It means that English Nature may increasingly act as an enabler, rather than as a full-time direct practitioner.

There will continue to be places, however, where English Nature will seek to own the land and manage it directly. Such Reserves are likely to lie in the aforementioned zones of high biodiversity or among rare and fragile habitats like lowland bogs that are at once threatened and unlikely to be acquired by another conservation body. It is probable that NNRs requiring relatively intensive management, such as grasslands, heaths and wetlands, or mosaics of different habitats, will remain under direct control. Such planning is, of course liable, to be upset by unforeseen events, which have surfaced at frequent intervals in the recent past. But as principles they do at least represent an attempt by English Nature to use its limited resources in areas where they will be most effective.

For the average visitor to National Nature Reserves, whether in search of rare wildlife, or beautiful countryside, or simply peace and quiet, such changes will happen largely off-stage. He or she may find a different design of sign or improved waymarking and information facilities on certain sites, but the view will remain much the same. Nature reserves are still our best guarantee that rare wild animals and plants can find a refuge, and that the richest parts of our natural heritage will be passed on intact to generations yet unborn. In their various guises—sanctuaries, outdoor museums and laboratories, test-beds for management techniques or simply as places to see wild plants and animals—National Nature Reserves have served England well these past 40 years. We had the advantage of an early start and the work of three centuries of English naturalists on which to draw. Through the management of nature reserves, we have learned a great deal about maintaining habitats, and restoring them from misuse, often in cases that would once have been written off as hopeless. England's National Nature Reserves may not boast the most dramatic scenery on the planet, but they do form a unique and wonderful record of how man and nature can still live together on a crowded island.

Selected Bibliography

Adams, W.M. 1986. *Nature's Place: Conservation Sites and Countryside Change.* Allen & Unwin, London.

Andrews, J. & Ward, D. 1991. The management and creation of reedbeds—especially for rare birds. *British Wildlife,* 3(2): 81–91.

Atkinson-Willes, G. L. (ed.) 1963. *Wildfowl in Great Britain.* HM Stationery Office, London.

Beebee, T. 1992. Trying to save the natterjack toad—a case study in amphibian conservation. *British Wildlife,* 3(3): 137–145.

Butterflies Under Threat Team 1986. *The Management of Chalk Grassland for Butterflies.* Focus on nature conservation No. 17. NCC, Peterborough.

Byfield, A. 1991. Classic British wildlife sites—the Lizard peninsula. *British Wildlife,* 3(2): 92–105.

Caufield, C. 1991. *Thorne Moors.* The Sumach Press, St. Albans.

Cherrill, A. 1993. The conservation of Britain's Wart-biter Bush-crickets. *British Wildlife,* 5(1): 26–31.

Chestney, B. 1993. *Island of Terns: Warden of Scolt Head.* Quiller Press, London.

Clapham, A.R. (ed.) 1978. *Upper Teesdale, The Area and its Natural History.* Collins, London.

Colebourn, P. & Gibbons, B. 1990. *Britain's Countryside Heritage.* Blandford, in association with the National Trust, London.

Cooke, A.S. 1986. *The Use of Herbicides on Nature Reserves.* Focus on nature conservation No. 14. NCC, Peterborough.

Dartington Amenity Research Trust 1978. *Self-guided Trails: An Appraisal.* Countryside Commission, Cheltenham.

Duffey, E. (ed.) 1967. *The Biotic Effects of Public Pressures on the Environment.* Monks Wood Experimental Station. Symposium No 3. Nature Conservancy, Huntingdon.

Duffey, E. 1971. The management of Woodwalton Fen: a multidisciplinary approach. *In:* Duffey, E. & Watt, A.S. (eds), *The Scientific Management of Animal and Plant Communities for Conservation*: 581–598. Blackwell, Oxford.

Duffey, E. 1974. *Nature Reserves and Wildlife.* Heinemann, London.

Duffey, E. *et al.* (eds) 1974. *Grassland Ecology and Wildlife Management.* Chapman & Hall, London.

English Nature 1992. First Report. Peterborough.

English Nature 1993. *Enact Magazine* 1, Nos 1–3. Peterborough.

Environmental Advisory Unit, University of Liverpool 1988. *Heathland Restoration: a Handbook of Techniques*. British Gas, Southampton.

Fisher, J. 1966. *The Shell Bird Book* Ebury Press and Michael Joseph, London.

Fuller, R.J. 1982. *Bird Habitats in Britain*. Poyser, Carlton.

Fuller, R.J. & Warren, M.S. 1990. *Coppiced Woodlands: their Management for Wildlife*. NCC, Peterborough.

George, M. 1991. *The Land Use, Ecology and Conservation of Broadland*. Packard Publishing, Chichester.

Gibbons, B. 1989–1994. Reserve Focus: Martin Down, Hampshire. *British Wildlife*, **1**(1): 41–43. North Meadow, Cricklade, Wiltshire. *British Wildlife*, **1**(4): 216–218. Derbyshire Dales National Nature Reserve. *British Wildlife*, **1**(6): 347–349. Braunton Burrows National Nature Reserve. *British Wildlife*, **2**(1): 42–44. Gait Barrows National Nature Reserve, Cumbria. *British Wildlife*, **2**(6): 359–361. Upper Teesdale National Nature Reserve. *British Wildlife*, **3**(4): 230–232. The Wyre Forest NNR, Hereford & Worcester. *British Wildlife*, **4**(4): 246–248. Thursley National Nature Reserve, Surrey. *British Wildlife*, **5**(3): 166–168. The Farne Islands, Northumberland. *British Wildlife*, **5**(4): 244–247.

Goodier, R. & Jeffers, J.N.R. 1981. Biosphere reserves. *Advances in Applied Biology*, **6**: 279–317.

Harding, P.T. & Rose, F. 1986. *Pasture-woodlands in Lowland Britain. A Review of Their Importance for Wildlife Conservation*. ITE, Huntingdon.

Henson, J. 1988. *Rare Breeds as Grazers for Nature Reserves*. Rare Breeds Survival Trust.

Hickin, N. 1971. *The Natural History of an English Forest. The Wild Life of Wyre*. Hutchinson, London.

Hillier, S.H., Walton, D.W.H. & Wells, D.A. (eds) 1990. *Calcareous Grasslands—Ecology and Management*. Proceedings of a British Ecological Society/NCC symposium at the University of Sheffield, 14–16 September 1987. Bluntisham Books, Huntingdon.

Holms, P. 1993. Dersingham: a conservation case-history. *Enact*, **1**(2): 4–5.

Hutchings, M.J. 1987. The population biology of the Early Spider Orchid. I. A demographic study from 1975 to 1984. II. Temporal patterns in behaviour. *Journal of Ecology*. **75**: 711–27; 729–42.

Hywel-Davies, J. & Thom, V. (eds) 1984. *The Macmillan Guide to Britain's Nature Reserves*. Macmillan, London.

Jefferson, R.G. & Crofts, A. (eds) 1993. *Lowland Grassland Management Handbook*. English Nature, Peterborough in association with the RSNC.

Johnson, A.L. & Dunham, K.C. 1963. *The Geology of Moor House*. Nature Conservancy Monograph No 2. HM Stationery Office, London.

Kaznowska, S. & Waller, C. 1993. Buying time for Benacre. *Enact*, **1**(3): 10–11.

Kirby, P. 1992. *Habitat Management for Invertebrates: A Practical Handbook*. RSPB/JNCC.

Lambert, D. 1993. Saltmarshes: managing for the future. *Enact*, **1**(3): 15–17.

Linsell, S. 1990. *Hickling Broad and its wildlife. The story of a famous nature reserve*. Terence Dalton, Lavenham.

Mabey, R. 1980. *The Common Ground.* Hutchinson in association with NCC, London.
Magnusson, M. & O'Connor, D.A. 1984. *Lindisfarne: the Cradle Island.* Oriel Press, Stocksfield.
McKibben, B. 1990. *The End of Nature.* Viking, Harmondsworth.
McVean, D.N. & Ratcliffe, D.A. 1962. *Plant Communities of the Scottish Highlands. A study of Scottish mountain, moorland and forest vegetation.* HMSO, London.
Ministry of Town and Country Planning 1947, repr. 1974. *Conservation of Nature in England and Wales.* Report of the Wild Life Conservation Special Committee (England and Wales). Cmd. 7122. HM Stationery Office.
Monke, B. 1980. *Castle Eden Dene. An Illustrated Guide.* Peterlee Development Corporation.
Moore, N.W. 1962. The heaths of Dorset and their conservation. *Journal of Ecology.* 50: 369–391.
Moore, N.W. 1987. *The Bird of Time: the Science and Politics of Nature Conservation.* Cambridge University Press, Cambridge.
Musgrave, M. 1993. Outfoxing the foxes. *Enact,* **1(1)**: 6–9.
Nature Conservancy 1949–65. *Annual Reports.* HM Stationery Office.
Nature Conservancy 1963. *Science Out of Doors.* Longmans, London.
Nature Conservancy 1968. *Nature Trails.* Leaflet published by the Nature Conservancy and distributed by Warne, London.
Nature Conservancy 1968. *Progress 1964–68.* Nature Conservancy, London.
Nature Conservancy Council 1986. *Nature conservation and afforestation in Britain.* NCC, Peterborough.
NCC 1975–1992. *Annual Reports.* Nos 1–6. HM Stationery Office. Nos 7–17. NCC, London and Peterborough.
NCC 1983. *A Handbook for the Preparation of Management Plans.* NCC, London.
NCC 1984. *Nature Conservation in Great Britain.* NCC, Peterborough.
NCC 1988. *Site Management for Nature Conservation: A Working Guide.* NCC, Peterborough.
Nicholson, E.M. 1957. *Britain's Nature Reserves.* Country Life, London.
Nicholson, M. 1970. *The Environmental Revolution. A guide for the new masters of the world.* Hodder & Stoughton, London.
O'Connor, D. & Townsend. 1993. Some effects of disturbance to wildfowl from bait-digging and wildfowling at Lindisfarne NNR, NE-England. *Disturbance of wildfowl on estuaries,* edited by N. Davidson and P. Rothwell. Wader Study Group Bulletin **60**, Special Issue, August 1993.
Oliver, F.W. 1928. Nature Reserves. *Transactions Norfolk and Norwich Naturalists Society,* **12**: 317–322.
Pearsall, W.H. 1917. The aquatic and marsh vegetation of Esthwaite Water. *Journal of Ecology,* **5**: 180–202.
Peterken, G.F. Revised edn. 1993. *Woodland Conservation and Management.* Chapman & Hall, London.
Peterken, G.F. & Jones, E.W. 1987. Forty years of Change in Lady Park Wood: the old growth stands. *Journal of Ecology,* **75**: 477–512.

Pollard, E., Hall, M.L. & Bibby, T.J. 1986. *Monitoring the Abundance of Butterflies 1976–1985*. Research & survey in nature conservation No. 2. NCC, Peterborough.

Poore, M.E.D. 1956. The ecology of Woodwalton Fen. *Journal of Ecology,* **44**: 455–492.

Purseglove, J. 1988. *Taming the Flood. A History and Natural History of Rivers and Wetlands.* Oxford University Press in association with Channel Four Television.

Rackham, O. Revised edn. 1990. *Trees and Woodland in the British Landscape.* Dent, London.

Ratcliffe, D.A. (ed.) 1977. *A Nature Conservation Review: the Selection of Biological Sites of National Importance to Nature Conservation in Great Britain.* 2 vols. Cambridge University Press, Cambridge.

Roberts, S. 1991. Reserve Focus. Holt Heath National Nature Reserve, Dorset. *British Wildlife,* **3(1)**: 34–36.

Rowell, T.A. 1988. *The Peatland Management Handbook.* Research & survey in nature conservation No. 14. NCC, Peterborough.

Rowell, T.A. 1988. The recent history of Wicken Fen, Cambridgeshire, England: a guide to ecological development. *Journal of Ecology,* **76**: 73–90.

Roworth, P. 1991. Reserve Focus. Thorne Moors National Nature Reserve. *British Wildlife,* **2(3)**: 164–166.

Sheail, J. 1976. *Nature in Trust: The History of Nature Conservation in Britain.* Blackie, Glasgow.

Sheail, J. 1987. *Seventy-five years in Ecology: the British Ecological Society.* Blackwell, Oxford.

Sheail, J. & Wells, T.C.E. 1983. The Fenlands of Huntingdonshire, England: A case study in catastrophic change. *In:* Gore, A.J.P. (ed.), *Mires: Swamp, Bog, Fen and Moor. Ecosystems of the World No. 4B. Regional Studies.* Elsevier, Amsterdam: 375–393.

Stamp, D. 1969. *Nature Conservation in Britain.* Collins New Naturalist, London.

Steele, R.C. & Welch, R.C. (eds) 1973. *Monks Wood. A Nature Reserve Record.* Nature Conservancy, Huntingdon.

Steele, R.C. & Welch, R.C. (undated c. 1973) Monk Wood. *A Native Reserve Record.* Natural Environment Research Council, Monks Wood.

Steers, J.A. 2nd edn 1960. *Scolt Head.* Heffer, London.

Tansley, A.G. 1946. *Our Heritage of Wild Nature: A Plea for Organised Nature Conservation.* Cambridge University Press, Cambridge.

Tansley, A.G. Revised edn. 1949. *The British Islands and their Vegetation.* 2 vols. Cambridge University Press, Cambridge.

Venner, J. 1993. Soft coast defences. The use–and misuse–of groynes on North Solent NNR. *Enact,* **1(3)**: 20–21.

Wall, T. 1993. Burning issues. *Enact,* **1(4)**: 12–14.

Waring, P. 1990. Conserving Britain's rarest moths. *British Wildlife,* **1(5)**: 266–284.

Warren, M.S. 1985. The status of the heath fritillary butterfly *Mellicta athalia* Rott. in relation to changing woodland management in the Blean Woods, Kent. *Quarterly Journal of Forestry,* **79**: 175–182.

Warren, M.S. & Fuller, R.J. 1990. *Woodland Rides and Glades: their Management for Wildlife.* NCC, Peterborough.

Wells, D.A. 1981. The protection of British rare plants in nature reserves. *In:* Synge, H. (ed.), *The Biological Aspects of Rare Plant Conservation.* 475–480. Wiley, Chichester.

Whitten, A.J. 1990. *Recovery: A Proposed Programme for Britain's Protected Species.* NCC, Peterborough.

Williams, R. 1992. *The Somerset Levels.* Ex Libris Press, Bradford on Avon.

Williamson, R. 1978. *The Great Yew Forest: the Natural History of Kingley Vale.* Macmillan, London.

Wright, M. 1993. Bracken versus Brettenham. *Enact,* **1**(**2**): 8–9.

Sites of England's NNRs

Key

1 Lindisfarne
2 Newham Bog
3 Coom Rigg Moss
4 Gowk Bank
5 Grain Heads Moss
6 Glasson Moss
7 Moor House
8 Castle Eden Dene
9 Tarn Moss
10 Upper Teesdale
11 Halsenna Moor
12 Blelham Bog
13 Asby Scar
14 North Fen
15 Rusland Moss
16 Roudsea Woods and Mosses
17 North Walney
18 Clawthorpe Fell
19 Park Wood
20 Gait Barrows
21 Ling Gill
22 Colt Park Wood
23 Scar Close
24 Forge Valley Woods
25 Lower Derwent Valley
26 Ribble Marshes
27 Ainsdale Sand Dunes
28 Cabin Hill
29 Rostherne Mere
30 Saltfleetby–Theddlethorpe Dunes
31 Derbyshire Dales
32 Wybunbury Moss
33 Gibraltar Point
34 Munston Meadows
35 Chartley Moss
36 Mottey Meadows
37 The Wash
38 Scolt Head Island
39 Holkham
40 Swanton Novers Woods
41 Winterton Dunes
42 Hickling Broad
43 Ludham Marshes
44 Bure Marshes
45 Barnack Hills & Holes
46 Castor Hanglands
47 Stiperstones
48 Wren's Nest
49 Downton Gorge
50 Wyre Forest
51 Chaddesley Woods
52 Moccas Park
53 The Flits
54 Bredon Hill
55 Buckingham Thick Copse
56 Holme Fen
57 Monks Wood
58 Upwood Meadows
59 Woodwalton Fen
60 Weeting Heath
61 Brettenham Heath
62 Thetford Heath
63 Cavenham Heath
64 Chippenham Fen
65 Benacre
66 Walberswick
67 Westleton Heath
68 Barton Hills
69 Knocking Hoe
70 Hales Wood
71 Orfordness–Havergate
72 Hamford Water
73 Colne Estuary
74 Blackwater Estuary
75 Dengie
76 Lady Park Wood
77 Highbury Woods
78 Cotswold Commons & Beechwoods
79 Wychwood
80 North Meadow, Cricklade
81 Cothill
82 Aston Rowant
83 Gordano Valley
84 Avon Gorge
85 Fyfield Down
86 Pewsey Downs
87 Swanscombe Skull Site
88 Leigh
89 High Halstow
90 The Swale
91 Blean Woods
92 Stodmarsh
93 Lundy Marine Nature Reserve
94 Braunton Burrows
95 Bridgewater Bay
96 Rodney Stoke
97 Ebbor Gorge
98 Shapwick Heath
99 Somerset Levels
100 Barrington Hill
101 The Lizard
102 Goss Moor
103 Golitha Falls
104 Dendles Wood
105 Yarner Wood
106 Bovey Valley Woodlands
107 Axmouth–Lyme Regis Undercliffs
108 Hog Cliff
109 Morden Bog
110 Holt Heath
111 Holton Heath
112 Arne, The Moors
113 Studland Heath
114 Hartland Moor
115 Stoborough Heath
116 North Solent
117 Martin Down
118 Prescombe Down
119 Wylye Down
120 Parsonage Down
121 Ashford Hill
122 Thursley
123 Beacon Hill, Warnford
124 Old Winchester Hill
125 Kingley Vale
126 Castle Hill
127 Lewes Down
128 Lullington Heath
129 Pevensey Levels
130 Ham Street Woods
131 Wye

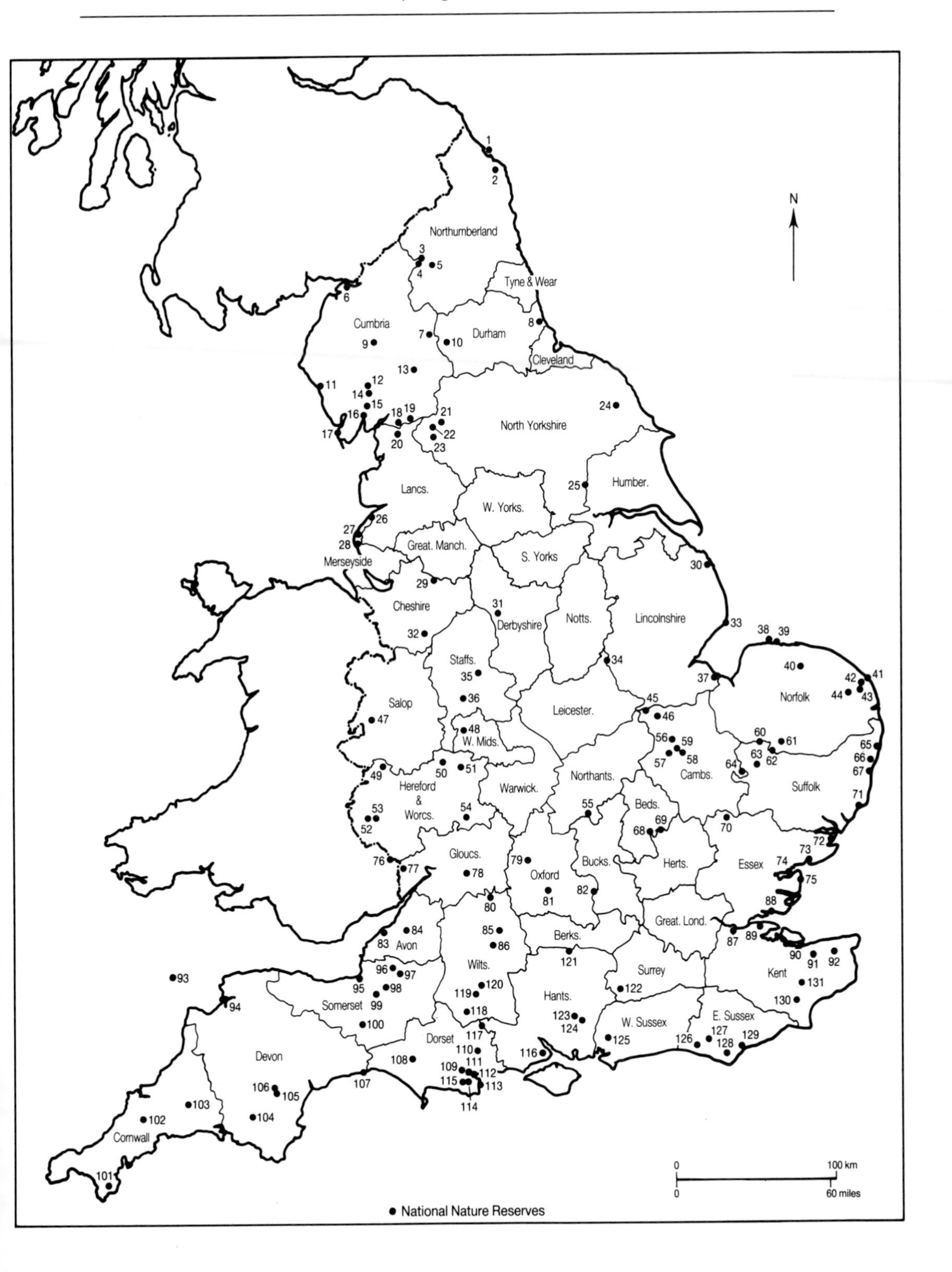
N
Northumberland
Tyne & Wear
Cumbria
Durham
Cleveland
North Yorkshire
Humber.
Lancs.
W. Yorks.
Great. Manch.
Merseyside
S. Yorks
Cheshire
Derbyshire
Notts.
Lincolnshire
Staffs.
Salop
Leicester.
W. Mids.
Norfolk
Hereford & Worcs.
Warwick.
Northants.
Cambs.
Suffolk
Beds.
Glouc.
Oxford
Bucks.
Herts.
Essex
Great. Lond.
Avon
Berks.
Wilts.
Kent
Surrey
Somerset
Hants.
W. Sussex
E. Sussex
Dorset
Devon
Cornwall
1
2
3
4
5
6
7
8
9
10
11
12
13
14
15
16
17
18
19
20
21
22
23
24
25
26
27
28
29
30
31
32
33
34
35
36
37
38
39
40
41
42
43
44
45
46
47
48
49
50
51
52
53
54
55
56
57
58
59
60
61
62
63
64
65
66
67
68
69
70
71
72
73
74
75
76
77
78
79
80
81
82
83
84
85
86
87
88
89
90
91
92
93
94
95
96
97
98
99
100
101
102
103
104
105
106
107
108
109
110
111
112
113
114
115
116
117
118
119
120
121
122
123
124
125
126
127
128
129
130
131
0
100 km
0
60 miles
• National Nature Reserves

APPENDIX 1

Gazetteer of England's National Nature Reserves

(at December 1993)

THIS gazetteer is a basic facts guide, covering the location, size, ownership, date of declaration, natural history highlights, details of management activities and the public facilities on each of England's 140 or so National Nature Reserves. The national grid reference given is at the approximate centre of the Reserve unless otherwise stated. The natural history highlights are necessarily selective, but are intended to indicate where the Reserve is *outstanding* or, in certain cases, where the presence of rare plants, birds or insects has a bearing on how the Reserve is managed. The management activities listed are those which are presently the most time-consuming or the most fundamental to the Reserve's well-being; I have omitted general estate maintenance like fencing, signs and path repairs which are common to nearly all Reserves. By the same token, I have also omitted biological survey and monitoring, which is a function of the majority of National Nature Reserves, except where they take up a significant amount of staff time and resources. Finally I have indicated the relative popularity of each Reserve, based on the estimated annual number of visitors, in one of three categories: low use (5000 or fewer visitors), medium use (5000–20,000), high use (20,000+). In the 'high use' Reserves, the object is often the beach, a viewpoint or a long distance footpath rather than the Reserve itself. Some Reserves have, in this sense, 'no use' in that access is restricted to permit holders. The Reserves are listed in alphabetical order. 'Section 35 Reserves', which are owned and managed by an 'approved body', are listed separately at the end. Further details of many of them are available in leaflet form from the appropriate English Nature office.

AINSDALE, MERSEYSIDE

SD 288102 (OS Sheet 108). 492 ha of sand dunes, wet dune slacks and planted pinewood along the Merseyside coast between Southport and Formby, owned by English Nature (1965). Best lime-rich dunes on NW coast, good flora incl. uncommon species, notable invertebrates, Natterjacks and Sand Lizards, passage waders. Scrub control, pine wood thinning, sheep grazing, cutting and mowing, erosion control, patrols, research, education. Open access, busy nature trail and path network, guided walks. Leaflet and educational material. High use (*c.* 250,000 visitors annually). Part of Sefton Coast management scheme, which also includes Cabin Hill NNR and Ainsdale and Birkdale Hills LNR, run by Sefton MBC.

Site manager: Michael Gee.

AQUALATE MERE, STAFFORDSHIRE

SJ 774204 (OS Sheet 127). 192 ha of open water, reedbed and fen, alder and willow carr and surrounding wet pasture, leased from a private landowner (1992). Largest and most diverse of the West Midland meres, rare example of kettle hole fen, good range of breeding and passage birds incl. heronry. Stockproofing for controlled grazing, ditch maintenance, cutting and mowing, water level control, scrub control, water quality research. Access for research purposes only.

Site manager: Tim Coleshaw.

ARNE, DORSET

SY 980886 (OS Sheet 195). Very minor 9 ha reedbed on S shore of Poole Harbour owned by English Nature (1985). Occasional reed cutting. Open access. The large RSPB Arne reserve is nearby.

Site manager: Mike Tuck.

ASBY SCAR, CUMBRIA

NY 648103 (OS Sheet 90). 166 ha of limestone scar and pavement and upland grassland at the head of Vale of Eden 10 km S of Appleby, part owned, rest by agreement with private owners (1987). Largest limestone pavement outside Ingleborough, impressively weathered with deep grikes and pits. Floristically less rich than

comparable sites (high altitude and grazing) but rare plants present. Sheep-grazed by lessee, otherwise non-intervention site. Open access. Low use.
Site manager: Terry Wells.

ASHFORD HILL, HAMPSHIRE

SU 562622 (OS Sheet 174). 20 ha of unimproved meadows, pasture and bordering broadleaved woodland 10 km SE of Newbury, owned by English Nature (1986). Olde England atmosphere, contrasting wet and dry (sandy) fields, thick hedges, flowery banks and streamsides. Excellent flora (235 spp.), invertebrate interest incl. notable butterflies. Seasonal and all-year grazing, hay-making, scrub cutting, ditch maintenance. Open access. Leaflet. Low use (*c.* 2000 visitors annually).
Site manager: Mick Finnemore.

ASTON ROWANT, OXFORDSHIRE AND BUCKINGHAMSHIRE

SU 732966 (OS Sheet 165). 127 ha of chalk grassland, scrub and beechwood around Beacon and Bald Hills on the Chiltern scarp 16 km NW of High Wycombe, partly owned by English Nature, partly leased or managed by agreement (1958 with subsequent extensions). Good mixture of prime Chilterns habitats incl. most of the characteristic plants and animals of the region. Unimproved grassland on N, S and E slopes, good mixed chalk scrub incl. juniper, succession of scrub to mature woodland, notable invertebrates, ponds. Bisected by the M40, cutting through 20 m of chalk ('Aston Remnant'). Sheep grazing, scrub cutting on rotation, traditional woodland management, research. Car park. Access on nature trail (booklet) and rights of way. Leaflet. Medium to high use.
Site manager: Mike Cox.

AVON GORGE, AVON

ST 553731 (OS Sheet 172). 63 ha of mature woodland, scrub, limestone grassland and crags on W side of Avon Gorge on the outskirts of Bristol, by agreement with the National Trust (1970). Ancient oak, ash and lime woods with rich flora (Leigh Woods), rare whitebeams and rock plants. Arch.: Iron Age hill fort. Limited coppicing and pollarding, scrub clearance, ride mowing, education. Open access, nature trail. Leaflet. High use (*c.* 20,000 visitors annually).
Site manager: Tony Robinson.

AXMOUTH–LYME REGIS UNDERCLIFFS, DEVON

SY 300901 (OS Sheet 193). 321 ha of unstable landslips overgrown by species-rich scrub and developing woodland along 8 km of the S Devon coast. Part owned (56 ha), the rest leased (120 ha) or by private agreement (1955). A real wilderness experience: best coastal landslip scenery in England, world's richest Lower Jurassic fossils, natural successions from open ground to woodland, rich flora and insect fauna. Mainly allowed to develop naturally; some scrub clearance and coppicing, cutting and mowing, path maintenance, education. South Devon coast path runs along full length, rough and slippery in places; access otherwise by permission. Best access for fossils is along beach. Leaflet. Medium use.

Hon. warden: Norman Barns.

Site manager: Phil Page.

BARNACK HILLS AND HOLES, CAMBRIDGESHIRE

TF 075046 (OS Sheet 142). 23 ha of limestone grassland at W end of Barnack village, leased from Burghley House Preservation Trust (1976). Oolitic grassland among ancient quarry workings (Barnack ragstone), good flora incl. Pasque Flower and Man Orchid, notable insects. Sheep grazed (autumn), scrub removal, species monitoring. Open access, car park, leaflet. Medium use (*c.* 12,000 visitors annually).

Site manager: Chris Gardiner.

BARRINGTON HILL MEADOWS, SOMERSET

ST 300170 (OS Sheet 193). 18 ha of unimproved hay meadow on S edge of Blackdown Hills, owned by English Nature (1987). Triangle of four fields on clay with old hedges and ponds. Good herb-rich grassland incl. large colony of Green-winged Orchids and other uncommon plants. Hay-making and after-grazing by cattle, pond restoration. Access by permission.

BARTON HILLS, BEDFORDSHIRE

TL 093295 (OS Sheet 166). 44 ha of chalk grassland, scrub and broadleaved woodland 8 km N of Luton, leased from Hexton Estate (1980, declared 1986). A knot of chalk hills, scarps and dry valleys with variety of aspect and sward, good chalk flora incl. Pasque Flower, notable insects, ancient woodland with large lime stools. Sheep grazing, scrub control, research, education. Open access. Leaflet. Medium use (*c.* 25,000 visitors annually).

Site manager: Graham Bellamy.

BEACON HILL, WARNFORD, HAMPSHIRE

SU 604226 (OS Sheet 185). 40 ha of chalk grassland, hazel scrub and developing woodland 1.6 km W of Warnford overlooking the Meon Valley, owned by English Nature (1986). Rich, S-facing chalk downland dotted with ant-hills, notable butterflies. Sheep-grazing with own flock, scrub removal, cutting and mowing, hazel coppicing, traditional woodland management. Car park, access on marked path. Leaflet.

Site manager: Mick Finnemore.

BENACRE, SUFFOLK

TM 530830 (OS Sheet 156). 393 ha of brackish pools, lagoon, reedbed, sand dunes, shingle beaches and broadleaved woodland on Suffolk coast 10 km S of Lowestoft, by agreement with Sir John Gooch (1987, extended 1993). Unusual variety of undisturbed coastal habitats incl. saline lagoon and extensive reedbeds, ancient pollard oaks. Passage birds, breeding terns, lagoon invertebrates. Coast and reedbed protection works incl. new berms, reed cutting, water level regulation, traditional woodland management. Closed Reserve apart from public hide and popular coastal path.
Site manager: Cliff Waller.

BLACKWATER ESTUARY, ESSEX

TL 940070 (OS Sheet 168). 1031 ha of remote mudflats and grazing marsh with fresh and brackish pools and ditches, mainly owned and managed by the RSPB; declared NNR 1983. With Colne Estuary and the Dengie flats (q.v.) one of the major staging posts and overwintering sites for waders and wildfowl on E coast. Common Seals. Mainly non-intervention. Public footpath along sea wall, otherwise by permission (small car park for permit holders at Old Hall Marsh Farm). Low use.
Site manager: Ian Black.

BLEAN WOODS, KENT

TR 109606 (OS Sheet 179). 90 ha of ancient oak, beech, chestnut and hornbeam woodland 2 km W of Blean village nr Canterbury, owned by English Nature (1953). Coppice-with-standards woodland with rides, glades and streambank. Famous for large colony of Heath Fritillary butterfly, outstanding invertebrates, good nesting birds. Coppicing, ride and glade maintenance, thinning. Common land. Open access on network of paths and rides, nature trail, leaflet. Medium use (*c.* 6000 visitors annually). RSPB's Church Wood reserve lies to immediate S; most of the ancient Blean Woods are now owned and managed by conservation bodies.
Site manager: David Maylam.

BLELHAM BOG, CUMBRIA

NY 364006 (OS Sheet 90). Tiny 2-ha *Sphagnum* bog with alder–willow carr at north end of Blelham Tarn, leased from the National Trust (1954). Bog formed over kettle hole. Minimum intervention. Blelham Tarn has been studied and monitored intensively for many years by the Freshwater Biological Association. Open access. Low use.
Site manager: Peter Singleton.

BOVEY VALLEY WOODLANDS, DEVON

SX 770804 (OS Sheet 191). 73 ha of mature broadleaved woodland along the rocky valley of the R Bovey between Manaton and Lustleigh, mostly owned by English Nature (1963 and later extensions). Relatively undisturbed woodland, mainly overgrown Sessile Oak coppice with scattered mature trees. Notable bryophyte and lichen flora with Atlantic and pollution-sensitive species, notable butterflies, Dormouse, birds of western oakwoods incl. Pied Flycatcher. Some coppicing, thinning and glade management, conifer and sycamore removal, but generally allowed to go wild. Access on rights of way, limited roadside parking. Leaflet. Medium use (*c.* 10,000 visitors annually).

Site manager: Phil Page.

BRAUNTON BURROWS, DEVON

SS 455338 (OS Sheet 180). 604 ha of sand dunes and dune slacks on N bank of the Taw/Torridge estuary, 11 km W of Barnstaple. Subleased from MoD, who lease it from the Christie Estate Trustees (1964). Finest lime-rich dune system in England, well-documented, high mobile dunes, rich flora with numerous rarities, important bryophytes and lichens. Limited paddock grazing with own Soay sheep, scrub control, dune stabilisation, footpath maintenance, education. Open access (except when army firing), two large car parks with information boards, board walk, guided walks, colour booklet. Nearby is Northam Burrows Country Park and the medieval Braunton Great Field. High use (*c.* 50,000 visitors annually).

Site manager: John Breeds.

BREDON HILL, WORCESTERSHIRE

SO 943397 (OS Sheet 150). 36 ha of limestone and neutral grassland, springs, scrub and woodland on hill 6 km SE of Pershore, owned by English Nature (1986). Prominent N-facing Cotswold outlier with characteristic tor-grass and tall brome-dominated unimproved grassland, active landslip, well-studied Badgers. Controlled grazing, scrub removal, thistle control trials. Access by permission, but local villagers allowed use. Low use.

Site manager: Malcolm Whitmore.

BRETTENHAM HEATH, NORFOLK

TL 925869 (OS Sheet 144). 236 ha of grass heath and bracken 6 km E of Thetford, leased from private estate (1982). Extensive grass-dominated Breck heath, periglacial soil patterns, Breckland birds. Restored from bracken by regular swiping; sheep grazing, scrub removal. Access by permission.

Site manager: Malcolm Wright.

BRIDGWATER BAY, SOMERSET

ST 267475 (OS Sheet 182). 2559 ha of mudflats, saltmarsh and grazing marsh on the Somerset coast at the mouth of the R Parrett 8 km NW of Bridgwater. Fenning Island is owned by English Nature, the rest leased from Crown Estate commissioners or by agreement with National Rivers Authority (1954, extended 1974). Wintering Wigeon, winter and passage waders, Shelduck moult, good flora on saltmarsh and low cliffs. Grazing, control of wildfowling, sea defence works. Open access, except to permit-only Stert Island and the hides on Fenning Island. Car park, hides, information board. Low use (*c.* 3000 visitors annually).
Site manager: Robin Prowse.

BUCKINGHAM THICK COPSE, NORTHAMPTONSHIRE

SP 708432 (OS Sheet 152). 45 ha of ancient broadleaved woodland in Whittlewood Forest, leased from private owners with purchase of standing timber (1990). Two copses separated by ancient track. Mainly relict ash–maple–hazel overstood coppice with giant over-mature oaks, good lichens and invertebrates centred on old oaks. Glade creation around ancient trees, coppicing, ride maintenance. Access for research only.
Site manager: Graham Bellamy.

BURE MARSHES, NORFOLK

TG 322157 (OS Sheet 134). 451 ha of open water, reedbed, fen meadow, dykes and alder carr in the Bure and Ant valleys, including Hoveton Great and Little Broad, Ranworth Broad, Cockshoot Broad, Decoy Broad and Woodbastwick Fen, owned, leased or by private agreement (1958, extended 1981). Excellent fen and freshwater flora, fine carr woodland, many notable invertebrates incl. Swallowtail, year-round birding incl. Bearded Tit, wintering duck and geese. Dyke management incl. suction dredging, mowing, scrub clearance, reed harvesting, water quality control experiment at Hoveton Great Broad, digging turf ponds, research, monitoring. Nature trail and hide at Hoveton Great Broad (via boat from Wroxham, April–September), walk-way and hide at Cockshoot Broad, access otherwise by permission. Leaflet, information sheet. Medium use (*c.* 5000 visitors annually). Norfolk Naturalists Trust information centre by Ranworth Broad (Apr–Oct).
Site manager: Rick Southwood.

CABIN HILL, MERSEYSIDE

SD 283050 (OS Sheet 108). 28 ha of sand dunes, dune slacks and abandoned cultivation 2 km SW of Formby, leased from private landowners (1991). Good dune slack flora incl. uncommon plants, Natterjack colony in flooded pits, reintroduced Sand

Lizards, wintering and passage waders. Cattle grazed (winter), cutting and mowing, pond construction. Open access, public path on seaward side. Leaflet. Medium use. Part of Sefton Coast management scheme with Ainsdale Reserve (q.v.).
Site manager: Michael Gee.

CASTLE EDEN DENE, DURHAM

NZ 435397 (OS Sheet 93). 221 ha of wooded gorge, owned by English Nature (1985), former LNR of Peterlee Development Corporation. Among the largest and least disturbed woods in NE England, largely native ash, oak, alder and yew, limestone grassland at seaward end, good spring flora, rare insects, bird migration route, red squirrels, active landslips. High level of estate work (repair of fences, stiles, bridges, etc), traditional woodland management, sycamore, Rhododendron and dead elm removal, path maintenance, patrols, education. Open access, popular 'green lung' of Peterlee/Durham area, 19-km footpath network. Leaflet. High use (*c.* 200,000 visitors annually).
Site manager: Chris McCarty.

CASTOR HANGLANDS, CAMBRIDGESHIRE

TF 117018 (OS Sheet 142). 90 ha of limestone grassland and scrub, ponds and broadleaved woodland 6 km W of Peterborough, leased from Forestry Authority and Milton Estates (1954). Good all-season natural history, ash-oak ancient woodland, good moths and butterflies incl. Black Hairstreak, amphibians incl. Crested Newt, bird-rich. Sheep grazing (autumn/winter), mowing and swiping, scrub management, traditional woodland management, ride, path and glade maintenance. Open access. Leaflet. Medium use (*c.* 8000 visitors annually).
Site manager: Chris Gardiner.

CAVENHAM HEATH, SUFFOLK

TL 751728 (OS Sheet 144). 204 ha of Breckland heath, grassland, valley fen and birch scrub 2 km W of Icklingham, mostly owned by English Nature (1952 and subsequent extensions). Includes Cavenham, Tuddenham and Roper's Heath and Ash Plantation. Finest dry acid heath in the Breck; bird-rich esp. in summer with breeding Nightjar, Gadwall, etc., notable invertebrates. Sheep and cattle-grazed under licence; fencing, scrub removal, heath restoration from arable. Car park, free access over 40 ha of heath; right of way over Tuddenham Heath; otherwise by permission. Information sheet. Medium use.
Site manager: Malcolm Wright.

CHADDESLEY WOODS, WORCESTERSHIRE

SO 914736 (OS Sheet 139). 102 ha of ancient oak woodland and conifer plantations on the Keuper Marl 5 km NW of Bromsgrove, owned by English Nature (1973). Large

Midlands-type wood, mainly mature oaks and overgrown hazel coppice with some hornbeam coppice and valley alders, small unimproved meadow. Nesting birds, notable insects. Restoration of conifers, traditional woodland management, cutting and mowing, pond maintenance. Access along paths and rights of way, car park, Jubilee Walk (booklet), leaflet. Medium use (*c.* 10,000 visitors annually).
Site manager: John Robinson.

CHARTLEY MOSS, STAFFORDSHIRE

SK 025282 (OS Sheet 128). 42 ha of peat bog and encroaching woodland in the Trent Valley, leased from a private owner (1963). Britain's best *Schwingmoore* (floating bog), skin of peat over a deep lake, good bog flora, rare insects, wilderness atmosphere. Habitat restoration by pine and birch removal and water level control, ride and glade creation, research, education. A dangerous site, hence access by permit only. Board walk, leaflet.
Site manager: Tim Coleshaw.

CHIPPENHAM FEN, CAMBRIDGESHIRE

TL 649693 (OS Sheet 154). 117 ha of fen meadow, reed and saw-sedge beds, fen carr and broadleaved woodland, 5 km N of Newmarket, leased from Chippenham Park Estate (1963). Rich and attractive fenland flora incl. rare plants, notable invertebrates esp. moths; bird-rich esp. in summer. Water level regulation and monitoring, water compensation scheme, sedge harvesting, cattle grazing by licensee, scrub control, ride maintenance, traditional woodland management, research. Access by permission. Information sheet. Low use (*c.* 2000 visitors annually).
Site manager: Malcolm Wright.

CLAWTHORPE FELL, CUMBRIA

SD 537786 (OS Sheet 97). 14 ha of limestone pavement, by agreement with English China Clays Ltd and private owner (1976). Reserve in two parts (1) an area of undamaged pavement surrounded by quarries, and (2) area of damaged pavement with encroaching scrub. Good flora. Minimal management. Access to first area (in hazardous working quarry) by permission only; second area crossed by public footpath. Low use.
Site manager: Rob Petley-Jones.

COLLYWESTON GREAT WOOD, NORTHAMPTONSHIRE AND CAMBRIDGESHIRE

TL 014004 (OS Sheet 141). 156 ha of ancient and semi-natural woodland and glades; properly three woods: Collyweston Great Wood, Easton Hornstocks and Wittering Coppice, all leased from the Cecil Estate Family Trust (1990). Relatively undisturbed

and diverse ancient woodland incl. extensive Small-leaved Lime coppice with rich flora. Ride and glade maintenance, coppicing. Access by permission (private estate and MoD weapons compound). Nearby is Bedford Purlieus Forestry Nature Reserve with similar types of semi-natural woodland and public access along rights of way.
Site manager: Chris Gardiner.

COLNE ESTUARY, ESSEX

TM 075155 (OS Sheet 168). 576 ha of grazing marsh, saltmarsh and mudflats at Brightlingsea Marshes and Mersea Flats; shingle spit at Colne Point. Intertidal zone leased from the Crown Estate Commissioners; Colne Point owned and managed by the Essex Naturalists Trust; NNR 1983. Branching estuary with five tidal arms, wintering wildfowl and waders, Common Seals, international importance for wintering Brent Geese and Sanderling, breeding Little Tern; many notable plants and insects on shingle, salt and freshwater marsh and sea walls. Mainly non-intervention. Open access at Cudmore Grove Country Park and on East Mersea dunes; elsewhere by permission. Essex Naturalists Trust visitor centre and hides at Fingringhoe Wick.
Site manager: Ian Black.

COOM RIGG MOSS, NORTHUMBERLAND

NY 691795 (OS Sheet 86). 36 ha of raised and blanket bog in Wark Forest, 16 km N of Haltwhistle, leased from Forestry Commission (1960). Relatively undisturbed *Sphagnum* bog, exhaustively studied. Research (esp. peat stratigraphy) and monitoring, planned water regulation by damming. Access (along forest tracks) by permission (vulnerable habitat and fire risk). Leaflet.
Site manager: Simon Walker.

COTHILL, OXFORDSHIRE

SU 460996 (OS Sheet 164). Tiny 2-ha portion of calcareous fen, reedbed, alder carr and woodland 8 km SW of Oxford, leased from National Trust (1956); one of earliest reserves (since 1916). Well-documented. Rare bryophyte-rich mire with rich flora. Sycamore and scrub removal, fen restoration, research. Leaflet. Access by permission (sensitive habitat).
Site manager: Mike Cox.

COTSWOLD COMMONS AND BEECHWOODS, GLOUCESTERSHIRE

SO 895135 (Buckholt Wood) (OS Sheet 162 and 163). 341 ha of mainly beech dominated woodland on scarp and dip slopes of the Cotswolds around Cranham,

Sheepscombe and Painswick, consisting of Workman's Wood (120 ha), Buckholt Wood (100 ha), Pope's Wood (26 ha), Saltridge Wood (51 ha), Blackstable Wood (26 ha), Rough Park (11 ha) and Lords and Ladies Wood (8.5 ha). Mainly by agreements with National Trust and private owners (1976, extended 1981). Large composite woodland reserve containing finest Cotswold beechwoods, ancient trees, wonderful atmosphere and views, locally rich flora with orchids, hellebores, etc, rare woodland snails. Managed using selection and shelterwood techniques aimed at mixed-age structure, glades and natural regeneration, some coppicing and pollarding, ride widening and maintenance. Some woodland left to develop naturally. Some common land (though grazing rights no longer exercised). Car park and open access to Buckholt Wood, rights of way or with permission on others. Leaflet. Medium use (*c.* 20,000 visitors annually).

Site manager: Malcolm Whitmore.

DENDLES WOOD, DEVON

SX 616616 (OS Sheet 191). 30 ha of mature deciduous woodland in valley of R Yealm on S side of Dartmoor, owned by English Nature (1965). Pedunculate Oak-dominated high forest, huge beeches, good bryophytes, lichens and ferns, spring birds incl. Pied Flycatcher. Mainly left to develop naturally. Access by permission. Leaflet.

Site manager: Phil Page.

DENGIE, ESSEX

TM 045030 (approx. centre) (OS Sheet 168). 2293 ha of tidal mudflats, shell-sand beaches and saltmarsh along E end of Dengie peninsula, leased from the Crown Estate Commissioners (1983). Large saltmarsh, wintering wildfowl and waders, incl. nationally important nos of Brent Geese, Knot, Sanderling and Grey Plover. Mainly non-intervention. Control of wildfowling and bait-digging, experimental saltmarsh protection using brushwood polders and wave-breaks. Restricted access but public footpath along sea wall. Car park and bird observatory run by Essex Naturalists Trust near St Peter's Chapel, Bradwell-on-Sea.

Site manager: Ian Black.

DERBYSHIRE DALES

SK 190657 (Lathkill Dale) (OS Sheet 119). 325 ha of limestone grassland and crag, broadleaved woodland and scrub, glades and streamcourses in the Peak District National Park. Declared NNR 1972, extended 1974 and 1981, made up of Lathkill Dale (140 ha, owned/leased), Monks Dale (69 ha, owned/leased/agreement), Cressbrook Dale (119 ha, mainly owned), Long Dale (7 ha, owned) and Biggin Dale (44 ha, mainly owned). Herb-rich unimproved grassland with uncommon flowers, notable bryophytes and lichens incl. montane species, notable insects, fine ashwoods and hazel coppice, crystal-clear streams (esp. Lathkill). Arch.: lead mining ruins. Geol.: cave systems (Lathkill). Maintaining stockproof fences and walls, scrub clearance, hazel coppicing, glade management, stream-bed restoration, path maintenance, education. Rights of way through all the dales. Booklet and series of leaflets on Lathkill, (incl. teacher's pack). Small display area at Reserve office at Over Haddon. Access to caves by permit from Derbyshire Caving Association. High use at Lathkill Dale; medium to low use elsewhere.

Site manager: Douglas Gilbert.

DERWENT GORGE AND MUGGLESWICK WOODS, DURHAM AND NORTHUMBERLAND

NZ 056490 (OS Sheet 87). 71 ha of riverine and gorge woodland in the Derwent valley 5 km SW of Consett, part owned, part leased from private owner (1992). Undisturbed woodland, good bryophytes and lichens, lead-mining history. Thinning, coppicing, control of sycamore. Some woodland left to develop naturally. Access on public footpaths. Low use.

Site manager: Simon Walker.

DOWNTON GORGE, HEREFORDSHIRE

SO 439739 (OS Sheet 137). 48 ha of mature deciduous woodland in ravine of R Teme 10 km W of Ludlow, leased principally from Primshire Ltd (1983, declared 1986). Sessile Oak, ash-elm, lime and alder woodland with fine old oaks and native limes, rich gorge flora, good epiphytic lichens, Otters and Polecats. Silurian fossils. Type site of 'picturesque landscape'. Conifer and sycamore removal, otherwise allowed to develop naturally. Access for research purposes only.

Site manager: Tom Wall.

DUNSDON FARM, DEVON

SS 295078 (OS Sheet 180). 38 ha of acid grassland and wet heath on Culm measures near Holsworthy, managed by private agreement (1992). One of best remaining unimproved Culm grasslands, series of small fields separated by thick hedges and small copses. Colourful summer flora of wet, acidic soils with uncommon species. Notable butterflies and moths, good breeding birds incl. small heronry, Dormouse. Cattle grazing (summer), winter burning, scrub control, cutting and mowing. Access by permission.

Site manager: John Breeds.

EBBOR GORGE, SOMERSET

ST 525486 (OS Sheet 182). 41 ha of ashwoods, hazel coppice, scrub and limestone grassland set in a steep-sided gorge and tributary valley, 5 km W of Wells, leased from

National Trust (1967). Characteristic Mendips ashwood incl. coppice, high forest and immature woodland; beautiful glade flora, good ferns and bryophytes in humid gorge, Badgers. Geolo: gorge, screes. Coppicing, glade maintenance, cutting and mowing, grazing, scrub management and removal, bracken control, pond creation, education. Open access, car park, picnic area. Walks with display panels; trail for disabled. Leaflet. High use (*c.* 30,000 visitors annually).
Site manager: Peter Mountford.

FENN'S, WHIXALL AND BETTISFIELD MOSSES, SHROPSHIRE AND CLWYD

SJ 489370 (Fenn's Moss), SJ 492362 (Whixall Moss), SJ 477355 (Bettisfield Moss) (OS Sheet 126). 509 ha of lowland raised bog, peat cuttings and encroaching woodland on the Welsh border 24 km N of Shrewsbury, part owned, part with peat winning lease from Bettisfield Park Estate Trustees (formal declaration expected 1994). Southernmost large raised bog, much cut over but retaining good mire flora with notable insects incl. Large Heath butterfly and White-faced dragonfly. Major habitat restoration project begun 1991 by blocking drains, hydrological survey and monitoring, bracken and scrub control. Access by permission (dangerous pits and ditches).
Site manager: Joan Daniels.

FINGLANDRIGG WOOD, CUMBRIA

NY 275568 (OS Sheet 85). 65 ha of mixed woodland, gorse and birch scrub, bog, heath and acid grassland, 12 km W of Carlisle, owned by English Nature (1992). Mosaic of unimproved habitats with good range breeding birds, Red Squirrel, notable insects. Partly common land. Sheep grazing, mowing and cutting, ride, glade and path maintenance, controlled burning; most woodland allowed to go wild. Open access. Low use.
Site manager: Frank Mawby.

THE FLITS, HEREFORDSHIRE

SO 375413 (OS Sheet 148 or 149). 21 ha of wet pasture, springs and streamside alders in the Wye valley between Preston-on-Wye and Blakemere, leased from Prudential Assurance and Mr C Dale (1986). Olde England flower-rich grassland and hedges, uncommon plants, outstanding subaquatic insects (soldier flies, snail flies, craneflies). Grazing, water level maintenance, scrub control. Access for research only.
Site manager: Tom Wall.

FORGE VALLEY WOODS, NORTH YORKSHIRE

SE 984864 (OS Sheet 101). 63 ha of ancient broadleaved woodland in the Derwent valley, 6 km W of Scarborough, by agreement with Scarborough Borough Council

(1977). One of largest ancient woods in N Yorks, former coppice ranging from oak through ash–elm to alder, with marshy glades on side of meltwater channel. Vernal flora, moderately rich in lichens and bryophytes. Coppicing, path, glade and ride maintenance, conifer, sycamore and dead elm removal, cutting and mowing, controlled grazing, some non-intervention. Car park. Access on public footpath, board walk, leaflet. Medium use (*c.* 10,000 visitors annually).
Site manager: Tim Dixon.

FYFIELD DOWN, WILTSHIRE

SU 135710 (OS Sheet 173). 248 ha of chalk downland 7 km W of Marlborough, leased from the Manton Estate (1956). Species-poor chalk grassland. Geomorph.: best site in Britain for sarsen stones, also coombes, terraces. Arch.: major Celtic, Romano-British and medieval field systems. Cattle and sheep grazing, scrub control, hazel coppicing, archaeological research. Geomorphological trail and handbook. Leaflet. Access on footpaths. Low use (*c.* 1000 visitors annually).
Site manager: Albert Knott.

GAIT BARROWS, LANCASHIRE

SD 480772 (OS Sheet 97). 106 ha of limestone pavement, scrub, woodland and freshwater 5 km E of Silverdale, owned by English Nature (1977 and later extensions). Finest low-level limestone pavement in Britain, surrounded by mixed broadleaved woodland. Rare marl lake (Hawes Water) with emergent fen and alder carr, rich wet meadows. Very rich flora (490 spp. vascular plants, 1000+ spp. fungi), notable butterflies and other insects, nesting and passage birds. Annual coppicing programme, ride, path and glade maintenance, birch control, hay-making and after-grazing, planned bog and marshland restoration. Much of the reserve is allowed to develop naturally. Access along rights of way, otherwise by permission. Leaflets, guided walks. High use.
Site manager: Rob Petley-Jones.

GLASSON MOSS, CUMBRIA

NY 235604 (OS Sheet 96). 93 ha of raised bog on the Solway plain 1.6 km S of Bowness-on-Solway, owned by English Nature (1967 and later extensions). Best preserved of the Solway mosses, extensive living moss carpet with excellent flora, notable bryophytes and invertebrates. Water level maintenance by damming, bog restoration, fire protection, bracken control, vegetation monitoring. Open access. Leaflet. Low use.
Site manager: Frank Mawby.

GOLITHA FALLS, CORNWALL

SX 223686 (OS Sheet 201). 18.5 ha of gorge and mature deciduous woodland along the R Fowey, 6 km NW of Liskeard, owned by English Nature (1990). Oak-dominated old coppice and rocky high forest, good bryophyte and lichen flora with many western (Atlantic) species. Arch.: disused copper mines and leat. Mainly left to develop naturally, some coppicing, thinning and sycamore removal, path maintenance. Open access, car park. Medium use (*c.* 15,000 visitors annually).

Site manager: Ian Davies.

GORDANO VALLEY, AVON

ST 435730 (OS Sheet 172). 66 ha of fen meadows, reedbed and fen carr on Walton and Weston Moors, 1.6 km east of Walton-in-Gordano, partly owned, partly under lease from the Miles Estate or by private agreement (1987). Wet meadows, broad ditches and rough corners, clear water dykes, marsh and meadow flowers, good bryophytes, breeding waders. Stratigraphic interest (peat record). Grazing and mowing, water level control, ditch maintenance. Access by permission except on public footpath. Leaflet. Low use.

Site manager: Tony Robinson.

GOSS MOOR, CORNWALL

SW 950600 (OS Sheet 200). 482 ha of wet and dry heath, bog, pools, and willow carr 1.6 km E of Indian Queens, leased from Falmouth Estate (1990). Shallow basin at headwaters of R Fal with rare plants and notable dragonflies. Cattle grazing, scrub clearance, ditch maintenance, fire protection, controlled burning. Crossed by A30 and minor roads. Low use.

Site manager: Ian Davies.

GOWK BANK, CUMBRIA

NY 679739 (OS Sheet 86). 15 ha of unimproved upland meadow and rough grazing by the R Irthing in Wark Forest, 10 km N of Haltwhistle, owned by English Nature (1991). Remote, traditionally managed hay meadows, with rich and colourful flora. Hay-making and after-grazing. Open access.

Site manager: Terry Wells.

GRAIN HEADS MOSS, NORTHUMBERLAND

NY 745735 (OS Sheet 86/87). 18 ha of raised and blanket bog, leased from Forestry Commission (1985). Isolated and relatively undisturbed bog system, one of a series in North Pennines known as the Irthinghead Mires. Living *Sphagnum* hummocks, hollows and lawns. Maintenance of water level by dams. Access by permission (vulnerable habitat, fire risk).

HALES WOOD, ESSEX

TL 573414 (OS Sheet 154). 8 ha of ancient coppice-with-standards woodland on chalky boulder clay, 5 km NE of Saffron Walden, leased from the Forestry Commission (1955). Semi-natural ash–maple–hazel wood, noted for Oxlips. Coppicing, 'dead hedge' fencing, ride and glade maintenance. Access by permission.

HALSENNA MOOR, CUMBRIA

NY 066007 (OS Sheet 89). 24 ha of raised bog, wet and dry heath and birch–willow carr on Cumbrian coast 3 km SE of Seascale, owned by English Nature (1990). Largest bog and heath on West Cumbrian plain, undisturbed site, neither burned nor grazed; notable beetles. Largely left to develop naturally, ditch and dyke maintenance, scrub control. Open access. Low use.

Site manager: Peter Singleton.

HAM STREET WOODS, KENT

TQ 008342 (OS Sheet 189). 97 ha of ancient coppice-with-standards woodland on Wealden clay, 6 km S of Ashford, owned by English Nature (1952). Oak standards, actively managed hazel, chestnut and hornbeam coppice, aspen groves with rides, glades, ponds and streams. Outstanding moths and other invertebrates, good songbird choir headed by Nightingales. Hit hard by '87 gale; coppicing, singling to high forest, thinning, ride and glade maintenance, track maintenance. Access on pathways, car park, woodland walks with display panels. Leaflet. Medium use.

Site manager: Bob Russell.

HAMFORD WATER, ESSEX

TM 235255 (OS Sheet 168). 688 ha of foreshore incl. mudflats, shingle and shell banks, saltmarsh and low dunes south of Harwich, leased from the Crown Estate Commissioners (1983). Tidal basin, major feeding area for overwintering waders and wildfowl, internationally important numbers of Brent Geese, Shelduck, Teal, Grey Plover, Sanderling and Black-tailed Godwit. Mainly non-intervention. Control of wildfowling, sea defence trials. Access by permission; but good views from public footpath along sea wall.

Site manager: Ian Black.

HARTLAND MOOR, DORSET

SY 950850 (OS Sheet 195). 243 ha of dry and wet heath with extensive valley mire system, 3 km SE of Wareham, part owned, part leased from the National Trust (1954

and later extensions). Large and well-documented heath with contrasting types of bog. Dorset heath and other good bog plants incl. bryophytes. Dartford Warbler, reptiles, invertebrates esp. dragonflies and ants. Birch removal, bracken and gorse control, fire protection. Access by permission (fire risk, vulnerable habitats) except permitted path on E side. Leaflet.
Site manager: Mike Tuck.

HICKLING BROAD, NORFOLK

TG 410220 (OS Sheet 134). 487 ha of open water, reed and sedge beds, marshes and damp woodland in the Thurne valley, owned and managed by the Norfolk Naturalists Trust (1958). Largest of the Broads and slightly brackish. Rare submerged plants esp. stoneworts, rich Broads fenland, Swallowtails, good all-year-round birding in reedbed and grazing marsh incl. breeding Bearded Tit, Bittern, Marsh Harrier, Gadwall, etc., wintering duck with good nos Teal and Shoveler. Reed and saw sedge harvesting, scrub clearance, mowing and grazing, water purification experiments, research and education. Hickling water trail (conducted boat tour) in summer, hides, nature trail. Sailing on Broad unrestricted; on land access on rights of way, elsewhere by permission from Norfolk Naturalists Trust. Leaflet, see also *Hickling Broad and its Wildlife* by Stewart Linsell (1990). High use.
Warden: F Russell (Norfolk Naturalists Trust).

HIGH HALSTOW, KENT

TQ 799763 (OS Sheet 178). 52 ha of oak woodland by the Thames estuary, by agreement with RSPB (1958). Largest heronry in Britain (Feb–Aug); otherwise bird-rich woodland and scrub incl. Nightingales and large rookery. Woodland ravaged by Dutch Elm disease and gales. Managed by RSPB as Northward Hill reserve. Hawthorn regeneration by felling coups, scrub management. Partly open access; heronry closed to visitors but distant viewing possible.
Reserve Warden: Alan Parker (RSPB).

HIGH LEYS, CUMBRIA

NY 064181 (OS Sheet 89). 9 ha of unimproved haymeadow and pasture near Rowrah village, owned by English Nature (1992). Well-preserved herb-rich northern haymeadow, with wet peaty areas. Traditional hay-making and after-grazing by cattle or sheep. Open access.
Site manager: Frank Mawby.

HIGHBURY WOOD, GLOUCESTERSHIRE

SO 540085 (OS Sheet 162). 47 ha of ancient broadleaved woodland on limestone in the Wye Valley 7 km SE of Monmouth, owned by English Nature (1986). Rich and

diverse broadleaved woodland including both native limes, fine spring flowers, wonderful views of valley. Coppice restoration, traditional woodland management, ride, glade and path maintenance, some woodland left to develop naturally. Access on footpaths. Medium use (*c.* 10,000 visitors annually, mainly on Offa's Dyke path).
Site manager: Malcolm Whitmore.

HOG CLIFF, DORSET

SY 615973 (OS Sheet 194). 88 ha of chalk grassland, scrub and ancient ash–maple–hazel woodland in three separate blocks—the main reserve, Southfield Down and Park Wood, 9.6 km NW of Dorchester. Owned by English Nature (1987). Downland slopes and dry valleys, notable chalk flowers and butterflies. Arch.: Celtic field system and settlement, lynchets, Roman road. Sheep and cattle grazing, scrub removal, coppicing and traditional woodland management. Open access. Leaflet. Low use.
Site manager: Mike Tuck.

HOLKHAM, NORFOLK

TF 892448 (at main access point, Lady Anne's Drive) (OS Sheet 132). 3925 ha (18 km^2) of sand dunes, saltmarsh, freshwater grazing marsh, intertidal mudflats and pine plantation on N Norfolk coast between Burnham Norton and Blakeney, by agreement with Holkham Estate (1967, and subsequent extensions). Some of best saltmarsh in Europe, vast numbers passage and wintering Pink-foot and Brent Geese and waders, tern colonies, Common Seal haul-out, small colony Natterjacks, good all-year-round birding. Most management carried out by estate and tenants incl. water level regulation, cattle grazing, dyke maintenance, pest control, research. Open access on dunes and foreshore, four car parks linked by Norfolk coast path, two hides. Colour booklet. High use.
Site manager: Ron Harold.

HOLME FEN, CAMBRIDGESHIRE

TL 205890 (OS Sheet 142). 259 ha of birchwood on fen peat with small areas of reedbed, heath, and open water, 10 km S of Peterborough, owned by English Nature (1952). Large lowland birchwood grown up on former fen, rare plants, fungi, notable insects. Famous Holme Fen post showing 4 m of peat shrinkage since 1851. Ride and glade mowing, water level control, dyke maintenance, mainly non-intervention. Hides by artificial meres. Access on marked paths. Low use. Leaflet.
Site manager: Alan Bowley.

HOLT HEATH, DORSET

SU 060040 (OS Sheet 195). 488 ha of wet and dry heathland, bogs, mature oak woodland and overgrown wood-pasture (Holt Forest) 6 km NE of Wimborne, leased from the National Trust (1985). One of the largest Dorset heaths, large bog system, reptiles, uncommon plants, outstanding insect fauna, usual heathland birds incl. Dartford Warbler and Nightjar. Common land. Fire protection, controlled burning and grazing, scrub removal. Open access, car park. Leaflet. Low use.

Site manager: Ian Nicol.

HOLTON HEATH, DORSET

SY 954914 (OS Sheet 195). 117 ha of heathland, recent pine woodland, wet woodland, reedbed and saltmarsh on NW shore of Poole Harbour, leased from Rank Organisation (1981). Diverse habitat range, Nightjars, reptiles. Pine removal, heather regeneration. Access by permission (fenced and locked, numerous hazards). Leaflet.

Site manager: Mike Tuck.

INGLEBOROUGH, NORTH YORKSHIRE

SD 767764 (OS Sheet 97). 698 ha of limestone grassland, pavement and scars, swallowholes and caves, upland heather moor, pasture and bog in the Yorkshire Dales National Park, mainly owned by English Nature (1992). Finest limestone 'karst' scenery in Britain incl. fine limestone pavement flora at Scar Close (NNR 1977), ashwood at Colt Park Wood (NNR 1962), extensive moorland and limestone pasture at South House Moor. Rich in bryophytes and lichens. Elaborate cave systems. Managed by agreement with local farmers esp. over stocking levels; maintaining stockproof boundaries, bog restoration, sycamore control, tree planting in gills; path maintenance, grassland research. Access on rights of way. Some pavement areas have deep grikes and are hazardous. High use (*c.* 80,000 visitors annually).

Site manager: Peter Corkhill.

KINGLEY VALE, WEST SUSSEX

SU 824088 (OS Sheet 197). 150 ha of yew forest, chalk grassland, scrub and broadleaved woodland on the South Downs, 7 km NW of Chichester. Owned by English Nature or leased from West Dean Estate (1952). Finest yew forest in Europe with marvellous ancient trees, good chalk flora, notable butterflies. Arch.: fine collection of monuments incl. bowl and bell barrows, field system and lynchet banks. Grazing by sheep and donkeys, cutting and mowing, ride and glade maintenance, scrub management, education. Part open access, car park with small field museum, waymarked walks, colour leaflet. Guided walks in summer. High use (*c.* 30,000 visitors annually). See *The Great Yew Forest. The Natural History of Kingley Vale*, by Richard Williamson.

Site manager: Richard Williamson.

KNOCKING HOE, BEDFORDSHIRE

TL 131308 (OS Sheet 166). 9-ha patch of chalk grassland, managed by agreement with private landowner (1958). Rare flowers, incl. Pasque Flower, Spotted Cat's-ear, Moon Carrot. Arch.: barrow, lynchets. Sheep and cattle grazing, swiping and mowing, scrub control, research. Access by permission.
Site manager: Graham Bellamy.

LADY PARK WOOD, GLOUCESTERSHIRE AND GWENT

SO 549144 (OS Sheet 162). 45 ha of ancient broadleaved woodland on steep bank of R Wye facing Seven Sisters Rocks, by long-term agreement with Forestry Authority (1985). Least disturbed wood in the Wye valley, long-term research site. Many types of native woodland, excellent flora incl. rich assemblages of calcicole lichens and bryophytes, both limes, rare whitebeams. Left to develop naturally, apart from perimeter sycamore control. Access on main paths and rights of way. Medium use on footpath (*c.* 10,000 walkers annually).
Site manager: Malcolm Whitemore.

LEIGH, ESSEX

TQ 830850 (OS Sheet 178). 257 ha of saltmarsh, mudflats and reclaimed grazing marsh, leased from Southend Borough Council and managed by Essex Naturalists Trust (1983). Over-wintering waders and wildfowl, incl. nationally important numbers of Brent Geese, Grey Plover, Knot and Redshank. Good flora and insect fauna on saltmarsh, sea wall, dykes and scrubby down inland, incl. rarities. Mainly non-intervention. Open access, small car park. Low use.
Site manager: Ian Black.

LEWES DOWNS

1. CASTLE HILL, EAST SUSSEX

TQ 371070 (OS Sheet 198). 47 ha of chalk grassland on the South Downs between Woodingdean and Kingston, leased from Brighton Borough Council (1975). Rich close-grazed turf on hill slopes and dry valleys, large colony Early Spider Orchid and other uncommon flowers, notable butterflies and moths, Wart-biter colony. Sheep (summer) and cattle (autumn) grazing. Access on right of way. Leaflet. Low use.

2. MOUNT CABURN, EAST SUSSEX

TQ 445090 (OS Sheet 198). 50 ha of chalk grassland on South Downs 3 km E of Lewes, by agreement with the Glynde Estate Trustees (1986). Herb-rich, mainly S-facing turf with rich flora, notable butterflies and moths. Arch.: large hill fort (fine

viewpoint). Sheep and cattle grazing, mowing, scrub control. Open access. Medium use.
Site manager: Malcolm Emery.

LINDISFARNE, NORTHUMBERLAND

NU 100420 at approx mid-point (OS Sheet 75). 3541 ha (36 km^2) of sand dunes, dune slacks, coastal grassland and heath, saltmarsh and tidal mudflats along Northumbrian coast from Cheswick Black Rocks to Budle Point, leased from the National Trust and Crown Estate Commissioners, and by agreement with private owners (1964 with later extensions). Atmospheric coast, lime-rich dune flora on Holy Isle, world's largest concentration of wintering Pale-bellied Brent Geese, international nos waders and wildfowl in winter and on migration, England's largest flock of Whooper Swans. Control of wildfowling and bait digging, spraying of Cord-grass (*Spartina*), sheep grazing, saltmarsh monitoring, education. Largely open access, information board, hide, leaflet. High use (*c.* 500,000 visitors to Holy Island each year).
Site manager: Phil Davey.

LING GILL, NORTH YORKSHIRE

SD 799785 (OS Sheet 98). 5-ha wooded limestone gorge, 8 km E of Chapel le Dale, owned by English Nature (1958). Subalpine ashwood with rich ungrazed flora incl. bryophytes, rare snails, stockproofed; rock exposures, non-intervention. Access by permission. Leaflet.
Site manager: Peter Corkhill.

THE LIZARD, CORNWALL

SW 720200 at approx mid-point (OS Sheet 203 and 204). 1375 ha (15.5 km^2) of serpentine heath, coastal grassland and cliffs on the Lizard peninsula, part owned (601 ha), part leased (615 ha) or by private agreement (1974, major extension 1990). Largest heathland reserve; unique serpentine flora with many rarities, superb dry and wet heaths on Goonhilly Downs, flower-rich sea cliffs, outstanding bryophytes and lichens. Geol.: serpentine rocks, 'crusair' boulders. Arch.: ancient settlements, hut circles, tumuli. Stock management, maintenance of fences and walls, provision of water supply, gorse control, fire protection, managed heather burning. Mainly open access, continuous coastal footpath. Leaflet. Medium use (low inland).
Site manager: Ray Lawman.

LOWER DERWENT VALLEY, NORTH YORKSHIRE AND HUMBERSIDE

SE 705435 at Wheldrake Ings (OS Sheet 106). 429 ha of unimproved flood meadow and wet pasture, marshes and alder wood in Derwent valley between Sutton upon

Derwent and Bubwith, part owned by English Nature, part by agreement with National Rivers Authority, Yorkshire Wildlife Trust and Carstairs Countryside Trust (1990). One of largest areas of unimproved meadowland in England, crossed by broad ditches. Excellent flora (397 spp.) incl. rarities, breeding duck and waders, good numbers passage birds, wintering wildfowl and Bewick's Swans. Hay-making and after-grazing by licensees, controlled wildfowling, water level regulation, ditch management, research. Car parks, four hides, access on rights of way. Leaflet. High use.

Site manager: Tim Dixon.

LUDHAM MARSHES, NORFOLK

TG 405177 (OS Sheet 134). 73 ha of unimproved or semi-improved pasture with drainage dykes in Thurne valley of the Norfolk Broads, owned by English Nature (1987). Dyke water varies from base-poor to moderately base-rich or saline; good aquatic flora and fauna, incl. Water Soldier and the rare Norfolk Aeshna dragonfly. Hay-making and stock grazing, maintenance of fences and gates, isolation of dykes from main drains, dyke maintenance. Access by permission. Low use.

Site manager: Rick Southwood.

LULLINGTON HEATH, EAST SUSSEX

TQ 545018 (OS Sheet 199). 63 ha of chalk heath and scrub on South Downs 4.8 km W of Eastbourne, leased from Forestry Commission (1955), owned by Eastbourne Water Company. Best chalk heath in Britain. Management a classic battle against encroaching scrub by mowing, grazing with own sheep and ponies, and scrub cutting, control of bracken and Willowherb. Arch.: Iron Age settlement and field system, Neolithic long barrow. Access on public bridleways and permitted path. Nature trail. Leaflet. Low use (*c.* 2000 visitors annually).

Site manager: Malcolm Emery.

MARTIN DOWN, HAMPSHIRE

SU 053188 (OS Sheet 184). 336 ha of chalk grassland, chalk heath and scrub 16 km SW of Salisbury. Part owned by English Nature, part by Section 35 agreement with Hampshire County Council (1977). Common land with grazing rights. A glorious downland landscape, mostly on flat or gently sloping ground. Long and short turf with the usual rich flora, all known types of chalk heath, outstanding butterflies, notable breeding birds. Arch.: barrows, linear earthworks, Celtic fields. Grazing with own sheep, cutting and mowing, traditional woodland management, scrub management, chalk heath restoration, pest control. Open access, two car parks. Leaflet. Medium use (*c.* 5000 visitors annually).

Site manager: Paul Toynton.

MOCCAS PARK, HEREFORDSHIRE

SO 340424 (OS Sheet 148 or 149). 39 ha of ancient wood-pasture with venerable trees 12.8 km E of Hay-on-Wye, by agreement with Baunton Trustees (1981). Magnificent old trees (mainly oak) in medieval deer park setting, later transformed by Capability Brown. Good lichen and fungus flora, outstanding dead-wood beetles, interesting lake. Tree planting, pollarding, monitoring. Access for research and escorted parties only.

Site manager: Tom Wall.

MONKS WOOD, CAMBRIDGESHIRE

TL 198800 (OS Sheet 142). 157 ha of ancient broadleaved woodland on calcareous boulder clay 5 km N of Alconbury. Owned by English Nature (1953). Well-documented ancient and semi-natural wood, mainly relict wet ash–maple coppice with oak and ash standards. Famous for butterflies incl. Black Hairstreak, good invertebrates generally, attractive ride and glade flora, Nightingales. Coppicing, ride and glade management, deer fencing, pond repairs and maintenance. Access by permission. Leaflet. See *Monks Wood. A Nature Reserve Record* (1973).

Site manager: David Massen.

MOOR HOUSE, CUMBRIA

NY 735325 (OS Sheet 91 and 92). 3894 ha (39 km^2) of blanket bog, heather moorland and upland pasture in North Pennines between the Eden and the Tees, owned by English Nature (1952). Reserve purchased for research and now the best-documented upland area in Britain. Extensive Cotton-Grass bog, rare example of unmanaged heather moor, rare limestone and mountain plants, good nos nesting waders esp. Golden Plover, Dunlin, Curlew, Snipe. Geol.: notable maze cave system at Knock Fell Caverns, mines with mineral interest. Common land with grazing rights. Major site for environmental monitoring, installation of new laboratory (1993); maintenance of roads, bridges, culverts and enclosures; mainly non-intervention. Access on rights of way, incl. Pennine Way. Medium use (*c.* 11,000 walkers annually).

Site manager: Terry Wells.

MORDEN BOG, DORSET

SY 913916 (OS Sheet 195). 149 ha of dry and wet heath, birch carr, recent pine woodland and valley mire 3 km N of Wareham, leased from Forestry Commission and Drax Estate (1956). Narrow 2 km-long valley bog, with flushes, old heather and old decoy ponds. Good insects incl. Large Marsh and Heath grasshoppers. Pine removal, fire protection, research. Access by peripheral public footpath, otherwise by permission. Leaflet.

Site manager: Mike Tuck.

MOTTEY MEADOWS, STAFFORDSHIRE

SJ 840130 (OS Sheet 127). 37 ha of hay meadows near Wheaton Aston, owned by English Nature (1982). One of best parcels of old damp meadowland in the Midlands, with Fritillaries, Marsh orchids and other wildflowers, bordered by thick hedges. Hay-making and after-grazing by licensees, maintenance of fences, ditches and hedges, water level control. Access by permission (breeding waders and vulnerable hay crop).

Site manager: Tim Coleshaw.

MUCKLE MOSS, NORTHUMBERLAND

NY 799668 (OS Sheet 86). 169 ha valley bog close to Hadrian's Wall, managed by agreement with private owners (1993). Patterned oligotrophic bog with pools, rare sphagna, notable insects. Management confined mainly to blocking drains to raise water levels, and removing conifers. Access by permission (sensitive site with deep pools and ditches).

Site manager: Simon Walker.

MUSTON MEADOWS, LEICESTERSHIRE

SK 824367 (OS Sheet 130). 9 ha of unimproved neutral grassland on Lias clay near Muston village, managed by agreement with Belvoir Estate (1983). Fine ridge-and-furrow grassland with old hedges, ditches and ponds. Rich flora (May–July) incl. large colony of Green-winged Orchid. Hay-making and after-grazing. Access on public footpath, otherwise by permission.

Site manager: Bob Lord.

NEWHAM BOG, NORTHUMBERLAND

NU 168295 (OS Sheet 75). 13 ha of fen and fen carr near Northumbrian coast, leased from Percy Northern Estates (1985). Spring-fed basin mire on former lake, birch–willow carr, wilderness atmosphere, rare plants and insects. Clearance of scrub to create open fen, pond excavations. Access by permission (sensitive habitat and hazardous).

Site manager: Phil Davey.

NORTH FEN, CUMBRIA

SD 358977 (OS Sheet 97). Tiny 2-ha reserve around the inflow stream at N end of Esthwaite Water, leased from the National Trust (1955). Classic example of hydrosere succession from open water through reedbed and fen to woodland, studied since

1900 by W H Pearsall and others. Esthwaite Water is one of world's most intensively studied lakes. Largely left to develop naturally. Open access. Low use.

NORTH MEADOW, WILTSHIRE

SU 095945 (OS Sheet 173). 40 ha alluvial flood meadow between Rivers Thames and Churn, close to the ancient borough of Cricklade, well known for its dazzling display of Fritillaries from late April to early May. Owned by English Nature (1973). One of the finest hay meadows in England. Traditional hay-making and after-grazing, seed harvesting, willow pollarding, monitoring. Access on public footpath (floods in winter). Leaflet and postcards. Medium use (*c.* 5000 visitors annually).
Site manager: Albert Knott.

NORTH SOLENT, HAMPSHIRE

SZ 418993 (OS Sheet 196). 763 ha of saltmarsh and grazing marsh, sand dunes, shingle islands and ridges, reedbeds, riverine meadows, estuarine mudflats and alder–willow woodland. Complex Reserve incl. Beaulieu River, Dark Water valley and linking 6 km of coast, by agreement with Beaulieu and Cadlands Estates (1980). Great variety of habitat and scenery, rich flora of brackish habitats and vegetated shingle incl. rarities. Breeding terns, largest Black-headed Gull colony (Gull Island), passage and wintering waders. Coast protection, regulating water levels, reedbed restoration, cutting and mowing, scrub control, education. Four large hides, bird sanctuary with hides at Needs Ore (permits from Beaulieu estate office). Public footpath along part of Beaulieu River, elsewhere by permission. High use (*c.* 20,000 visitors annually).
Site manager: James Venner.

NORTH WALNEY, CUMBRIA

SD 177724 (OS Sheet 96). 144 ha of sand dunes, dune slacks, shingle, dune heath, saltmarsh and tidal mudflats at the N end of Walney Island, near Barrow-in-Furness. Leased to English Nature from Vickers Shipbuilding & Engineering Ltd and Boughton Estates, managed by Cumbria Wildlife Trust (1991). Geomorph.: barrier island with raised beach; good dune slack flora (360 spp.) incl. 'Walney Geranium', vegetated shingle, good amphibians incl. Natterjacks, big wader roosts, winter wildfowl. Arch.: Neolithic finds. Sheep grazing (introduced 1992), fencing, patrols, limited dune stabilisation, scrub and bracken removal, education. Open access. Leaflet, guided walks. High use (*c.* 25,000 visitors annually). South Walney reserve also managed by CWT.
Warden: Trevor James (Cumbria Wildlife Trust).

OLD WINCHESTER HILL, HAMPSHIRE

SU 645209 (OS Sheet 185). 63 ha of chalk grassland, mixed scrub, yew wood and broadleaved woodland 3 km S of West Meon, owned by English Nature (1954).

Popular reserve with splendid views, horseshoe-shaped escarpment, good flora on slopes incl. uncommon flowers, large stand of juniper, notable butterflies. Arch.: Iron Age hill fort, Bronze Age tumuli. Sheep-grazing with own flock, scrub cutting, hazel coppicing, traditional woodland management, research and education. Parking spaces, picnic area, nature trail, guided walks in summer. Access on paths. Leaflet. High use (*c*. 30,000 visitors annually).

Site manager: Mick Finnemore.

ORFORDNESS – HAVERGATE, SUFFOLK

TM 430480 (OS Sheet 169). 228 ha of tidal mudflats, saltmarsh, shingle and brackish lagoons on the Suffolk coast S of Aldeburgh, part owned by English Nature, remainder by agreement with RSPB (1954, extended 1977). Of physiographic interest as best example of shingle spit (Shingle Street) and cuspate foreland; second largest area vegetated shingle, birds incl. famous Avocet colony, wintering and passage waders/wildfowl, large gullery, good saltmarsh, rare invertebrates esp. spiders. Non-intervention. Access by boat, hide overlooking scrape. Havergate Island is RSPB nature reserve. Low use (*c*. 2000 visitors annually).

Site manager: Cliff Waller.

PARK WOOD, CUMBRIA

SD 565778 (OS Sheet 97). 15 ha of ashwood SW of Hutton Roof village, owned by English Nature (1981). Example of rare northern calcareous ashwood with hazel, Wych Elm and maple, spring birds, good flora. Ride, glade and path maintenance, controlled cattle grazing in summer, mainly non-intervention. Open access. Low use.

PARSONAGE DOWN, WILTSHIRE

SU 055415 (OS Sheet 173). 276 ha of chalk grassland and grass ley on S edge of Salisbury Plain between Shrewton and Winterbourne Stoke, owned by English Nature (1981). One of the finest chalk grasslands in England, rich flora mainly on gentle slopes, the product of 70 years of stable, low intensity farm practices. Arch.: Celtic field system and medieval ridge and furrow. Maintained as part of farm with own sheep and cattle (incl. longhorns), lambing and calving on open down, back-up land harvested for winter feed. Access by permission (working farm, dangerous bulls). Leaflet.

Site manager: Bill Elliott.

PEVENSEY LEVELS, EAST SUSSEX

TQ 670058 (OS Sheet 199). 54 ha of flood pasture and drainage dykes between Pevensey and Bexhill, owned by English Nature (1985). Superb aquatic flora and fauna in dykes, Marsh Frog, 20 spp of dragonflies, many rarities incl. Fen Raft Spider. Breeding Yellow Wagtail, Snipe, Redshank, etc., wintering waders and wildfowl. Wildlife enhancement scheme, cattle grazing, water level control, dyke maintenance. Access by permission, but good roadside birdwatching. Leaflet, plans for hide. Low use.

Site manager: Malcolm Emery.

PEWSEY DOWNS, WILTSHIRE

SU 106637 (OS Sheet 173). 166 ha of chalk grassland at S edge of Marlborough Downs, overlooking Vale of Pewsey. Part owned by English Nature, part leased from New College Oxford (1968 with later extensions). Impressive, almost bare, chalk scarp winding between hill tops. Among finest examples of western chalk grassland, rich flora incl. uncommon species. Notable butterflies, Badger setts on open down, sarsen stones. Arch.: Neolithic causeway camp, long and round barrows, Wansdyke, lynchets, field system, White Horse. Sheep and cattle grazing, Ragwort and scrub control. Open access, car park. Leaflet. Medium use (*c.* 5000 visitors annually).

Site manager: Albert Knott.

PRESCOMBE DOWN, WILTSHIRE

ST 985255 (OS Sheet 184). 47 ha of chalk grassland 2 km NW of Ebbesbourne Wake, privately owned and managed by agreement (1982). Impressive double coombe at head of dry valley. Fine short-grazed S-facing chalk sward with ant-hills, notable butterflies and moths. Sheep and cattle grazed, scrub control. Access by permission (working farm). Leaflet.

Site manager: Paul Toynton.

REDGRAVE AND LOPHOM FEN, SUFFOLK

TM 050797 (OS Sheet 144). 125 ha of base-rich fen and damp woodland 8 km W of Diss, owned or leased by the Suffolk Wildlife Trust (NNR 1993). Varied fen vegetation incl. mixed sedge and reedbeds, flushes, open pools, *Molinia* grassland and sallow carr. Noted for rare invertebrates incl. the Fen Raft Spider. Cutting reed and saw-sedge, scrub clearance, water-level control and pumped water to top-up the main Raft Spider pools, path mowing. Open access, car park, board walk and waymarked path, leaflet. Medium use.

Field officer: Arthur Rivett (Suffolk Wildlife Trust).

RIBBLE MARSHES, LANCASHIRE AND MERSEYSIDE

SD 390240 (approx centre) (OS Sheets 102 and 108). 4112 ha (39 km^2) of grazed and ungrazed saltmarsh, tidal mud and sandflats in the Ribble estuary, 3.2 km N of

Southport, owned by English Nature or leased from Duchy of Lancaster (1981, extended 1991). Among largest grazed saltings in Britain; major wintering and staging post on W coast, immense flocks Pink-footed Goose and Wigeon, high-tide wader roosts with international nos Dunlin, Knot and Bar-tailed Godwit. Licensed cattle grazing, ditch/dyke maintenance, controlled wildfowling, bird monitoring; strategy for whole estuary. Open access except central sanctuary at Banks Marsh. Leaflet, plans for other facilities. High use (*c.* 250,000 visitors annually). Sandbanks to seaward form part of Southport wildfowl refuge.

Site manager: Dick Lambert.

RODNEY STOKE, SOMERSET

ST 490510 (OS Sheet 182). 35 ha of ashwoods and limestone grassland on SW scarp of the Mendips, overlooking Rodney Stoke village and Somerset Levels, owned by English Nature (1957). Two wild rocky woods flanking a dry valley; characteristic Mendips flora incl. Blue Gromwell, good invertebrates, Badgers. Sheep and cattle grazing, some hazel coppicing and lime pollarding, thinning, ride widening, scrub control. Public footpath between woods, otherwise access by permission. Leaflet. Low use.

Site manager: Peter Mountford.

ROSTHERNE MERE, CHESHIRE

SJ 744843 (OS Sheet 118). 152 ha of open water and reedbed with wet pasture, small woods and willow-beds, characteristic of N Cheshire plain. Mainly owned by English Nature (1961). Large, undisturbed and well-documented mere, roost site for duck, gulls, cormorants, etc. Coppicing, ride, path, hedge and glade maintenance, scrub control, cutting and mowing, controlled grazing, research, education. Bird observatory (run jointly with Manchester Ornithological Society). Access otherwise by permission. Leaflet, bird 'tick list'. Medium use (*c.* 6000 observatory permits annually).

Site manager: Martin Davey.

ROUDSEA WOOD AND MOSSES, CUMBRIA

SD 332824 (wood); SD 337826 (Fish House Moss) (OS Sheets 96 and 97). 388 ha of ancient broadleaved woodland, raised bog, valley fen and foreshore at the head of Morecambe Bay, 6 km NE of Ulverston, leased from private estate (1955, extended 1981). Contrasting woods on spurs of limestone (ash, yew) and slate (Sessile Oak), separated by a fenny valley, extensive bogs to E (Deer Dike Moss and Fish House Moss). Superb wild area with rare plants, unusual ecological transitions, spring birds, dormouse, notable invertebrates esp. in bogs. Arch.: stone barns, lime kilns, potash pits, bark peeler's huts, etc. Coppicing, thinning, ride, glade and path maintenance, conifer removal, rhododendron removal, bog restoration. Footpath network; small car park for permit holders. Leaflet. Low use.

Site manager: Peter Singleton.

RUSLAND MOSS, CUMBRIA

SD 334886 (OS Sheet 97). 24 ha of wet and dry heath, bog, marsh and willow carr, and raised bog with encroaching pines, leased from private estate (1958, extended 1964). Final stage of hydrosere succession from open water to bog. Good flora incl. Royal Fern, possibly native pines, heronry. Scrub and Rhododendron clearance. Open access.

SALTFLEETBY-THEDDLETHORPE DUNES, LINCOLNSHIRE

TF 499873-480933 (OS Sheet 113 & 122). 440 ha of sand dunes, saltmarsh, mudflats and freshwater marsh along 6 km of the Lincs coast between Saltfleet Haven and Mablethorpe North End. Part owned, otherwise leased from Crown Estate Commissioners (1966). Best lime-rich dunes between Wash and Humber with good dune flora, maritime fen, saltmarsh with drifts of Sea Lavender, breeding Little Tern and Natterjack, bird migration route, haul-outs of Common and Grey Seal. Physiographic interest as accreting dune system. Sheep and cattle-grazing (autumn), cutting and mowing, Sea Buckthorn removal, dyke maintenance, scrub cutting, dune stabilisation, pond/scrape maintenance. Open access with seven car parks on landward side. Leaflet. High use (*c.* 100,000 visitors annually).

Site manager: Graham Weaver.

SCOLT HEAD ISLAND, NORFOLK

TF 788466-848460 (OS Sheet 132). 737 ha of saltmarsh, sand dunes, shingle and mudflats, leased from National Trust and Norfolk Naturalists Trust (1953). One of England's oldest nature reserves, owned by NT since 1923. Object of classic studies in coastal erosion and accretion, extensive saltmarsh, one of the world's great terneries (Sandwich, Common and Little Terns); huge flocks of Brent and Pink-footed Geese in winter. Mainly non-intervention; predator control, research and education. Access by arrangement with local boat owners at Brancaster Staithe, possible 2–3 h before and after high water. Visitors excluded from ternery in breeding season. Crossing marshes by foot not advised. Leaflet, nature trail. Medium use. See *Island of Terns* (1993) by Bob Chestney.

Site manager: Colin Campbell.

SCOSKA WOOD, NORTH YORKSHIRE

SD 913725 (OS Sheet 98). 10 ha of ashwood and limestone grassland on NE facing slope of Littondale between Litton and Arncliffe in Yorkshire Dales National Park, owned by English Nature (1992). Herb-rich flora incl. Baneberry, ashwood with flushes, scar ledges and tufa springs. Sycamore removal, limited sheep grazing. Access on public footpath.

Site manager: Peter Corkhill.

SHAPWICK HEATH, SOMERSET

ST 424405 (OS Sheet 182). 304 ha of fen meadows, wet heath, Bog Myrtle, birch carr and peat bog on the plain between the Polders and R Brue, 6 km W of Glastonbury. Part owned, part leased or by private agreement (1961, extended 1982). Best peat bog on Somerset Levels, good general natural history with many uncommon plants and invertebrates. Arch.: Sweet Track (Neolithic walkway), stratigraphic interest (pollen record in peat). Grazing, hay-making, pumped irrigation system, water level regulation, ditch maintenance, scrub control. Large part worked for peat, destined to be flooded. Access on right of way or by permission. Leaflet. Low–medium use.
Site manager: Robin Prowse.

SOMERSET LEVELS

ST 418381 (OS Sheet 182). 300 ha of wet, peaty grassland on the Levels around Shapwick village, with scattered parcels of land at Southlake Moor, King's Sedgemoor, Moorlinch, Tealham and Tadham Moors and Westhay Moor, all owned by English Nature (1990). Old grassland, ditch flora, breeding waders. Grazing and hay-making (rented out), ditch maintenance, willow pollarding. Access by permission. The major nature reserve on the Levels is West Sedgemoor, managed by the RSPB. Low use.
Site manager: Robin Prowse.

THE STIPERSTONES, SHROPSHIRE

SO 368992 (at Devils Chair) (OS Sheet 126 & 137). 448 ha of heather moor, acid grassland and crag with smaller areas of hay meadow, oak coppice and bog 14.5 km SW of Shrewsbury, mainly owned by English Nature (1982). Wonderful area steeped in history, inspiring numerous writers and artists. Several types of heath with northern and southern types, southernmost native red grouse, notable lichens on rocks. Geomorph.: periglacial features incl. frost-shattered quartzite tors, stone polygons and stripes. Arch.: lead mines (mainly outside NNR), Iron Age hill fort, Bronze Age cairn. Common grazing. Cutting and controlled burning, coppicing. Open access but beware severe weather on exposed areas. Leaflet. Medium use (*c.* 15,000 visitors annually).
Site manager: Tom Wall.

STOBOROUGH HEATH, DORSET

SY 941855 (OS Sheet 195). 109 ha of wet and dry heathland and former agricultural land 2 km SE of Wareham, owned by English Nature (1985). Fine viewpoint, good heather and grass heath, rare insects. Heathland birds incl. Dartford Warbler, Hobby, etc. Cattle and horse grazing, heathland restoration, scrub management, fire protection. Access by permission.
Site manager: Mike Tuck.

STODMARSH, KENT

TR 229601 (OS Sheet 179). 163 ha of flood meadow, reedbed, shallow lagoons and alder carr in the Stour valley, 9 km NE of Canterbury, owned by English Nature (1968). Good all-year-round birding, incl. breeding Savi's and Cetti's Warblers, Bearded Tit and Bittern, rare migrants, wintering wildfowl, Hen Harrier roost. Good wetland flora incl. rarities. Reed harvesting, cutting and mowing, cattle grazing, scrub control, dyke maintenance, willow pollarding, education. Open access except to the reedbeds. Car park, nature trail with display panels and hide, trail for disabled. Leaflet. High use (*c.* 14,000 visitors annually).

Site manager: Paul Burnham.

STUDLAND AND GODLINGSTON HEATHS, DORSET

SZ 020840 (OS Sheet 195). 631 ha of sand dunes, wet and dry heath, damp woodland, freshwater and foreshore at S entrance to Poole Harbour, leased from National Trust (1962, extended 1978). Dramatic and extensive Dorset heathland, unusual heather-covered sand dunes, shallow lagoon of Little Sea with interesting plants and winter duck, notable dragonflies and other invertebrates, rare reptiles, wildfowl roost and feeding grounds, a good place to see Dartford Warbler. Hazel coppicing, scrub and pine control, fire protection, education. Open access, observation hut and display centre overlooking Little Sea, four other hides, two nature trails (leaflets). High use (*c.* 250,000 visitors annually). Large car park and nearby visitor centre run by National Trust.

Site manager: Rees Cox.

THE SWALE, KENT

TR 034673 (OS Sheet 178). 220 ha of freshwater grazing marsh, saltmarsh and mudflats at SE corner of the Isle of Sheppey. Mostly owned by English Nature, 52 ha leased from Accrep Ltd (1976). Good all-year-round birding with breeding Marsh Harrier, Avocet, Black-tailed Godwit, Little Tern, etc., nationally important numbers of Brent and White-fronted Geese, Wigeon, Gadwall, Shoveler, Grey Plover and Ruff in winter, big harrier roost, Marsh Frog. Geomorph.: cockle-shell spit at Shellness. Cattle and sheep-grazing; pumped water regulation in dykes, bunded fields, dyke maintenance. Car park and access on paths to six hides overlooking flood pasture. Leaflets. Medium use (*c.* 6000 visitors annually). Nearby RSPB Elmley reserve.

Site manager: Steve Clarke.

SWANSCOMBE SKULL SITE, KENT

TQ 599743 (OS Sheet 177). 2 ha gravel pit near Thames estuary, owned by English Nature (1954). Discovery site of Swanscombe skull (1935), 'the English Adam',

earliest known skull of *Homo sapiens*. Basic maintenance. Car park, commemorative stones, open access. Low use. Display of skull casts, mammoth bones and flint implements found on site at the nearby Swanscombe Centre.
Site manager: Steve Clarke.

SWANTON NOVERS, NORFOLK

TG 015313 (OS Sheet 133). 79 ha of ancient and semi-natural woodland with rides and glades, by agreement with Hastings Estate (1974). Complex of woods consisting of Swanton Great Wood, Swanton Little Wood, Barney Wood, Guybon's Wood and two medieval hedges. Large ancient wood with long history of coppice management; magnificent Small-leaved Lime and Sessile Oak coppice, rare Bird Cherry–alder woodland, rich flora. Coppicing, traditional woodland management, ride, glade and path maintenance, scrub control. Access for research purposes only.
Site manager: Ron Harold.

TARN MOSS, CUMBRIA

NY 400275 (OS Sheet 90). 16 ha of raised bog and fen at watershed between Keswick and Penrith, leased from Lonsdale Estate Trust (1990). Unusual basin mire at 270 m with relatively undisturbed acid bog, poor fen and mesotrophic swamp; unusually free from invading scrub. Non-intervention. Open access.

THETFORD HEATH, SUFFOLK

TL 845800 (OS Sheet 144). 94 ha of lime-rich grassland and heath, 3 km W of Thetford by agreement with Norfolk Naturalists Trust (1958). One of best species-rich heaths in the Breck with rare plants, notable lichens, periglacial frost patterning, Breckland birds, invertebrates incl. rare spiders. Sheep grazing, rotovating surface, scrub control. Access by permission.
Site manager: Malcolm Wright.

THORNE MOORS, SOUTH YORKSHIRE

SE 723154 at centre (OS Sheet 112). 73 ha of cut-over raised bog, dykes, birch scrub and broadleaved woodland S of the Humber between Goole, Thorne and Crowle, owned (but not yet formally declared) by English Nature (1991). Reserve likely to be extended to *c.* 800 ha in near future. English-Nature-owned area forms most intact part of the largest raised bog in England, all cut-over but regenerating on wet ground; bleak but atmospheric. Extensive Cotton-grass mire between dry heathery baulks, notable plants and insects incl. Large Heath butterfly; good breeding birds incl. Nightjar and Nightingale. Restoration of bog by water level regulation and scrub clearance; research. No public rights of way but pedestrian access being developed.

Leaflet. Low use. *Thorne Moors* (1991) by Catherine Caufield describes the fascinating history and personalities of the place.
Site manager: Peter Roworth.

THORNHILL MOSS AND MEADOWS, CUMBRIA

NY 174485 (OS Sheet 85). 12 ha of wet meadow and valley mire 3 km S of Abbeytown, owned by English Nature (1992). Unimproved fragment of the Solway Plain, ranging from acid bog through poor fen and Bog Myrtle to richer types of fen. Water level regulation, grazing, mowing, scrub cutting. Access on footpath.
Site manager: Frank Mawby.

THRISLINGTON, DURHAM

NZ 324325 (OS Sheet 88). 24 ha of limestone grassland and scrub (but no plantation!) 2 km S of West Cornforth, by agreement with Redland Aggregates (1992). Best magnesian limestone grassland in Britain, good flora and insect fauna. 4.5 ha of grassland was successfully dug up and transplanted nearby in advance of quarry face. Cattle and sheep grazing, scrub control, after-care of turves. Open access. Booklet.
Site manager: Simon Walker.

THURSLEY, SURREY

SU 901415 (OS Sheet 186). 326 ha of heathland and bog 9 km SE of Farnham, owned by English Nature, managed with co-operation of Surrey Wildlife Trust. Reserve in two sections, forming part of Thursley Common. Finest of the Surrey heaths with superb wet heath and bog, outstanding dragonflies centred on bog pools, good reptiles, invertebrates of dry heath and birds incl. Nightjar, Curlew, Hobby and Dartford Warbler. Common land. Heather and bracken cutting. Pine, birch and bracken control, water level control, fire prevention, heath reinstatement, research, major educational use. Open access, car park, board walk. Leaflets. High use (*c.* 25,000 visitors annually). Nearby heathland nature reserves at Witley Common (nature trail) and the popular Frensham Common (National Trust-owned Country Park and Local Nature Reserve).
Site manager: Simon Nobes.

UPPER TEESDALE, DURHAM

NY 815308 at Cow Green car park (OS Sheet 92). 3493 ha of grouse moor and sheep walk, blanket bog, limestone grassland and flushes, hay meadows, juniper scrub, subalpine woodland and river shingle at the head of Teesdale, by agreement with the Earl of Strathmore, Lord Barnard and their tenants (1963, 1969). World famous flora—'the Teesdale assemblage'—rich in bryophytes and lichens, variety of rare habitats, colourful hay meadows (May–June). Geol: whin sill with High Force and Cauldron Snout waterfalls. Arch.: many artefacts of mining history. Management by field-by-field agreements with dalesmen; juniper regeneration project by local clearing and fencing, ditch/dyke maintenance, erosion control, research, education. Car park, display boards, nature trail (leaflet). Visitor centre at Bowlees with nature trail, run by Durham Wildlife Trust. Access on rights of way only. Booklet. High use (*c.* 125,000 visitors annually).

Site manager: Ian Findlay.

UPWOOD MEADOWS, CAMBRIDGESHIRE

TL 251825 (OS Sheet 142). 6 ha of permanent pasture on calcareous clay 4 km SW of Ramsey, by agreement with Cambs and Beds Wildlife Trust (1980). Old pasture with rich flora incl. large colony of Green-winged Orchid, thick hedges and ponds. Arch.: fine ridge and furrow system with 'S-bends'. Cattle-grazed (summer), control of scrub and 'weeds'. Car park, open access.

Site manager: David Massen.

WALBERSWICK, SUFFOLK

TM 466737 (at Westwood Lodge car park) (OS Sheet 156). 582 ha of heath, grazing marsh, reedbed, woodland, intertidal mudflats, saltmarsh and shingle on Suffolk coast between Blythburgh and Walberswick, by agreement with Blois estate (1972). Foreshore leased from Crown Estate Commissioners, Angel Marshes owned by English Nature. Britain's largest reedbed at Westwood Marshes; first class bird reserve with breeding Bittern, Bearded Tit, Avocet, Marsh Harrier, Woodlark, good numbers waders and wildfowl in winter and on migration. Notable moths, dragonflies, etc. Bracken and scrub control, cutting and mowing, reed harvesting, dyke maintenance, water level control, controlled burning. Access on rights of way, hide on Blyth estuary. Leaflet. RSPB Minsmere reserve a few miles to S covers similar range of habitats but with better public facilities.

Site manager: Cliff Waller.

THE WASH, LINCOLNSHIRE

TF 560265 (OS Sheet 131). Original Reserve on 97 ha of saltmarsh and mudflats at Lutton and Kirton Outmarsh (1986), but conclusion of a lease of 9899 ha of mainly intertidal sand and mud from the Crown Estate Commissioners in 1992 (extended 1993) makes this easily the largest nature reserve in England. Major overwintering area and staging post for migrating arctic birds incl. large flocks of Brent Geese, Shelduck, Knot, Dunlin, Oystercatcher and other waders; important Common Seal

area, extensive saltmarshes. Controlled grazing; mainly non-intervention. Open access. Small hide on Lutton Outmarsh. Other nature reserves on the Wash are managed by RSPB and Lincs Trust for Nature Conservation.
Site manager: Bob Lord.

WEETING HEATH, NORFOLK

TL 955880 (OS Sheet 144). 137 ha of close-grazed calcareous grassland and bracken, by agreement with Norfolk Naturalists Trust (1958). Best place in Britain to watch Stone Curlews from well-placed hides (small charge). Also Nightjar, Long-eared Owl, Crossbill, etc. good Breck flora incl. rarities, notable invertebrates. Sheep grazing, rotovating surface, bracken and Willowherb control, pest control. Car park, access to four hides (6000–7000 visitors annually), otherwise by permission. Information sheet.
Site manager: Malcolm Wright.

WESTLETON HEATH, SUFFOLK

TM 455695 (OS Sheet 156). 47 ha of heath and bird scrub on Suffolk Sanderlings, owned by English Nature (1956). Largest of the Sanderling heaths. Good birds incl. Nightjar; insects incl. Silver-studded Blue butterfly. Controlled burning, birch removal, firebreak maintenance. Car park, part open access, otherwise by permission. Leaflet. Close to RSPB Minsmere reserve and the National Trust's Dunwich Heath. Medium use (*c.* 8000 visitors annually).
Site manager: Cliff Waller.

WINTERTON DUNES, NORFOLK

TG 487214 (OS Sheet 134). 109 ha of sand dune, dune slack and dune heath on the Norfolk coast 3 km N of Winterton village, managed by agreement with Cimec Ltd (1956). Acidic dunes with well-developed slacks, good flora, breeding Nightjar, Little Tern, Natterjack; good invertebrates incl. rare moths. Physiographic interest as largest Norfolk dune system. Rhododendron removal, scrub control, cutting and mowing, pond maintenance. Open access, car park on Winterton beach. Leaflet. Medium use.
Site manager: Rick Southwood.

WOODWALTON FEN, CAMBRIDGESHIRE

TL 230846 (OS Sheet 142). 208 ha of reedbed, fen carr, birch and alder woodland and fen pasture 5 km W of Ramsey, leased from RSNC (1954). One of England's oldest

nature reserves (1919). Well-documented patchwork of fenland habitats, rich flora in mown or grazed fen, ditches and peat cuttings, notable moths, dragonflies, beetles and spiders, Chinese Water Deer. Dyke and drove maintenance, water level control, cutting and mowing, cattle grazing, Large Copper project, research and education. Two hides. Leaflet. Permitted path, otherwise by permission.
Site manager: Alan Bowley.

WREN'S NEST, BOROUGH OF DUDLEY

SO 937917 (OS Sheet 139). 35 ha of fossil-rich cliffs and quarries on a limestone promontory in the heart of a Midlands city, by agreement with Dudley MBC and the Earl of Dudley (1956). First geological NNR, and the only truly urban NNR in England. World famous Silurian fossils esp. trilobites, sea-lilies, corals and molluscs, collected over past 200 years; habitats incl. ashwood, limestone grassland and ponds. Interesting mining history. Clearance of geological exposures, traditional habitat management, path repair. Educational reserve. Car park, geological trail and handbook, colour leaflet. Open access on numerous waymarked paths, platform view of Seven Sisters Cavern, barge trips from Black Country Museum. Geological collections and display in Dudley Museum. Plans (currently in abeyance) for visitor centre with teaching facilities. High use.
Site managers: Tim Coleshaw (English Nature). Nick Williams (Dudley MBC).

WYBUNBURY MOSS, CHESHIRE

SJ 698502 (OS Sheet 118). 17 ha of floating peat bog and surrounding woodland and wet pasture in a hollow close to Wybunbury village near Nantwich, owned by English Nature (1955). Fine well-documented floating mire (*Schwingmoor*), second only to Chartley Moss. Good bog flora and numerous rare and remarkable invertebrates. Birch and pine removal, monitoring of water level, holding tank and pump for diverting polluted water, research. Board walk, leaflet. A dangerous place, hence access by permission.
Site manager: Martin Davey.

WYCHWOOD, OXFORDSHIRE

SP 338165 (OS Sheet 164). 261 ha of mature broadleaved woodland with rides, ponds, limestone grassland and old limestone quarries, 3 km SW of Charlbury by private agreement (1955). Well-documented large ancient wood, mainly ash–maple–hazel woodland, formerly coppice, now mainly high forest with good ride and glade flora, clear calcareous pools, notable invertebrates incl. Roman Snail. Ride mowing, forestry operations. Access restricted to agreed footpath.

WYE, KENT

TR 054469 (OS Sheet 179). 133 ha of chalk and neutral grassland, scrub and ash–hazel woodland on North Downs, 3 km E of Wye. Owned by English Nature (1961 with later extensions), formerly called Wye and Crundale Downs. Chalk scarp with series of deep coombes, incl. classic dry valley, the Devil's Kneading-trough. Rich chalk flora, noted for orchids, rare invertebrates. Sheep-grazing with own flock, cattle grazing by licencees; thinning and coppicing, scrub control. Car park at viewpoint and open picnic area, nature trail with numbered posts and leaflet; access otherwise on rights of way. Leaflet. Medium use.

Site manager: Bob Russell.

WYLYE DOWN, WILTSHIRE

SU 002362 (OS Sheet 184). 34 ha of chalk grassland in dry valley 2 km S of Wylye, owned by English Nature (1981). Close-grazed chalk turf, dotted with ant-hills, rich flora. Arch.: prominent Celtic field system, lynchets. Cattle (Ayrshire herd) and sheep grazed. Access by permission. Leaflet.

Site manager: Paul Toynton.

WYRE FOREST, WORCESTERSHIRE

SO 753763 (OS Sheet 138). 549 ha of native Sessile Oak, birch and alder woodland with rides, glades, meadows and streams in ancient Royal Forest. Part owned (194 ha), part leased from Forestry Commission or by private agreement (1978 with later extensions). Text book example of woodland management for nature conservation containing high forest, overgrown and recently restored coppice, glades, plantations and non-intervention areas. One of largest native woods in England, well-documented, fine specimen trees, good woodland birds, outstanding invertebrates. Ambitious programme to reinstate coppice from 60–80-year-old oaks inside fenced plots, thinning, ride and glade management, removal of conifers and Rhododendron, grazing and hay-cutting in numerous grassy clearings, research and education. Open access along paths. Forestry Authority information centre with large car park. Leaflet, see also *The Natural History of an English Forest* (1971) by Norman Hickin. Medium to high use (*c.* 25,000 visitors annually).

Site manager: John Robinson.

YARNER WOOD, DEVON

SX 778787 (OS Sheet 191). 150 ha of ancient broadleaved woodland on fringe of Dartmoor, 5 km W of Bovey Tracey, owned by English Nature (1952). Sessile Oak high forest and old coppice, some birchwood and heath. Dormouse, spring birds incl. Pied Flycatchers, good lichen flora. Arch.: copper mine, charcoal hearths and pottery

leat. Conifer and beech removal, thinning, ride and glade maintenance, education. Open access to nature trails, car park, small field museum, two trails with numbered posts and leaflets, hide. Medium use (*c.* 12,000 visitors annually).
Site manager: Phil Page.

THE DERSINGHAM RESERVE, NORFOLK

(NOT A NATIONAL NATURE RESERVE BUT MANAGED BY ENGLISH NATURE)

TF 685295 (OS Sheet 132). 167 ha of heath and valley mire near the Norfolk coast S of Dersingham, leased from and managed by agreement with Sandringham Estate (1991), but not formally declared as NNR for legal reasons. Extensive heath and undisturbed bog, nesting Nightjar, Shelduck, Curlew, Tree Pipit, etc. Heath and mire restoration by removal and control of invasive Rhododendron, bracken, pine seedlings and scrub, mowing and swiping to maintain heather, research. Public access on woodland paths, otherwise by permission. Medium use. Nearby is Dersingham Country Park and the RSPB's Snettersham reserve.
Site manager: Phil Holms.

SECTION 35 NATIONAL NATURE RESERVES

DUNCOMBE PARK

SE 607828 (OS Sheet 109). 103 ha of ancient wood–pasture by the R Rye, nr Helmsley, owned and managed by Duncombe Park Estate; NNR 1994. Broadleaved woodland with old trees, river shingle and sandbanks, lime-rich and neutral permanent grassland. Outstanding insect fauna incl. many rarities esp. of dead wood and riverine habitats, nesting birds incl. Pied Flycatcher, Wood Warbler, all three woodpeckers. Management aimed at maintaining present habitats; some native tree-planting to replace dead elms.

BASSENTHWAITE LAKE, CUMBRIA

Declared NNR in autumn 1993. Home of the rare whitefish, the Vendace, threatened by pollution and competition from introduced coarse fish. Managed in co-operation with the Lake District National Park Authority, National Trust and neighbouring landowners and users.

THE FARNE ISLANDS, NORTHUMBERLAND

NU 230370 (OS Sheet 75). 96.7 ha of vegetated and unvegetated offshore islands, owned and managed by the National Trust since 1925, NNR 1993. Large breeding colonies of auks, gulls and terns, including a few pairs of Roseate Terns. Large Grey Seal colony (currently *c.* 4000). Bird and seal monitoring, cutting docks, escorting parties. Summer wardens. High use (35,000–50,000 boat-borne visitors annually). Leaflet.
Warden: John Walton (National Trust).

GIBRALTAR POINT, LINCOLNSHIRE

SK 556581 (OS Sheet 122). 414 ha of sand dune, saltmarsh and freshwater grazing marsh on the Lincs coast, 5 km south of Skegness. Local Nature Reserve (1952) owned by Lincs County Council and East Lindsey District Council, leased and managed by Lincs Trust for Nature Conservation; NNR (1985). Dynamic dune and marsh system, bird migration route, high tide wader roosts, breeding Little Terns, reintroduced Natterjacks. Cattle grazing, cutting and mowing, water level control, dyke maintenance, scrub and Willowherb control, stabilisation of dunes. Open access, car park, bird observatory, information centre, residential field centre, hides. Booklet. High use.

Site manager: Carl Hawke (Lincs Trust for Nature Conservation).

GREENLEE LOUGH, NORTHUMBERLAND

NY 767697 (OS Sheet 87). 57 ha of open water, reedswamp, birch–willow carr, and unimproved pasture in Northumberland National Park 2 km N. of Hadrian's Wall, by agreement with the National Park Authority and Forestry Commission (1992). Upland mesotrophic lake (a rare habitat) with natural hydrosere through reedbed and poor fen to developing woodland. Water level regulation, tree planting, Rhododendron control. Guided walks. Access on right of way, elsewhere by permission from Park Authority.

Manager: Derek Proudlock, Northumberland National Park Authority.

MALHAM TARN, NORTH YORKSHIRE

SD 890668 (OS Sheet 98). 137 ha of open water, raised bog and fen in the Yorkshire Dales National Park, between Arncliffe and Settle, owned and managed by the National Trust; NNR 1992. Best example of marl lake in Britain with associated raised bog and calcareous fen, fen carr and planted woods. Well documented site, used by residential field centre on N shore run by Field Studies Council. Scrub cutting esp. willow, blocking drains on Tarn Moss, pond clearance. Car parks, 1.6-km-long board walk across fen, hide with display board. Access by permit obtainable from National Trust office at Waterhouses. Leaflet. High use.

Warden-naturalist: Alastair Clunas (National Trust).

MARTIN DOWN, HAMPSHIRE

SU 053188 (OS Sheet 184). 336 ha of chalk grassland, chalk heath and scrub 16 km SW of Salisbury. Part owned by English Nature, part by Section 35 agreement with Hampshire County Council (1977). For details, see main listing.

SLAPTON LEY, DEVON

SX 826441 (OS Sheet 202). 190 ha of shingle, freshwater, reed swamp, willow carr and broadleaved woodland along S Devon coast nr Slapton village. Owned by Whitley Wildlife Conservation Trust, leased and managed by Field Studies Council;

NNR 1993. Shingle bar damming eutrophic freshwater lake (the Ley), of physiographic interest. Rich and varied flora, strange floating islands, bird-rich incl. Cetti's Warbler, wildfowl. Stock management, woodland management by coppicing, natural regeneration and replanting, reed cutting. Major educational site; residential natural history courses at Field Centre, guided walks (July–Sept), nature trails, board walks, hide. Booklet, bird checklist. Part open access, car parks at Slapton Bridge and Torcross. High use (*c.* 20,000 visitors annually).

Reserve officer: Chris Riley (Field Studies Centre).

WICKEN FEN, CAMBRIDGESHIRE

TL 553703 (OS Sheet 154). 255 ha of fen and fen carr, owned and managed by the National Trust since 1899; NNR 1993. Reedbeds and sedge (*Cladium*) fen, ditches, open water (brick ponds) and peat diggings; birch and sallow carr. Rich flora incl. rare plants. Notable breeding birds incl. Bearded Tit and *c.* 2500 wildfowl in winter. Management to maintain diversity—sedge and reed cutting, water-proofing of banks to maintain water level, experimental peat cutting, scrub control, cutting of litter fields and droves. Educational use. Public footpaths. Access to 3.2 km nature trail and boardwalk by permit (from the William Thorpe visitor centre). High use (>30,000 visitors annually).

Head warden: Tim Bennett (National Trust).

APPENDIX 2

England's National Nature Reserves Summary of tenure (as at October 1993)

By area

Tenure	*Area declared (ha)*
Owned	14,091
Leased	29,394
Nature Reserve Agreement	13,107
Held by an approved body	743
Total	57,335

By number

Tenure	*Number of reserves*
Owned	46
Leased	40
Owned and leased	9
Nature Reserve Agreement	20
Held by an approved body	3
A mixture of the above	22
Total number of NNRs	140

By habitat

Main habitat	*Number of NNRs*	*Total hectarage*
Coastland	22	33,292
Woodland	36	4197
Upland	5	8885
Peatland	20	2396
Open water	7	1082
Lowland grass and heath	50	7566

The total number of NNRs listed above slightly exceeds the actual number of NNRs because some sites are listed more than once across the habitat classifications.

APPENDIX 3

International Designations on England's National Nature Reserves

1. RAMSAR SITES

These are defined as wetlands of international importance especially as wildfowl habitat. Signatories to the Ramsar Convention (1973) are committed to designate such areas and 'use them wisely'. The following NNRs have been proposed or designated as Ramsar sites.

Name	*County*	*Area (ha)*	*Status*	*Date designated or submitted to Dept of Environment*
Bridgwater Bay	Somerset	2703	Designated	5 January 1976
Chippenham Fen	Cambridgeshire	115	Designated	11 March 1992
Dersingham Bog	Norfolk		Proposed	
Esthwaite Water (incl. North Fen NNR	Cumbria	134	Designated	7 November 1991
Gibraltar Point	Lincs	414	Designated	5 March 1993
Hamford Water	Essex	2179	Designated	8 June 1993
Irthinghead Mires (incl. Coom Rigg Moss and Grains Head Moss NNRs)	Cumbria and Northumberland	608	Designated	17 July 1989
Lindisfarne	Northumberland	3123 502	Designated Designated	5 January 1976 11 March 1992
Lower Derwent Valley	Humberside/ N Yorks	1089	Designated	8 June 1993
Malham Tarn	North Yorkshire		Proposed	
Mid-Essex Coast	Essex	627	Designated	11 March 1992
Minsmere–Walberswick (incl. Walberswick NNR)	Suffolk	1697 306	Designated Designated	5 January 1976 19 May 1992
Norfolk Broads (Bure Marshes and Hickling Broad NNRs)	Norfolk	1304	Designated	5 January 1976

1. RAMSAR SITES—continued

Name	*County*	*Area (ha)*	*Status*	*Date designated or submitted to Dept of Environment*
North Norfolk Coast (incl. Holkham and Scolt Head Island NNRs)	Norfolk	7700	Designated	30 January 1989
North Pennine Moors (incl. Moor House and Upper Teesdale NNRs)	Cumbria/Durham		Proposed	
Orfordness–Havergate	Suffolk		Proposed	
Pevensey Levels	East Sussex		Proposed	
Redgrave and South Lophom Fens	Norfolk/Suffolk	125	Designated	15 February 1991
Rostherne Mere (as first part of proposed Midland Meres and Mosses)	Cheshire	79	Designated	24 July 1981
Ribble Estuary	Lancashire		Submitted	1 March 1991
Solway Mosses (incl. Glasson Moss NNR)	Cumbria		Proposed	
Somerset Levels and Moors (incl. Shapwick Heath and Somerset Levels NNRs)	Somerset		Proposed	
Southampton Water and Solent Marshes (incl. North Solent NNR)	Hampshire		Proposed	
Stodmarsh	Kent		Proposed	
The Swale	Kent	5790	Designated	17 July 1985
Thorne and Hatfield Moors	South and East Yorkshire		Proposed	
Thursley, Hankley and Frensham Commons (incl. Thursley Common NNR)	Surrey		Proposed	
The Wash	Lincolnshire and Norfolk	63,135	Designated	30 March 1988

2. SPECIAL PROTECTION AREAS

Under the EC Birds Directive (1979), community governments must designate Special Protection Areas to conserve the habitat of certain rare or vulnerable birds and regularly occurring migratory birds. Governments commit themselves to avoid polluting or disturbing such sites, or allowing them to deteriorate. Many sites qualify both as Special Protection Areas and Ramsar sites, which is why this list has much in common with the last one.

Name	*County*	*Area (ha)*	*Status*	*Date designated or submitted to Dept of Environment*
Breckland Heaths (incl. Weeting, Thetford, Brettenham and Cavenham Heath NNRs)	Norfolk and Suffolk		Proposed	
Derwent Ings	North and East Yorkshire	783	Designated	17 July 1985
Dorset Heathlands (incl. Studland, Hartland Moor, Stoborough, Holt and Holton Heaths and Moroden Bog NNRs)	Dorset		Proposed	
Farne Islands	Northumberland	97	Designated	17 July 1985
Gibraltar Point	Lincolnshire	414	Designated	5 March 1993
Hamford Water	Essex	2179	Designated	8 June 1993
Lindisfarne	Northumberland	3625	Designated	11 March 1992
Lower Derwent Valley	N Yorks/ Humberside	1089	Designated	8 June 1993
Mid-Essex Coast	Essex	627	Designated	11 March 1992
Minsmere–Walberswick	Suffolk	2000	Designated	27 March 1990
Moor House	Cumbria	3894	Designated	31 August 1982
Norfolk Broads	Norfolk		Proposed	
North Norfolk Coast	Norfolk	7701	Designated	20 January 1989
Orfordness–Havergate	Suffolk	117	Designated	31 August 1982
Pevensey Levels	East Sussex		Proposed	
Ribble Estuary	Lancashire	2182	Designated	31 August 1982
Somerset Levels and Moors	Somerset		Proposed	
Southampton Water and Solent Marshes	Hampshire		Proposed	
Stodmarsh	Kent		Proposed	
The Swale	Kent	5790	Designated	17 July 1985
Thorne and Hatfield Moors	South and East Yorkshire		Proposed	
Thursley, Hankley and Frensham Commons	Surrey		Proposed	
The Wash	Lincolnshire and Norfolk	63,135	Designated	30 March 1988
Yorkshire Dale Moorlands (incl. Ingleborough NNR)	North Yorkshire and Cumbria		Proposed	

3. BIOSPHERE RESERVES as designated by UNESCO in 1976/77

Name	Region	Area (ha)	Year listed
Braunton Burrows NNR	SW England	596	1976
North Norfolk Coast Biosphere Reserve	East Anglia	5497	1976
Moor House—Upper Teesdale Biosphere Reserve	NW/E England	7399	1976

4. BIOGENETIC RESERVES

This is a Council of Europe network of wildlife sites established to conserve 'representative examples of European flora, fauna and natural areas and to encourage biological research'. The UK reserves were selected from two habitat types identified as priorities by the Council of Europe, namely lowland heaths and dry grasslands, and included in the network in March 1992:

Arne NNR, Dorset
Castle Hill NNR, Sussex
Cavenham Heath NNR, Suffolk
Hartland Moor NNR, Dorset
The Lizard NNR, Cornwall
Morden Bog NNR, Dorset
Old Winchester Hill NNR, Hants
Parsonage Down NNR, Wilts
Pewsey Down NNR, Wilts
Studland NNR, Dorset
Thursley Common NNR, Surrey

5. EUROPEAN DIPLOMA SITES

The Committee of Ministers of the Council of Europe instituted the European Diploma in 1966 as a mark of recognition for protected landscapes, reserves and natural features for their outstanding European interest. The Diploma is awarded at the request of Governments of Member States.

The awards are classified under three categories namely:

(A) Concerned with the protection of flora and fauna and requires for inclusion legal protection, provision of wardens, absence of development and no public access without special authorisation.
(B) Concerned with the protection of landscape and required for inclusion legal protection and regulation of public access.
(C) Concerned with social and recreational functions of an area with the maintenance of its biological or aesthetic characteristics.

There are currently five UK European Diploma sites, three of which are in England namely:
Peak Park Category C awarded 1966 (includes NNRs within the National Park).
Minsmere Reserve Category A awarded 1979 (RSPB reserve).
Purbeck Heritage Coast Category C awarded 1984 (includes NNRs on Purbeck Coast).

APPENDIX 4

National Nature Reserves Some Key Events 1899–1993

1899 'The first nature reserve'—nine strips of land at Wicken Fen—is designed by the National Trust (other candidates could be Breydon Water, Norfolk (1888), Abbotsbury Swannery (before 1393) or even the Farne Islands under St Cuthbert (AD 676)).

1910 Charles Rothschild buys Woodwalton Fen as a private nature reserve, later presented to the SPNR.

1913 British Ecological Society is founded by A G Tansley and others.

1915 Rothschild sends list of important nature sites to the Ministry of Agriculture.

1923 Scolt Head Island is presented to the National Trust.

1925 The Farne Islands is purchased by public subscription and presented to the National Trust.

1926 Norfolk Naturalists Trust purchase Cley Marshes as the first County Trust nature reserve.

1927 Large Copper butterflies from Holland are introduced at Woodwalton Fen.

1932 First RSPB nature reserve is designated at Dungeness.

1939 Publication of A G Tansley's *The British Islands and their Vegetation*.

1942 The Nature Reserves Investigation Committee (NRIC) is set up.

1945 NRIC produces its final list of nature and geological reserves. The Dower report on National Parks recommends a permanent body of government to take charge of wildlife conservation. The Wild Life Conservation Special Committee meets for first time.

1947 The Special Committee's report, White Paper Cmd. 7122, is published.

1949 March: A Royal Charter is granted to the Nature Conservancy by the King. November: The National Parks Act empowers the Conservancy to establish, maintain and manage National Nature Reserves.

1951 March: Holme Fen is purchased for £5000. November: The first NNR in Britain is declared, at Beinn Eighe in NW Scotland.

1952 May: The first batch of NNRs in England is declared: Cavenham Heath, Ham Street Woods, Holme Fen, Kingley Vale, Moor House, Piltdown Skull site and Yarner Wood. August: First Local Nature Reserve in England is designated at Gibraltar Point, Lincs.

1953 Floods along east coast. Monks Wood, Blean Woods and Swanscombe Skull NNRs are declared. Myxomatosis is confirmed in Britain. Piltdown Skull is revealed as a hoax, and NNR designation quietly dropped.

1954 Scolt Head Island is declared a NNR, the first area to be leased from National Trust. Conservancy headquarters moves to Belgrave Square, London. Old Winchester Hill and Castor Hanglands NNRs are declared. The first Forestry Nature Reserve is designated: Waterperry Wood in Oxfordshire. Furzebrook research station in Dorset opens.

1955 The first NNRs in a National Park are established—Roudsea Wood, Blelham Bog and North Fen, all in the Lake District. The Conservancy also declares Bridgwater Bay, Axmouth–Lyme Regis landslip, Hartland Moor and Wybunbury Moss as NNRs. First Wildfowl Refuge is established, on the Humber. Sir Arthur Tansley dies.

1956 Lullington Heath, Fyfield Down, Winterton Dunes and Wren's Nest are declared NNRs. The Treasury recognises category of Reserve Warden as 'a departmental class peculiar to the Nature Conservancy'.

1957 Cattle are introduced to Woodwalton Fen. An agreement is signed over the future of wildfowling at Caerlaverock NNR. *Britain's Nature Reserves* is published. Dedication of Tansley memorial stone at Kingley Vale.

1958 Four Norfolk Naturalists Trust-owned Reserves are declared NNRs. Commons Select Committee investigate Nature Conservancy. Public inquiries held to hear objections made to Conservancy's bye-laws at Bridgwater Bay and to hear the Conservancy's objections to the siting of a nuclear power station at Dungeness. The Council of Nature sets up the Conservation Corps (now the British Trust for Conservation Volunteers).

1959 Several Reserves are damaged by fire, including an arson blaze at Hartland Moor.

1960 The Duke of Edinburgh visits Orfordness NNR.

1961 Wye and Crundale Downs and Shapwick Heath are declared NNRs.

1962 100th NNR in Britain is declared. Experimental ponds are dug at Woodwalton Fen. Arctic winter from December 1962–March 1963.

1963 National Nature Week in May. New Reserves are declared at Chartley Moss, Chippenham Fen, Bovey Valley Woods and Upper Teesdale. Monks Wood Experimental Station opens. 'Countryside in 1970' conference.

1964 International Biological Programme launched, based at Moor House (ceases 1974). Biological Records Centre established. Braunton Burrows and Lindisfarne declared NNRs. Sheep introduced to Aston Rowant.

1965 Nature Conservancy becomes part of the newly established Natural Environment Research Council (NERC). Ainsdale Dunes declared NNR.

1966 Second National Nature Week. Nature trails established on several Reserves. Commons authorises building of reservoir at Cow Green in Upper Teesdale.

1967 Ebbor Gorge, Glasson Moss and Holkham declared NNRs.

1968 Stodmarsh declared NNR. Countryside Act establishes Countryside Commission and extends power of local authorities in 'the wider countryside'. Grade of Warden Naturalist abolished. Motorway built through Aston Rowant.

1970 European Conservation Year. Conservancy publishes *Twenty-One Years of Conservation*. Prime Minister and Prince of Wales visit Monks Wood.

1971 UNESCO 'Man and the Biosphere' programme introduces concept of Biosphere Reserves.

1972 Derbyshire Dales NNR declared.

1973 Nature Conservancy Council Act replaces Nature Conservancy with the NCC. UK ratifies the Ramsar Convention on wetlands. First NCC Reserve, Chaddesley Wood, declared.

1976 Summer of drought: fires damage much of Hartland Moor, Thursley Common, Glasson Moss and the recently declared Lizard NNR. First batch of Ramsar sites designated.

1977 *A Nature Conservation Review* published. Gait Barrows NNR opened in ceremony to mark Queen's Silver Jubilee. Geological Conservation Review begins.

1978 The Ribble estuary bought by private developers. SPNC conference on nature reserves.

1979 NCC purchases the Ribble as NNR after starting Compulsory Purchase proceedings. Large Blue butterfly declared extinct. EEC ruling introduces Special Protection Areas for wild birds and their habitats.

1980 World Conservation Strategy is launched in 32 countries. Parsonage Down is purchased by the NCC on favourable terms and declared next year.

1981 The Wildlife and Countryside Act becomes law. A new era for nature conservation in Britain.

1982 The Stiperstones NNR is declared. Farming versus conservation in the Somerset Levels. The first batch of Special Protection Areas is designated.

1983 Essex coast Reserves declared.

1984 NCC publishes *Nature Conservation in Great Britain* and moves main office to Peterborough. Gibraltar Point is declared a NNR, the first to be managed by 'an approved body' under Section 35 of the Wildlife and Countryside Act.

1985 NCC takes over responsibility for Castle Eden Dene. Eleven new NNRs in England declared, including Holt Heath, Stoborough Heath and Holton Heath in Dorset.

1986 NCC publishes *Nature Conservation and Afforestation in Britain.* First Marine Nature Reserve designated around Lundy. First round of Environmentally Sensitive Areas announced.

1987 European Year of the Environment. New batch of Reserves designated including Gordano Valley, Benacre and Hog Cliff. October gale damages 12 NNRs. Manpower Services youth opportunity schemes cease.

1988 Secretary of State for the Environment, Nicholas Ridley, 'invites' NCC to consider 'privatising' some of its owned NNRs and places embargo on new land purchases. *Site Management Plans for Nature Conservation* is published. The Broads Authority is given a set of sharper teeth by the Broads Act.

1989 Embargo on new NNRs continues. Thorne Moors is damaged by fire. Ridley announces the dismemberment of the NCC into separate bodies for England, Scotland and Wales.

1990 Embargo lifted. NCC purchase Fenn's, Whixall and Bettisfield Mosses to save the area from further commercial peat extraction. Lower Derwent Valley is declared a NNR.

1991 English Nature comes into being on 2 April. Cabin Hill becomes first new NNR shortly afterwards. Countryside Stewardship Scheme launched. Conference titled '*Nature Reserves—who needs them*?' is held at Birmingham University. English Nature offers special grants for Devon Culm Measures and Pevensey Levels. NNR strategy is 'made available'. UK ratifies EC Habitats Directive.

1992 The Wash becomes England's largest National Nature Reserve. English Nature launches its Living Coast campaign. Informal agreement over future of peatlands made with Fisons.

1993 Farne Islands, Malham Tarn, Slapton Ley, Wicken Fen and Bassenthwaite become 'Section 35' Reserves. NNRs to be included on Ordnance Survey maps. English Nature launch the land management magazine, *Enact.*

Index

The most substantial mentions are indicated in **bold**